Digital Transformation in Accounting and Auditing

Arif Perdana · Tawei Wang
Editors

Digital Transformation in Accounting and Auditing

Navigating Technological Advances for the Future

palgrave
macmillan

Editors
Arif Perdana
Monash University
BSD City, Tangerang Selatan, Indonesia

Tawei Wang
DePaul University
Chicago, IL, USA

ISBN 978-3-031-46208-5   ISBN 978-3-031-46209-2 (eBook)
https://doi.org/10.1007/978-3-031-46209-2

This Palgrave Macmillan imprint is published by the registered company Springer Nature Switzerland AG
The registered company address is: Gewerbestrasse 11, 6330 Cham, Switzerland

Preface

Charting the Digital Path in Accounting and Auditing: Navigating Technological Advances for the Future

This book explores the landscape of digital transformation in accounting and auditing domain. This book provides professionals, academics and educators with diverse perspectives in the domain, driven by the dynamic developments in technology and the changing demands of the digital age.

The book is divided into four themes, each offering a perspective on the advanced accounting domain in the digital age. The first theme, "Digital Disruption in Accounting: Adapting to the Changing Paradigm," explores the profound impact of digital transformation on traditional accounting practices. The chapters in this theme address the barriers accounting institutions face in integrating digital capabilities into their academic programs. This emphasize the urgent need for accountants to stay abreast with the rapidly evolving technological advances. The second theme, "Empowering Accountants: Embracing Technology Skills for Success," the chapters examine the relevant competencies and skills essential for accountants in the digitalization age. The chapters on this theme analyze the discrepancy between required and actual skills, accountants' attitudes towards technological advances, and their significance to accounting education. The third theme, "The Technological Frontier: Transforming Accounting and Auditing Practices," examines advanced technologies such as artificial intelligence (AI), data analytics, and blockchain. The chapters highlight the transformative potential of these technologies and analyze their impact on decision-making, automation, and the audit process. The fourth theme, "Innovation in Practice: Applying Technology to Accounting and Auditing," explains the different areas in which innovating with digital technology in accounting and auditing domain is critical. This chapter examines how accounting and auditing practices intersect with various technology and industries and uncovers each sector's unique challenges and opportunities in digital transformation.

Part 1: Digital Disruption in Accounting: Adapting to the Changing Paradigm

The accounting profession has changed significantly with the advent of digital technologies, resulting in a necessary reassessment and realignment of practices and procedures. This section contains chapters addressing the complex dynamics of digital transformation in accounting and auditing. It explores the obstacles academic institutions face when adapting their curricula to incorporate contemporary digital competencies.

Chapter 1 analyzes the influence of digital transformation on the accounting profession and industry, along with the challenges accounting schools encounter when attempting to integrate pertinent digital skills and competencies into their educational offerings. The invention of the Internet has revolutionized the way work is performed. Therefore, accounting has shifted from physically sifting through documents to communicating online. The COVID-19 pandemic has led to the need for virtual audits and digital technologies to account for this even more apparent. Accounting schools have gradually updated their curricula to include computerized information systems and software skills, but there is a growing need for additional digital skills, such as AI, Big Data, Blockchain, and cloud computing. The article suggests a hybrid approach to teaching these skills and emphasizes that universities should support and incentivize accounting schools to adapt to digital disruptions. Inaction to address this disruption may hinder the advancement of the accounting profession, while timely adaptation may lead to better educational outcomes for accounting graduates.

Chapter 2 presents the impact of digital transformation on accounting industry. This emphasizes that the industry must combine digital technologies with adept personnel and impactful leadership to leverage the full potential of digital technologies. The articles contained in this chapter underscore the significance of leveraging digital to enhance the decision-making processes, optimize business operations, drive operational efficiency, and augment accounting productivity. The chapter also acknowledges the challenges and risks associated with automation and resistance to changes related to digital transformation. Finally, the article outlines several contributions that can help organizations manage digital transformation.

Chapter 3 addresses the significant impacts of technological advances and digital transformation on accounting and auditing. With the increasing use of information technology and digital transformation in businesses, accountants are increasingly positioned as strategic partners driving business growth. Through technology tools and systems, accountants can improve operational visibility, thoroughly investigate issues, and provide critical perspectives for informed decision-making. Likewise, accountants are anticipated to possess the flexibility to adeptly respond to digitally driven business models and IT infrastructure, illustrating the progressive evolution of their responsibilities. This chapter presents a comprehensive analysis of the effects of digital transformation on various sectors, including retail and distribution, healthcare services, financial services, and the public sector. The chapter aims to examine the ways in which digital transformation can present diverse prospects and challenges for accountants and auditors.

Chapter 4 examines the phenomenon of digital transformation in accounting by analyzing a corpus of 243 academic journal articles on digital transformation. It also identifies research trends in IS and compares them with the existing knowledge of digital transformation in accounting. The results show a significant increase in accounting research related to digital transformation, especially in the areas of security and blockchain/ big data. On the other hand, the IS field focuses on digital and social media, automation software, digital platform ecosystems, and the value these technologies can bring to an organization. The results presented are intended to improve accounting researchers' knowledge of ongoing digital transformation research in their fields and to identify promising avenues for future research.

Part 2: Empowering Accountants: Embracing Technology Skills for Success

In this age of rapid technological advancement, the mastery of specific technical and digital skills and competencies is essential for accounting professionals. This theme revolves around the pivotal role of technological expertise in accounting and the dynamic skill requirements of accountants today.

Chapter 5 highlights the importance of digital technology skills for accountants and the gap between the required and actual skills. Previous research has identified various digital technology competencies needed in accounting, including IS management, data analytics, and digital transformation. However, a limited understanding of the presence and importance of these competencies exists across accounting functions, career stages, and practices. This study examines the skills of accountants in these areas and finds inconsistencies between the required and existing digital technology skills across skill groups and accounting fields. These findings have implications for accounting practices, education, and professional organizations. This study underscores the need to close the skills gap and incorporate relevant digital technology skills into accounting curricula and professional programs.

Chapter 6 delves into the perspectives of accountants regarding digital technologies and their implications in fostering the establishment of technological competencies in accounting. Accountants' perspectives on digital technologies have received insufficient focus, despite the increasing significance of accounting competencies. The chapter aims to provide a comprehensive insight into accountants' attitudes toward technology and their impact on the acquisition of digital technology skills and competencies. The researchers performed a cross-sectional survey and utilized content analysis to explore accountants' attitudes by analyzing their open-ended responses. The results indicate that majority of accountants perceive digital technologies as inconsequential to their professional responsibilities, lack of motivation to adopt or acquire proficiency in digital technologies, or exhibit limited confidence in their ability to attain digital literacy. The presence of these unfavorable beliefs may considerably impede the progress of digital transformation of accounting, unless proactive measures are taken by industry leaders, professional association, and educational organizations. This chapter holds significant relevance for professionals in the accounting domain.

Part 3: The Technological Frontier: Transforming Accounting and Auditing Practices

The proliferation of innovative technologies fundamentally changes the terrain of accounting and auditing, presenting professionals working in these fields with multiple challenges and groundbreaking prospects for change. In this section, we examine the impact of emerging technologies such as AI and Blockchain on accounting and auditing practices. We assessed their impact on decision-making processes, automation techniques, data analytics, and audit protocols.

Chapter 7 focuses on two strategies, the step-in and step-forward strategies that accountants can use to drive digital transformation in their organizations. This strategy recognizes the need for accountants to work with technology to complete tasks that cannot be fully automated. This strategy encourages accountants to leverage technological advances to develop new tools and drive digital transformation. This study provides examples of how these strategies can be implemented in different areas of accounting and auditing. It also discusses the importance of universities and educational institutions in supporting the development of new skills and competencies that accountants need to implement effectively.

Chapter 8 explores the implications of AI on accounting, specifically focusing on its effects on management accounting. This demonstrates how AI can effectively streamline repetitive tasks, minimize human fallibility, and furnish real-time financial information. The authors propose the necessity for additional investigation to elucidate the complex dynamics linking technology and accounting, as well as to identify the evolving proficiencies and competencies that accountants will require in the age of AI. The chapter identifies four dimensions impacted by AI in management accounting: Financial, Customer, Operational, and Organizational. The article concludes that while AI will change the role of accountants, it will not eliminate them, but will augment their skills and present new avenues for engaging in value-added activities.

Chapter 9 provides an analysis of the transformative role of the blockchain technology in the financial industry. It emphasizes its implications for accounting and auditing. Blockchain has the potential to revolutionize conventional financial practices by automating tasks and improving data accuracy. Despite the potential for blockchain to substitute for certain elements of the audit process, auditors retain their crucial function in examining transactions, assessing reliability, and evaluating organizational accounting practices. This article highlights the significance of auditors modifying their protocols to leverage blockchain technology and efficiently address the associated risks. It also highlights the importance of establishing robust regulatory frameworks and cultivating collaborative alliances between policymakers and industry stakeholders to enable seamless integration of blockchain technology.

Part 4: Innovation in Practice: Applying Technology to Accounting and Auditing

The field of accounting and auditing extends beyond mere numerical calculations and encompasses a wide range of applications in various fields and industries. In this section, we examine the complex nuances of accounting and auditing principles in various fields such as financial services, environmental sustainability, and digital transformation in business. We conducted a comprehensive analysis to assess the impact of these applications on the roles of accountants and auditors and their changing expectations in their respective industries.

Chapter 10 extensively evaluates scholarly publications on the prospective use of blockchain technology in accounting and auditing. The accounting industry is encountering novel challenges and intricacies resulting from the emergence of blockchain. This study conducted a semi-systematic literature review to analyze 80 articles sourced from leading accounting journals worldwide. Analyzing accounting journals published worldwide shows an increase in research articles on accounting information systems (AIS) and auditing. This study also examines important theoretical constructs such as triple-entry accounting, smart contracts, continuous auditing, accountability, and governance. Finally, this chapter presents potential research areas and questions that will enable a more comprehensive analysis of the impact of blockchain technology on accounting and auditing.

Chapter 11 analyzes the use of AI in automated decision systems (ADM) and the ethical and legal considerations involved. Although ADM offers significant benefits in accelerating and improving decision-making processes, organizations must consider the critical elements of privacy, fairness, and accountability. Establishing clear and robust policies and protocols is essential for promoting accountability for all ADM actions. Increasing the use of AI in decision-making may require an overhaul of conventional accountability practices. Accounting professionals can potentially improve corporate transparency and accountability, while identifying and mitigating potential biases in ADM.

Chapter 12 provides a comprehensive examination of the pivotal role that technology and data play in expediting advancement in environmental, social, and governance (ESG) objectives. It shows the use of ESG information and resources by corporations to effectively recognize, monitor, and address the potential ESG risks and their implications for operational activities. Owing to the emergence of advanced technologies such as the Internet of Things (IoT), AI, and sensory mechanisms, companies are able to collect and examine large amounts of data about their supply chains and business operations. Nonetheless, using technology in ESG recognizes the importance of competent data management and accurate data to monitor ESG performance and avoid barriers to technological risk and overreaching. This article describes methods for effectively using data to strengthen ESG goals, optimize benefits, and mitigate the associated risks.

Chapter 13 analyzes the impact of modern technological advances on the accounting profession in Japan, highlighting, in particular, the customized computer systems and digitization that were introduced from the 1990s to the present. This highlights the increasing use of computer-assisted audit techniques (CAAT) and digital documentation in audit procedures, which increases auditor efficiency and competence. Despite progress in this area, there are still barriers to overcome, such as the lack of competency in data analysis technologies and limitations in the existing infrastructure. The industry seeks to integrate advanced CAAT and digital work papers to achieve higher efficiency levels. It is essential to address and overcome barriers such as software options, cost, and the need for thorough training. Strategies include developing cost-effective CAAT-specific software and incorporating comprehensive CAAT courses into academic programs.

In summary, our book provides a detailed examination of the impact of digital innovation and evolving technologies on accounting and auditing. Chapters address several facets, including the challenges accounting institutions encounter in modernizing their technological capabilities and the importance of academic institutions in facilitating this transformation. This book highlights the implementation of AI in streamlining workflows and enhancing the proficiency of accounting professionals. This book highlights how digital transformation impacts organizations' workflows, decision-making mechanisms, and accounting systems. It further also highlights the significance of bridging the disparity between the anticipated and current digital technology skills and competencies. Additionally, it explains accountants' attitudes towards technological advances, the impact of blockchain technology on accounting and auditing practices, and the ethical implications associated with automated decision-making systems. It also explores how technology and data can help accelerate the ESG initiatives. Overall, this study provides a comprehensive understanding of the intricacies and implications of digital transformation and emerging technologies in accounting and auditing and offers noteworthy perspectives on challenges and prospects.

BSD City, Tangerang Selatan, Indonesia — Arif Perdana
Chicago, USA — Tawei Wang

Contents

Notes on Contributors

Sandy Arief is an assistant professor at the Faculty of Economics and Business Universitas Negeri Semarang (UNNES), Indonesia. He received his Ph.D. in Accounting and Corporate Governance from Macquarie University, Sydney, Australia, with an "Award" (Dissertation with no corrections/revisions). His Ph.D. focuses on organizational culture, leadership, and employee empowerment in using information systems and their subsequent impact on organizational innovation and performance. He publishes scholarly works in reputable national and international journals and media.

He is a Harvard Business Review Advisory Council member, Communications and Technology for Society Research Group at the University of Sydney Business School, and the Center for Positive Organizations. He is also a certified trainer and consultant for the ARC Australia Consulting Firm. His recent consulting clients are the state-owned airport authority Angkasa Pura I, Department of Foreign Affairs and Trade (DFAT) Australia, Department of Cooperatives and SMEs Central Java, and many more. He is currently an assessor for the Ministry of Education, Culture, Research and Technology (MoECRT), Indonesia; an expert reviewer for the Australia–Indonesia Research Collaboration funded by the Department of Foreign Affairs and Trade (DFAT), Australia; and an academic reviewer for the Indonesia Endowment Funds for Education. He received the 2020 Emerging Scholar Award from the Organization Studies Research Network at the University of Illinois in Chicago, USA.

Saru Arifin is currently a research fellow in the Faculty of Social Science at Universitas Islam Internasional Indonesia. He is a permanent lecturer at the Faculty of Law, Universitas Negeri Semarang, Indonesia. His publications related to Public International Law, Human Rights Law, Constitutional Law, and Legislation studies were published by Routledge, Brill, and SAGE and indexed by Scopus. Besides committed member of numerous international organizations, Arifin is in active positions as director of programs of the Institute for Migrant Rights in Cianjur, West Java, Indonesia (2016–Present), head of law and Human Rights Advocacy Clinics (2018–2020), board editor, and reviewer of numerous National and International journals. He is about to complete a Ph.D. titled Strengthening Indonesia's Migrant Workers Legislation: Reality and Necessity under the Faculty of Law, University of Pecs, Hungary.

Rajitha Basnayake Independent Management and Communication Technology consultants with 35+ years of extensive experience in ICT and Business Management.

Rajitha currently serves on the Board of Asia Asset Finance PLC, subsidiary of Mutooth India as Senior Independent Non-Executive Director, as well as Chairman of Evoke International Ltd, the leader in the Digital Entertainment industry in Sri Lanka. He is also a chairman/ member of several board committees. Furthermore, he functions as a senior management consultant at Latex Green (Pvt) Ltd., the regional leader in the Natural Latex Foam industry.

During his career, he spearheaded ICT operations of Asia Capital Group Sri Lanka, a highly diversified conglomerate as Group Chief Information Officer, Director of Software Development arm, and held key Senior Management positions in ICT at The Lion Brewery Ceylon Ltd as Head of Information Technology and Manager Information Systems at Richard Pieris Group. He has extensive experience as Director Advisory services at Ernst & Young, where he has played a pivotal role as an expert in Strategy, Process transformation projects involving ADB, UNIDO, ICTA, high-profile e-government initiatives in transportation, judicial system, education, central bank, stock exchange, and several other assignments as Project Director. He was also a visiting lecturer for an MSc in the Information Technology study program conducted by the Informatics Institute of Technology Sri Lanka in collaboration with Keele University UK.

Rajitha holds a Master's Degree in IT with Distinction from Keele University UK, Professional membership of the British Computer Society UK (MBCS), Executive Diploma in Business Administration with Distinction from the University of Colombo, and full qualifications from the Australian Computer Society.

Paolo Biancone Professor in business administration and accounting at the University of Turin, Department of Management "Valter Cantino". Chartered accountants, auditors, freelance journalists, and authors of numerous publications on accounting, social entrepreneurship, and tourism management. He is the Editor-in-Chief of the European Journal of Social Impact and Circular Economy and the European Journal of Islamic Finance. Finally, over the years, he has been the scientific coordinator of multiple European projects, such as H2020 Avangard, to study proper business models for electric mobility and Erasmus + on social entrepreneurship.

Jacqueline Birt is a professor of accounting and deputy dean at the University of Washington Business School. She has more than 35 years of experience as an accounting educator and is a co-author of one of the leading financial accounting textbooks in Oceania. Jac's research areas include international financial reporting standards and accounting education. She was the former president of the Accounting and Finance Association of Australia and New Zealand (AFAANZ) and has been a board director since 2011. Jac is the current chair of the Chairs in Accounting and Finance in Australia and New Zealand. Jac supervises Ph.D. students in AI, digital disruption, accounting education, and sustainability accounting.

Richard Busulwa teaches undergraduate and postgraduate financial accounting, management accounting, and accounting information systems at Swinburne University of Technology. He has worked as a CFO, divisional finance manager, management accountant, and financial analyst within small, medium-sized, and large complex organizations. Richard's research explores different digital technology advancements, how they drive disruption, and their implications for particular industries, business functions, and professions. He is the co-author of Digital Transformation in Accounting and the author of Navigating Digital Transformation in Management.

Assistant Professor in Business Administration and Accounting at the University of Turin, Department of Management "Valter Cantino" Co-lecturer, Ph.D. Program in Torino and didactic programs in several institutions, such as the Wroclaw University of Business and Economics, the University of Palermo, and the University of Torino. His research interests include new technology applications in accounting, auditing, and accountability and the application and management of new technologies in the health sector, such as blockchain and artificial intelligence. Finally, he deals with the Islamic economy and finance.

Davide Calandra Assistant Professor in Business Administration and Accounting at the University of Turin, Department of Management "Valter Cantino Co-lecturer, Ph.D. Program in Torino and didactic programs in several institutions, such as the Wroclaw University of Business and Economics, the University of Palermo, and the University of Torino. His research interests include new technology applications in accounting, auditing, and accountability and the application and management of new technologies in the health sector, such as blockchain and artificial intelligence. Finally, he deals with the Islamic economy and finance.

Adrian Gepp is a professor of Data Analytics at Bangor Business School, Bangor University, UK. Adrian is also a member of the Center of Data Analytics and Bond Business School at Bond University, Australia. With Adrian as the leader, the Bond Data Analytics teaching team received an Australian award for university teaching citations for their outstanding contributions to student learning. In his research, Adrian used modern data analytics to better understand issues such as fraud detection, business failure prediction, and money laundering to specify only a few. Adrian is also on the editorial boards of multiple academic journals and a fellow of the Royal Statistical Society.

Clarence Goh is an assistant professor of Accounting (practice) and director of Professional Development at the School of Accountancy, Singapore Management University (SMU). His research examines the judgment and decision-making of users of financial and nonfinancial information. His work has been published in international accounting journals and in leading media outlets. He is also the co-editor of two recent books, "Riding the Waves of Disruption" and "Charting the Future of Accountancy with AI." Before joining SMU, Clarence led the Asia-Pacific

Corporate Research team at Jones Lang LaSalle (Corporate Solutions). He also held various accounting and finance appointments with Deutsche Bank, Barclays Capital, and the Institute of Singapore Chartered Accountants. Clarence is a fellow of CPA Australia, a chartered accountant of Singapore, and a member of the American Accounting Association.

Sheng-Feng Hsieh is an assistant professor of accounting at the National Taiwan University, Taiwan. He earned his doctoral degree at Rutgers, the State University of New Jersey, and master's and bachelor's degrees at National Taiwan University. He was one of the recipients of the 2022 American Accounting Association (AAA) Strategic & Emerging Technologies (SET) Section Outstanding Dissertation Award. His research interests include accounting for and auditing digital assets, emerging technologies in accounting and auditing, and text mining. His works have been published in the *Journal of Accounting, Auditing, and Finance*, *International Journal of Accounting Information Systems*, *International Journal of Digital Accounting Research*, etc.

Ridoan Karim is a lecturer at the Department of Business Law & Taxation, School of Business, Monash University Malaysia. He taught and researched business, international trade, and cyber law. Being a passionate researcher and academic, Ridoan has widely published in peer-reviewed journals and presented papers at several national and international conferences in other areas of interest, i.e., "energy, environment and natural resources law," "science, technology and law," "privacy and data protection law," "Asian and comparative law," etc. Ridoan acted as a consultant and fellow in projects funded by the University of Malaya, Malaysia, and the Monash Data Futures Institute (MDFI). Ridoan Karim holds a Doctor of Philosophy (Ph.D.) from the University of Malaya, Malaysia. He also obtained a Master of Business Administration (MBA) from the University of Chichester, UK, a Master of Comparative Laws (MCL) from International Islamic University Malaysia (IIUM), and a Bachelor of Laws (LLB) from BRAC University, Bangladesh.

Ho Yew Kee is a professor of accounting and cluster directors, business, communication, and design. In his current position, he oversees the faculty and undergraduate programs under the Business, Communication, and Design Cluster. Previously, he was Head of the Department of Accounting at NUS Business School.

Professor Ho obtained his Bachelor (First Class) and Master of Economics degrees from Monash University, Australia. He also obtained his Master of Science in Industrial Administration and Ph.D. software (Carnegie Mellon University, USA). Professionally, he is a fellow of CPA Australia, a fellow of Chartered Accountants Singapore, a chartered financial analyst (CFA), and a fellow at the Singapore Institute of Directors. He has been widely published in academic and practitioner journals.

Professor Ho has held directorships in Singapore to list companies and government entities such as Ngee Ann Polytechnic, Accounting and Corporate Reporting Authority (ACRA), Singapore Tax Academy, and Charity Council; charities such as St Luke Eldercare, Dover Park Hospice, National Kidney Foundation, and Prison Fellowship Singapore, among others. He is on the advisory board of the Institute of Certified Management Accountants, Sri Lanka, Deakin University Integrated Reporting Centre, Australia, and Ngee Ann Polytechnic Diploma in Business Studies, among others.

Professor Ho serves as a financial consultant and expert witness for litigation. His consulting work included the valuation of companies, stock options, financial planning, and the evaluation of companies.

Federico Lanzalonga Candidate in Business and Management at the University of Turin—Department of Management "Valter Cantino". Lecturer of business administration and accounting at the "Università del Piemonte Orientale." Research Fellow at Społeczna Akademia Nauk, Łódź. His research interests include new technology applications in accounting, auditing, accountability, and knowledge management in the circular economy. Finally, he deals with the Islamic economy and finance field.

Po-Lin Li is now working as an auditor at Deloitte, Taiwan. He earned his master's degree in accounting from National Taiwan University (NTU), Taiwan. He worked as an intern for Tax and Legal Department of Deloitte and Corporate Banking of Taishin International Bank during his study at NTU. He also conducted many projects of industry analysis in Taiwan Master of Business Administration (TMBA). His research focuses specifically on the blockchain and its impact on the accounting and auditing.

Grainne Oates is an associate professor of Accounting at Swinburne University of Technology. Grainne's research is mainly in the areas of innovative educational technology. She was the founder of Quitch, a widely adopted Edutech platform focused on enhancing student engagement and learning through gamification and puzzle-based learning. Quitches are used globally to enhance engagement with accounting curricula at the professional body certification, university degree, and secondary school levels.

Arif Perdana diverse research spotlights the transformative role of digital technology, including algorithmic systems, automated decision-making, data analytics, and blockchain across sectors such as finance, education, and healthcare. He provided crucial insights into digital technology adoption challenges and sector-specific strategies. His ongoing studies concentrate on responsible AI in finance, blockchain business applications, and machine learning algorithms, showcasing his comprehensive portfolio and commitment to digital strategies.

Arif is currently an associate professor at Monash University specializing in digital strategy, data science and analytics, and sustainable digital transformation. Over a decade in academia at various institutions, such as Singapore Institute of Technology, Aarhus University, and the University of Queensland, he has gained rich expertise. His experience spans IT services and finance, lending depth to his academic insights. Since December 2022, he has directed Monash University's Action Lab Research Network, Indonesia.

Securing notable funding from Singaporean institutions, Australian agencies, and Indonesian government/corporate sources, Arif's work is notable. The major projects encompass the Monash Data Future Institute, Whyte Fund, Research Grant Bank Indonesia, Ministry of Education, Singapore Academic Research Fund Tier 1 Grant, and Singapore Institute of Technology Ignition Grants. Arif adeptly educates executives and professionals in information systems and analytics, holding workshops in Singapore such as Data Analytics for Professionals, Robotic Process Automation, and more. His research focuses on information systems journals, and he presents at conferences on accounting information systems, primary accounting, and mainstream information systems.

Silvana Secinaro Professor in business administration and accounting at the University of Turin, Department of Management "Valter Cantino". Chartered accountants, auditors, freelance journalists, and authors of numerous publications on accounting, social entrepreneurship, and tourism management. He is the editor-in-chief of the European Journal of Social Impact and Circular Economy and the European Journal of Islamic Finance. Finally, over the years, he has been the scientific coordinator of multiple European projects, such as H2020 Avangard, to study proper business models for electric mobility and Erasmus + on social entrepreneurship.

Seck Tan is an associate professor at the Singapore Institute of Technology. His research focuses on environmental economics with reference to the valuation of environmental goods and services, environmental accounting, and resource management applied to poverty-rich economies. He is an applied economist with broad research interests in policy analysis and policy recommendations for sustainable development and evidence-based public policy formulation in relation to energy and environmental issues. Seck was quoted and interviewed on issues related to sustainable development policies, environmental policies, and climate change.

Tawei Wang is a KPMG/Neil F. Casson Endowed Professor at DePaul University. He is also an associate dean of Faculty and Research at the Driehaus College of Business. He received his Ph.D. from the Krannert Graduate School of Management, Purdue University, in 2009. His research interests include information security and IT management. His papers have appeared in several leading journals, including *Accounting Horizons*, *Auditing: A Journal of Practice and Theory*, *Communications of the Association for Information Systems*, *Decision Support Systems*, *European Journal of Information Systems*, *International Journal of Information Management*, *Information and Management*, *Information Systems Journal*, *Information Systems Research*, *International Journal of Accounting Information Systems*, *Journal of Accounting and Public Policy*, *Journal of Banking and Finance*, and the *Journal of Information Systems*. He is an associate editor of Information and Management and the co-senior editor of the *Journal of Information Systems*. He was a Fulbright Specialist who developed data analytics curricular for accounting programs. He was also involved in the development of the cybersecurity curriculum guidelines by ACM. He was a speaker at the Institute of Internal Auditors, and Institute of Management Accountants (ISACA), and a panelist at the Federal Reserve Bank Charlotte. He was selected as a KPMG James Marwick professor in Residence in 2018. He was the president of the American Accounting Association (AAA) Midwest Region and the president of the AAA Accounting Information Systems section.

Chinthake Wijesooriya is an academic with practitioners. He has over 15 years of academic experience and 15 years of industry experience. Chinthake's industry experience spans information system design, development, and maintenance. He possesses extensive academic experience in Information Systems, Data Science, Postgraduate/Undergraduate/Industry teaching, course coordination, program development, and consulting. Further, he conducted research on Data Science and Formal and Informal Online Learning Systems.

Chinthake currently works as a full-time academic at the RMIT University Vietnam and his previous academic experience includes work at the University of Queensland (2007–2021) and HELP University (2021–2023), where he was the program leader for the Master of Data Science program. He was instrumental in developing industry engagements in academic projects, particularly under the Master of Data Science program. He was a guest speaker at numerous institutions including Universitas Indonesia, Universiti Malaysia Terengganu, Malaysia, and CERT Sri Lanka.

China's industry experience includes but is not limited to, consulting with CSL and EDS (Lanka), FJ Benjamin (Singapore), Jaques Martin (NZ), Andrews Partners (NZ), and Enterprise Rent a Car (USA). He has played a pivotal role in system development and management, digital transformation, and the implementation of disaster recovery strategies in these companies.

Chinthake holds a Ph.D. in Information Systems from the University of Queensland, which explores the impact of formal and informal learning systems on actual and perceived performance. Additionally, he has Masters in Information Systems from the University of Queensland, BSc (CS) from Webster University, USA, and Executive Diploma in Business Administration from the University of Colombo, a member of the Association for Information Systems (AIS).

Ju-Chun Yen is an associate professor at the Graduate Institute of Accounting and the Department of Finance at National Central University, Taiwan. She received her Ph.D. in accounting in 2015 from National Taiwan University, Taiwan. Her research interests include accounting information systems and financial accounting. Her research has been published in various journals, including *Accounting & Finance, Auditing, A Journal of Practice & Theory, International Journal of Accounting*

Information Systems, *Journal of Accounting and Public Policy*, *Journal of Database Management*, and *Journal of Information Systems*.

Kevin Ow Yong is an Associate Professor of Accounting at the Singapore Institute of Technology. He holds a first-class honor degree (with University Medal) in Accounting from Nanyang Technological University and received his PhD degree from Duke University. He had previously worked at Peking University as an associate professor, Singapore Management University as an assistant professor, and Singapore Airlines as a regional accountant and financial analyst. Prof. Ow Yong currently sits on the UAFRS Advisory Council with Valens Research. He is a Chartered Accountant Journal Editorial Advisory Panel member at the Institute of Singapore Chartered Accountants (ISCA). He had previously served on the Candidate Programme Committee with the CFA Society (Singapore). He was on the advisory board of Brahm Centre, a non-profit charity organization, as their Finance Advisor. He has also served as Head of the Accounting Technology and Innovation Center (AccTech). He is currently a member of the university's Institutional Review Board, Research Integrity Committee, and Sustainability Education Committee.

Keiji Yumiba President of SanKei Biz Consulting, Corp., and Representative Director of the International Computer Auditing Education Association of Japan (ICAEA JAPAN) is a blend of audit mastery and technological acumen. Over 25 years, Keiji honed his computer-assisted audit techniques (CAATs) prowess as a Certified Public Accountant (CPA) at Chuo Shinko Audit Corporation. His influence extended beyond introducing innovative information systems within audit firms, including a groundbreaking audit documentation support system from an overseas partner. Joining Deloitte Touche Tohmatsu LLC. Keiji expanded its reach as a partner in 2007, leaving a mark on human resource development during auditing.

In 2017, Keiji's vision led to the founding of SankeiBizCon and ICAEA JAPAN, where he now drives CAATs adoption and shapes proficient practitioners. An authority in industry governance, Keiji, contributed to the Internal Control Study Expert and Planning Expert Committees at the Japanese Institute of Certified Public Accountants.

Keiji's educational dedication is clear, teaching the Audit Case Study III (CAATs) course at Aoyama Gakuin University in 2020. His impact will further expand with the "Practical Digital Audit Exercise" endowed course at Kansai University Accounting School. Keiji Yumiba's journey exemplifies pioneering vision, dedication, and reshaping audit practices in today's digital landscape.

List of Figures

List of Tables

PART I

Digital Disruption in Accounting: Adapting to the Changing Paradigm

CHAPTER 1

Incorporating Digital Skills in Accounting Education

Ho Yew Kee

Introduction

The invention of the Internet ushered in a new paradigm for getting work done. Information moves at a much faster speed than anyone can imagine. Responses to inquiries used to take days through snail mail or through expedient facsimiles. These were thoroughly replaced by almost instantaneous responses through emails, online chats, and voice over internet protocols (VOIP).

The accounting profession provides attestation, information creation, and decision-making support services using financial data. This has been done primarily through physical sightings of hardcopy documents. The development of information technology, particularly the invention of the Internet, has systematically and significantly changed the way accounting services are offered. This was most evident in the 2020 and 2021 global

H. Y. Kee (✉)
Singapore Institute of Technology, Singapore, Singapore
e-mail: Yewkee.Ho@Singaporetech.edu.sg

A. Perdana and T. Wang (eds.), *Digital Transformation in Accounting and Auditing*, https://doi.org/10.1007/978-3-031-46209-2_1

pandemics, where auditing had to be conducted virtually because businesses and economies were closed to accountants and auditors for onsite physical work for periods of time.

In the 1960s and 1970s,[1] the introduction of computerized information technology, information systems, and electronic data processing became key accounting courses taught in accounting schools. Over the years, the emergence of more sophisticated computerized information systems,[2] such as enterprise resources and planning systems, plus the use of accounting software, has added to the necessary digital skills[3] needed to train accountants. It is inconceivable today for any accounting graduate to not use a spreadsheet.

A third wave of digital technologies, that "*transform and expand the types and sources of data used by accountants*" further stretched the digital skills of accountants.[4] Moll and Yigitbasioglu (2019) commented that "*scholars have not given sufficient attention to these technologies and how these technologies affect the everyday work of accountants. Research is urgently needed to understand the new kinds of accounting required to manage firms in the changing digital economy and to determine the new skills and competencies accountants may need to master to remain relevant and add value.*"

Many articles have addressed the need for accounting schools to incorporate digital skills into their curricula.[5] Accounting schools have systematically updated their curricula to ensure that accounting students are well-versed with the changing digital skills that impact the accounting profession over time. This is to ensure that accounting graduates can be dovetailed to the digital transformation taking place in the accounting profession. Otherwise, accounting graduates are left behind. However, with the increased speed of change in the set of digital skills, there are significant discussions that accounting schools are struggling to update

[1] Knudsen (2020), Porter and Heppelmann (2014), Granlund and Mouritsen (2003).

[2] Porter and Heppelmann (2014), Rom and Rohde (2007), Davenport (1998).

[3] For simplicity, digital skills for the rest of this chapter represents information technology and digital knowledge and skills.

[4] Knudsen (2020).

[5] Brink and Stoel (2019), Leitner-Hanetseder, Eisl, et al. (2021), Kotb et al. (2019), Al-Htaybat et al. (2018), Pan and Seow (2016).

their curricula and provide relevant digital skills to meet these new challenges.

This chapter seeks to paint a picture of what the future of accountants would look like in the face of the digital transformation of the accounting profession. It then surveys the literature and opinions of practitioners on the key digital skills that accountants would be required to be proficient in. Third, it covers what accounting schools need to do to ensure that accounting students are adequately trained and prepared for these current and emerging digital skills. Finally, it discusses the challenges faced by accounting schools in meeting the new digital skill requirements for accountants in the future.

Future of Accountants—The Great Digital Disruption

In the Future of Jobs Report 2020 by the World Economic Forum (WEF, 2020), technological adoption will be a high priority for companies, and Fig. 1.1 shows the share of technologies likely to be adopted by 2025 by surveyed companies. Accountants will not be spared of this digital disruption as the companies they have worked in evolve digitally. It will be a tragedy if accountants lack the digital skills to service their clients.

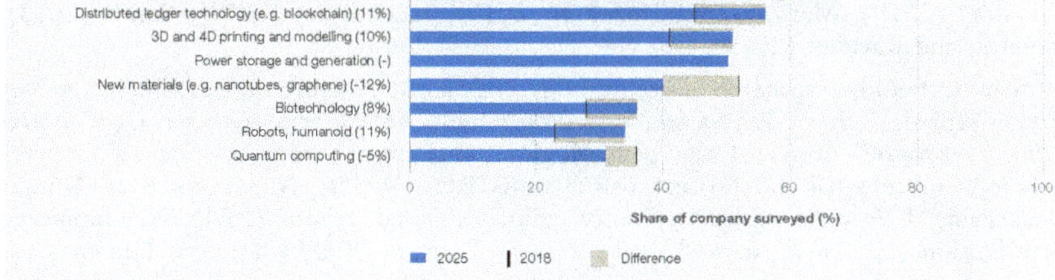

Fig. 1.1 Technologies likely to be adopted by 2025 (*Source* Future of Works, WEF, 2020 [Figure 18])

Many articles have been published on the digital disruption of the accounting profession arising from emerging technology trends.[6] For example, Moll and Yigitbasioglu (2019) reviewed the role of four Internet-related technologies[7] that have the potential to change the work of accountants and argued for more research to understand how these four Internet-related technologies can be better understood. These four technologies are artificial intelligence, big data, blockchain, and cloud computing (collectively called ABBC). This is not surprising as the "Pathways Commission on Accounting Higher Education: Charting a National Strategy for the Next Generation of Accountants" by the American Accounting Association (AAA) and the American Institute of Certified Practicing Accountants (AICPA) had sounded the need to relook at accounting education in the light of emerging technologies as early as 2012. Recommendation 4[8] highlights the use of technology. The need to incorporate digital skills into accounting education may be an existential challenge for educators and schools. This is because the new generation of accounting students is a digital-native. They are more at home with emerging technologies, and if accounting educators are unable to speak their native language, the accounting profession would seem less attractive and relevant to them. This is articulated in the face of the rapidly changing practice of accounting, especially in the area of technology, which will play an increasingly prominent role.

A key question is how emerging technology will change the role of an accountant or the accounting profession in general. Undoubtedly, the

[6] Leitner-Hanetseder, Eisl, et al. (2021), Berikol and Killi (2021), Kamau (2021), Brink and Stoel (2019), Marrone and Hazelton (2019), Hutchinson (2019), Smith (2018), Asonitou and Kavoura (2019).

[7] The technology space in accounting is constantly evolving. For example, ACCA (2022) remarked that "*Professional accountants must be equipped with the right digital skills in response*." Some of the technologies transforming the future of accountancy include: Current—robotic process automation (RPA), wiFi6, AI, Internet of Things, Blockchain; 1–3 years—Edge inference chip, extended reality (XR), 5G, biometric identification (ID); 3–5 years—Visual internet of things (ViOT), artificial human assistant, autonomous driving; >5 years—quantum computing, 6G, satellite internet and brain–computer interface. The sky is the limit when it comes to the technology of tomorrow.

[8] "*Transform learning experiences to reflect current and emerging technologies and global trends in business*" (Pathway Commission, 2012).

uniqueness of humanity in the form of creativity, agility, dynamic decision-making in uncertainties, analytical thinking in unstructured environments, and other human traits will continue to exemplify the best of an accountant. Nonetheless, more routine, structured, and mundane tasks can be automated and performed using emerging technologies. For instance, Kokina et al. (2021) advocate the five distinct roles of an accountant in the face of ever-improving Robotic Process Automation (RPA): identifier,[9] explainer,[10] trainer,[11] sustainability,[12] and analyzer.[13] The key to this article is that the accountant will play different roles in the face of emerging technology, and they will not be simply eliminated. Accountants play key roles in teaching and training emerging technologies to perform the roles traditionally performed by accountants.

Many have also advocated that one key role of accountants in the face of emerging technology is to become business consultants or advisors where technology cannot mimic. However, this is too simplistic, as it assumes that the ultimate endpoint or the peak of the accounting professional role is being an advisor or consultant. The work of an accountant comprises a whole spectrum of business processes. Accountants will have to deploy technologies throughout the spectrum of their work, and technology must be a tool that an accountant can use skillfully to perform his job more efficiently and effectively. Consider the example of auditing. In the past, auditors could only draw samples and offer opinions based on them. With technology, an auditor can study a large percentage of transactions, if not the entire population. However, the auditor still needs to offer an opinion based on the large sample examined. This allows the

[9] Accountants would play the Identifier role by identifying and specifying the role to be played by the technology or types of technology to enable it to analyse and understand the business processes.

[10] Accountants would play the Explainer role by bridging the knowledge and information gap to allow the developers of technologies to construct the relevant technology to carry out the business processes.

[11] Accountants would play the Trainer role by training and shaking down the technology created to ensure that it fulfills its role in the business professes.

[12] Accountants would play the Sustainer role by developing performance KPIs or accuracy metrics to ensure that the technology developed is fit for purpose and is deployed effectively and efficiently to carry out the business processes.

[13] Accountants would play the Analyser role by analysing and offering of judgment on how the results and performance of the business processes by the deployed technology would change given differing inputs.

auditor to perform his work more efficiently and effectively using the technology available to examine a large sample or population.

Therefore, equipping accounting students with emerging technology has become an existential requirement to deal with the future of an accountant. A way to conceptualize the development of the training of an accounting student over time is summarized in Fig. 1.2.

The "Pillar Approach" emphasizes the technical accounting skills of an accountant to discharge his professional responsibility. Deep knowledge of each of the core areas (pillars) of the technical accounting domain is required. This has been the primary emphasis of accounting schools since time memorial.

As accountants are more than technicians, they serve as advisors and analysts. The requirement for soft skills which generally includes those skills which are typical of "humanity" like communication, listening, negotiation, and critical thinking, among others are crucial for the success of a professional accountant. This resulted in the "T-Shape Approach"[14]

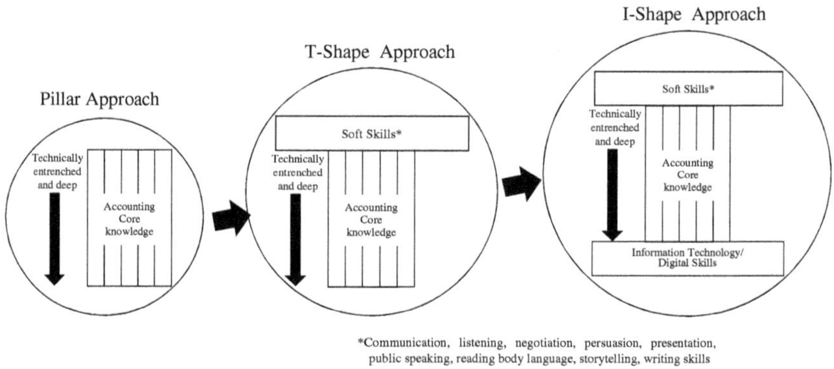

Fig. 1.2 Progressive development of training for accountants (*Source* Author)

[14] David Epstein in his book "Range: Why generalists triumph in a specialized world" used the T-shape concept to represent someone who is technically deep and yet has breadth which incorporates general skills. This is very different from the concept in this chapter as "T-shape Approach" requires the accountant to have both the technical skills and soft skills. The impartation of both technical and soft skills is the imperative of accounting schools.

for the training of accountants. These soft skills are required, in addition to the technical accounting skills traditionally learned by accounting students.[15]

With the advent of new digital technologies, the traditional technical and soft skills knowledge and training of accountants will have to be undergirded by the foundation of digital skills. This is to ensure that accountants can compete and be competent in the digital world. This gives rise to the "I-Shape Approach" in the training of accountants.

However, the duration of accounting programs has not increased. This creates a challenge, as more content is added to the accounting curriculum (as shown by the enlarged circles) with a hard-constrained duration.

The above characterization of the progressive development of training for accounting students immediately results in two key challenges for educators: First, the content space for each accounting core knowledge type continues to increase. For example, 23 International Accounting Standards (IASs) were introduced between 1975 and 1985. By 2022, there will be 24 IAS and 15 International Financial Reporting Standards (IFRS)[16] and numerous interpretations from the International Financial Reporting Interpretations Committee (IFRICs). The content space for financial accounting standards alone has more than doubled. The same can be said for auditing, taxation, valuation, and many other existing and new topics in accounting. Take another example. The increased complexity of mathematical models used in financial reporting adds to the content space. In 1982, the most sophisticated mathematical model was the net present value calculation introduced in IAS 17: Accounting for Leases. Fast forward to 2022, the binomial and Black–Scholes option pricing models are choices available in the pricing of financial instruments for financial reporting purposes. Additionally, Monte Carlo simulations can be used in IFRS 13: Fair Value Measurement for the computation of credit valuation adjustment (CVA) and debit valuation adjustment (DVA).

Second, the introduction of soft and digital skills has taken up more curriculum time. In a world where increasing content is introduced into the curriculum, it could result in under-coverage of some of the key

[15] Rebele and St. Pierre (2019).

[16] International Accounting Standards (IASs) were first released in 1975 and new standards are called International Financial Reporting Standards (IFRSs) from 2003 onward.

content or an information overload for the students. This runs the risk of having "half-baked" accountants who are not adequately trained in the multi-content accounting curriculum.

In the case of the "I-Shape Approach," it is inevitable that the training of accountants must incorporate the needed digital skills that will drive the future of accounting profession. The challenge is to determine what kind of digital skills accounting students need to possess so as to be capable and competent accountants in the new digital world, given the constraint of the limited duration of the accounting program.

Key Emerging Digital Skills of Accountants

Discussions on the impact of digital disruption on accounting have been vigorous, as there is a key view that accounting jobs can be severely reduced by the automation of processes pertaining to more repetitive and rule-based tasks (Agygemang et al., 2019; Frey & Osborne, 2017). However, there are also optimism of new opportunities[17] if the accounting profession leverages new possibilities by re-inventing itself in the digital age. The general conclusion from the literature is that for an accountant to perform his role well in the future, he must be equipped with the necessary digital skills to handle this digital disruption.[18]

In a survey of companies in the financial service sector by the World Economic Forum (WEF, 2020), the top five technologies to be adopted in 2025 are cloud computing, encryption and cybersecurity, big data analytics, artificial intelligence, and e-commerce and digital trade. Distributed ledger technology (blockchain) has eighth position (Fig. 1.3).

Some immediately identified changes in the accounting field include big data analytics, data visualization, machine learning, cloud computing, cybersecurity, methods to deal with structured and unstructured data, artificial intelligence, and automated repetitive processing capabilities.

The challenge is to determine the key digital skills and knowledge in digital disruption that are essential for accounting students to be knowledgeable given the fact that digital disruption is evolving rapidly and curriculum time is limited.

[17] Leitner-Hanetseder, Lehner, et al. (2021).

[18] Seow et al. (2021), Leitner-Hanetseder, Eisl, et al. (2021), Moll and Yigitbasioglu (2019), Tan and Laswad (2018), van Laar et al. (2017), Howcroft (2017).

SN	Technology	Financial Services (%)
1	Cloud computing	98
2	Encryption and cyber security	95
3	Big data analytics	91
4	Artificial intelligence (e.g. machine learning, neural networks, NLP)	90
5	E-commerce and digital trade	90
6	Internet of things and connected devices	88
7	Text, image and voice processing	88
8	Distributed ledger technology (e.g. blockchain)	73

Fig. 1.3 Technologies likely to be adopted by 2025, by share of companies surveyed, from the Financial Services Sector (*Source* Future of Works, WEF 2020 [Figure 19—abstract])

The literature is filled with discussions and opinions on the four key digital skills that accountants ought to have.[19] They are ABBC: artificial intelligence,[20] big data,[21,22] blockchain,[23] and cloud computing.[24,25] Existing IT knowledge in spreadsheets, ERP, and information systems are assumed. The following provides brief descriptions of the importance of the four digital skills that accountants ought to have.

[19] Moll and Yigitbasioglu (2019), Gulin et al. (2019).

[20] Leitner-Hanetseder, Lehner, et al. (2021), Rane and Lahane (2020), Ukpong et al. (2019), Kokina and Devenport (2017), Appelbaum and Nehmer (2017), Sutton et al. (2016).

[21] Cockcroft and Russell (2018), Appelbaum, Kogan, Vasarhelyi, et al. (2017), Arnaboldi et al. (2017), Janvrin and Watson (2017), McKinney et al. (2017), Enget et al. (2017), Sledgianowski et al. (2017), Alles (2015), Vasarhelyi et al. (2015), Krahel and Titera (2015), Schneider et al. (2015), Warren et al. (2015), Wilder-James (2012).

[22] In the area of big data, it will include data analytics. Lawson and Street (2021), Andiola et al. (2020), Oesterreich and Teuteberg (2019), Richardson and Shan (2019), Ballou et al. (2018), Cunningham and Stein (2018), Dzuranin et al. (2018), Appelbaum, Kogan, Vasarhelyi, et al. (2017), Kokina et al. (2017), Tang et al. (2017), Wang and Cuthbertson (2015).

[23] Cai (2021), Felski and Empey (2020), Dai and Vasarhelyi (2017).

[24] Brandas et al. (2015), Cambridge (2018).

[25] In the context of cloud computing, cybersecurity and encryption are generally assumed as part of the knowledge for cloud computing.

Artificial Intelligence

Neely and Cook (2011) comment on the major impact of new technologies, particularly artificial intelligence (AI), on the accounting profession and that AI has the "*potential to massively transform existing professional occupations and task profiles.*" The use of AI in accounting is not new as it was in the 1980s; auditors were already toying with "expert systems" in which the system "*assists decision maker, replace the decision maker or train the decision maker*" for auditing purposes (O'Leary, 1986). The introduction of software robots in robotic process automation (RPA) is a natural progression in taking over routine tasks defined by structured rules, processes, or protocols. With the continuing improvement in computer technologies in terms of computational power and storage, it is expected that software will be able to provide "*more and more support in non-routine tasks that require decisions on complex and novel situations and flexibility*" (Autor & Dorn, 2013; Frey & Osborne, 2017; Guthrie & Parker, 2016; Leitner-Hanetseder, Lehner, et al., 2021).

Despite the fact that AI-based digital technology is making small but systematic inroads into the accounting and finance profession, there are high hopes that AI-based software robots can be deployed in highly complex tasks, such as fraud detection and liquidity planning (Brynjolfsson & McAfee, 2014; Skrbis & Jacqueline, 2019). Lehner et al. (2020) advocate the possibility that AI will be a key link that will proceed stepwise toward a "Fully Autonomous Accounting System" (FAAS). Letner, et al. described FAAS as a "*firm-wide, fully autonomous, self-aware and self-improving accounting system. The centre of an FAAS is a state-based, multi-functional, deep-learning network as artificial intelligence (AI) that is able to holistically simulate and potentially outpace human-cognition and decision-making processes. This AI manages structured and unstructured data and regulations from various sources and delivers timely and apt information to the right audience in the right format.*"

Accountants need to be educated on the opportunities, risks, and limitations afforded by AI to stay ahead of their game.

Big Data/Data Analytics

Gartner (2012) defines big data as "*high-volume, high velocity and/or high-variety information assets that demand cost-effective, innovative forms of information processing that enable enhanced insight, decision making and process automation*." In recent times, a fourth "V" is attached to big data, namely, veracity. A large dataset may contain errors and would require a significant amount of verification and data cleansing. Accountants must be educated on the knowledge and understanding of big data.

ICAEW (2019) documents three key reasons that accountants need to pay attention to why big data is a modern phenomenon. First, advances in computing power allow for the processing of large datasets, which we have never been able to do. For example, accountants primarily use Excel to process data for computation, summarization, transformation, and analysis. Excel 2003 has a maximum combination of 65,536 rows with 256 columns, which was significantly enhanced in Excel 2007, reaching 1,048,576 rows by 16,384 columns (enlargement by 1024 times the number of cells). Nonetheless, as the dataset becomes larger, the use of Excel as a key data manipulation tool may be lacking. In today's standard, Excel is not a good tool for handling large datasets because of its efficiency and effectiveness, notwithstanding the amount of storage capacity needed or computing power. The second reason for the prevalence of big data is the variety of data sources. Many articles on big data in accounting advocate that accountants would need to consider the massive amount of data generated from social media, mobile technology and devices, open source data, and the Internet of Things. The data from these sources may have financial implications for companies that accountants cannot ignore in their work. Big data allows for the bridging, amalgamation, triangulation, confirmation, and management of data from these varied datasets. Finally, IT infrastructure has allowed for the collaboration and sharing of numerous datasets in the cloud or offsite at a scale that has never been possible previously. Given the presence of big data, accountants must have the necessary digital skills to manage, analyze, and join the dots in big data to provide a valuable information-based service.

In addition, the availability of big data also allows greater opportunities for data analytics, data visualization,[26] decision-making, verification, and fact-finding (Schneider et al., 2015; Warren et al., 2015). For example, with big data, auditors may not need to perform random or limited sampling for audit tests. Technically, auditors can perform a 100% check of the data to arrive at their audit opinions because the data are available in a digital form. Krahel and Titera (2015) argued that financial reporting

[26] Janvrin et al. (2014).

and auditing standards may have to evolve in the face of big data and the processes that generate them. This is needed to "*add value and relevance to the accounting profession, empower end users, and improve efficiency of the capital markets*." Alles (2015) warns that "*auditors cannot stray too far from the practices of their clients since their credibility with and respect of those clients are the basis of the value added that they provide.*" Accountants cannot miss this key digital skill and knowledge.[27]

Blockchain

Blockchain is a digital representation of a traditional accounting ledger that is supposed to be immutable, as accounting ledgers were not meant to be changed once the transactions were recorded. Blockchain is a digital ledger technology where transactions that are approved by peers are distributed globally in networks of computers with the key attribute where the transaction, and hence the information, can be verified in real time (Smith, 2018). Accounting has traditionally been carried out in printed hardcopies, and the hardcopies are immutable proof of the existence of transactions. One way to view blockchain is as a digitalized form of an accounting ledger. The concept of blockchain will have a significant affiliation with accounting because a traditional view of accounting is that it is a recording, processing, and communication of information arising from past transactions. Blockchain is a digital technology in which accounting can be digitally conducted.

Deloitte (2019) published survey results showing increasing signs of blockchain's maturity and its increasing use in fintech, technology, media, telecommunications, life sciences, healthcare, and the government. Therefore, it is not surprising that individuals hail blockchain as one of the "*most promising emerging technologies that has the potential to vastly transform the accounting and auditing profession*" (Felski & Empey, 2020). In fact, Dai and Vasarhelyi (2017) comment that "*blockchain has served as a potentially transformative information technology expected to be as revolutionary as the internet.*" Its vast potential lies in auditing, as blockchain can provide an important conduit for verifying accounting transactions in a virtual environment. Cai (2021) postulates that blockchain can be the third entry in the current double-entry accounting system outside the

[27] Janvrin and Watson (2017) called this (big data) a "new twist to accounting."

bounds of a company.[28] This third entry in blockchain has the advantage that it can be verified in an efficient manner in which fundamental trust and transparency are addressed by the attributes of the blockchain (i.e., distributed recordings and immutable). This could potentially usher in the simplification of audits or even the demise of traditional audit procedures and processes. The audit will be blockchain focus, rather than checking traditional records in hardcopies. For example, audit confirmation of account balances may be a thing of the past if auditors have access to the blockchain to confirm the account balances directly, rather than obtaining an account confirmation from the clients of the auditee. Accounting students will do well to be educated on blockchain.

Cloud Computing/Cyber Security

The Covid-19 pandemic has demonstrated the relevance and importance of cloud-based solutions and services. It has been demonstrated in the Covid-19 pandemic that the accountant's role in analytics, compliance control, and monitoring with reporting and data governance can all be done in the cloud away from physical presence in the office. Accountants need to be well-versed with the skills and knowledge needed to navigate and perform their roles in this new cloud environment. In addition, as information, processes, and works are done in a virtual environment, accountants need to be highly sensitized to the increased risk of cybersecurity as "all-the-eggs" in the cloud basket can be compromised in a single cyber breach. Accountants performing audit and risk management advisory would need to be well-versed in cybersecurity for them to perform their roles as auditors and evaluators of the system and processes of their clients.

Given the need to incorporate digital skills into accounting education, three critical questions need to be addressed. First, how much depth do accounting students need in each of these areas? Second, what are the best ways to impart digital skills to accounting students given an already packed curriculum? Finally, what are the current challenges faced by accounting schools in addressing the requirements of these new digital skills?

[28] Psaila (2017) writing on Deloitte Malta article hailed blockchain as a game changer for the audit profession.

With respect to the question of depth, it is important to note that the accounting program is never meant to train and produce data or computer scientists. Therefore, reasonable functional knowledge of these technologies and their applications in accounting may be sufficient. There is a discussion on whether accounting education should include the learning of programming languages, such as Python or R, as these are the basic computer programming languages that are useful for machine learning and data analytics.[29] One school of thought is that it is good to have if the students have an aptitude to learn, and there are opportunities or spaces in the curriculum to allow the acquisition of programming skills. An alternative school of thought is that this is not necessary, as accountants generally do not need programming skills in their daily work. The jury is still out as the world evolves further. In the world of emerging technologies, accountants should be encouraged to adopt a lifelong learning approach as new technologies will soon replace current technologies, and accountants must constantly retool themselves to cope with new technologies.

The remaining two questions are addressed in the following two sections.

Imparting Digital Skills in Accounting Schools

As alluded to earlier, the current accounting curriculum is already packed because of the continuous enlargement of the content space with no lengthening of the accounting program's duration. The duration of the accounting program is a hard constraint that forces every accounting school to optimize the learning outcomes given the key imperatives (technical, soft, and digital skills) in accounting education (that is. the I-Shape Approach).

In carefully selecting the required digital skills (e.g., the four core digital skills [ABBC]: artificial intelligence, big data, blockchain, and cloud computing), the key challenge is how these digital skills should be imparted to accounting students.

Currently, there are two key methods for imparting digital skills to accounting students.[30] One of the most popular approaches is the "silo approach," in which each course on information technologies or digital

[29] Schoute (2019).

[30] Lafond et al. (2016).

skills stands on its own with very minimal linkages to other key accounting technical knowledge. For example, a course in data visualization or big data, where the knowledge and examples are general business-related and scarcely cover any accounting domain. A second approach is the integrated or linked approach, in which digital skills are embedded in core accounting technical courses. For example, big data is taught and applied in the context of an audit or forensic accounting course.

The choice of either the method or the hybrid approach has its own challenges. For the silo approach, specific digital skills can be adequately covered by faculty members who are experts in those digital skills. Digital skill courses may be taught by faculty from another discipline, such as computer science or information technology. It could be in a course on the Accounting Information System (AIS).[31] This approach has been used by some schools to teach quantitative methods for business (or statistics for business) by faculty members who are not from business or accounting schools. This method has the advantage of providing a deep coverage of digital skills. However, the digital skills taught are not directly related to the accounting discipline, and students may have difficulties applying this knowledge to their technical accounting knowledge. Learning is performed using an unconnected silo approach.

The integrated approach has the significant advantage of imparting digital skills in the context of technical accounting knowledge. This hastens learning, as the digital skills acquired are directly relevant to the context of accounting. Lafond et al. (2016) report that the integrated or linked approach "*hold stronger perceptions about the role of technology in accounting than students in the stand-alone computer science courses.*"

The challenge in the integrated or linked approach is that the accounting educator would have to significantly re-scope accounting courses to incorporate the digital skills to be taught. Accounting faculty must be capable of integrating or using digital skills in technical accounting courses without sacrificing the learning outcomes of technical accounting knowledge. Alternatively, the accounting course must be co-taught by faculty from accounting and computer science or information schools.

Integrated or linked accounting courses require examples, illustrations, assignments, and projects that include digital skills or knowledge. It

[31] Pan and Seow (2016).

is likely that such an approach would require significant redrafting of the accounting course. The worst-case scenario is that neither technical accounting knowledge nor digital skills will be taught or learned well in this integrated approach.

A possible hybrid approach is to provide silo courses on digital skills and knowledge at the foundation level to accounting students, and thereafter, weave the advanced digital skills into technical accounting courses. For example, there will be an introductory course on big data and various digital skills in big data, data analytics, cybersecurity, etc. Thereafter, digital skills in big data are applied in accounting technical courses, such as auditing, forensic accounting, or advanced management accounting. Figure 1.4 illustrates this approach.

The advantage of the hybrid approach is that digital skills are assumed to have been acquired in a standalone foundation course on digital skills. These digital skills are applied in technical accounting courses through examples, illustrations, and assignments. This is almost similar to the current approach in which Excel or Advanced Excel is taught as a standalone course and Excel knowledge is used in examples and applications in other accounting technical courses. This approach has the advantage of allotting time for the purposeful acquisition of digital skills with the subsequent application of those digital skills to the accounting technical domain.

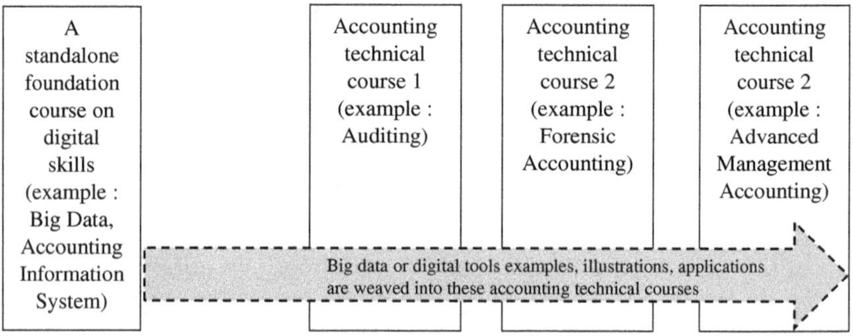

Fig. 1.4 Hybrid approach in weaving standalone digital knowledge and skills courses into accounting technical courses (*Source* Author)

This brings us to the final topic of the challenges faced by accounting schools, given their need to equip accounting students with these new digital skills.

Resource Needs for Imparting Digital Skills

Moll and Yigitbasioglu (2019) note that despite the advent of new technologies and their impact on the accounting profession, they observe that "*few university accounting programmes cover issues related to how accounting is interlinked with digitisation.*" A constrained and crowded curriculum has been explained as a possible source of this bottleneck. Two other factors may have contributed to this challenge.

First, there must be a well-defined governance mechanism to encourage accounting schools to review their curricula and incorporate these technological changes into their curricula. This may include the need to provide the necessary infrastructure and resources for accounting schools to include digital skills in their curricula. Infrastructure or hardware investment may be non-trivial, as new computer labs and software will have to be funded with additional manpower to manage these new infrastructures. If accounting schools are left to their natural evolution in their curriculum review to address the digital skills challenge, progress may be too slow. For example, most accounting schools refresh their curriculum periodically, such as once every five years. In this dynamically changing world, if the curriculum is refreshed once every five years with new digital skills, this would mean that the first batch of graduates with new digital skills from the refreshed curriculum will hit the accounting profession market with a lag of four years. It could even be up to nine years in the worst-case scenario. In the world of digitalization, this is too slow, and the lag can impede the progress of the accounting profession. The worst outcome is that accounting schools will be deemed irrelevant to the needs of the accounting profession. Therefore, accounting schools may need to constantly and continuously review their curricula in order to incorporate new technologies. Accounting schools need to obtain sound and good advice and guidance from the accounting profession and accreditation bodies to select and incorporate key digital skills into the crowded curriculum. Discipline will have to be exercised to create space in the crowded curriculum to accommodate these new digital skills by reviewing and even possibly jettisoning some of the existing topics or streams in the curriculum. This may mean slaughtering sacred and pet topics or reducing the number of courses for a particular stream of knowledge.

Second, one key factor is the availability of accounting educators who are skilled and knowledgeable in imparting these digital skills. There are numerous discussions which suggest that the state of accounting education is failing to equip students with these digital skills because "*technological developments 'out-pace' educators' abilities to remain updated*."[32] This problem can be exasperated by educators who teach digital natives from Gen Y and Gen Z can address this problem. The "generation" and "experience" gaps can result in resistance by accounting educators to introduce these new technologies into the curriculum, even though there is a sense of importance and urgency.[33] An extreme example illustrates this divergence. In its recommendations to university accounting educators and program leaders, PWC (2015) suggested that in the technical skills needed in undergraduate accounting programs, basic programming skills using contemporary programming languages such as Python or Java should be incorporated into the training alongside Microsoft Excel, Access, and both structured and unstructured databases such as SQL, MongoDB, and Hadoop. Looking at the profile of the current accounting educators in accounting schools, unless accounting educators are highly progressive and kept up to date on these technological developments, most would object to the need to incorporate programming languages or new digital technologies into the accounting curriculum. Watty et al. (2016) are of the opinion that the biggest inhibitor to the adoption of new technologies in accounting education is resistance from accounting educators. There seems to be a digital divide between accounting educators and students, arising from accounting educators' lack of technological literacy (Lewis et al., 2013; Prensky, 2001). It is possible that younger and technologically well-equipped accounting educators would venture to take this untrodden path, and the divide is less severe than articulated (Kennedy et al., 2008). Accounting schools face the enormous challenge on how to pivot or "re-educate" senior accounting educators who may be digitally deficient or disrupted to retool themselves in this push to incorporate digital skills into the curriculum.

[32] Al-Htaybat et al. (2018).

[33] Rebele and St. Pierre (2019), Watty et al. (2016).

Therefore, the hardwares and "heartwares" (accounting educators) are the two key considerations in the resource needs of accounting schools to impart digital skills effectively in their curricula.

Conclusion

Civilizations do not disappear overnight, nor do professional practices or jobs become obsolete in a short period of time. Nonetheless, these do disappear because of the erosion of their relevance, as signs and influencing factors are ignored over time. Accounting education is probably experiencing one of the most challenging periods of history, as its relevance may be determined by its ability to reinvent itself in light of digital disruption. There are quarters of disquiet that accounting schools are not producing graduates who are able to navigate the digitally disrupted world of accounting professional practices. Given that the future of accountants will be significantly disrupted by technology, accounting schools must identify the key digital skills that they need to incorporate into their accounting curriculum. This chapter identifies four possible key digital skills (ABBC): artificial intelligence, big data, blockchain, and cloud computing. The accounting curriculum constantly overflows with enlarged content space in all technical accounting domains and soft skills. Nonetheless, these new digital skills must be incorporated into the accounting curriculum. This chapter recommends a hybrid approach in which foundational digital skills can be introduced to the curriculum on a standalone basis, with the applied and advanced knowledge being integrated into the rest of the technical accounting courses for illustrations, applications, and contextual learning. Finally, universities will have to relook their governance mechanism to incentivize and support accounting schools to pivot toward incorporating digital skills into the accounting curriculum. This may necessitate additional investment in teaching and learning infrastructure and the retraining of existing accounting educators or the hiring of new accounting educators with relevant digital skills.

The key challenge is that every day of inaction to address this digital disruption to the accounting profession from the supply side will set back the progress of the accounting profession. However, accounting schools that urgently address this digital disruption would likely reap significant payoffs in the enhanced educational outcomes of accounting graduates (Fogarty et al., 2016).

References

Al-Htaybat, K., von Alberti-Alhtaybat, L., & Alhatabat, Z. (2018). Educating digital natives for the future: Accounting educators' evaluation of the accounting curriculum. *Accounting Education, 27*(4), 333–357.

Alles, M. G. (2015). Drivers of the use and facilitators and obstacles of the evolution of Big Data by the audit profession. *Accounting Horizons, 29*(2), 439–449.

Andiola, L. M., Masters, E., & Norman, C. (2020). Integrating technology and data analytic skills into the accounting curriculum: Accounting department leaders' experiences and insights. *Journal of Accounting Education, 50*, 100655.

Appelbaum, D., Kogan, A., & Vasarhelyi, M. (2017). Big data and analytics in the modern audit engagement: Research needs. *Auditing: A Journal of Practice and Theory, 36*(4), 1–27. https://doi.org/10.2308/ajpt-51684

Appelbaum, D., Kogan, A., Vasarhelyi, M., & Yan, Z. (2017). Impact of business analytics and enterprise systems on managerial accounting. *International Journal of Accounting Information Systems, 25*, 29–44.

Appelbaum, D., & Nehmer, R. (2017). The coming disruption of drones, robots, and bots: How will it affect CPAs and accounting practice? *CPA Journal, 87*(6), 40–45.

Arnaboldi, M., Busco, C., & Cuganesan, S. (2017). Accounting, accountability, social media and big data: Revolution or hype? *Accounting, Auditing and Accountability Journal, 30*(4), 762–776.

Asonitou, S., & Kavoura, A. (2019). Accounting, technology and entrepreneurship education—Current trends and perspectives. *Zeszyty Naukowe Małopolskiej Wyższej Szkoły Ekonomicznej w Tarnowie, 44*(4), 65–78.

Association of Chartered Certified Accountants (ACCA). (2022). *Accounting for a better world: Priorities for a transforming profession.*

Autor, D. H., & Dorn, D. (2013). The growth of low-skill service jobs and the polarization of the US labor market. *The American Economic Review, 103*(5), 1553–1597. https://doi.org/10.1257/aer.103.5.1553

Ballou, B., Heitger, D. L., & Stoel, D. (2018). Data-driven decision-making and its impact on accounting undergraduate curriculum. *Journal of Accounting Education, 44*, 14–24.

Berikol, B. Z., & Killi, M. (2021). The effects of digital transformation process on accounting profession and accounting education. In K. T. Çalıyurt (Ed.), *Ethics and sustainability in accounting and finance, Volume II, accounting, finance, sustainability, governance and fraud: Theory and application*. Springer. https://doi.org/10.1007/978-981-15-1928-4_13

Brandas, C., Megan, O., & Didraga, O. (2015). Global perspectives on accounting information systems: Mobile and cloud approach. *Procedia Economics and Finance, 20*, 88–93.

Brink, W. D., & Stoel, M. D. (2019). Analytics knowledge, skills, and abilities for accounting graduates. In *Advances in Accounting Educations: Teaching and Curriculum Innovations* (pp. 23–43). Emerald Publishing Limited.

Brynjolfsson, E., & McAfee, A. (2014). *The second machine age: Work, progress, and prosperity in a time of brilliant technologies*. W. W. Norton.

Cai, C. W. (2021). Triple-entry accounting with blockchain: How far have we come? *Accounting and Finance, 1*, 71–93.

Cambridge, J. (2018, October 3). *Cloud business and closing the gap between accounting theory and practice: A case study of accountingpod*. Available at SSRN: https://ssrn.com/abstract=3317955

Cockcroft, S., & Russell, M. (2018). Big data opportunities for accounting and finance practice and research. *Australian Accounting Review, 28*(3), 323–333.

Cunningham, L. M., & Stein, S. E. (2018). Using visualization software in the audit of revenue transactions to identify anomalies. *Issues in Accounting Education, 33*(4), 33–46.

Dai, J., & Vasarhelyi, M. A. (2017). Toward blockchain-based accounting and assurance. *Journal of Information Systems, 31*(3), 5–21.

Davenport, T. H. (1998). Putting the enterprise into the enterprise system. *Harvard Business Review, 76*(July), 121–131.

Deloitte. (2019). *Deloitte's 2019 global blockchain survey*. https://www2.deloitte.com/content/dam/insights/us/articles/2019-global-blockchain-survey/DI_2019-global-blockchain-survey.pdf

Dzuranin, A. C., Jones, J. R., & Olvera, R. M. (2018). Infusing data analytics into the accounting curriculum: A framework and insights from faculty. *Journal of Accounting Education, 43*, 24–39.

Enget, K., Saucedo, G. D., & Wright, N. S. (2017). Mystery Inc.: A Big Data case. *Journal of Accounting Education, 38*, 9–22.

Epstein, D. (2019). *Range: Why generalists triumph in a specialized world*. Riverhead Books.

Felski, E. A., & Empey, T. B. (2020). Should blockchain be added to the accounting curriculum? Evidence from a survey of students, professionals and academics. *The Accounting Educators' Journal, XXX*, 201–218.

Fogarty, T., Zimmerman, A., & Richardson, V. (2016). What do we mean by accounting program quality? A decomposition of accounting faculty opinions. *Journal of Accounting Education, 36*, 16–42.

Frey, C. B., & Osborne, M. A. (2017). The future of employment: How susceptible are jobs to computerization? *Technological Forecasting and Social Change, 114*, 254–280.

Gartner. (2012). *What is big data?—Gartner IT glossary—Big data*. Available on the internet at https://www.gartner.com/it-glossary/big-data/. Accessed 30 Dec 2018.

Granlund, M., & Mouritsen, J. (2003). Special section on management control and new information technologies. *European Accounting Review, 12*(1), 77–83. https://doi.org/10.1080/0963818031000087925

Gulin, D., Hladika, M., & Valenta, I. (2019, September). Digitalization and challenges for the accounting profession. *ENTRENOVA* 12–14.

Guthrie, J., & Parker, L. D. (2016). Whither the accounting profession, accountants and accounting researchers? Commentary and projections. *Accounting, Auditing and Accountability Journal, 29*(1), 2–10. https://doi.org/10.1108/aaaj-10-2015-2263

Howcroft, D. (2017). Graduates' vocational skills for the management accountancy profession: Exploring the accounting education expectation-performance gap. *Accounting Education, 26*(5–6), 459–481.

Hutchinson, G. (2019, June 10). *Accounting in 2040: 4 Ways the industry will (probably) change in 20 years.* Retrieved from Going Concern: https://goingconcern.com/future-accounting-jobs-new-york-fort-lauderdale-sponcon/

ICAEW. (2019). *Big data and analytics: The impact on the accountancy profession.*

International Accounting Standards Board. International Accounting Standard (IAS) 17: Accounting for Leases (1982).

International Accounting Standards Board. International Financial Reporting Standard (IFRS) 13: Fair Value Measurement (2011).

Janvrin, D. J., Raschke, R. L., & Dilla, W. N. (2014). Making sense of complex data using interactive data visualization. *Journal of Accounting Education, 32*(4), 31–48.

Janvrin, D. J., & Watson, M. (2017). Big data: A new twist to accounting. *Journal of Accounting Education, 38*, 3–8.

Kamau, C. G. (2021). *Accounting profession: Steps into the future (African perspective).* Available at SSRN: https://ssrn.com/abstract=3946885

Kennedy, G., Dalgarno, B., Bennett, S., Judd, T., T. Gray, K., & Chang, R. (2008). Immigrants and natives: Investigating differences between staff and students' use of technology, in Hello! Where are you in the landscape of educational technology? In *Proceedings ASCILITE Conference* (pp. 484–492), ASCILITE.

Knudsen, D. R. (2020). Elusive boundaries, power relations, and knowledge production: A systematic review of the literature on digitalization in accounting. *International Journal of Accounting Information Systems, 36*, 100441.

Kokina, J., & Davenport, T. H. (2017). The emergence of artificial intelligence: How automation is changing auditing. *Journal of Emerging Technologies in Accounting, 14*(1), 115–122.

Kokina, J., Gilleran, R., Blanchette, S., & Stoddard, D. (2021). Accountant as digital innovator: Roles and competencies in the age of automation. *Accounting Horizons, 35*(1), 153–184.

Kokina, J., Pachamanova, D., & Corbett, A. (2017). The role of data visualization and analytics in performance management: Guiding entrepreneurial growth decisions. *Journal of Accounting Education, 38*, 50–62.

Kotb, A., Abdel-Kader, M., Allam, A., Halabi, H., & Franklin, E. (2019). Information technology in the British and Irish undergraduate accounting degrees. *Accounting Education, 28*(5), 445–464. https://doi.org/10.1080/09639284.2019.1588135

Krahel, J., & Titera, W. (2015). Consequences of big data and formalization on accounting and auditing standards. *Accounting Horizons, 29*(2), 409–422.

Lafond, C. A., McAleer, A. C., & Wentzel, K. (2016). Enhancing the link between technology and accounting in introductory courses: Evidence from students. *Journal of the Academy of Business Education, 17*, 95–108.

Lawson, J. G., & Street, D. A. (2021). Detecting dirty data using SQL: Rigorous house insurance case. *Journal of Accounting Education, 55*, 100714.

Lehner, O. M., Forstenlechner, C., Leitner-Hanetseder, S., & Eisl, C. (2020). *The dynamics of artificial intelligence in accounting organisations: A structuration perspective*. Working Paper Series, Hanken School of Economics, Helsinki.

Leitner-Hanetseder, S., Eisl, C., Knoll, C., & Lehner, O. M. (2021). Need for advanced IT skills for accountants—What does accounting education literature tell us? *Business Education and Accreditation, 13*(1), 57–69.

Leitner-Hanetseder, S., Lehner, O. M., Eisl, C., & Forstenlechner, C. (2021). A profession in transition: Actors, tasks and roles in AI-based accounting. *Journal of Applied Accounting Research, 22*(3), 539–556.

Lewis, C. C., Fretwell, C. E., Ryan, J., & Parham, J. B. (2013). Faculty use of established and emerging technologies in higher education: A unified theory of acceptance and use of technology perspective. *International Journal of Higher Education, 2*(2), 22. https://doi.org/10.5430/ijhe.v2n2p22

Marrone, M., & Hazelton, J. (2019). The disruptive and transformative potential of new technologies for accounting, accountants and accountability. *Meditari Accountancy Research, 27*(5), 677–694.

McKinney, E., Jr., Yoos, C., & Snead, K. (2017). The need for 'skeptical' accountants in the era of big data. *Journal of Accounting Education, 38*, 63–80.

Moll, J., & Yigitbasioglu, O. (2019). The role of internet-related technologies in shaping the work of accountants: New directions for accounting research. *The British Accounting Review, 51*, 1–20.

Neely, M. P., & Cook, J. S. (2011). Fifteen years of data and information quality literature: Developing a research agenda for accounting. *Journal of Information Systems, 25*(1), 79–108.

Oesterreich, T. D., & Teuteberg, F. (2019). The role of business analytics in controllers and management accountant's competence profiles: An exploratory study on individual-level data. *Journal of Accounting and Organizational Change, 15*(2), 1–27.

O'Leary, D. (1986). Expert systems in a personal computer environment. *Georgia Journal of Accounting, 7*(Spring), 107–118.

Pan, G., & Seow, P. S. (2016). Preparing accounting graduates for digital revolution: A critical review of information technology competencies and skills development. *Journal of Education for Business, 91*(3), 166–175.

Pathways Commission. (2012). *Charting a national strategy for the next generation of accountants.* http://commons.aaahq.org/files/0b14318188/Pathways_Commission_Final_Report_Complete.pdf

Porter, M. E., & Heppelmann, J. E. (2014, November). How smart, connected products are transforming competition. *Harvard Business Review, 92*(11), 64–88.

Prensky, M. (2001). Digital natives, digital immigrants part 1. *On the Horizon, 9*(5), 1–6.

PricewaterhouseCoopers (PwC). (2015). *Data driven: What students need to succeed in a rapidly changing business world.* http://www.pwc.com/us/en/faculty-resource/assets/pwc-data-driven-paper-feb2015.pdf

Psaila, S. (2017). *Blockchain: A game changer for audit processes?* Available on the internet at https://www2.deloitte.com/mt/en/pages/audit/articles/mt-blockchain-a-game-changer-for-audit.html. Accessed 7 June 2022.

Rane, S. P., & Lahane, R. B. (2020). The future of accounting and finance: Artificial 23.

Rebele, J. E., & St. Pierre, E. K. (2019). A commentary on learning objectives for accounting education programs: The importance of soft skills and technical knowledge. *Journal of Accounting Education, 48*, 71–79. https://doi.org/10.1016/j.jaccedu.2019.07.002

Richardson, V. J., & Shan, Y. (2019). Data analytics in the accounting curriculum. *Advances in accounting education: Teaching and curriculum innovations* (pp. 67–79). Emerald Publishing Limited.

Rom, A., & Rohde, C. (2007). Management accounting and integrated information systems: A literature review. *International Journal of Accounting Information Systems, 8*(1), 40–68.

Schneider, G., Dai, J., Janvrin, D. J., Ajayi, K., & Raschke, R. L. (2015). Infer, predict, and assure: Accounting opportunities in data analytics. *Accounting Horizons, 29*(3), 719–742.

Schoute, M. (2019). Teaching python to management accounting students: An illustration using support department cost-allocation methods. *The Accounting Educators' Journal, XXIX*, 137–161.

Seow, P. S., Goh, C., Pan, G., Yong, M., & Chek J. (2021). Embracing digital transformation in accounting & finance. *CPA Australia and Singapore Management University School of Accountancy.*

Skrbis, Z., & Jacqueline, L. B. (2019). Technology, change, and uncertainty: Maintaining career confidence in the early 21st century. *New Technology, Work and Employment, 34*(3), 191–207. https://doi.org/10.1111/ntwe.12151

Sledgianowski, D., Gomaa, M., & Tan, C. (2017). Toward integration of Big data, technology and information systems competencies into the accounting curriculum. *Journal of Accounting Education, 38*, 81–93.

Smith, S. S. (2018). Digitization and financial reporting—How technology innovation may drive the shift toward continuous accounting. *Accounting and Finance Research, 7*(3), 240–250.

Sutton, S. G., Holt, M., & Arnold, V. (2016). The reports of my death are greatly exaggerated—Artificial intelligence research in accounting. *International Journal of Accounting Information Systems, 22*, 60–73.

Tan, L. M., & Laswad, F. (2018). Professional skills required of accountants: What do job advertisements tell us? *Accounting Education, 27*(4), 403–432.

Tang, F., Norman, C. S., & Vendrzyk, V. (2017). Exploring perceptions of data analytics in the internal audit function. *Behaviour and Information Technology, 36*(11), 1125–1136.

Ukpong, E. G., Udoh, I. I., & Essien, I. T. (2019). Artificial intelligence: Opportunities, issues and applications in banking, accounting, and auditing in Nigeria. *Asian Journal of Economics, Business and Accounting, 10*(1), 1–6.

van Laar, E., van Deursen, A. J. A. M., van Dijk, J. A. G. M., & de Haan, J. (2017). The relation between 21st-century skills and digital skills: A systematic literature review. *Computers in Human Behavior, 72*, 577–588.

Vasarhelyi, M. A., Kogan, A., & Tuttle, B. M. (2015). Big data in accounting: An overview. *Accounting Horizons, 29*(2), 381–396.

Wang, T., & Cuthbertson, R. (2015). Eight issues on audit data analytics we would like researched. *Journal of Information Systems, 29*(1), 155–162.

Warren, J., Moffitt, K., & Byrnes, P. (2015). How big data will change accounting. *Accounting Horizons, 29*(2), 397–407.

Watty, K., McKay, J., & Ngo, L. (2016). Innovators or inhibitors? Accounting faculty resistance to new educational technologies in higher education. *Journal of Accounting Education, 36*, 1–15.

Wilder-James, E. (2012). What is Big data—An introduction to the big data landscape. https://www.oreilly.com/radar/what-is-big-data/. Accessed 7 June 2022.

World Economic Forum. (2020). Future of Jobs Report 2020.

CHAPTER 2

Digital Transformation in Accounting: The Nexus Between Technology, Leadership, and Beyond

Sandy Arief

Introduction

In today's business landscape, organizations are required to constantly face rapid changes in technological advancements, inevitably reshaping business models, internal processes, products, or services (Loonam et al., 2018). Digital transformation is defined as transformation "concerned with the changes digital technologies can bring about in a company's business model, ...products or organizational structures" (Hess et al., 2020, 124). Digital possibilities need to come together with skilled organizational members and leaders in order to reveal its transformative power. Therefore, digital transformation requires both technology and people. In addition, digital transformation is considered as the merging of physical and digital processes into decentralized systems, representing a major change in social and organizational operations (Gonçalves et al.,

S. Arief (✉)
Universitas Negeri Semarang, Semarang, Indonesia
e-mail: sandy.arief@mail.unnes.ac.id

A. Perdana and T. Wang (eds.), *Digital Transformation in Accounting and Auditing*, https://doi.org/10.1007/978-3-031-46209-2_2

2022; Matt et al., 2015). It affects all aspects of people's lives, as organizations and society change their structures, and the economy and businesses reinvent their value-creation process.

In recent years, scholarly attention, particularly in the information systems literature, has been steadily increasing, leading to a significant increase in the number of studies addressing different technological and organizational aspects of digital transformation. Therefore, this chapter aims to provide a descriptive, comprehensive analysis of the accounting field by critically assessing how digital transformation affects organizations. This objective is approached in two steps. First, I provide a systematic literature review on digital technology in accounting. By reviewing the literature on digital transformation, I hope to derive implications for technology adoption and development in the accounting field. Second, this chapter contributes to the advancement of this field by elaborating on significant factors of digital transformation that integrate other areas, such as the role of leadership, the importance of future transformation in accounting, and the implications of digital transformation on future jobs. I find that the important leadership perspective on digital transformation has thus far been neglected in the literature. Further, the impact of digital transformation on organizational members and work-related outcomes has been identified as an important research direction. Accordingly, this chapter contributes to the literature by providing new perspectives and possible explanations for the limited literature on future transformation in accounting and its impact of digital transformation on future jobs.

Thus, the impact of digital transformation on accounting is significant. Previous studies have addressed the association between digital transformation and accounting from different perspectives, with different research tools, and within a distinct study. From a management perspective, organizations rely on various types of computer-based information systems that use hardware, software, and other forms of information technology for decision-making processes. Management also applies information systems to support their organization's activities, including marketing, production, accounting, finance, human resources, and other areas that are supported and integrated through the common system (Laudon & Laudon, 2011; O'Brien & Marakas, 2011; Stair & Reynolds, 2020). Increasingly, management is becoming aware that information is a resource of strategic importance, with technology being used to support information resources to gain competitive advantages (Laudon &

Laudon, 2011). Hence, owing to the ubiquitous and prominent use of information systems, including digital transformation in organizations, working to improve information systems and ensuring that they function at peak performance using the most efficient and readily available technology is of utmost importance.

The demand for effective information technology is evident in both the academic literature and the corporate world, and a review of the literature highlights the significant impact of information systems on reducing costs, increasing efficiency, improving product innovation, and enhancing productivity (Carvalho & Guerrini, 2017; Kakhki & Gargeya, 2019; Kim & Jee, 2007; Nwankpa & Roumani, 2014; Queiroz et al., 2018). Over the last few decades, there has been an increase in information systems research, which has changed and shaped the way organizations operate and produce goods and services. For example, Phornlaphatrachakorn and NaKalasindhu (2021) show that digital transformation is of great significance in influencing accounting information and the quality of financial reports, thereby increasing the effectiveness of strategic decision-making processes. Parlak (2020) explained that digital transformation has a tangible impact on the accounting profession, from memorizing, classifying, and summarizing to analyzing and discussing financial statements, establishing the system, and ensuring the effective continuity of the system. In addition, Nguyen et al. (2021) concluded that digital transformation processes will allow managers to take advantage of the effort related to accounting work and attendant errors to search for customers and focus on improving product quality and increasing the organization's competitiveness and positions. Further, Othman and AL-Dweikat (2021) found that there is a tangible impact of managing the risks of digital transformation in making appropriate information that serves the makers and users of accounting data. Consequently, it is necessary for organizational members of the accounting profession to use the developed systems to effectively adapt to this transformation process.

However, automation also increases the risk of jeopardizing the quality of information (Korhonen et al., 2020). Hence, although the abundance of data suggests that the decision-making process is more rational, there is an increase in complexity as a challenge for organizations to utilize digital automation (Bromwicha & Scapens, 2016). In addition, resistance to change has been elaborated with respect to digital transformation. In general, it can be said that change in the digital sphere is, at least conceptually, a highly disruptive enterprise, with a focus on fundamental transformations of both practices and products (Loonam et al., 2018). However, when it comes to resistance to change, the researched construct is often technology implementation, and the researched "resistances" were actually related to the rejection of specific (new) technologies (Laumer, 2016). Although many theorists have argued that the implementation and consequent adoption of new technologies is the first step toward more fundamental digital transformations (Berghaus & Back, 2017; Matt et al., 2015; Murdoch & Fichter, 2017; Vial, 2019), the notion that digital transformation must always be disruptive has also been challenged by some (Furr & Shipilov, 2019).

Hence, the importance of this chapter comes from the growing interest in exploring digital transformation in the corporate environment. The remainder of this chapter is organized into four sections. The next section provides a relevant literature review on digital technology in accounting, followed by a discussion of the rationale for the association between leadership and digital transformation. The final two sections discuss the future of accounting and its implications for future work.

Digital Technology in Accounting

I will focus on some types of digital technology, such as Robotic Process Automation (RPA), Artificial Intelligence (AI), Blockchain, Business Intelligence (BI), and Big Data, and present their relevance and impact as per these studies.

Robotic Process Automation (RPA)

Robotic Process Automation (RPA) is widely used for accounting purposes to automate well-defined repetitive tasks. It is a relatively new technology that comprises software agents called "bots" that mimic the manual path taken by a human being through a variety of computer applications when performing certain tasks in a business process (Syed et al., 2020). RPA can be found at the intersection of repetitive task automation and digital task performance. The most suitable processes for RPA are based on rules and repetitions that do not require frequent changes and are mostly free of exceptions (Deloitte, 2019). Gartner (2020) pointed out that the global revenue in the RPA software market is expected to reach the US$ 1.89 billion mark by 2021, an increase of 19.5% by 2020, with the prospect of continuing growth in the double digits until 2024.

This exponential growth of the RPA product market stems from the perception of the impacts of these automations on the optimization of the quality, speed, and productivity of processes, important gains for organizations seeking cost reductions, and remaining competitive in the market. Consequently, accounting professionals are interested in rethinking their processes in terms of automation and deepening their understanding of the matter.

RPA studies have recently focused on analyzing their impact on business. It is worth mentioning that most market research was developed by major accounting firms that applied RPA to achieve cost savings and increase operational efficiency in tax and consulting services. For example, since 2018, KPMG has been working in partnership with a global leader in Enterprise RPA to help customers automate manual business processes (KPMG, 2017). Further, a survey conducted by Deloitte, one of the largest RPA consultants on 523 organizations worldwide, showed a projection of a 22% reduction in operating costs and an improvement of 88% in the accuracy of information generated by automated processes with the implementation of RPA.

From an accounting perspective, manual and repetitive audit tasks such as reconciliations, internal control tests, and detailed tests can be automated. With automation, accountants or auditors can allocate more resources to complex audit areas or investigate potential anomalies, leading to higher audit quality (Moffitt et al., 2018). Many areas of finance and accounting involve tasks that interact with multiple systems, contain high levels of processing transactions, and require few decisions to make. The potential for RPA use in these areas is high. One example of an RPA application in the accounting field is related to taxes. For example, after the creation of automation software, robots are configured to perform repetitive processes such as sending applicative functions to a tax authority portal (Zhang et al., 2005). Therefore, the potential of RPA is both numerous and of considerable impact: rationalization of daily tasks, cost reduction, performance, and productivity gains, but also improvements in human *know-how* within the organization.

It is worth noting that the automation of RPA is only part of the digital transformation process. Other factors, such as the revision of procedures and professional development, are essential for its deployment. A study by EY (2019) revealed that 30–50% of initial RPA projects failed during their implementation. The main critical points highlighted include the absence of process risk analysis, professional preparation, solution testing, access controls, and management of changes. In addition, Kokina and Blanchette (2019) explained that various restrictions on the use of RPA exist because organizations benefit from the automation of only a few processes, which are structured and repetitive, based on rules, and involve digital input. Other sources point to difficulties in understanding the process and managing the changes involved (PWC, 2020). Therefore, it is important for academics and accounting professionals to assess the benefits and potential risks of implementing RPA.

Although RPA provides significant improvements in business operations, it still has limitations in terms of unstructured data. To expand the capabilities of RPA, AI and cognitive technologies have been adapted, and a new form of automation has evolved named Intelligent Process Automation (IPA). IPA is a new technology that combines fundamental process redesign with RPA and machine learning (Zhang, 2019). IPA can replace human effort in processes that involve aggregating data from multiple systems or taking a piece of information from a written document and entering it as standardized data input (Lievano-Martínez et al., 2022). It is a suite of business process improvements and next-generation tools that assist knowledge workers by removing repetitive, replicable, and routine tasks (Ansari et al., 2019). In addition, it can radically improve customer journeys by simplifying interactions and accelerating processes. IPA mimics the activities carried out by humans and learns to do them even better. IPA promises radically enhanced efficiency, increased worker performance, reduced operational risks, and improved response times and customer experiences (Berruti et al., 2017). IPA leverages data-driven optimization and pattern mining to automate business processes to interpret user behaviors, and undeniably works as a catalyst for business growth (Berruti et al., 2017; Lievano-Martínez et al., 2022). AI advancement provides a solid foundation for IPA to improve process efficiency in automated and optimized workflow and business processes (Chakraborti et al., 2020).

Artificial Intelligence (AI)

AI is gaining attention in the accounting discipline. From a practical point of view, AI refers to machines, algorithms, or programs that draw inspiration from or imitate human skills, such as understanding natural language, identifying visual objects, or reasoning in various forms (Sutton et al., 2016). AI includes innovations, such as machine learning and natural language processing, as well as statistical techniques known for decades, such as classification and grouping (Sutton et al., 2016). In some studies, this technology has been defined as synthetic intelligence or computer system intelligence that simulates intellectual functions. Practically, AI technologies perform tasks that require human intelligence, such as extracting meaning from images, texts, or speech; detecting patterns and anomalies; and making recommendations, predictions, or decisions. These include machine learning, deep processing, and natural language generation (Deloitte, 2019). Hence, AI is a sophisticated tool capable of learning using training protocols. AI has three areas of action, namely description, prediction, and prescription. The three fields of action can be described as follows: the description represents the knowledge and understanding of the researched data (what happened); the purpose of the prediction is to use historical information to decipher the future (what will happen); and the purpose of the prescription is to obtain the best results (what needs to happen).

Many scholars examine the effects of AI on accounting. For example, Chase and Shim (1991) and O'Leary (1991) investigated the application of AI in useful devices to facilitate the organization, storage, and application of intelligence in accounting database systems. AI is used by professionals and organizations such as the *Big Four*, which have their own robots capable of automatically recognizing data, entering invoices, and generating financial reports, as well as detecting fraudulent invoices, assisting with tax returns, and reduced processing (Zhang et al., 2005). However, the ability of AI to see faster and further than the human eye can also allow for the detection of errors, gaps, or similarities in accounting documents (Iansiti & Lakhani, 2014). It is not a question to replace accountants but rather to strengthen their skills and capacities. AI has developed a world of accounting and can be used for many accounting objectives. This implies significant changes in the areas of accounting practices and transfers of some practices, including consulting, certification, and tax reporting, to a virtual level. AI focuses on the "logical part" of the tasks while the professional accountant focuses more on the "emotional part." This technological tool constitutes a competitive advantage for the accounting department as well as for the company owing to its unprecedented capacity in the continuous production of internal and external data (Iansiti & Lakhani, 2014).

Blockchain and Cryptocurrency

In a business that heavily depends on the transfer and exchange of strategic data, blockchain plays an important role in certifying the authenticity and integrity of a digital coin without trusted third parties and heralds a real revolution. Similar to all digital innovations, accountants do not seem to be left behind. It seems appropriate to highlight the characteristics and implications of blockchain technology in the accounting profession (Carlozo, 2017).

Blockchain is characterized by three principles: transparency, data protection, and decentralization (Desplebin et al., 2021). This technology has specific characteristics that enhance the functionality of continuous accounting and provoke fruitful digitizing of the accounting profession. Financial or non-financial information, which is approved by the consensus protocol of the blockchain and then downloaded and integrated into the blockchain platform, cannot be modified without an easily visible and verifiable trace (Casino et al., 2019). It is all about the immutability characteristic of the blockchain platform. The blockchain platform, which is constituted as a decentralized construction, provides more extensive communication of information (Bonsón & Bednárová, 2019). Likewise, the information charged to specific data blocks is encrypted and can only be unlocked using a specific combination of public and private keys (Carlozo, 2017). Furthermore, this control solution proposed by the blockchain allows for the possibility of defining degrees of transparency, which makes it possible to have both a definable register and ledger, public, or private. One of the advantages of blockchain platforms is that they offer real-time features that ensure the integrity and transparency of everyone involved. Other advantages are expected with the use of blockchain in accounting, as shown in Table 2.1.

Even though the technology has the potential to reshape capital markets as a whole, tension still needs to be considered in relation to the social and political barriers that prevent blockchain proliferation. In addition, blockchain expansion comes with some barriers, posing questions regarding cybersecurity and scalability. Accounting professionals will not be the central authority of a blockchain but will likely remain the party responsible for a company's financial reports, as required by regulations for corporate governance purposes (Tan & Low, 2019). Accounting professionals should be aware of blockchain's impact on accounting

Table 2.1 Blockchain resources and applications in accounting

Blockchain resources	*Potential impact on accounting*
Triple entry	The triple entry by which the system automatically confirms the debitt /credit entry registered for each party in a transaction would ensure greater accounting reliability
Entries registered in real time	Streamlines the production of reports and financial statements. Help identifying hidden accounts or incorrect entries
Traceability of historical data	Accuracy and efficiency in financial management and performance in general
Speed of access to numbers	Useful management information, avoiding poor practices and bottlenecks in management. Significantly reduces the time required to verify accounting entries. The scope of the audit in relation to the analysis becomes more aggregated and accessible to accountants
Automated taxation	Mitigate tax evasion by providing an immutable platform through which taxes can be collected in real time
Smart Contracts	Streamlines the registration process by instantly updating account information and tracking supply chains through real-time analyses

Source Karajovic et al. (2019)

services. In addition, they must acquire new skills to adapt to changes in work requirements for existing and emerging accounting positions.

Blockchain ecosystems are composed of cryptographic hashes that represent information input (McAliney & Ang, 2019). The cryptographic hash protects the validity and accuracy of information and the integrity of data integrity (Smith, 2018). Cryptocurrencies are gaining worldwide popularity. They are virtual currencies supported by decentralized systems that use cryptography and blockchain for security, which engender trust by making it difficult to counterfeit (Ramassa & Leoni, 2021). Although not tangible as commodities and notes, cryptocurrencies are created as an alternative form of currency and offer three money functions as a medium of exchange, a unit of account, and a store of value (Radford, 1945). Further, cryptocurrency can be considered a sub-class of crypto-assets, which have been defined by the European Financial Reporting Advisory Group (EFRAG) as digital representations of value or contractual rights created, transferred, and stored on a distributed ledger technology

(DTL) network, that is, blockchain (Tan & Low, 2019). In the field of accounting and auditing, cryptocurrency features revolutionize how accounting data are accessed, as they allow all actors in the chain to obtain history, real-time updating, and final reporting.

Cryptocurrencies have several advantages. First, it engenders trust via this sequence of verification and confirmation and through the transparency offered by the public ledger, which is shared among all nodes of the network. Second, it may provide a valid alternative for exchanging goods and services in jurisdictions where central banks and institutions are not trustworthy. Third, transaction costs are reduced to a minimum because there is no need for a third party to confirm the transaction, and there are no fixed costs related to software purchase or system access (Ram, 2018; Tan & Low, 2019). However, cryptocurrencies have significant disadvantages. First, the network participants are pseudo-anonymous; it is difficult to trace the identity of the users, making cryptocurrencies a potential tool for illegal activities such as money laundering or black-market purchases. Second, there are significant doubts related to the intrinsic value of a currency due to its high volatility and intangible nature. Third, cryptocurrency is striving to become an accepted payment method owing to its technical complexity and volatility (Ram, 2018; Tan & Low, 2019).

Consequently, it is not surprising that cryptocurrencies have been under the radar of governments, central banks, and financial markets in recent years. Some accounting scholars have raised concerns about the absence of specific provisions within current accounting standards (Procházka, 2018; Ram, 2018). In this specific issue, cryptocurrency holdings are suggested as a new asset class with unique characteristics that make them a different financial investment that requires new and specific regulations (Ram, 2018). In contrast, other scholars consider cryptocurrency holdings aligned with the current definitions of assets and liabilities in the International Accounting Standards Board (IASB) Financial Reporting Framework and neglect any need for accounting regulations (Tan & Low, 2019). However, while scholars disagree with the treatment of such new items, they all agree that guidance on how to account for such items should be provided clearly by the relevant accounting standard setters (Lowe et al., 2020; Ram, 2018; Tan & Low, 2019).

Business Intelligence (BI) and Big Data

The increasing volume of information and its potential in strategic business management demand a structure and control that makes the decision-making process more efficient. BI is a set of techniques and tools for acquiring and transforming raw data into meaningful and useful information for business analysis purposes (Appelbaum et al., 2017). It is a set of techniques and tools that aims to support decision-making and monitoring of companies' results.

Previous studies examined the relationship between BI and Big Data. For example, Kowalczyk and Buxmann (2015) highlight that BI supports specific accounting tasks, such as profitability analysis. Peters et al. (2016) examined the quality of BI (infrastructure integration, functionality, and self-service) and its effect on diagnostic performance measurement capabilities. In addition, the reach of Big Data for existing accounting practices, such as influencing budgeting processes (Moll & Yigitbasioglu, 2019); presents several opportunities for accounting professionals with exploratory analysis in Big Data and BI (Richins et al., 2017), among others.

Belfo and Trigo (2013) highlighted that BI involves processes such as data mining, process mining, statistical analysis, predictive analysis, and predictive modeling, which can support various management accounting issues, such as forecasting, or other management support concerns, such as identifying and analyzing strategic options, decision support, and business risk management. There are numerous advantages of employing BI, such as increasing the velocity of decision-making with reliable data, enhancing the efficiency of operations, and optimizing processes. Hence, BI facilitates the decision-making process within organizations because of the ease of viewing analysis and reporting resulting from the processes. To ensure the reliability of the information used in BI, a structured and consistent database, that is, Big Data, is needed (Coyne & McMickle, 2017). Janvrin and Watson (2017) pointed out that Big Data has three features: volume as described by large amounts of machine data, transactions, and social media interactions; speed, which covers a high rate at which large amounts of data are created, processed, and become obsolete; and variety as the different data sources containing text, audio, video, image, and other data types.

In the accounting field, Big Data presents large amounts and new forms of structured, unstructured, and semi-structured data; hence, alternative methods of data management and reporting (Perkhofer et al., 2019). While datasets are now larger than ever (Big Data) and better analytical software data (BI) are available, the main goal of accounting has always been the same, which is to create and provide information for internal and external decision-makers. For this reason, these digital technologies should be deployed simultaneously in organizations to ensure efficient data analysis.

Leadership in Digital Transformation

Leadership is considered a critical factor in digital transformation (McQuade, 2006; Yang et al., 2014). A lack of leadership or an ineffective leadership style is a major impediment to the success of information systems (Banks et al., 2016; Neubert et al., 2013; Sumner, 2000). In the context of digital transformation, leaders play an essential role in affecting organizational members' behavior, as leaders are those who integrate new information systems or transform organizational practices and processes (Arvidsson et al., 2014; O'Reilly et al., 2010). Additionally, leaders play a pivotal role in influencing and shaping organizational behavior, adapting to external changes, providing guidance for organizational members as they face challenges, and ensuring continuous progress and development (Hernandez et al., 2011; House et al., 2002; Karahanna & Watson, 2006; Odumeru & Ogbonna, 2013). Further, leaders also play an important role in encouraging organizational members to develop new ideas or improve work procedures for the benefit of the organization (Kappelman et al., 2019; Schmitt et al., 2016; Zhu et al., 2005). In particular, the complex and knowledge-intensive nature of information systems requires leadership to direct teamwork processes and outcomes (Kappelman et al., 2019).

Leadership plays a pivotal role in engaging information system leaders and business leaders in the digital transformation of respective organizations. Leadership plays a critical role in guiding a leader's vision and generating new propositions that impact successful digital transformation (Sebastian et al., 2020; Yokoi et al., 2019). To achieve the quality of digital transformation, it takes commitment from top management as well as the involvement of top management as a user in the development of digital transformation.

The literature is deficient in considering the role of top management in implementing and supporting such initiatives. In particular, organizations can no longer expect that the deployment of tangible resources, such as information systems, will automatically result in enhanced organizational performance. Rather, they must consider the influence of human and knowledge resources; for example, the influence of leadership style on the association between the use of information systems and organizational performance, especially given that human resources are considered to be an organization's most pivotal resource (Abualoush et al., 2018).

Based on the new institutional theory (NIT) perspective, leadership is considered a fundamental aspect of organizational values and belief systems when organizations change over time, and leadership must also change and adapt (Biggart & Hamilton, 1987). Organizations have shifted to digital transformation by changing how they operate and deliver their products/services by promoting digital cultures (Chierici et al., 2020). It would not be possible without leaders who create platforms for this and drive stakeholders toward action (Sainger, 2018). Leaders can help organizations succeed in the digital age through three habits: (1) following the trends of emergent technologies, (2) determining the direction of the digital change and investment strategy, and (3) leading the team to change effectively and efficiently. In addition, leaders with digital transformation mindsets, also known as "digital leaders," can build collaborative networked organizations and create digital competencies (Bresciani et al., 2021; Frankowska & Rzeczycki, 2020).

The notion of digital leadership was introduced to address the competence that leaders must develop in today's digital environment. El Sawy et al. (2020) defined digital leadership as the capacity of doing the right things for the strategic success of digitalization for the enterprise and its business ecosystem. Imran et al. (2020) identified five critical competencies of digital leaders. First, *digital vision* requires leaders to envision and communicate with people in the digital future of the organization. Second, *digital knowledge* refers to a good understanding of digital tools and how a specific technology impacts customer business. Third, *failing fast*, the capability to fail and learn quickly to manage resources for the organization with efficient tasks and stop something that does not work. Fourth, *empowerment*, the delegation of power toward subordinates to ensure powerful digital transformation, encouraging participation in decision-making, expressing confidence in high performance, and helping organizational members to be part of this whole transformation process.

Finally, ***managing diverse teams***, and managing each team member inclusively to deliver complex projects in a digital transformation context, leaders need to develop cross-functional teams.

Digital transformation is more far-reaching than technology (Hadžiosmanović et al., 2012). If we look at how the digital market is evolving, it is clear that people are constant and at the heart of digital evolution (Lee et al., 2016). Harnessing the collective intelligence of employees, partners, and customers is a critical success factor in digital transformation (Choi et al., 2014; Khan et al., 2016). According to Klaus Schawb, Founder, and Executive Chairman of the World Economic Forum, these technologies have the power to connect businesses in a "global digital and virtual system and the related flow of ideas and services" (Singh & Fhom, 2017). The impact of digital transformation on business removes all borders and replaces old economies of scale (Kurosawa et al., 2017; Yar, 2006).

According to a study conducted by McKinsey & Company in 2016 calculated that "digital flows—which were practically nonexistent just 15 years ago—now exert a larger impact on GDP growth than the centuries-old trade in goods" (Friedberg et al., 2016). The study also revealed that a "45-fold increase in the amount of cross-border bandwidth from 2005 to 2016 and predicted another 5-fold increase by 2022" (Kurosawa et al., 2017).

In 2019, another study entitled "Measuring the Digital Transformation: A Roadmap for the Future" published by the Organisation for Economic Co-operation and Development (OECD) showed a roadmap with nine action steps to help countries monitor the process of digital transformation and its impacts on the economic environment (Schwab, 2019). The first four steps are directed to build a new generation of stakeholders, a new generation of data, and indicators capable of dealing with the challenges of digital transformation: make the digital economy visible in global economic statistics, understand the cross-country economic impacts of business digital transformation, measure well-being in the digital age, and design new and interdisciplinary approaches to data collection. The next five action steps are directed toward specific areas of interest: fast-accelerating transformative digital technologies, global data infrastructure, data flows and skills in the digital era, trust in online environments, and governments' digital strengths and policies.

Digital transformation has developed a new practical paradigm for economic value (Fischbacher-Smith, 2016). A survey from 2019 revealed that between 2013 and 2016, five economies of the world—the USA, China, Japan, Chinese Taipei, and Korea—developed between 70% and 100% of cutting-edge digital technologies. Digital business transformation under digital technology is based on technology entities. In less than 25 years, Amazon has grown from a startup e-commerce store to the world's second-largest traded company, revolutionizing retail, cloud computing, and other web services. Apple became the world's first trillion-dollar company in 2018, barely a decade after it released its first iPhone (Schwab, 2019).

Cyber Accounting—The Future of Accounting?

Cyber accounting is a growing issue. The exponential growth of new technologies, sustained by the increasing number of mobile and wireless devices and services, requires customers to respond in real time to their demands, which represents a vast digital technology exploration field for today and future economic entities, reshaping the accounting departments, and connecting them with cybersecurity from a new intelligence perspective: cyber accounting (Schwab, 2019).

From the perspective of an economic entity, cyber accounting is a new force of accounting in the digital business landscape. The objective is to make a significant, reliable, and positive impact on the finance department, by redefining key performance indicators and specifically real profits, creating new business models, developing revolutionary business solutions for all types of economic entities, covering accounting services, bookkeeping, TAX filing, and VAT reporting services as "technology building blocks" (Okamoto & Takashima, 2015) with the expansion in maximizing the value of financial data even if the threat of cybersecurity risk still exists. To navigate the threat of cybersecurity, cyber accountants work intensively with cybersecurity professionals to identify system errors, develop and implement strategic plans to protect assets, and evaluate the need to execute specific internal controls to close data security gaps (Stefanescu et al., 2019).

With respect to practitioners, cyber accounting is a new business language in which accounting and finance speak to the public. Cyber accounting will assist future leaders in building a strong economic entity by developing a better business model. The classical accounting procedures in which accountants "processed invoices, purchase orders, or deliver orders on paper documents which manually were introduced in computer systems, coded, and finally transmitted to the managers for approval and payment" is replaced by "automated workflow process and software that analyses, recognises, directs, and exports data into a company's ERP systems" (Karanja, 2017).

ERP systems are considered the most essential and critical information systems and are widely used to integrate all the functions of a business process into a unified and efficient enterprise system (Davenport, 2000; Dechow & Mouritsen, 2005; Kirmizi & Kocaoglu, 2020). In recent years, Enterprise Resource Planning (ERP) systems have been used as comprehensive integrated systems by most companies and organizations. ERP systems have also been widely implemented by many organizations worldwide and are considered the most rapidly growing systems in operational areas (Koksalmis & Damar, 2021; Molla & Bhalla, 2006; Zhang et al., 2005).

ERP systems were initially implemented to help re-engineer organizations around the principles of real-time data integration, which led to greater transactional and reporting efficiencies (Aremu et al., 2019; Carvalho & Guerrini, 2017; Davenport, 2000; Dechow & Mouritsen, 2005). As organizations gain more experience in managing them, ERP systems have evolved into a platform for developing decision-support applications across the entire organization. This was a somewhat unexpected but well-documented benefit of ERP system implementation (Chou & Chang, 2008; Holsapple & Sena, 2001). Currently, with the significant growth in the use of real-time corporate analytics and big data applications, ERP system implementation has become even more crucial. Current ERP system research shows that users are even more focused on how to leverage the data from ERP systems for better decision-making (Lemonakis et al., 2018; Seethamraju & Sundar, 2013; Mukwasi & Seymour, 2012; Kallunki et al., 2011). Furthermore, some ERP experts are pushing for even tighter integration with decision-support functions and are promoting a new wave of "integrated analytics" to support improved reporting and provide greater operational insights (Holsapple et al., 2019; Ruivo et al., 2020; Shi & Wang, 2018). ERP systems are now viewed as key assets from which corporations can leverage a huge amount of data generated by their various applications. For example, Umran Hasan, the senior manager of Product Marketing at Microsoft Dynamics ERP, stated that machine learning, predictive analytics, and the Internet of Things are all areas that customers want to get more from, with their ERP systems being the key to enabling them to gather such information and to make sense of it all for their business (Holsapple et al., 2019).

ERP systems have a relatively large global market share. According to a study by Allied Market Research, the ERP market is expected to reach $41.69 billion with a Compound Annual Growth Rate (CAGR) of 7.2% by 2020 (Chaudhari & Ghone, 2015). Sun et al. (2016) found that 66% of ERP projects achieved less than 50% of expected benefits. Therefore, in view of such high failure rates, both researchers and managers continue to analyze the antecedent factors influencing the extent of ERP system use and the subsequent impact on the success of ERP systems.

Digital transformation, which is available in real time for millions of economic entities and the force of cyber accounting, has positive notes for organizations. For example, improving cloud-based software solutions for managing financial documents, reducing processes and routes invoices from 30 to 2 days, reducing processing costs per invoice from $13.00 to about $2.00, increasing the opportunities to capture early payment discounts from only 20% to 80% of the time (Chen et al., 2015), and rebuilding an automated relationship with suppliers and leaders on payment deadlines, approval workflows, and management decisions based on financial reports (Stefanescu et al., 2019).

Digital Transformation and Future Jobs

Several factors have impacted the accounting profession in recent years, including digital transformation (Petani et al., 2021). Based on a large survey conducted by Chartered Accountants Australia and New Zealand (CAANZ), most survey respondents considered information technology (IT) to be the biggest perceived driver of occupational change over the next 10 years (CAANZ, 2016). Similar concerns have been raised in studies that address the potential impacts of automation on various professions (Frey & Osborne, 2017; Tschang & Almirall, 2020), including those that specifically focus on accounting (Guthrie & Parker, 2016; Kokina & Blanchette, 2019).

The adoption of new technologies, such as RPA and AI, continues to increase productivity, and while digitalization is increasing the demand for high-skilled workers, it is expected that a large proportion of medium- and low-skilled jobs (characterized as back-office work) will be eliminated in the near future (Tschang & Almirall, 2020). Consequently, concerns are being raised about the future of the accounting profession owing to digital transformation and what accountants need to do to remain relevant (Moll & Yigitbasioglu, 2019).

There is no exception that the accounting and auditing professions will change sooner rather than later because of the digital transformation that we are presently in. When time-consuming tasks are performed by machines, professionals can focus on adding more value to their customers, which reduces both the cost and time spent on the given tasks. The automation of regular accounting processes will lead accountants and auditors to focus on more specific tasks, because many of the earlier tasks will be done by automation. Traditional accounting procedures, such as in-house and travel invoicing, will be replaced by computers. Auditing processes will be automated and there will be advanced tools to detect risk and fraud. Future auditors will be able to focus on analyzing outputs instead of using several hours to collect information from financial statements (Forbes, 2018). While some jobs may be at risk, new technologies and practices, such as Big Data analytics (Richins et al., 2017) and blockchain (Tan & Low, 2019) are giving rise to new opportunities for accountants, although such technologies may potentially impact professional jurisdictions and lead to turf wars (Abbott, 1988; Sikka & Willmott, 1995).

The automation of accounting tasks coupled with other technologies also puts downward pressure on traditional accounting roles such as taxation (Tadros, 2019). However, revenue from commercial services, including advisory services that involve risk and technology, is experiencing strong growth (FT, 2021). Furthermore, while in 2020, the total revenue of the *Big Four* was US157 billion, it is predicted that in the future, 80% of their revenue will be sourced from advisory services (Nixon, 2016).

The future jobs of accountants and auditors will use sophisticated information systems and artificial intelligence to analyze, report, and develop targeted outputs. Sophisticated information systems will handle data security by connecting different parts of the financials, which will become part of Big Data. The revolution is changing the tasks related to management accounting and financial accounting. In the future of management accounting, tasks will be more precise and detailed because of the computer's ability to collect and gather the information needed for managers to make the correct decisions. Accountants in the field can then focus more specifically on preparing and analyzing data for those who are interested. The problem that accountants may face is the overwhelming amount of information available. This means that the accountants' jobs will be about recognizing relevant and important information to be able to make decisions. These tasks require strong communication skills to share the most important results in a clear way (Guthrie & Parker, 2016). Although computers are taking over, one important fact is that the quality of the data remains important. To produce quality data, there is a need for someone who can transfer information and serve as a service agent when transferring knowledge to the systems (Kokina & Blanchette, 2019).

In contrast, professions considered to be at the greatest risk of extinction are those wherein tasks are repetitive and there is little social interaction (Frey & Osborne, 2017). Now that we have seen what kinds of jobs might be offered in the future, we need to figure out how we can adapt and overcome to be the kind of employee companies will be looking for. To start, basic knowledge of accounting and auditing will always be necessary; thus, the skills mentioned here are needed in addition to what accountants and auditors should already somewhat know. To overcome this issue, we have broken the skills down into more technical skills/"hard skills" and then so-called "soft" and then the so-called soft skills, which are not always taught in conventional education.

National and international professional associations also play a crucial role in defining the profiles of the skills needed to prepare professionals in the current context. They defined guidelines to update the course curricula. Examples are the American Institute of CPAs (AICPA) and the National Association of State Boards of Accountancy (NASBA). In 2021, they presented the AICPA and NASBA CPA Evolution Model Curriculum. According to Taylor and Dustin (2021), the curriculum covers the content necessary for all future CPAs (the Core on Accounting and data analytics, Auditing and AIS, and Tax), as well as three separate disciplines (business analysis and reporting, information systems, control, tax compliance, and planning). After analyzing the program, it can be seen that the AICPA Curriculum increases the coverage of the CPA exam in the area of IT, namely, information systems and data science.

Finally, and more importantly, from a normative perspective (Alzola, 2017; Stahl & Flick, 2011), research needs to bring in different voices from society about how ethical boundaries need to be in place when it comes to the decision-making of technology-powered accounting systems (Dwivedi et al., 2019; Glikson & Woolley, 2020; Munoko et al., 2020). In the past few years, there has been an ongoing debate on AI-related ethical considerations. AI ethics is a set of guidelines that function as a "code of conduct" to think, solve, design, and implement an AI system ethically to cope with a given situation (McGrath & Gupta, 2018; Rogerson et al., 2019).

The role of cultural standards and the position of the organization must be revisited. For example, in entrepreneurship research with recent discussions on hybrid business models, environmental, social, and commercial factors need to be considered when making strategic decisions. Such factors may be under-represented as unstructured and less quantifiable non-financial information may be harder to process and considerably scarcer than the "hard" and easy-to-digest financial information. From the current literature on digital accounting, it becomes clear that any ethical considerations need to be enforced by rules and regulations and can no longer be based on managers' personal human values of managers (Kellogg et al., 2019; Kirkpatrick, 2016; Kovacova et al., 2019; Martin, 2019). AI answers how a data-derived strategy should be put into place needs to be carefully monitored, and a socially accepted way of integrating people, planets, and profit thoughts into the mere functionalist approaches of non-human actors has to be found in a process that includes more than industry and policymakers. Further, ethical considerations—as far as such considerations are possible on a meta-level without a cultural context—will need to be inserted as rules, and the impact of a potential sample bias in machine learning has to be looked at from various critical perspectives. Hence, agency theory may interplay well with sociological and philosophical approaches to create a solid foundation of what the role of ethics should be in digital technology-based accounting (Bogt & Scapens, 2019).

Conclusion

Digital transformation in accounting plays a key role in creating strategic value and guiding business operations. It facilitates process standardization, technical automation, and continuous analysis. In addition, digital transformation in accounting fosters continuous improvements in the quality, accuracy, and efficiency of human activities. This chapter offers four contributions that can help organizations in the context of digital transformation. First, the chapter responds to the call to provide a relevant literature review on digital technology in accounting and how this influences organizations. Therefore, the chapter adds to the scant literature on the adverse impact of digital transformation to support organizations in achieving their objectives. Second, this chapter contributes to the literature by investigating the relationship between leadership and digital transformation. The role of leadership in digital transformation is a pervasive theme in existing literature. However, literature on the role of leadership in digital transformation is still nascent. The concept of how leadership induces digital transformation has not yet been explored. Third, the chapter enriches the limited literature and insights into the future of accounting and cyber accounting. This chapter can serve as the basis for future research to explore cyber accounting and expand it to yield further insights in other areas, such as knowledge management. Finally, there is a pressing need to explore the impact of digital transformation on future employment. As organizations prepare to meet the demands of the digital age, they must understand the challenges that lie ahead. This means focusing on managing the transition to a future workforce, as an implication of digital transformation. Organizations should transform their human resources functions and processes to cater to the shift in approach needed to hire and retain talent with new skills in demand. Organizations that make significant changes in their own processes stand to gain a substantial competitive advantage over those that adhere to their current approach. To survive and thrive in the digital age means embracing digital technology, leading organizations with digital mindsets, predicting future transformation, and responding rapidly to build an adaptive, future-ready workforce that can support a strong and robust organization.

References

Abbott, A. (1988). *The system of professions—An essay on the division of expert labour*. The University of Chicago Press.

Abualoush, S., Masa'deh, R., Bataineh, K., & Alrowwad, A. (2018). The role of knowledge management process and intellectual capital as intermediary variables between knowledge management infrastructure and organization performance. *Interdisciplinary Journal of Information, Knowledge, and Management*, *13*, 279–309.

Alzola, M. (2017). Beware of the watchdog: Rethinking the normative justification of Gatekeeper liability. *Journal of Business Ethics, 140*(4), 705–721.

Ansari, W. A., Diya, P., Patil, S., & Patil, S. (2019). A review on robotic process automation-the future of business organizations. In *2nd International Conference on Advances in Science & Technology (ICAST)*.

Appelbaum, D., Kogan, A., Vasarhelyi, M., & Yan, Z. (2017). Impact of business analytics and enterprise systems on managerial accounting. *International Journal of Accounting Information Systems, 25*, 29–44.

Aremu, A. Y., Shahzad, A., & Hassan, S. (2019). Factors affecting enterprise resource planning adoption on firms' performance among medium-sized enterprises. *International Journal of Supply Chain Management, 8*(1), 308–315.

Arvidsson, V., Holmström, J., & Lyytinen, K. (2014). Information systems use as strategy practice: A multi-dimensional view of strategic information system implementation and use. *The Journal of Strategic Information Systems, 23*(1), 45–61.

Banks, G. C., McCauley, K. D., Gardner, W. L., & Guler, C. E. (2016). A meta-analytic review of authentic and transformational leadership: A test for redundancy. *The Leadership Quarterly, 27*(4), 634–652.

Belfo, F., & Trigo, A. (2013). Accounting information systems: Tradition and future directions. *Procedia Technology, 9*, 536–546.

Berghaus, S., & Back, A. (2017). Disentangling the fuzzy front end of digital transformation: Activities and approaches. In *CIS 2017 Proceedings* (p. 4).

Berruti, F., Nixon, G., Taglioni, G., & Whiteman, R. (2017). Intelligent process automation: The engine at the core of the next-generation operating model. *Digital McKinsey*, p. 9.

Biggart, N. W., & Hamilton, G. G. (1987). An institutional theory of leadership. *The Journal of Applied Behavioral Science, 23*(4), 429–441.

Bogt, H. J., & Scapens, R. W. (2019). Institutions, situated rationality and agency in management accounting: A research note extending the Burns and Scapens framework. *Accounting, Auditing and Accountability Journal, 32*(6), 1801–1825.

Bonsón, E., & Bednárová, M. (2019). Blockchain and its implications for accounting and auditing. *Meditari Accountancy Research, 27*(5), 725–740.

Bresciani, S., Ferraris, A., Huarng, K. H., & Malhotra, A. (2021). Digital transformation as a springboard for product, process and business model innovation. *Journal of Business Research, 128*, 204–210.

Bromwicha, M., & Scapens, R. W. (2016). Management accounting research: 25 years on. *Management Accounting Research, 31*, 1–9.

CAANZ, 2016. *The future or work: How can we adapt to survive and thrive*. Chartered Accountants Australia and New Zealand. https://www.charteredaccountantsanz.com/news-and-analysis/insights/research-and-insights/the-future-of-work. Accessed 9 Aug 2021.

Carlozo, L. (2017). What is blockchain? *Journal of Accountancy, 224*(1), 29.

Carvalho, H. L., & Guerrini, F. M. (2017). Reference model for implementing ERP systems: An analytical innovation networks perspective. *Production Planning & Control, 28*(4), 281–294.

Casino, F., Dasaklis, T., & Patsakis, C. (2019). A systematic literature review of blockchain-based applications: Current status, classification and open issues. *Telematics and Informatics, 39*, 55–81.

Chakraborti, T., Isahagian, V., Khalaf, R., Khazaeni, Y., Muthusamy, V., Rizk, Y., & Unuvar, M. (2020, September). From robotic process automation to intelligent process automation. In *International Conference on Business Process Management* (pp. 215–228).

Chandi, N. (2018). Accounting trends of tomorrow: What you need to know. *Forbes.*

Chase, M. D., & Shim, J. K. (1991). Artificial intelligence and big six accounting. A survey of the current uses of expert systems in the modern accounting environment. *Computers and Industrial Engineering, 21*(1–4), 205–209.

Chaudhari, S., & Ghone, A. (2015). ERP Software Market by Deployment (On-premises Deployment and Cloud deployment) and Function (Finance, Human Resource, Supply Chain and others)—*Global Opportunity Analysis and Industry Forecast, 2013–2020 Research.* Retrieved February 9, 2019, from https://www.alliedmarketresearch.com/ERP-market

Chen, H., Ge, L., & Xie, L. A. (2015). User authentication scheme based on elliptic curves Cryptography for Wireless Ad Hoc Networks. *Sensors, 15*, 17057–17075.

Chierici, R., Tortora, D., Del Giudice, M., & Quacquarelli, B. (2020). Strengthening digital collaboration to enhance social innovation capital: An analysis of Italian small innovative enterprises. *Journal of Intellectual Capital, 22*(3), 610–632.

Choi, Y., Lee, D., Kim, J., Jung, J., Nam, J., & Won, D. (2014). Security enhanced user authentication protocol for wireless sensor networks using elliptic curves cryptography. *Sensors, 14*, 10081–10106.

Chou, S., & Chang, C. (2008). The implementation factors that influence the ERP (enterprise resource planning) benefits. *Decision Support Systems, 46*, 149–157.

Coyne, J., & McMickle, P. (2017). Can blockchains serve an accounting purpose? *Journal of Emerging Technologies in Accounting, 14*(2), 101–111.

Davenport, T. H. (2000). *Mission critical: Realizing the promise of enterprise systems*. Harvard Business Press.

Dechow, N., & Mouritsen, J. (2005). Enterprise resource planning systems, management control and the quest for integration. *Accounting, Organizations and Society, 30*(7–8), 691–733.

Deloitte. (2019). Automation with intelligence. *Deloitte Insights*, p. 28.

Desplebin, O., Lux, G., & Petit, N. (2021). To be or not to be: Blockchain and the future of accounting and auditing. *Accounting Perspectives, 20*(4), 743–769.

Dwivedi, Y. K., Hughes, L., Ismagilova, E., Aarts, G., Coombs, C., Crick, T., Duan, Y., Dwivedi, R., Edwards, J., Eirug, A., Galanos, V., Vigneswara Ilavarasan, P., Janssen, M., Jones, P., Kar, A. K., Kizgin, H., Kronemann, B., Lal, B., ... Williams, M. D. (2019), Artificial Intelligence (AI): Multidisciplinary perspectives on emerging challenges, opportunities, and agenda for research, practice and policy. *International Journal of Information Management*, *57*, 101994.

El Sawy, O. A., Kræmmergaard, P., Amsinck, H., & Vinther, A. L. (2020). How LEGO built the foundations and enterprise capabilities for digital leadership. In *Strategic Information Management* (pp. 174–201). Routledge.

EY. (2019). *Five design principles to help build confidence in RPA implementation*. https://www.ey.com/pt_ao/consulting/five-design-principles-to-help-build-confidence-in-rpa-implement

Fischbacher-Smith, D. (2016). Breaking bad? In search of a (softer) systems view of security ergonomics. *Security Journal, 29*(1), 5–22.

Frankowska, M., & Rzeczycki, A. (2020). Reshaping supply chain collaboration—The role of digital leadership in a networked organization. In *Working Conference on Virtual Enterprises* (pp. 353–364). Springer.

Friedberg, I., McLaughlin, K., Smith, P., Laverty, D., & Sezer, S. (2016). STPA-SafeSec: Safety and security analysis for cyber-physical systems. *Journal of Information Security and Applications, 29*, 1–12.

Frey, C. B., & Osborne, M. A. (2017). The future of employment: How susceptible are jobs to computerisation? *Technological Forecasting and Social Change, 114*, 254–280.

FT. (2021). Big Four post strongest performance since Enron as advisory business booms. *Financial Times*. https://www.ft.com/content/95a0c80b-1262-42c3-ac5b-bb693e06d3c4. Accessed 11 Apr 2022.

Furr, N., & Shipilov, A. (2019, July–August). Digital doesn't have to be disruptive. *Harvard Business Review*. Online via https://hbr.org/2019/07/digital-doesnt-have-to-be-disruptive

Gartner. (2020). https://www.gartner.com/en/information-technology/glossary/digitalization. Accessed 5 May 2022.

Glikson, E., & Woolley, A. W. (2020). Human trust in artificial intelligence: Review of empirical research. *The Academy of Management Annals, 14*(2), 627–660.

Gonçalves, M. J. A., da Silva, A. C. F., & Ferreira, C. G. (2022). The future of accounting: Will digital Accounting: How will digital transformation impact the sector? *Informatics, 9*(19), 1–17.

Guthrie, J., & Parker, L. D. (2016). Whither the accounting profession, accountants and accounting researchers? Commentary and projections. *Accounting, Auditing & Accountability Journal, 29*(1), 2–10.

Hadžiosmanović, D., Bolzoni, D., & Hartel, P. H. (2012). A log mining approach for process monitoring in SCADA. *International Journal of Information Security, 11*(4), 231–251.

Hernandez, M., Eberly, M. B., Avolio, B. J., & Johnson, M. D. (2011). The loci and mechanisms of leadership: Exploring a more comprehensive view of leadership theory. *The Leadership Quarterly, 22*(6), 1165–1185.

Hess, T., Matt, C., Benlian, A., & Wiesböck, F. (2020). Options for formulating a digital transformation strategy. In *Strategic information management* (pp. 151–173). Routledge.

Holsapple, C., & Sena, M. (2001). Beyond transactions: The decision support benefits of enterprise systems. *Journal of Decision Systems, 10*, 65–85.

Holsapple, C., Sena, M., & Wagner, W. (2019). The perceived success of ERP systems for decision support. *Information Technology and Management, 20*(1), 1–7.

House, R., Javidan, M., Hanges, P., & Dorfman, P. (2002). Understanding cultures and implicit leadership theories across the globe: An introduction to project GLOBE. *Journal of World Business, 37*(1), 3–10.

Iansiti, M., & Lakhani, K. R. (2014). Digital ubiquity: How connections, sensors, and data are revolutionizing business. *Harvard Business Review, 92*(11), 90–99.

Imran, F., Shahzad, K., Butt, A., & Kantola, J. (2020, July). Leadership competencies for digital transformation: Evidence from multiple cases. In *International Conference on Applied Human Factors and Ergonomics* (pp. 81–87). Springer.

Janvrin, D. J., & Weidenmier Watson, M. (2017). Big Data: A new twist to accounting. *Journal of Accounting Education, 38*, 3–8.

Kakhki, M., & Gargeya, V. B. (2019). Information systems for supply chain management: A systematic literature analysis. *International Journal of Production Research, 57*(15–16), 5318–5339.

Kallunki, J. P., Laitinen, E. K., & Silvola, H. (2011). Impact of enterprise resource planning systems on management control systems and firm performance. *International Journal of Accounting Information Systems, 12*(1), 20–39.

Kappelman, L., Johnson, V., Torres, R., Maurer, C., & McLean, E. (2019). A study of information systems issues, practices, and leadership in Europe. *European Journal of Information Systems, 28*(1), 26–42.

Karahanna, E., & Watson, R. T. (2006). Information systems leadership. *IEEE Transactions on Engineering Management, 53*(2), 171–176.

Karajovic, M., Kim, H. M., & Laskowski, M. (2019). Thinking outside the block: Projected phases of blockchain integration in the accounting industry. *Australian Accounting Review, 29*, 319–330.

Karanja, E. (2017). The role of the chief information security officer in the management of IT security. *Information & Computer Security, 25*(3), 300–329.

Kellogg, K., Valentine, M., & Christin, A. (2019). Algorithms at work: The new contested terrain of control. *The Academy of Management Annals, 14*(1), 366–410.

Khan, S., Gani, A., Wahab, A. W. A., Shiraz, M., & Ahmad, I. (2016). Network forensics: Review, taxonomy, and open challenges. *Journal of Network and Computer Applications, 66*, 214–235.

Kim, M. K., & Jee, K. Y. (2007). Factors influencing strategic use of information technology and its impact on business performance of SMEs. *ETRI Journal, 29*(4), 497–506.

Kirkpatrick, K. (2016). Battling algorithmic bias. *Communications of the ACM, 59*(10), 16–17.

Kirmizi, M., & Kocaoglu, B. (2020). The key for success in enterprise information systems projects: Development of a novel ERP readiness assessment method and a case study. *Enterprise Information Systems, 14*(1), 1–37.

Kokina, J., & Blanchette, S. (2019). Early evidence of digital labor in accounting: Innovation with robotic process automation. *International Journal of Accounting Information Systems, 35*, 100431.

Koksalmis, G., & Damar, S. (2021). An empirical evaluation of a modified technology acceptance model for SAP ERP system. *Engineering Management Journal, 34*(2), 201–216.

Korhonen, T., Selos, E., Laine, T., & Suomala, P. (2020). Exploring the programmability of management accounting work for increasing automation: An interventionist case study. *Accounting, Auditing & Accountability Journal, 34*, 253–280.

Kovacova, M., Kliestik, T., Pera, A., Grecu, I., & Grecu, G. (2019). Big data governance of automated algorithmic decision-making processes. *Review of Contemporary Philosophy, 18*, 126–132.

Kowalczyk, M., & Buxmann, P. (2015). An ambidextrous perspective on business intelligence and analytics support in decision processes: Insights from a multiple case study. *Decision Support Systems, 80*, 1–13.

KPMG. (2017). Rise of the Humans: The Integration of Digital and Human Labor. https://advisory.kpmg.us/articles/2017/rise-of-the-humans-1.html. Accessed 1 July 2022.

Kurosawa, K., Ohta, H., & Kakuta, K. (2017). How to make a linear network code (strongly) secure. *Designs, Codes and Cryptography, 82*(3), 559–582.

Laudon, K. C., & Laudon, J. P. (2011). *Essentials of management information systems*. Pearson.

Laumer, S. (2016). Why do people reject technologies? A literature-based discussion of the phenomena "resistance to change" information systems and managerial psychology. In *ECIS 2011 Proceedings* (p. 60).

Lee, C., Lee, C., & Kim, S. (2016). Understanding information security stress: Focusing on the type of information security compliance activity. *Computers & Security, 59*, 60–70.

Lemonakis, C., Sariannidis, N., Garefalakis, A., & Adamou, A. (2018). Visualizing operational effects of ERP systems through graphical representations: Current trends and perspectives. *Annals of Operations Research, 294*, 401–418.

Lievano-Martínez, F. A., Fernández-Ledesma, J. D., Burgos, D., Branch-Bedoya, J. W., & Jimenez-Builes, J. A. (2022). Intelligent process automation: An application in manufacturing industry. *Sustainability, 14*(14), 8804.

Loonam, J., Eaves, S., Kumar, V., & Parry, G. (2018). Towards digital transformation: Lessons learned from traditional organizations. *Strategic Change, 27*(2), 101–109.

Lowe, A., Nama, Y., Bryer, A., Chabrak, N., Dambrin, C., Jeacle, I., Lind, J., Lorino, P., Robson, K., Bottausci, C., Spence, C., & Svetlova, E. (2020). Problematizing profit and profitability: Discussions. *Accounting, Auditing & Accountability Journal, 1233*(4), 753–793.

Martin, K. (2019). Ethical implications and accountability of algorithms. *Journal of Business Ethics, 160*(4), 835–850.

Matt, C., Hess, T., & Benlian, A. (2015). Digital transformation strategies. *Business & Information Systems Engineering, 57*(5), 339–343.

McAliney, P. J., & Ang, B. (2019). Blockchain: Business' next new "It" technology—A comparison of blockchain, relational databases, and Google Sheets. *International Journal of Disclosure and Governance, 16*(4), 163–173.

McGrath, J., & Gupta, A. (2018). Writing a moral code: Algorithms for ethical reasoning by humans and machines. *Religions, 9*(8), 240–252.

McQuade, S. (2006). *Understanding and managing cybercrime*. Allyn & Bacon.

Moffitt, K. C., Rozario, A. M., & Vasarhelyi, M. A. (2018). Robotic process automation for auditing. *Journal of Emerging Technologies in Accounting, 15*(1), 1–10.

Moll, J., & Yigitbasioglu, O. (2019). The role of internet-related technologies in shaping the work of accountants: New directions for accounting research. *British Accounting Review, 51*(6), 100833.

Molla, A., & Bhalla, A. (2006). ERP and competitive advantage in developing countries: The case of an Asian company. *The Electronic Journal of Information Systems in Developing Countries, 24*(1), 1–19.

Mukwasi, C. M., & Seymour, L. F. (2012). Enterprise resource planning business case considerations: A review for small and medium-sized enterprises. *Journal of Innovation Management in Small & Medium Enterprises, 2012*, 1.

Munoko, I., Brown-Liburd, H. L., & Vasarhelyi, M. (2020). The ethical implications of using artificial intelligence in auditing. *Journal of Business Ethics, 167*(2), 209–234.

Murdoch, D., & Fichter, R. (2017). From doing digital to being digital: Exploring workplace adoption of technology in the age of digital disruption. *International Journal of Adult Vocational Education and Technology, 8*(4), 13–28.

Neubert, M. J., Wu, C., & Roberts, J. A. (2013). The influence of ethical leadership and regulatory focus on employee outcomes. *Business Ethics Quarterly, 23*(2), 269–296.

Nixon, R. (2016). *12 Predictions on the Future of the Accounting Profession.*

Nguyen, M. T., Nguyen, Q. H., & Nguyen, T. H. (2021). Digital transformation in the business: A solution for developing cash accounting information systems and digitizing documents. *Science and Technology Development Journal, 24*(2), 1975–1987.

Nwankpa, J., & Roumani, Y. (2014). Understanding the link between organizational learning capability and ERP system usage: An empirical examination. *Computers in Human Behavior, 33*, 224–234.

O'Brien, J. A., & Marakas, G. M. (2011). *Management Information Systems* (10th ed.). McGraw Hill.

Odumeru, J. A., & Ogbonna, I. G. (2013). Transformational vs. transactional leadership theories: Evidence in literature. *International Review of Management and Business Research, 2*(2), 355–361.

Okamoto, T., & Takashima, K. (2015). Achieving short ciphertexts or short secret-keys for adaptively secure general inner-product encryption. *Designs, Codes and Cryptography, 77*(2), 725–771.

O'Leary, D. E. (1991). Artificial intelligence and expert systems in accounting databases: Survey and extensions. *Expert Systems with Applications, 3*(1), 143–152.

O'Reilly, C. A., Caldwell, D. F., Chatman, J. A., Lapiz, M., & Self, W. (2010). How leadership matters: The effects of leaders' alignment on strategy implementation. *The Leadership Quarterly, 21*(1), 104–113.

Othman, O. H. O., & AL-Dweikat, M. F. S. (2021). The impact of digital transformation risk management on the credibility of accounting information in Jordanian commercial banks. *Psychology and Education Journal, 58*(2), 3893–3904.

Parlak, N. (2020). *Change of the accounting profession in the age of digital transformation*. Academic Studies in Social Sciences.

Perkhofer, L. M., Hofer, P., Walchshofer, C., Plank, T., & Jetter, H. C. (2019). Interactive visualization of big data in the field of accounting: A survey of current practice and potential barriers for adoption. *Journal of Applied Accounting Research, 20*(4), 497–525.

Petani, F. J., Ramirez, C., & Gendron, Y. (2021). Special issue on digitalization, work, and professions. *Critical Perspectives on Accounting, 79*, 1–3.

Peters, M. D., Wieder, B., Sutton, S. G., & Wakefield, J. (2016). Business intelligence systems use in performance measurement capabilities: Implications for enhanced competitive advantage. *International Journal of Accounting Information Systems, 21*, 1–17.

Phornlaphatrachakorn, K., & NaKalasindhu, K. (2021). Digital accounting, financial reporting quality and digital transformation: Evidence from Thai listed firms. *The Journal of Asian Finance, Economics and Business, 8*(8), 409–419.

Procházka, D. (2018). Accounting for bitcoin and other cryptocurrencies under IFRS: A comparison and assessment of competing models. *The International Journal of Digital Accounting Research, 18*(24), 161–188.

PWC. (2020). *Tax technology & digital.*

Queiroz, M., Tallon, P. P., Sharma, R., & Coltman, T. (2018). The role of IT application orchestration capability in improving agility and performance. *The Journal of Strategic Information Systems, 27*(1), 4–21.

Radford, R. A. (1945). The economic organisation of a POW camp. *Economica, 12*(48), 189–201.

Ram, A. J. (2018). Bitcoin as a new asset class. *Meditari Accountancy Research, 27*(1), 147–168.

Ramassa, P., & Leoni, G. (2021). Standard setting in times of technological change: Accounting for cryptocurrency holdings. *Accounting, Auditing & Accountability Journal, 35*(7), 1598–1624.

Richins, G., Stapleton, A., Stratopoulos, T. C., & Wong, C. (2017). Big data analytics: Opportunity or threat for the accounting profession? *Journal of Information Systems, 31*(3), 63–79.

Rogerson, S., Miller, K. W., Winter, J. S., & Larson, D. (2019). Information systems ethics–challenges and opportunities. *Journal of Information, Communication and Ethics in Society, 17*(1), 87–97.

Ruivo, P., Johansson, B., Sarker, S., & Oliveira, T. (2020). The relationship between ERP capabilities, use, and value. *Computers in Industry, 117*, 1–15.

Sainger, G. (2018). Leadership in digital age: A study on the role of leader in this era of digital transformation. *International Journal on Leadership, 6*(1), 1.

Schmitt, A., Hartog, D., & Belschak, F. (2016). Transformational leadership and proactive work behaviour: A moderated mediation model including work engagement and job strain. *Journal of Occupational and Organizational Psychology, 89*(3), 588–610.

Schwab, K. (2019). *Globalization 4.0. A New Architecture for the Fourth Industrial Revolution. A call for engagement.* World Economic Forum.

Sebastian, I. M., Ross, J. W., Beath, C., Mocker, M., Moloney, K. G., & Fonstad, N. O. (2020). How big old companies navigate digital transformation. In *Strategic information management* (pp. 133–150). Routledge.

Seethamraju, R., & Sundar, D. K. (2013). Influence of ERP systems on business process agility. *IIMB Management Review, 25*(3), 137–149.

Shi, Z., & Wang, G. (2018). Integration of big-data ERP and business analytics (BA). *The Journal of High Technology Management Research, 29*(2), 141–150.

Sikka, P., & Willmott, H. (1995). The power of independence: Defending and extending the jurisdiction of accounting in the UK. *Accounting, Organizations and Society, 20*(6), 547–581.

Singh, A., & Fhom, H. C. S. (2017). Restricted usage of anonymous credentials in vehicular ad hoc networks for misbehavior detection. *International Journal of Information Security, 16*(2), 195–201.

Smith, S. (2018). Implications of next step blockchain applications for accounting and legal practitioners: A case study. *Australasian Accounting, Business and Finance Journal, 12*(4), 77–90.

Stahl, B. C., & Flick, C. (2011). ETICA workshop on computer ethics: Exploring normative issues. *Privacy and Identity Management for Life, 532*, 64–77.

Stair, R., & Reynolds, G. (2020). *Principles of Information Systems*. Cengage Learning.

Stefanescu, C., Comanescu, L. E., Buhusi, C., & Bilcan, G. A. (2019). Cyber security for cyber accounting-tool for the digital ENTERPRISE. *Academic Journal of Economic Studies, 5*(3), 138–144.

Sumner, M. (2000). Risk factors in enterprise-wide/ERP projects. *Journal of Information Technology, 15*(4), 317–327.

Sun, H., Ni, R. L., & Ng, C. Y. (2016). A stage-by-stage assessment of enterprise resource planning implementation: An empirical study from Hong Kong. *Journal of Global Information Technology Management, 19*(2), 104–127.

Sutton, S. G., Holt, M., & Arnold, V. (2016). The reports of my death are greatly exaggerated—Artificial intelligence research in accounting. *International Journal of Accounting Information Systems, 2*, 60–73.

Syed, R., Suriadi, S., Adams, M., Bandara, W., Leemans, S., Ouyang, C., ter Hofstede, A. H., van de Weerd, I., Wynn, M. T., & Reijers, H. A. (2020). Robotic process automation: Contemporary themes and challenges. *Computers in Industry, 115*, 103162.

Tadros, E. (2019). Automation cuts into profit at firms. *Financial Review*.

Tan, B. S., & Low, K. Y. (2019). Blockchain as the database engine in the accounting system. *Australian Accounting Review, 29*(2), 312–318.

Taylor, J., & Dustin, D. (2021). AICPA, NASBA publish revised CPA evolution Model curriculum. *Journal of Accountancy* (News Article). Accessed 10 July 2022.

Tschang, F. T., & Almirall, E. (2020). Artificial intelligence as augmenting automation: Implications for employment. *Academy of Management Perspectives, 35*(4), 642–659.

Vial, G. (2019). Understanding digital transformation: A review and a research agenda. *The Journal of Strategic Information Systems, 28*(2), 118–144.

Yang, C. N., Wu, C., & Wang, D. S. (2014). A discussion on the relationship between probabilistic visual cryptography and random grid. *Information Sciences, 278*, 141–173.

Yar, M. (2006). *Cybercrime and society*. Sage.

Yokoi, T., Shan, J., Wade, M., & Macaulay, J. (2019, June). *Digital vortex 2019—Continuous and connected change*. Global Center for Digital Business Transformation, IMD and CISCO.

Zhang, C. (2019). Intelligent process automation in audit. *Journal of Emerging Technologies in Accounting, 16*(2), 69–88.

Zhang, Z., Lee, M. K., Huang, P., Zhang, L., & Huang, X. (2005). A framework of ERP systems implementation success in China: An empirical study. *International Journal of Production Economics, 98*(1), 56–80.

Zhu, W., Chew, I. K., & Spangler, W. D. (2005). CEO transformational leadership and organizational outcomes: The mediating role of human–capital-enhancing human resource management. *The Leadership Quarterly, 16*(1), 39–52.

CHAPTER 3

Digital Transformation in Redefining the Role of the Finance and Audit Professional of the Future

Chinthake Wijesooriya and Rajitha Basnayake

Introduction

Today, organizational dependency on Information Systems is significant, and information technology has become an integral enabler of business operations and strategies. Business digitalization has redefined and transformed the way organizations function across different areas and sectors, deliver products and services, across channels catering to customers, and fulfilling stakeholders' expectations. Over the years, digitalization of Information Systems has been instrumental in data processing, process automation, process transformation, implementation of new business strategies, facilitating decision-making at levels namely operational, tactical, and

C. Wijesooriya (✉)
RMIT University Vietnam, Ho Chi Minh City, Vietnam
e-mail: chinthake.wijesooriya@rmit.edu.vn

R. Basnayake
Board of Asia Asset Finance PLC, Colombo, Sri Lanka
e-mail: rajitha.basnayake@asiaassetfinance.lk

A. Perdana and T. Wang (eds.), *Digital Transformation in Accounting and Auditing*, https://doi.org/10.1007/978-3-031-46209-2_3

strategic, becoming an indispensable fabric enabling operations and decision-making of private and public sector organizations. Further Rapid developments in the Internet, cloud computing mobile applications, digitally driven data collection methodologies, Data Science, artificial intelligence, and digitally enabled business models have significantly transformed various business processes, business models, and competition. The enormous Wealth of databases created by these business systems opened doors to gain more insights into business operations and information using business intelligence, which facilitated the identification of trends and opportunities by slicing and dicing data to provide competitive advantage.

These developments significantly transformed the day-to-day roles of all CFOs, finance leaders, finance professionals, and the auditing profession. The role of finance professionals has evolved to "business partners" and is now considered a mission-critical role across all cross-functional teams right up to strategic leadership teams. It is crucial for financial professionals to gain visibility of operations, diagnose challenges and opportunities, assess implications in the short and long run, perform simulations on options, and advise/influence decision-makers across operational to strategic with alternatives on short-term or strategic solutions. To excel at this role, they have been significantly empowered through digital transformation.

As organizational transformations are underpinned by digital transformation and tools, the functions of audit professionals, internal auditors, and external auditors have also been empowered when a new dimension of complexity is brought to their audit programs. The role of the internal auditor is enriched to a true business partner where they could create value addition as catalysts for change, process improvement, risk management, governance, compliance matters, and industry insights. For external auditors, digitalization in organizations brings added complexity into their audit programs and methodologies, as they are required to quickly adapt to changes in the digitally enabled business models of their clients, grasp the IT-enabled business processes, information systems, IT infrastructure, and system controls that demand a new breed of audit professionals.

However, Finance and Auditing professionals have benefitted immensely from digitalization. As back-office financial management systems, risk management, costing systems, HR, and treasury management systems that integrate front-end systems together with business ecosystems connecting banks, suppliers, and customers, including other core business functions, instantly update financials and enable finance professionals to track data to the source of the transaction, and for the auditors providing insights into audit trails, workflows, and internal control perspectives.

Therefore, the aim of the following sections is to explain the abstract view of various industries and business domains, the level of digitalization, and its impact on the Accounting and Auditing profession. This chapter discusses how current and evolving landscapes of digitalization unfold endless possibilities augmenting the quality of decision-making and advisory roles of finance and auditing professionals involved in some key industry sectors, namely, supply chain driven businesses into retail and distribution, healthcare services, and insurance business from the financial service sector. The authors further elaborate how digitalization and e-government initiatives of the public sector empower Finance and Auditing professionals who need to be the catalysts driving government financial management systems and governance functions delivering higher-quality citizen-centric services to the public.

Digital Transformation

Digital transformation is the process of using digital technologies to automate business processes and functionalities in order to meet changing business and market requirements. Over the years, the use of technology to automate and improve business processes has increased progressively. With technological improvements such as improved hardware and software capabilities together with improvements on the Internet, companies discovered innovative process transformation initiatives through technology enablement, which eventually created new business models and opened new horizons for products/services and information, augmenting the quality of decision-making.

However, the core processes and functionalities of the business remain highly valued, as they provide the foundation for business success. Digital practices that support the business operational domain, digital enablement of operations, business structural domain (business ecosystem, business capability), and business strategic goals (e.g., customer-focused business services) are the core ingredients of digital transformation (Open Group, 2022). Accordingly, digitalization could include, but is not limited to, the use of internet and document management systems, workflow management systems, data capture methods, bar codes, QR, RFID, blockchain, openness of technology platforms, interfacing technologies such as EDI, API, Artificial intelligence, and related technologies such as robotic process automation, chatbots, and machine learning, which has brought a new dimension, improving data capture, data processing, decision support, intelligence, and reporting systems. Blockchain facilitates digitized tamperproof ledger systems while enhancing the accuracy and security of the information (CPA, 2023); therefore, digital practices must focus on the operational domain, structural domain, and strategy domain and have been the consistence emphasis highlighted by the Open Group (2022). The Open Group is a global consortium that advises businesses through technological standards and recommendations.

In the early stages of technological development, particularly the Internet, companies used technology to automate business processes and connect suppliers, customers, and banks. With the advent of enterprise resource planning (ERPs) designed for various business/industry verticals and the development of web-based applications and software capabilities, organizations were able to automate multi-site, multi-company, multi-financial core business processes, linking customers, stakeholders, and functions, allowing them to digitally capture information. Digital data can have many different forms, such as manual data entry, automated reading from barcodes, QR codes, scanning for images, text, and web scraping, which have varying levels of abstraction, as well as a significantly increased amount of data. Due to the amount and complexity of data, it was necessary to store and process data aided by data warehousing, data mining, analytics, and business intelligence. In addition, capturing data digitally allows organizations to improve data quality, consisting of immediate data collection, improved consistency, availability, and accuracy. Further, technological advances have increased customer/business partner touch points, improved workflow, and improved controls to enhance data. Improved data quality helps organizations obtain better information for decisions. In the early stages of digital transformation, organizations emphasized the process and functional architecture of information systems (Fig. 3.1). Over time, digitalization of business processes has resulted in a large collection of business data. These data indicated that the data analysis could inform about the business better, such as a better understanding of customers, markets, and products they sell.

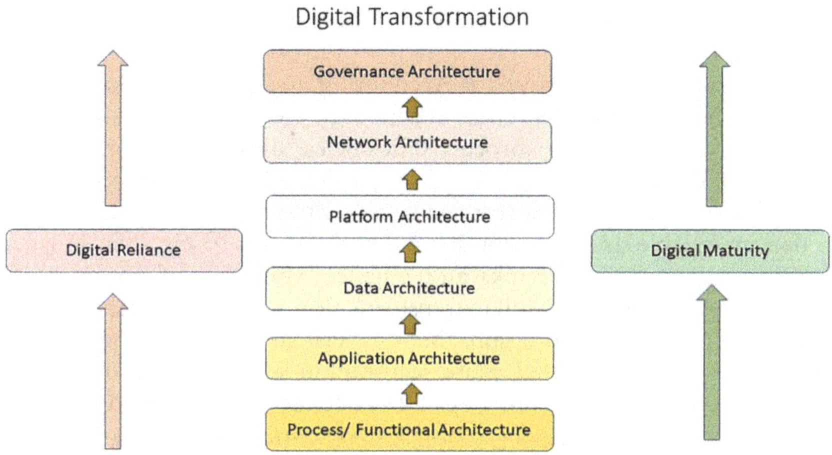

Fig. 3.1 Modified from Open group (2022) enterprise architecture framework

Increased focus on specific aspects of businesses, such as customer relationship management, has triggered organizations to develop various other aspects of business applications. Progressively, organizations have incorporated application architecture and data architecture, followed by network architecture, platform architecture, and governance architecture (Fig. 3.1). The increased use of digitalization, together with specialized applications such as mobile applications, requires the use of APIs to maximize the benefits of the applications. The progress of technology-enabled business processes has extended the use of technology to business intelligence, data analytics, cloud systems, and security. Increased digitalization allows organizations to capture and process data faster, receive information faster, and develop business intelligence. These digitally enabled capabilities have become a driving force in business decisions, and increased reliance on technology highlights the necessity to maintain the quality of the digital environment. Therefore, there has been a continuous effort to develop technology that supports business needs. Currently, we note the development of business interests in blockchain, cryptocurrency, and the Internet of Things, which are yet to be matured. However, the increasing development and progression of these new technologies indicate their increasing usefulness in businesses, which would present a series of new challenges and opportunities for Accounting and Auditing professionals.

It is, therefore, imperative for Accounting and Auditing professionals to realize how they can leverage technology to improve organizational productivity, performance process efficiencies, and decision-making to gain competitive advantage. Digital transformation has now become an integral part of the Public Sector to improve citizen-centric service models to deliver reliable and superior state-sector services to citizens. Finance professionals of Central Banks and Finance Ministries of governments increasingly rely on the digital transformation of public sector institutions to gain visibility and ensure that financial and funding requirements are monitored and allocated. State-sector audit services are also required to play a role in implementing reliable systems, business processes, and controls to assess and gain a reasonable assurance that governance and reporting mechanisms function within expected norms.

Many organizations have implemented data analytics, AI, and machine learning to improve strategic decision-making capabilities. Business process improvements and transformation perspective businesses integrate digitally enabled customer/service-centric capabilities into value chains for process efficiency and have now been moving to new-generation ERP on cloud platforms using full-stack SaaS platforms aiming for new growth avenues so that all digital channels/solutions could be integrated with core business systems. Many organizations now deploy Robotic Process Automation (RPA) to improve the efficiencies of repetitive/time-consuming functions, relieving Finance and Audit teams to focus on more value-adding tasks.

Current Landscape on Digital Transformation in Accounting and Auditing

Accounting keeps the financial aspect of the organizations in order, while auditing provides assurance and opinion on the credibility of the accounting in the organizations. The technology facilitates Accounting and Auditing to track transactions, improves efficiency, consistency, information availability, and stores information. Thus, the development and capabilities of the technology-enabled Accounting and Auditing complex and highly valued skills. The ultimate objective of digitization now goes beyond producing accurate, timely, and relevant information for decision-making. With increased interest in customer relationships, the objectives of digital systems should ideally focus on customer-centric business models that integrate with the entire business ecosystem. Data capture at customer touch points on digital platforms enables businesses to develop better business intelligence regarding customers and markets. Thanks to the technology, specifically the Internet, a massive amount of data collected over the years by businesses has provided a valuable information resource for better understanding of the business while facilitating information for better decisions. Data collected, however, require transformation before analysis to make sense of the data. The growth of data warehouses, data mining, business intelligence, and analytics shows the importance of data and data processing in organizations. Technological developments have progressively changed business processes, especially accounting and auditing. Financial management, together with management accounting professionals, requires comprehensive knowledge of technologically enabled business processes and the applications of technology in accounting processes. Such knowledge could provide more insights into cross-functional business processes and performance to advise top management on financial status and projections.

With improved network, communication, hardware, and software capabilities supported by advanced databases, software development tools, operating system platforms, highly improved technology, and specialized tools such as analytics, decision-making has become easier and faster, connecting all levels of the organization. The use of technology in organizational processes is not limited to Accounting and Auditing. The extent of the impact of information technology on accounting is further reflected by the Auditing Standards announced by leading professional accounting bodies such as Chartered Accountants England and Wales and AACSB 2018 Accounting Accreditation to incorporate information technology (AACSB, 2018). In addition to setting standards, the importance of digital engagement through the necessary active applications of information technology in accounting and financial processes has been noted by the CFA Institute (Institute, 2021, 2022). Today, businesses operate more globally than their predecessors do. Therefore, accounting reports require data to be captured, processed, and reported in a global context. This situation creates the need for internationally acceptable financial reporting, and hence, the need for international financial reporting standards (KPMG, 2022). International Financial Reporting Standards (IFRS) is a non-profit organization that sets international standards for financial reporting. IFRS sets two forms of standards:

the International Accounting Standards and the International Sustainability Standards Board. Accounting Standards explain how a company prepares its financial statements, while Sustainability Standards explain how a company reports sustainability-related information (IFRS, 2022). Digital environments can provide more accurate and faster data capture and processing, resulting in accurate and timely information.

The incorporation of information technology knowledge in accounting is necessary for accountants to be relevant to the reality of contemporary businesses and to refine business/accounting processors. Accountants, therefore, are able to understand how the data have been collected, stored, processed, and reported, and appreciate the capabilities of information systems. More importantly, the accountant role today requires a proper understanding of the applications of technology in business processes and how to maximize the potential of technology-enabled business processes. Finance professionals play a role in Operational Finance and Strategic Finance. The operational Finance professional has his radar focused on companies' financial processes and business processes in relation to their systems. Through digital operational finance, the professional role is empowered, enabling him to analyze business performances, stabilize finances, and bring process improvements. Strategic Finance management professionals, while well-informed and aware of operational finance functions and the status of current and past financials, have a broader role to play, formulating tactical and strategic directions, and advising company management.

Online businesses, such as Facebook, Google, eBay, and Uber, present additional challenges owing to the nature of their online business operations. Online businesses could cross national boundaries and require addressing different country regulatory requirements along with other complexities such as cultural differences and technological challenges (inconsistencies). Therefore, online businesses must be able to capture the necessary (additional) data for analysis and local/global reporting requirements. Additionally, there is an increased demand for environmental responsibility for organizations that are required to capture environmental data for analysis and reporting (Hillary, 2004; Malhotra et al., 2013).

Further, recent developments in digital technologies have caused significant improvements in government process reengineering and digitization of government/public sector services, e-government services including citizen-centric services, and technology improvements in government accounting and financial reporting systems. These state-sector institutions, organizations, and state-owned enterprises are being funded and monitored by the Government Treasury. Integration with Government treasury enabled by these institutions through digitalization brought a massive improvement in managing public finances and the implementation of public sector accounting standards, reporting and monitoring mechanisms, and public sector auditing standards. Today, technology-based processes are able to capture the necessary data comprehensively at the right time, and these processes and information would have financial implications that need to be reflected in the accounting systems of the organization. Organizational performance is ultimately measured by the financial results.

While performing these activities, organizations need to ensure that such transactions are performed in compliance with organizational policies, follow standard operational procedures, adhere to prescribed authority limits and accounting policies, meet budgets, and satisfy the regulatory framework of the industry. Thus, auditing brings good governance to enterprises, providing reasonable assurance of controls, business systems in place, and reporting systems in place to stakeholders. There are various types of audits performed by the organization, including internal audits, financial accounting audits, project audits, quality audits, information technology/application controls/general control audits, compliance audits, and Forensic Audits. All these audits will have to be performed in computerized environments; thus, digitalization also has a significant impact on auditing. While technology makes auditing easier, it can bring added complexities for audit professionals when the automation boundary is further extended due to the digitalization of business partners, customers, or end user processes compared to back-office accounting record verifications. Here, the transactions need to be tracked from source to record and from record to report. Moreover, cybersecurity, while being a catalyst and imperative for growth, can also cause the downfall of an organization if risks are not adequately managed. Hence, in this digital age, audit professionals in their teams should have specialists equipped with above-average cybersecurity skills, IT infrastructure management skills, and business domain knowledge to assess the effectiveness and control environments of clients' IT architectures and operations. This invariably adds complexity to auditors in their audit plans, programs, execution, and risk-based audit approaches to assess risks stemming from cybersecurity strategies, IT infrastructure consisting of network/hardware/software operating systems OS/DBMS/middleware, server farms, business applications, application controls, access controls, compliance environment, governance, and implementation mechanisms specific to the organization (Fig. 3.2).

Auditors are now increasingly using technology to improve the efficiency, productivity, and reliability of their audits. With the use of technological solutions, the importance of on-site financial statement audits has been decreasing. Although some on-site work cannot be totally eliminated, more interaction, that is, client and auditor, would take place in virtual rooms using technology solutions such as MS Team, and their proprietary communication tools and work can be performed on e-Audit solutions connecting to clients' workplace from Auditor's offices. This

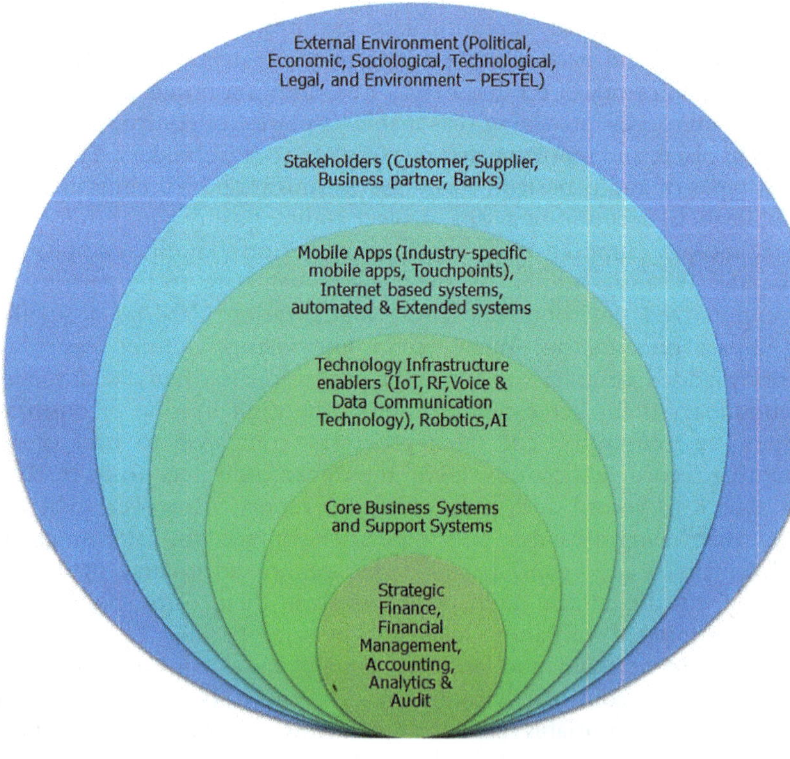

Fig. 3.2 Scope of financials—accounting and auditing (*Source* Authors)

adds significant value to the client because subject matter experts of the auditor could get involved, probably from many parts of the world, when discussing key audit matters requiring judgment. For the auditor, travel costs and travel time would be significant savings in terms of resource pool and availability; for the client, additional out-of-pocket expenses of audit experts could be avoided and saved.

Many leading international audit firms, including the Big 4 audit firms, EY, Deloitte, PWC, and KPMG, set high-quality standards for statutory and financial statement audits. The use of technology has become an integral part of audits. They use sector-specific trained professionals, skills and e-audit solutions, workflow-based tools that allow documents to be accessed online, and specific risk analysis solutions that facilitate risk-based audits. Their technological solutions facilitate collaboration with clients, carrying sector-specific business processes and financial transactions, and reporting while assessing the control environment. Such tools can scan billions of transactions in seconds, discard exceptions, or indicate risk factors. Many such tools have developed algorithms that replicate auditors' decision-making capabilities in transaction reviews. Customized RPA processes with software robot trace exception, reconciles, and improves the process quality, reliability, and accuracy. They also use audit query tools on client databases to perform transaction reviews, data mining, etc.

However, auditor statement of work (SOW) has become increasingly complex with the evolution of cloud computing, SaaS services, cybersecurity issues, data protection laws, regulators requiring technology risk management and resilience, and client-specific IT governance issues, which are indispensable elements influencing the auditor's opinion on the reliability of the systems and record-keeping of the organization. Hence, audit teams are required to revisit their SOWs, approach and methodologies, audit plans, and engagement letters every time they meet clients because at least one of these factors would change when auditors' next visit is due. The role of the internal auditor has also been evolving into a business partnering role, where they largely contribute to Change Agents, highlighting risk, governance, compliance, and process issues. The internal auditor, being a part of the organization's reporting directly to the board, closely monitors key business functions using the technologies deployed by the organizations. Internal auditor reporting on current systems would bring useful insights for systems/process improvements and would unfold business cases for new system implementations. The impact on accounting and auditing professionals continues with the rapid developments in technologies but varies according to different businesses and industry sectors and the extent to which digitalization has been used in respective organizations. The professionals, however, need to sharpen their skills in visualizing the technology options available; ROI/value addition derived through digitalization and above all facilitates implementing such solutions to improve productivity, decision-making, and competitive advantage of their organizations; therefore, the following sections aim to explain the abstract view of various industries, business domains, the level of digitalization, and its impact on the Accounting and Auditing profession.

Digitization in Various Industry Models and Implications on Financial Management Systems and Auditing

Case for Supply Chain and Logistics Management

The supply chain is the nucleus of manufacturing/distribution businesses. These businesses aim to acquire the resources they need to fulfill customer demand while managing cost, quality, timeliness, supply chain speed, cash flows, optimized inventory, and resilience within the defined performance indicators of the business. Technological advances have significantly increased organizational processes, interactions, and complexities. However, technology has facilitated the management of organizational challenges while enabling new opportunities. The increased use of technology in business provides an increased number of digital touch points for organizations that can be used to collect data on various aspects of the business. For example, businesses can communicate with suppliers using automated functions such as automated reorders. Once the reorder level is reached, an automated reorder can be created. Pending reorders could warn suppliers that they were informed about the impending order to better prepare. Such process can be fully automated while inclusion of a manual intervention provides additional options.

automated, whereas the inclusion of a manual intervention provides additional options. Automated reorder, together with manual intervention, could be an additional check of the order when confirming an order. When an order is placed, payments must be applied, which can be finalized once the order is received. If the order has been placed on credit, it must be recorded promptly, as the final payment must be settled at a later stage. All pending orders (and payments) through finalized transactions can be managed digitally. Being able to track the status of the orders, payments, and inventory could help organizations be better informed, resulting in better understanding of the state of the business, improved communication with the suppliers, better control of financials, and improved customer service. Usually, the process and payments are financially related because the accountant must be aware of the processes relevant to the payments. The overall result is improved efficiency and service level. In integrated financial management systems, these transactions are updated in purchases, accounts payable, and cash management systems for payment planning. The weighted cost of items purchased is updated instantly, and supplier performance tracking systems indicate any deviations between planned delivery and actual delivery dates, indicating supplier reliability.

Therefore, accountants and auditors require in-depth knowledge of the uses of technology and technology-enabled business processes. They must be aware of the technology, its characteristics, and how to use it in business processes. Many technological devices are in use in supply chain processes. Examples include regular desktops, laptops, tablets, tracking and tracing devices, barcode readers, QR code scanners, GPS, mobile devices, and business-specific devices. During Covid-19, companies were forced to automate many systems, particularly supply chain processes, to minimize human interaction. Thanks to Covid-19, during the last few years, new technologies such as the Internet of Things (IoT), blockchain, AI and machine learning, robotics, and process automation have been used extensively, and technology has attracted increased interest. With the increased use of new technologies, the complexity of accounting and auditing has changed. The result is the need for new technological knowledge in the accounting and auditing profession. New knowledge is not limited to the internal uses of the technology, as most processes (e.g., Supply Chain Process) today involve multiple organizational services through various technologies. Multinational conglomerates may form part of the supply chain process. It consists of parent companies and subsidiaries that perform specific chain functions. Digitalization has enabled complex business partnerships and collaborations through multi-currency, multi-company, and multi-site ERP with comprehensive financial management/consolidation capabilities at the center (Gartner, 2022). Therefore, improvements in technological knowledge must be dynamic for accountants and auditors. Consequently, the use and development of new technologies could become more significant in the next few years.

IoT refers to objects that have sensors, data processing capabilities, dynamic re-aligning/adjusting capabilities, and software to connect and communicate with other devices. Examples of such devices are alarm systems and cameras. 5G is a technology with a greater bandwidth, which significantly improves internet-based services. A greater speed could transfer data faster, thus quicker processing of the services. The blockchain technology ensures that transactions are validated, recorded, encrypted, and traceable. They significantly improve the speed of processes and strengthen their traceability. Blockchains are expanding into other business sectors, and supply chains can use tracing to the origin of goods. Machine learning can be used to analyze, compute, and make decisions in real time. The processing speed is significantly higher than that of humans. Machine learning increases productivity and accuracy, resulting in a better supply chain. Automation and robots have been used in supply chains for several years. However, with the application of IoT and AI, robots have become far more capable than their predecessors. They can be used for operations, warehousing, tracking, quality control, and sorting. Even though these technologies seem to be beyond the functions of accountants and auditors, they must have knowledge of the technology, its functionality, capabilities, and how they have been used in the business. These new professional knowledge developments regarding the new technology must, therefore, be dynamic.

Supply Chain integrates many different business sectors, including suppliers, warehousing, shipping, transport, professional consultants such as legal and financial consultants, manufacturing, distributors/stockists, retail shops, e-commerce platforms, customer service (during and after sales), financial services, and marketing. All of these businesses could be part of a supply chain. Individual organizations usually pay attention to internal matters and their direct impacts. However, for success, it is necessary for all participants in the supply chain to be connected and function as a single unit. If one of the participating businesses fails to deliver expectations, the downstream impact could be a bullwhip effect. The following presents broader supply chain management and specific industry impacts:

Digital Disruption in Supply Chain Management

Supply chain management is a process that includes obtaining raw materials for production, making the product, and getting the product to the customer. Therefore, the supply chain process includes inbound logistics, operations, outbound logistics, marketing, sales, and services (Porter, 1997, 2011). Supply chain management integrates, synchronizes, and orchestrates all physical, financial, and information flows that organizations and their value chain partners need to fulfill demand for their goods and services (Gartner, 2022). Often, these products or services are provided by multiple specialized organizations, business units, or departments. For example, suppliers, shipping companies delivering raw materials, distributors, dealers, local and regional warehouses, national and international companies delivering various services, retail outlets, sales force consumers using mobile platforms, networking and communication services provided by technology companies, legal and other professional services, and customs and border control by government organizations are some of the significant organizations involved in the supply chain process. In addition, third-party services and sub-contractors provide numerous services within a supply chain process. The megaprocesses of the supply chain can be categorized into.

- **Sourcing and Purchasing**
- **Demand Planning and Supply Chain Planning**, Supply chain resilience, which consists of making to stock/make to order strategies, material requirement, labor, resource, capacity planning, supply chain resilience building, model stock planning
- **Fleet Management and Transport Inbound and Outbound**
- **Production Planning and Management**
- **Warehouse Operations and Distribution** (inbound, storage/ warehouse operations/stock control, distribution requirement planning to regional warehouses, and outbound delivery to distributor/ dealer), Timely Replenishments are critical to ensure availability.
- **Store Operations** (chain of retail outlets if retailing is covered in scope, shelf stock management, feeder store management, and model stock strategy)
- **After sales Services**

Through these processes, supply chain organizations manage demand forecasting, choose and manage suppliers (including contract manufacturers), plan for and manufacture products (having acquired the raw materials), store and deliver finished goods (using logistics or third-party logistics providers (3PLs) to coordinate and schedule orders and deliveries), and manage products that are returned, defective, or in excess of needs.

All these organizations use Internet-based technology for communication, tracking, shipping, and many other functionalities. To Maximize and derive benefit of the digital transformation to an organization, the whole supply chain process (from start to the end) is to be analyzed, process improvement opportunities identified, and mapped to digital enablers to gain superior process efficiencies and visibility. New generation ERP, SCM, APM/EAM solutions, IoT, Robotics, and warehouse automation have added a new dimension to SCM function, enabling end-to-end tracking, integration, and speed of execution as critical success factors in the supply chain. Therefore, the organization must ensure that organizational processes are optimized to build resilience, optimize costs, and gain a competitive advantage.

Therefore, Information Systems and digital enablers could play a critical role in supporting data capturing, processing, and analyzing internal (organizational) as well as external (supply chain) data. Consequently, organizations must apply digital transformation with a holistic approach, using organizational objectives as a guide while supporting the supply chain process. Such a holistic view by the organization allows all processes and functions to be aligned for a common objective. For example, the objective of the supply chain could be to build competitive advantage through trade-offs between cost optimization and resilience, maximize the service efficiency, and the overall quality of the supply chain, which requires all organizations in the supply chain process to function harmoniously, which will enable organizations for better planning, feasible forecasting, maximizing availability, and improving the processing times so that the product gets faster to the market and minimizes costs. Even though the accountant may be responsible for the financials of the organization, the accountant must be aware of the performance indicators, costs, bottlenecks, cash out flows/inflows, and projections and actuals attached to each of the processes. Today, senior finance professionals' CFOs play a major role in managing cash outflows, inventory carrying costs along the supply chain, and evaluating various scenarios and alternatives to optimize costs while bridging the demand plan and order fulfillment.

Role of the Finance Professional and Auditor in Supply Chain-Driven Organization

Therefore, accountant/finance professionals should be equipped to provide a financial perspective of supply chain planning, forecasting, sourcing, managing production costs/process efficiencies, mitigating supply chain risks, minimizing capital tied up inventory, minimizing supply chain operation costs, optimizing distribution strategies/channels, and finally making the products available on shelf/to the customer. Therefore, accountants must understand the cross-functional implications of supply chain process complexity. Hence, significant judgement is required from the accountant in procurement, pricing strategies, production, plant management/ engineering and other related services, warehousing, distribution, marketing channels, business partners, sales, retail network, taxes, and profitability. Further, due to the availability of information and capabilities, the new-generation ERP was equipped with strong SCM. Production, asset performance management systems, and BI systems finance professionals can shed light on supply chain performance and process improvements for.

- Shorter order cycle time, planning and forecasting, fulfilling customer demand, and improving service aspects
- Production planning and execution providing insights/ implementing controls on cost of raw material, conversion costs, overhead costs, factory waste, and product defects
- Minimize planned maintenance and downtimes, improve availability through APM/EAM integrations
- Inventories i.e., raw materials, semi-finished, WIP, and Finished goods
- Warehouse operational costs
- Transport, shipping costs, and alternatives
- Activities involving distributor/dealer and retail network

Auditors in such environments find ample information and visibility from operations to financial records, clear audit trails, and reports to track exceptions. E-Auditing systems now have the capability to build audit plans and execute them in a system environment, enabling audit professionals to identify exceptions, malpractices, and inefficiencies. Today, business processes consist of numerous services delivered by internal, external, local, and global service providers. The auditing function therefore requires multidimensional views to understand the highly complex business networks enabled through digital transformation. Key capabilities these organizations would require provide useful insights into cross-functional integration requirements that could be enabled through digital transformation. The capability blueprint for the manufacturing/distribution business with a supply chain-enabled process framework is depicted below. This diagram further illustrates the capabilities provided to enterprise strategic decision-making, financial management, cost accounting, and analytics. Tightly integrated platforms similar to these provide reasonable assurance on the process framework to auditors (Fig. 3.3).

CEOs (chief executive officers) look up to their CFO (Chief Financial Officer) to provide feasibility studies of such projects, including the strategies of funding them with various supply chain scenarios and business models. Such decisions need to be aided by digitalization, which has already been happening in ERP systems such as SAP, IFS, Oracle EBusiness/Net suite, and Microsoft Business Central. Even solutions, such as SAGE and many open-source ERP solutions, possess these capabilities. Application system solutions can run on various Operating Systems (OS) and BMS platforms with accessibility from anywhere and the majority on various other mobile platforms. POS/retail store management systems, warehouse automation systems, EAM systems, and SFA added more complexity and value data, providing insights on managing supply chains. Among all cash flow management skills, the ability to project projections and juggles with funding strategies requires deep insights into the internal and external processes of the business. More analytics will be required to visualize how to finance the complex and highly volatile business domains. More information is required on transactions, borrowing portfolios, credit facilities, lending rates, and associated financial costs to strike the best deal to lower the financial costs of the organization. While the accountant should secure finances for the ongoing operations, he should have visibility on revamps required and new investments required to develop the business.

Banks and financial institutions play pivotal roles in these operations; thus, the banker's role in this digital ecosystem is indispensable. Having

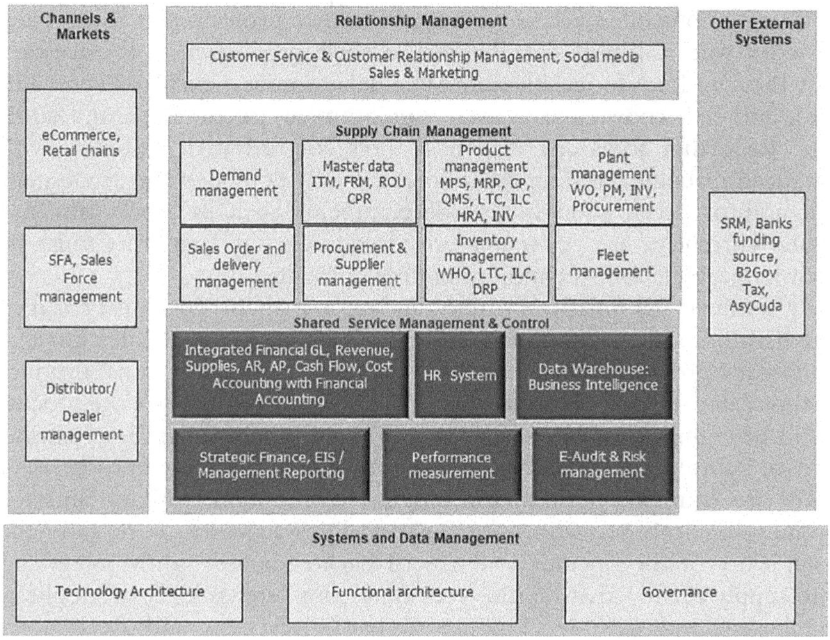

Fig. 3.3 Supply chain integrating with financials—application architecture (*Source* Authors)

them linked to organizational systems via Internet banking platforms supplies the fluid and confidence needed for digital platforms for organizations dealing with stakeholders along the supply chain processes. Such connectivity and integration facilitate the faster processing of financial transactions that can be verified, traced, and secured.

Accountants cannot forget their faithful companion Excel spreadsheets. Spreadsheets are still useful and the inclusion of analytical functions in spreadsheets is improving. However, because of the nature of the amount of data, amount of data, range of data, variety of data, multiuser needs, and the immediacy of information requirements, it is necessary to consider databases that are capable of handling large amounts of data as a viable option. Today, databases are capable of storing large amounts of data, supporting various data processing methods (analytical tools/ methods), facilitating data sharing (relational/non-relational, cloud), and facilitating controlled access and security. Since professionals today need to work with a lot of data related to their profession, it is necessary that they are knowledgeable about the data (sources, characteristics, and use), and this knowledge is more significant for accountants and auditors. Reporting tools and analytical tools coupled with BI suites with advanced machine learning capabilities digitally equipped the accountant and auditor. Even though new developments such as blockchain and digital currencies are yet to mature, accountants and auditors must be knowledgeable about technological development.

In summary, all functions within the supply chain process must collaborate harmoniously to maximize efficiency. This approach requires integration of the processes, obtaining raw materials to deliver the final product to the customer, as well as maintenance/service. Even though the process could be complex, such integration provides a platform for the organization to capture the necessary information for accounting purposes. All ERPs are equipped with strong supply chain models, with variants for business verticals providing the functionalities required to support the complexity of the operation. Financial back-ends are tightly integrated into supply chain activities, thus providing complete visibility of supplies/purchasing and payable (Procure to pay), Revenues and Receivables (Order to cash), Record to report, Plan to produce, Plan to Inventory, Forecast to Delivery processes to finance and audit professionals so that data capture and integration facilitate transaction tracing, comprehensive dataset, and better supply chain view (internal and external) could be achieved. Therefore, digitalization in the supply chain intensified connections between parties participating in the chain and activities interdependent along the chain. To unlock opportunities in the digital supply chain, supplying information to finance leaders and technologies that could expedite supply chain execution must be explored with SCM and IT Professionals. All such enablers make the organization planning sharper, optimize the cost base, and achieve the speed required to deliver the product, the critical success factor of the organization.

The auditor digitally disrupted SCM models present a series of challenges, including starting from cybersecurity rights down to the transaction in ERP systems and legacy systems in operation in that organization. This means that they will be required to assess the control environment and risks associated with what can go wrong scenarios to formulate their audit plans and programs. Their teams will have specialized information systems professionals that focus on cybersecurity and IT infrastructure.

Cloud computing, heterogeneous platforms/applications, platforms, and telco platforms. ERP environments would be heavily specialized in business verticals and solutions, such as SAP, Oracle, NetSuite, IFA, or Microsoft family. Hence, the auditor coming to such environments must be familiar with the modules, integrations, and typical pitfalls associated with ERP products; thus, it would be advantageous for auditors to ideally hold ERP product/module certifications in such environments so that the risks associated with solutions could be factored into their audit programs.

Case for Healthcare Industry

Patients are at the core of healthcare services. Therefore, optimal patient care is the best healthcare service. All healthcare activities must contribute to the healthcare process to make patient care effective and efficient. Healthcare services include primary care (general practitioner, specialist, and allied health), personal health, and other complementary services (Medtech, 2022). Healthcare involves internal and external stakeholders, including patients, doctors, medical and other support staff, professional organizations, government, and other stakeholders, such as insurance services. The processes of healthcare services are therefore diverse, such as the recent developments in applications of technology in healthcare services that have been transformed rapidly during the last five years.

Patient-centric healthcare service models represent the basic framework depicted in the following diagram (Fig. 3.4).

Covid-19 pandemic has forced us to prioritize healthcare over all other services. An increased number of patients and the need to care for them as well as to protect others from Covid-19 is a simple task. Most governments and health services consider digital transformation a viable choice to facilitate and maintain patient care while protecting others from Covid-19. This choice required changes to existing practices to use the technology and educate staff and patients about it. Some of these practices could continue even after the Covid-19 challenges as they improve the extent of the services provided to patients. For example, telehealth or telemedicine can be used.

Digital Transformation in Healthcare Sector

The digital transformation of healthcare services has improved tremendously. Telemedicine facilitates the delivery of health services using internet/telecommunication technology, where healthcare providers are

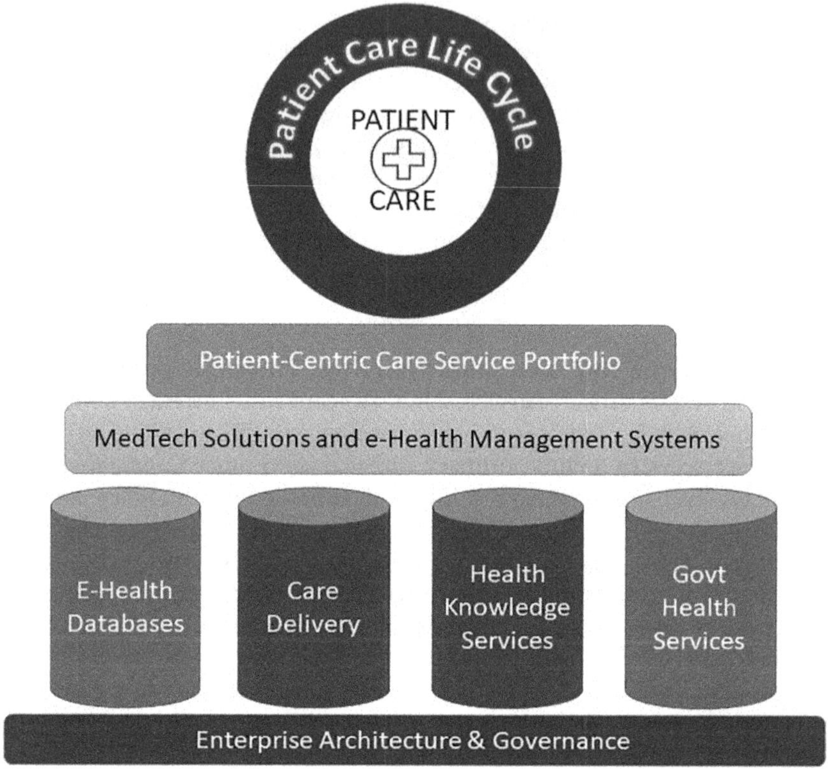

Fig. 3.4 Patient-centric care (*Source* Authors)

given the functionality required to remotely evaluate, diagnose, and treat patients. They typically cover all aspects of patient online consultations and related services, such as delivery of medicine, ambulance services, referrals to specialists, and monitoring the health of wearables. Wearable technology in healthcare represents electronic devices that patients can wear, such as Fitbits and smartwatches, which capture data on users' personal health and body changes due to activities. These devices capture and transmit a user's health information to a doctor or hospital monitoring system in real time.

Examples of digital healthcare applications include mobile healthcare apps in mobile phones, smart devices such as wearable monitoring devices (e.g., pacemakers and hearing aids), digital health records that include documents, images, and videos, and telehealth. In addition, there is increased interest in applications of blockchain technology that improve access, security, scalability, and privacy; artificial intelligence that supports independence; and analytics in big data that enable informed decisions. Healthcare data include a wide range of data types, such as documents, images, and many other forms; hence, the importance of big data analytics in healthcare. Big data demand purposeful data capture, cleaning, and processing for a clear objective, where data analytics could be instrumental for data analysis for better decisions. The complexity of these processes highlights the need for business professionals to have better technological knowledge. Therefore, it is paramount that accounting professionals develop technological knowledge as they become better conversant about business processes. Therefore, accounting professionals are better able to contribute to digital transformation in organizations. However, a lack of comprehensive knowledge (i.e., professional accounting knowledge combined with technological knowledge) could result in poor decision-making. These eHealth services have significantly transformed the workflows, data, financial information, access, and decision-making capabilities of all key stakeholders, including but not limited to patients, hospital doctors, community nurses, physiotherapists, hospital group managers/ service groups in care delivery, and GPs. Accounting and Audit professionals thus gain the visibility of entire end-to-end workflows, affecting their financials.

Technology with artificial intelligence in healthcare (e.g., X-ray and CT scans) highly improves non-invasive diagnostic measures and provides evidence-based information for decisions. These specialized services may not be provided by doctors' medical centers. In such situations, the patient's medical information is shared through specialized services. Sharing such information requires patient consent and following the regulatory body guidelines. Similarly, capturing accounting-related information is far more challenging because the process involves multiple organizations. For example, financial transactions for a medical service could involve a patient's bank/credit card company, bank for the medical lab where the X-ray has been taken, government medical support systems, insurance companies, and the bank for doctor's medical center. Each of these organizations has its own financial institution, and the transaction can be processed through several financial institutional processes. This technology facilitates the accurate and quick processing of such transactions. The accountant must understand the complete process, information constraints, such as patient consent, and the state of the data in each part of the process.

Healthcare application systems are capable of providing insights from healthcare services, as these systems are able to capture valuable data that improves the ability to measure and improve practice performance and the financial position of the organization. Technology, including advanced database systems, can provide high availability, control, monitoring, and recovery systems of data. Healthcare systems, therefore, can capture the actual process and patient data into a powerful knowledge base to assist in decision-making (Medtech, 2022). Its interactive dashboards and reports help analyze and track practice performance. These capabilities allow accountants to be informed decision-makers with increased responsibility.

AI and machine learning are currently used in healthcare. There are applications that facilitate the improvement of medical diagnoses and pharmaceutical companies in their R&D efforts to develop new products. Smart sensors with IoT, such as wearables, open up new possibilities in healthcare monitoring patients and devices, namely clinical and administrative functions. This enables the healthcare staff to respond to events and treatments involving patient care expeditiously. This space of innovation is now termed the Internet of Medical Things (IoMT), which minimizes human error. The major categories include emergency response intelligent systems, sensors planted in logistic/transport systems, healthcare mobility services monitoring patients, and in-hospital systems.

- Patient-Centric Aspect of Healthcare in Digital Transformation:

  Ethics: Patients are customers of healthcare services. Medical issues can create a vulnerable situation for patients and their dependents. This vulnerability makes medical professionals more responsible for their actions. Accounting information is always linked with medical information about a patient's case. Medical expenses can be paid by patients, government support, or insurance services. When medical services require ongoing treatment, it is necessary to capture and manage payments with the respective medical records. The protection of medical records and accounting information requires further attention. The protection of information requires sufficient and comprehensive data capture. The captured data must be stored promptly in a suitably designed database to facilitate proper use of the data. Accountants should be capable of discussing medical information and (medical) processes with database designers so that ethical issues are managed and suitable controls are in place. Therefore, accounting professionals can be involved in all stages of the digital transformation process. Due to the complex nature of digital accounting systems, accountants must continue to be up to date with the technology and be aware of the ethical and professional responsibilities in relation to accounting information.

Customer-focused: Digital transformation can improve the customer service capabilities of an organization. For example, accounting information can be more accurate and immediate, thus enabling timely and comprehensive tracking. Financial information about patients could be relatively challenging in medical cases, as several organizations are involved. Through the integration streamlining of information systems (e.g., systems used by patients' financial organizations (banks), healthcare service providers (hospitals), insurance, and government services), patients can be provided with accurate and timely information. Properly integrated systems can extract the necessary information when required. Such integration could require APIs and application systems to function harmoniously while accurately processing information. Additionally, it is necessary to ensure the accuracy and security of the information, as well as ethical issues. These processes, as well as the relevant financial information, must be available and known to accountants and auditors. Only then will they know the state of the financial aspect of the business. This understanding helps service providers deliver effective customer services.

Refined Knowledge and Skills: Medical professionals and accounting professionals require knowledge of the digital systems, data (source, path, state, and use), regulatory requirements (local, national, and global), and knowledge of the relevant internal and external processes related to the digital environment. Knowledge development is a dynamic process owing to continuing developments in technology and changes in working environments. Professionals today must have comprehensive computer literacy, system knowledge, and data knowledge.

One of the challenges faced by medical professionals is their knowledge of the technology. Users of the technology could find it difficult to keep up with technological development; hence, they may not have sufficient knowledge to use the new technology. Another issue is that all participants in a process require knowledge of the technology, which provides a better understanding of the process and decisions. However, the technology could help address industry requirements, regulatory requirements (compliance, social, privacy, ethical, and legal), and organizations to make informed decisions. This technology allows businesses to capture data much better than before.

Implications on the Role of the Finance Professional and Auditor
Finance and governance are key aspects of enterprise functions in healthcare service delivery. Digital transformation has enabled many possibilities connecting all participants in this ecosystem, populating data up to the financial records, and creating a source to record the trace route to the auditor. Various models have been developed to formulate capability blueprints for the healthcare sector by integrating digital capabilities. The following capability blueprint released by eHealth Ireland (ehealthireland, 2022) provides a logical arrangement of portfolios integrated with key functions (Fig. 3.5).

Care delivery, care administration, planning and funding, supply chains, and facility management are core functions that are tightly integrated. Furthermore, these systems cannot fail; thus, they are safety critical, and downtime cannot be tolerated as lives are dependent on systems. Safety–critical systems are those systems whose failure could result in a loss of life or cause a catastrophic event due to a malfunction of a critical task. Hence, finance and auditing professionals in healthcare require an understanding of the technology, systems, data (location, data table/attributes, validations, and formats), sequence of the process, integration, rollback procedures, constraints, auditing requirements, and application systems. In addition, regulatory requirements demand the reporting of environmental and ethical issues. To be competitive, maintain reputation, and ensure good governance, organizations must ensure that they address these regulatory requirements.

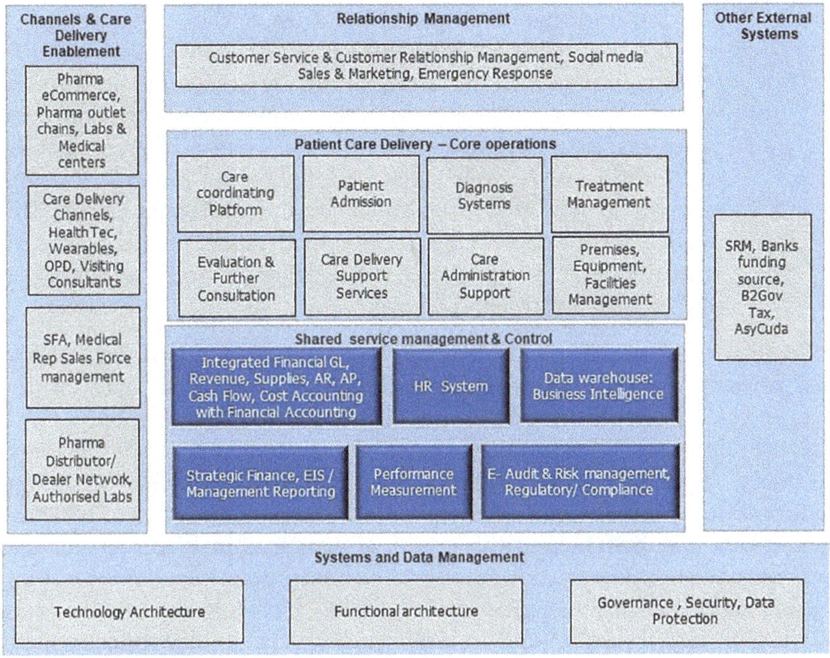

Fig. 3.5 HealthCare integrating with financials—application architecture (*Source* Authors)

Managing the healthcare supply chain is also a critical factor in this equation, as a resilient supply chain is imperative to support safety–critical systems and resilience to combat rising costs. Supplies to healthcare are a crucial factor to ensure continuity in optimizing procurement and logistics costs and making it affordable to patients and consumers. Thus, supply chain visibility and resilience are required, and financial professionals need to play a pivotal role in this process. Another challenge for finance professionals is to ensure that funding lines support these operations. Hence, cash flow projections in these healthcare organizations must be meticulously planned. Fortunately, information requirements to fulfill these needs can be accessible through digitalization capabilities open to the healthcare business sector.

- Professional Responsibility

> Medical information is one of the most sensitive types of information, and trust in managing medical information securely is critical. Patients in care are usually not in a position of bargaining power. Their vulnerability must be noted in medical processes. Accountants in this situation are no different, as they have additional responsibility for information security, sharing, and reporting, including ethical and security issues. In this regard, accountants and auditors must respect patients' consent and adhere to the government and industry body guidelines, as well as organizational directions.

In healthcare situations, staff in multiple departments, organizations, and physically different locations are able to track the state of the required financial information and share necessary information with internal and external organizations (e.g., laboratories, insurance, and hospitals). Tracking and sharing such financial information are not limited to mobile devices. For example, the increasing acceptance of blockchain technology and XBRL indicates evolving standards in financial practices that specifically impact accounting and auditing practices (ARCA, 2022; XBRL, 2022). Healthcare practices are usually busy because of the nature of the services they provide. Emergencies and urgent healthcare situations clearly have an impact on other responsibilities such as ensuring the proper use of financial and other information. Such situations are usually managed by administrative and financial staff, but the financial information responsibility of the organization cannot be discounted. XBRL provides greater accuracy of financial information, thus better reliability, sharing, and reuse of financial information through tags, better data management through real-time data monitoring, and easier documentation through XBRL taxonomies (Deloitte, 2022). These XBRL characteristics could support the improvement of financial service quality, which could improve overall healthcare.

Transactions can occur through regular countersales, online direct bank transfers, and other devices. Even though it may not be popular yet, other payment modes such as cashcard/ipay88 (payments by bank accounts using mobile phones), PayPal, and evolving new technology (e.g., digital currency, digital payments) could be noted (Exabytes, 2022). This is because contemporary accountants must be more proactive in understanding technological development than their predecessors. The use of PayPal is more acceptable than digital currencies, but digital currencies seem to be progressing (Barclays, 2022). For example, Tesla's efforts to accept digital currency. Therefore, accountants today must be familiar with evolving alternative payment methods.

Today, people frequently use online payments, as they are relatively convenient and linked to the user's bank account, deemed to be an acceptable risk. In medical payments, information about the payee and transaction details must be recorded. Although the amount of data that can be captured is high, organizations usually capture the minimum required information, as any additional information could pose a risk with more responsibility to protect data. The information they capture will be linked to the patient, and the organization (healthcare service) is responsible for the safe use of the information. However, maintaining data integrity of the payments and insurance information with the respective medical information could be increasingly challenging with the increased use of new technology owing to insufficient knowledge about new systems.

Auditors' roles in healthcare are far more complex in terms of processes, as they are safety–critical systems. This list is unusually long, and the scope would include assessing, evaluating, and improving care delivery, care administration, health record maintenance, and security. In other words, this would entail a comprehensive, in-depth evaluation of the practices and processes in healthcare facilities. Internal audit teams would assess the control environment and mitigate risks, the external audit team would provide assurance on financial reporting, standards, and systems, and third-party audits would be carried out by specialized teams reviewing regulatory compliance, practices, or specialized aspects of care delivery. Digitally enabled processes would provide useful information on data flows, audit trails, and access controls, while minimizing downtime. Auditors can use specialized e-audit solutions and the RPA to run their audit programs. While specialist audits/skills on HealthTech digital products are required, including complex IT infrastructure, domain-specialized auditors would be required to assess back-office systems, care delivery, care administration, facilities management, compliance/regulatory, pharmaceuticals, treatment, consultants, patient record handling, security, etc.

Case of Financial Services Insurance

The financial service sector broadly comprises banking, payment services, investments, and insurance. This sector plays a pivotal role in the economy. Our focus in this study is narrowed down to the insurance industry, which is an area where the exploits of digital transformation are not often discussed. The insurance industry typically caters to contracts between the insurance company and the policyholder, where the policyholder will pay the insurance company premiums to mitigate the risks that are undertaken by the insurer. In this exchange, the insurance company pays a lump sum to the beneficiaries after losing or damaging the insured property/life of the policyholder. Investopedia further explains that the company pools the client's risk to ease the burden of client loss. Insurance policies are used to hedge against the risk of financial losses that may result from damage to the insured or from liability for the damage or injury caused to the third party.

There are two types of insurance policies: life and non-life. Other than life insurance, non-life insurance contains a wide range of policies covering many other specific contingencies or perils. The list includes health, homeowners, auto, business premises, assets, marine, travel, professional indemnity, and so on. The insurance sector has many characteristics and processes. In the context of the sales process, the agent or broker approaches prospects to provide them with a financial risk management plan. The agent/broker typically uses CRM, which is used to track and monitor sales activities, new leads, and marketing content generation. After securing a prospect, the customer will sign up through policy management software in which the details of the policy are drafted, details of the customer's information (personal details, financial details), and signed policies are stored. These details were stored and sent to the underwriter for underwriting.

Underwriting is a process in which the underwriter (representing the insurance company) determines the level of risk that the company is willing to take on the insured and, if so, provides the premium price for the coverage (Investopedia, 2022). Underwriters use underwriting software or Enterprise Risk Management (ERM) to automate the underwriting process. In life insurance, actuarial services evaluate major risk factors such as the customer's age, gender, medical history, and occupation. For example, a woman in her 40s will have a higher premium than a woman in her 20s as there is a higher risk of death.

Once the underwriting has been approved, the payment will be processed, and the contract between the insurance company and policyholder will be enforced according to the terms and conditions. Depending on the company, policyholders can view their policies on a mobile app or a website. These apps and websites keep track of premium payments, claims, and policy information. They can also offer customer support with regard to changing payment methods, payment frequency, personal information, and so on.

Claims play an important role in the life insurance industry. Upon death, beneficiaries will need to submit documents and information that are managed by a claim management department (usually software is used). Through this, the company is able to track policy information, payments, and other claims related to support. Apart from the traditional plans provided by life insurance, some companies also offer investment-linked policies (also known as Universal Life Insurance). Investment-linked policies are life insurance policies that have an investment aspect. These policies integrate insurance coverage and investment, as a portion of the premium is paid toward investment funds of the policyholder's choice. This enables flexibility in the policyholder's part fund switching can take place depending on the rate of return and even top-up on the investment component. To offer integrated investment plans, the company must strictly follow and comply with the regulations of the country. Additionally, they must have an application system that allows policyholders to track their investments and make changes. Another type of plan offered by insurance companies in many countries is the takaful plan. Takaful plans are insurance plans that follow Shariah Law. These plans work in the same way as conventional insurance plans, providing coverage permissible by Shariah Law.

Digital Transformation in Insurance industry

In the insurance business, with recent technological developments, innovative models are compelled to gain competitive advantage and achieve critical success factors. While business priorities always revolve around KPIs, such as reducing costs, customer 360 relationship management, customer experience, speed to market, underwriting efficiency, claims efficiency, mitigating risks, growing revenue, digitalization, and recent developments in Fintech space have caused insurers to launch innovative InsureTech family products transforming insurance industry customer touch points and core business processes.

InsureTech is a family of products created to transform core business- and customer-centric processes leading to customer touchpoints in all aspects of delivering products and services in the insurance industry. Many insurers have launched innovative products and processes to achieve market speed and customer service excellence. Reengineered processes include dynamically priced policies tailored to fit customer-specific needs and hitherto non-existent service risk mitigation, claims processing, advisory options via mobile apps, auto-monitoring devices, GPS tracking devices, and IoT technologies. Today's needs are diverse, requiring speedy solutions in situations involving travel, business startups requiring short-term plans, and health insurance within minutes or hours. The customer is advised and navigated through various options with AI engines and chatbot interfaces, enabling him to configure the policy on his own with the aid of the insurance advisor.

Other innovative features in mobile apps include:

a. Claims processing: Information on claims can be captured via a mobile application. The customer can capture the incident and record so that the claims estimates and related/dependent activities are automatically processed.
b. Payment solutions: Payment solutions are integrated with mobile apps and premium payments, claims, and refunds can be processed with credit cards or any financial institution. Partner firms working with insurance companies are also connected to the ecosystem, so that the customer obtaining such services and payment settlement becomes far more convenient.
c. Risk Mitigation: Some insurance companies have introduced functionalities that capture customer driving habits and records through IoT and mobile apps. With these records, insurance companies can tailor premiums based on the risks associated with driving patterns so that those who drive recklessly are penalized with a higher premium for their auto insurance.
d. Customized Underwriting: Some insurance companies track data read from customer wearables by collecting data on their changes in key health indicators. With this, they can now tailor customized premiums outside the normal price configurator model.

InsureTech solutions are now becoming more intelligent with AI and machine learning. The data collected from various sources are thus used to formulate risk models, predictions, and risk mitigation measures so that future losses can be significantly reduced while getting their clients to pay higher premiums. Advance Analytics are also indispensable in insurance, and customer analytics, risk analytics, treasury, and portfolio management analytics are being extensively used.

In the insurance industry, key technologies are widely used worldwide, namely Customer Relationship Management software (CRM), insurance workflow automation software, and Enterprise Resource Planning software (ERP). CRM application systems can be used to connect agents to a centralized portal that digitalizes many insurance processes. Not only will it manage leads but it will also allow the agent to verify new policy sales, cross-sell and upsell, field operations, and team management, which streamlines many processes to be more efficient. Insurance workflow automation is a software which arranges, monitors, controls, and coordinates different business processes that involve human resources, sales and marketing, lead management, and more. This is very useful in terms of workflow management as it provides a central platform from lead generation to policy issuance.

The role of the actuary in insurance is another function that benefits from digital transformation. Actual professionals can now use the developments of data science to unlock new methods to assess risks or develop complex and robust models aided with AI and machine learning to capture more insights into the data. They juggle with large amounts of data with customers, agents, sales force interactions/events, and data getting populated in real time in structured and unstructured big data warehouses. Even actuarial professionals now find that a high level of IT literacy is a competitive advantage in their careers and adds to the armor of professional competencies. They add significant value to their organizations and become catalysts in the innovation agenda of these firms.

Investment portfolio management in insurance is another mission-critical function in insurance to ensure choosing the best investment option out of range investment strategies with available funds and the current portfolio. Today's technology and vast amount of computing power allow investment managers to access consolidated databases, data models, and tools for evaluating investment options. These applications are instantly connected through e-banking, investment banking, trading, and money dealer platforms. Solutions enable return on investments, buy sell options, and cash flow projections.

ERP solutions designed specifically for insurance companies can help track customer credentials, transactional amounts, and legal agreement data. By integrating ERP and CRM, companies can effectively manage operations and customer relationships. This software allows auditors and accountants to streamline their processes as it provides them with financial documents recorded by the software. This software aids in the operation and automation of the company, leaving more room for efficiency and productivity. By having a centralized database, customers, agents, and operations can easily access data, real-time analytics, and reports. These technologies will aid auditors and accountants, as these data are easily accessible and much more accurate because of higher security and automation, which reduces the risk of human errors. In addition, upcoming technologies, such as AI, blockchain, and InsureTech, are gaining popularity. Many of the above software already have AI integrated, but future trends will see that AI can be integrated into daily lives that allow more personalized premiums through connected devices (smart watches, Amazon Alexa, etc.) and cognitive technologies. AI can also automate underwriting and claims, thereby providing a more efficient system. Blockchain can enhance security and fraud detection in the life insurance industry. This not only improves the added value for policyholders but also reduces costs and increases business opportunities and potential. InsureTech companies design processes that are data- and technology-driven, capturing $2.7 billion of investments in 2015. These upcoming trends will force accountants and auditors to be digitally savvy.

Role of Auditors and Accountants in the Insurance Industry

Since digital transformation has become an integral element in the insurance industry, the role of finance professionals is becoming more challenging with the changes and process reengineering taking place with technology enablement, although finance professionals gain more visibility of information and process flows. Systems are updated promptly with end-to-end workflows from customer touch points, brokers, agents, and insurance advisors, enabling finance professionals to obtain a bird's eye view of the implications of their day-to-day cash flows, funding requirements, and risks.

The following diagram depicts the basic application architecture and business capability blueprints from a functional perspective of insurance (Figs. 3.6 and 3.7).

Finance professionals, in addition to core business issues, must have their people, processes, and technology to address the following enterprise management functions as well as digital transformation: their day-to-day financial management functions involving payable/receivables, cash flows, and investments. The list includes, but is not limited to,

- Treasury and portfolio management, investment options, evaluations
- Actuarial
- Tax
- Reinsurance
- Legal, process management, records management
- Marketing, channels, branch network, and distribution network
- Partner, Commissions, brokerage management
- Sales force management
- HR processes
- Procurement
- Customer relationship management
- Corporate performance management
- Compliance/regulatory matters involving the regulator
- IT strategy, data management, and security
    - New operating models based on digital transformation initiatives
    - IT projects involving cloud, mobile apps, process reengineering
    - Cybersecurity
    - Technology investments, cost benefit analysis
    - Advance Analytics
    - AI & machine learning projects

Given the complexity of automated transactions, finance professionals are required to extensively explore auto reconciliations, RPA-assisted routines, and regular control reports to finance teams, including exception reporting. Similarly, the digitally transformed insurance company presents a series of challenges to the auditor, starting from IT infrastructure and application portfolios right down to transactions and reporting. Hence, auditors will have to assess the risks and control environment associated with cybersecurity measures, infrastructure management, mobile

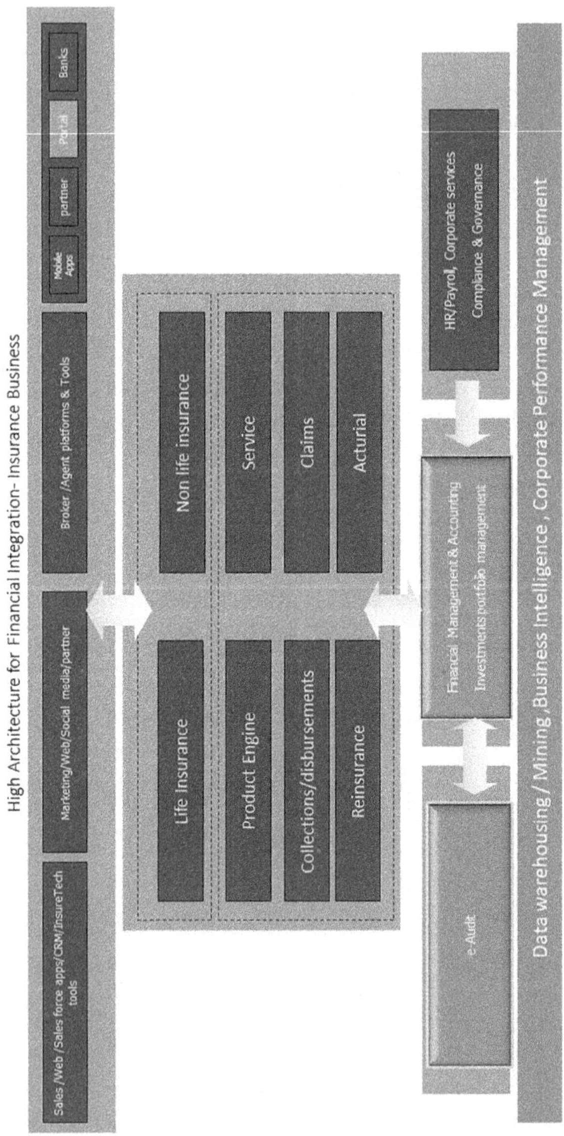

Fig. 3.6 High level architecture for financial integration—insurance business (*Source* Authors)

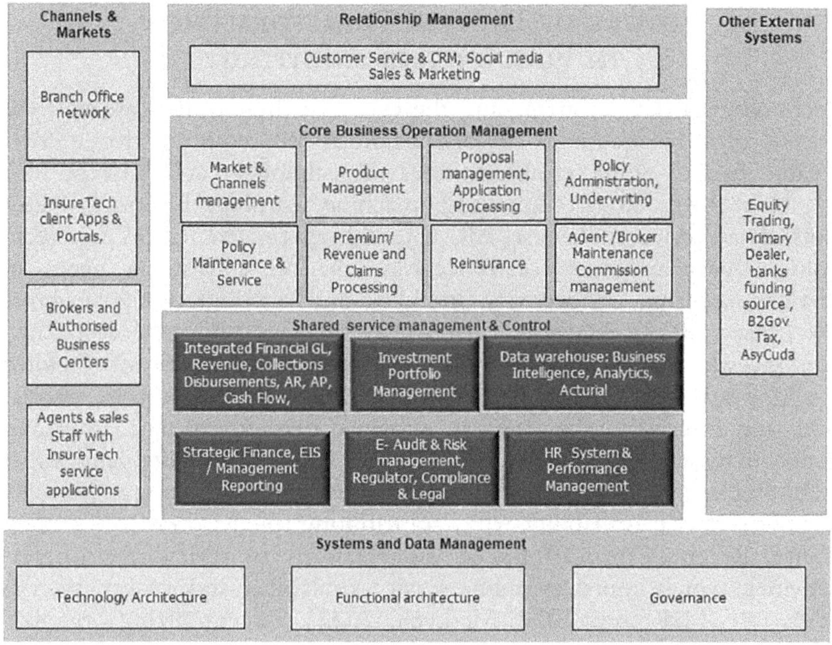

Fig. 3.7 Insurance business integrating with financials—application architecture (*Source* Authors)

and core business applications, access controls, process workflows, financial reporting, analytics platforms, financial models, governance environment, and compliance, and the list is endless.

However, auditors could still use e-Audit software solutions sitting outside to track the reliability of the information, control environment, application controls, etc. RPA is another useful option that can be incorporated into automated audit routines. Auditor-specialized teams on Cybersecurity and IT infrastructure, apps, and back-office connectivity would assess risks, threats, and vulnerabilities so that the potential threats and vulnerabilities, control deficiencies, and data inconsistencies could be identified and provided as input so that systems could be reinforced and made robust.

Future of Digital Transformation in Finance and Auditing

Technological developments and the evidence thus far indicate that the use of digital technology in organizations will continue for a foreseeable future. Some significant uses of technology are Fintech, IoT, AI, blockchain, cloud computing, machine learning, Robotics, RPA/Bots, data science, metaverse, AR/VR, and cryptocurrencies. These technologies have an impact on process automation, consistency, access to services, security, connectivity, mobility, and distributed infrastructure (McKinsey, 2022). Machine learning has been used in decision-making, and investments in applied machine learning are significant. Applied machine learning can be used for data analysis, classification, prediction, and forecasting, resulting in informed decision-making. Improved connectivity enabled by 5G/6G cellular, wireless, satellite, and other technologies has improved connections and faster processing. Mobility improves service availability, while contributing to environmental sustainability. Recent Covid-19 forced organizations to review their online activities, which improves online service availability and quality, such as telehealth (McKinsey, 2022; Medtech, 2022). Decentralizing organizational services through the use of Web3 aims to protect digital ownership rights and influence changes in business operations. Cloud computing facilitates the distribution of computer resources while improving the availability, security, and reliability of data. These technologies are yet to be fully mature, but investments in the development of the technology are significant (McKinsey, 2022). The use of technology is not limited to the above examples, but is critical for organizational competitiveness and sustainability. Increased digital transformation, government support for digitalization, and awareness of digital technology contribute to organizations investing in digital transformation (Penneo, 2022).

The evolving landscape indicates that there will be major implications, many positives, and challenges, namely to the finance workplace, workforce, work content, and the processes with the new technology introduced to organization and technology evolving outside the organization perimeter influencing how a finance professional interacts with suppliers, customers, service providers, banks, regulators, and stakeholders. Many organizations with technology-enabled operating models will start opening offshore offices to implement multi-site, multi-company, multi-currency systems, use blockchain, and cryptocurrencies with work processes supporting cross-border operations with different regulations and cultures. Consequently, auditors will be required to observe these developments closely and ensure their efficiency, productivity, quality of service, and meet client expectations amidst the fast-paced digital disruption of business models, portfolios of solutions, and technology platforms used while adding value to their clients' operations.

It is observed that at the current speed of innovation, the following areas would significantly transform finance workplaces for which finance and audit professionals should be geared to if they are not up to date. The capability to ride these waves of digital disruption would be a competitive advantage for these professions. Below, we present the business domain and technologies that will be significantly transformed within the next few years.

- Cloud computing, SaaS, cloud-based ERPs: New service models will evolve. ERPs significantly simplify processes and workflow-driven solutions, making finance professionals more productive. This could also indicate a major change in the business model or a change in the operating model in some divisions of the company. New service models would open new doors for new subsidiary companies providing a range of services; some businesses with industry expertise would explore BPO, competency centers, or professional services for specific industries. Mergers and Acquisitions need more planning and careful assessment of systems and IT due diligence, as the technology platforms of buy and sell side companies are diverse, and finance professionals will have to play a pivotal role in deriving and evaluating these new models.
- Digital document management and signatures would be implemented, especially in Asian countries, creating extra workload for auditors trying to ascertain integrity, confidentiality, and authenticity. However, finance professionals must play a key role in process mapping and business process reengineering to make use of these solutions. Industry-specific solution verticals would be further refined in the future so that investment in ERPs could be protected with the next upgrade. Finance professionals, therefore, will have to play a leading role in formulating IT strategy, business process reengineering, and performing cost/benefit analysis of these investments. Proliferation of API will begin to emerge with many systems trying to talk to the back-end. CFO and auditors will have to be

prepared to spend hours with other teams trying to resolve data messes if these interfaces are not properly monitored. This could mean that more special assignments to auditors can simultaneously provide additional headaches in audit plans and SOW.

- Finance professionals find more time to devote to their Strategic Finance and value-added functions, which could make CXO happy and ultimately benefit the organization.
- Chatbots, RPAs, and AI, including machine learning, will become indispensable in some organizations to become competitive. In such organizations, finance professionals must be equipped with specific skills to add value to the organizational strategy.
- Cryptocurrencies and Blockchain: Accounting standards for cryptocurrencies will emerge, giving more clarity to accounting and professionals, although no standards from IFRS exist other than IFRS 13 fair value measurement (ACCAGlobal.com). The IAS currently plants it under the IAs. Digital currencies will gain wider acceptance over a period of time, although they cannot be considered equivalent to cash as they currently inherit the risk of changes in value. Accountants will find their business partners accepting digital currencies in their transactions with the organization. This means that future accountants and auditors should understand the digital ledger; thus, we have a new layer of complexity. They must familiarize themselves with blockchain cryptography, cryptocurrency digital mining, and digital ledgers spread through a network of computers. More challenges would surface in assessing cryptocurrency risks, visualizing and accounting for investment volatilities, and implications on balance sheet and company valuations.
- Integration capabilities with extended ERP solutions such as CRM, EAM, SCM, warehouse automations, 3PL/$PL operations, robotics in manufacturing, IoT, Mobile Applications, B2B, e-commerce, SRM, e-procurement, e-government, e-banking, neo-bank models, and customer-centric core banking platforms will increase significantly.

    - Healthcare sector will enhance digitally enabled services.
    - AR/VR, 5G, and Metaverse open up new possibilities of technology use cases for the quantum leap in telco, digital entertainment, media/entertainment, leisure, and hospitality sector service-delivery models.

  - Financial services stock trading, investment banking, asset management, and insurance digitally enabled business models would evolve with AI, machine learning, Analytics, and CRMs.

- Amidst these digital disruptions, finance professionals will have to trace the data flows to their GL and related modules, the complexity of their data sources and transaction volume, and the speed at which the data change grows. His work will become real time in time to come when all touch points are integrated. This adds complexity to the auditor's audit plans, and he/she is required to deploy more audit professionals with a blend of technology and financial auditing capabilities.
- New technology tools that would be useful for finance professionals will be available in the market. New generation finance staff using these tools and performing financial modeling could make senior finance staff guess the reliability and quality of work performed. This would compel senior professionals to train themselves in these technologies or obtain professional certifications.
- Public sector aiming smart state: People would be demanding more digital solutions from government departments and state-sector organizations, as the proliferation of digital applications has already made citizens' lives easier. Rapid urbanization, environmental protection, laws, utilities provided by the government, government regulations, complex tax cultures, and fiscal management policies would make digitalization imperative for future governments. Investing in digital initiatives in the public sector would be among the top priorities of the government agenda, as digitally enabled government services attract businesses and Foreign Direct Investments that benefit the country, economy, and happier citizens in the near future. Some governments have already attempted to set up one-stop shops to deliver citizen-centric e-gov services. These portals would grow significantly, and public sector finance professionals and auditors of the Auditor General's office will have to sharpen their technology to know how to carry out their professional roles in these environments. However, they will immensely benefit from these digital platforms and processes as they will be using standard back-end financial applications built in the government financial regulations and public sector accounting standards in the time to

come, processes, and reporting platforms integrated into government treasury. However, data protection, information security, and robust and highly secure investigations would be mandatory, which would be managed by a new arm of national security. The Ministry of Finance and the Government Treasury will find a consolidated repository of financial information in their consolidated databases, enabling public finance management, government revenue management, allocation of funding to public sector services, and monitoring these government departments and projects easier through these integrated databases and reporting platforms, even if the infrastructure is provided by the government cloud, digital signatures, security services, project management services, and National Audit services with e-Audit platforms. Governments could explore new revenue models and services using these digital platforms so that such revenues can be used to improve the quality of the services to be delivered to citizens.

Conclusion

Technology has significantly transformed the way we live, how businesses operate, and how governments deliver their services. The impact of digital transformation is significant in almost all the business sectors. Farming technology is indispensable, even in agribusiness. Therefore, CXO professionals, entrepreneurs in their business strategy formulation, and decision-making roles are required to consider digital transformation as an indispensable and critical success factor for the business and an essential companion in their day-to-day lives. However, it is imperative that such digital transformation initiatives aim to improve customer experience. Two key dimensions, namely customer experience and financial performance, ROI, and payback, must be appraised when evaluating projects. All these projects add more data for organizations' data lakes and large amounts of unstructured data, which eventually require further analysis, causing changes to reporting formats and frequency of reporting. This would mean that a finance professional in Data Scientist/Data Analyst shoes is needed in the finance team to assist and add value to the CFO, which provides insights on business performance. This skill would be required in the auditor team to track exceptions or to perform forensic audits exploring data lakes. Although AI has not invaded the lives of audit professionals, it would soon become a reality where audit professionals would be compelled to use AI in their audit programs to improve productivity and audit findings. This means that auditors must be equipped with skills in ML, NLP, and distributed ledger technology.

Hence, the Finance and Auditing professionals today need to be equipped with multiple skills consisting of business knowledge, professional knowledge, technological knowledge and are also required to keep abreast of developments specially in technology and digitally enabled business models/processes as they are required to play crucial role managing finance, governance, resources while advising the business. How they deliver value to their organization now depends heavily on the extent to which digital transformation is being used in their organization and the tools utilized to facilitate decision-making.

References

AACSB. (2018). 2018 Eligibility Procedures and Accreditation Standards for Accounting Accreditation. In: AACSB.

ARCA. (2022, December 11, 2020). About XBRL. https://www.acra.gov.sg/xbrl-filing-and-resources/about-xbrl

Barclays. (2022). Should the Federal Reserve create a digital dollar? Barclays—Should the Federal Reserve create a digital dollar?

CPA, A. (2023). Embracing digital transformation in accounting and finance.

Deloitte. (2022). What is XBRL? What is XBRL?

ehealthireland. (2022). Key capability areas. https://www.ehealthireland.ie/knowledge-information-plan/new-health-service-capabilities/key-capability-areas/

Exabytes. (2022). Top 8 Malaysia online payment solutions in 2021. https://www.exabytes.my/blog/top-8-malaysia-online-payment-solutions/

Gartner. (2022). What is supply chain management? https://www.gartner.com/en/topics/supply-chain-management

Group, O. (2022). The open group: Leading the development of open, vendor-neutral technology standards and certifications. https://www.opengroup.org/about-us/what-we-do

Hillary, R. (2004). Environmental management systems and the smaller enterprise. *Journal of Cleaner Production, 12*(6), 561–569. Environmental management systems and the smaller enterprise

IFRS. (2022). IFRS—Who we are. https://www.ifrs.org/about-us/who-we-are/

Institute, C. (2021, October 2018). Comment letter on SEC RFI on digital engagement practices and digital investment advice. In *Millennials and investing*.

Institute, C. (2022). *The new age of special purpose acquisition companies—What investors should know*. https://www.cfainstitute.org/advocacy/policy-positions/new-age-of-special-purpose-acquisition-companies

Investopedia. (2022, October 28, 2021). Personal finance insurance. https://www.investopedia.com/terms/i/insurance-underwriter.asp

KPMG. (2022). Guides to financial statements. https://home.kpmg/xx/en/home/services/audit/international-financial-reporting-standards/ifrs-illustrative-financial-statements.html

Malhotra, A., Melville, N. P., & Watson, R. T. (2013). Spurring impactful research on information systems for environmental sustainability. *Mis Quarterly, 37*(4), 1265–1274. http://search.ebscohost.com/login.aspx?direct=true&db=bth&AN=91906263&site=ehost-live

McKinsey. (2022). The top trends in tech. https://www.mckinsey.com/business-functions/mckinsey-digital/our-insights/the-top-trends-in-tech-2021

Medtech. (2022). Empowering health with the best of breed practice management and personal health management solutions. https://medtechglobal.com/global/about-us-global/

Penneo. (2022). What are the main trends driving digital transformation in accounting? https://penneo.com/blog/audit-accounting-digitization/

Porter, M. E. (1997). Competitive strategy. *Measuring Business Excellence, 1*(2), 12–17. https://doi.org/10.1108/eb025476

Porter, M. E. (2011). *Competitive advantage of nations: creating and sustaining superior performance*. Simon and Schuster.

XBRL. (2022). An Introduction to XBRL. https://www.xbrl.org/the-standard/what/an-introduction-to-xbrl/

CHAPTER 4

A Topic Modeling-Based Review of Digital Transformation Literature in Accounting

Ju-Chun Yen and Tawei Wang

Introduction

Digital transformation (DT) has proliferated and become an important topic for both researchers and practitioners in recent years. There are various definitions of DT (Vial, 2019). Still, a general concept of DT is "a process that aims to improve an entity by triggering significant changes to its properties through combinations of information, computing, communication, and connectivity technologies" (Vial, 2019, 118). In other words, DT indicates the process by which firms embed technologies to fundamentally change their businesses. To perform DT, companies must go through several gradual phases and levels (Liew et al., 2022). The first phase is digitization, which transforms analog data into a digital form.

J.-C. Yen
National Central University, Taoyuan City, Taiwan
e-mail: jcyen@ncu.edu.tw

T. Wang (✉)
DePaul University, Chicago, IL, USA
e-mail: david.wang@depaul.edu

A. Perdana and T. Wang (eds.), *Digital Transformation in Accounting and Auditing*, https://doi.org/10.1007/978-3-031-46209-2_4

The second phase is digitalization, which means using digital technologies to change a business model and move to digital business to generate new revenue. Finally, firms can create new digital business models.

As DT has started changing the entire business environment and creating new business models, it is important to understand the extent to which accounting researchers and practitioners understand how DT has changed their own or their customers' business models. For example, auditors can now utilize better tools, such as robotic process automation (RPA) or artificial intelligence (AI), to perform audit tasks for clients who have completed digitization. In addition, as digitalization and DT have changed or created new business models for clients, auditors need sufficient knowledge to understand clients' business models and assess their business risks. Thus, it is important for accounting and auditing researchers and practitioners to have a good understanding of how DT will change businesses and how it will support accounting work (Forbes, 2021).

To understand the research trends related to DT in the accounting field, we explore the current literature related to DT over the past decade in both fields of information systems (IS) and accounting (Acc). We adopted the literature review approach in Gurcan et al. (2021) by performing a textual analysis with the probabilistic topic model of latent Dirichlet allocation (LDA) on the abstracts of research papers. By comparing the trends of topics in both fields, we observed which topics about DT have been developed in the IS field and which topics about DT are focused in the Acc field. Thus, we can provide potential future research directions for accounting researchers regarding what has been developed in the IS field but has not been introduced to the Acc field.

Review of Literature Review of Digital Transformation

IS researchers have addressed DT and reviewed the related literature from different perspectives. Henriette et al. (2015) analyzed 13 DT studies from 2006 to 2014 and found that about half of them were case studies. Morakanyane et al. (2017) retrieved 53 DT studies and organized them into a conceptual matrix of DT characteristics, drivers, and key impacts. Reis et al. (2018) used a qualitative approach of bibliometric analysis and a quantitative approach to content analysis to review DT literature around the world and found that DT literature started to increase significantly in

2014. Vial (2019) used an inductive approach to review the DT literature by searching relevant keywords within IS literature in three databases (AIS Library, Business Source Complete, and ScienceDirect). By analyzing 282 works, Vial (2019) summarizes the definition of DT and establishes the building blocks of the DT framework.

Some researchers have focused on how DT has been applied to specific fields through literature reviews, such as business and management (Kraus et al., 2022; Verhoef et al., 2021), financial sectors (Cziesla, 2014), environmental sustainability (Feroz et al., 2021), etc. However, we do not find any DT literature that focuses on the accounting field. While DT has been significantly changing the business environment, as an accountant or auditor, it is essential to understand how DT impacts fundamental accounting and auditing. Therefore, in this study, we aim to fill this gap by performing a systematic literature review of DT in accounting and compare it with DT in IS to understand the current discussion and potential future direction in research.

Research Design

Sample

We followed steps similar to those in de Bakker et al. (2019), Han et al. (2023), and Vial (2019) as our fundamental literature review approach. First, we selected top academic journals in the fields of accounting (Acc) and information systems (IS) as the search pool. Because there are two journals in the accounting field, Journal of Information Systems and the International Journal of Accounting Information Systems, generally regarded as cross-discipline journals between Acc and IS, we also include these two journals in the search pool and mark them as the "Acc/IS" field. In summary, our search pool includes 24 journals, consisting of eight journals in the IS field, two in the Acc/IS field, and two in the Acc field. A list of the journals is presented in Table 4.1.

Next, we searched for journal articles related to digital transformation between 2012 and 2022 from the search pool. Specifically, we searched for the term "digital transformation" in all fields (title, abstracts, keywords, etc.) in each journal's search panel. We first used an RPA program to search and collect articles automatically, and then manually organized and confirmed the content. At this initial step, we collected 324 journal articles related to digital transformation, consisting of 274 in

Table 4.1 Overview of journal articles in the sample

Field	*Journal*	*# of articles including "digital transformation"*	*# of articles excluded*	*# of articles in the final sample*
IS	European Journal of Information Systems	50	(5)	45
	Information Systems Journal	33	(13)	20
	Information Systems Research	41	(21)	20
	Journal of Information Technology	34	(4)	30
	Journal of Management Information Systems	22	(5)	17
	Journal of the Association for Information Systems	24	(4)	20
	Management Information Systems Quarterly	32	(11)	21
	The Journal of Strategic Information Systems	38	(9)	29
	Subtotal of IS journal articles	274	(72)	202
Acc/IS	International Journal of Accounting Information Systems	13	(0)	13
	Journal of Information Systems	13	(2)	11
	Subtotal of Acc/IS journal articles	26	(2)	24
Acc	Accounting Horizons	6	(0)	6
	Accounting, Organizations and Society	0	(0)	0
	AUDITING: A Journal of Practice & Theory	1	(1)	1
	Contemporary Accounting Research	1	(0)	1
	European Accounting Review	1	(0)	1
	Journal of Accounting, Auditing & Finance	0	(0)	0
	Journal of Accounting and Economics	0	(0)	0

(continued)

Table 4.1 (continued)

Field	*Journal*	*# of articles including "digital transformation"*	*# of articles excluded*	*# of articles in the final sample*
	Journal of Accounting Research	5	(5)	0
	Journal of Business Finance & Accounting	0	(0)	0
	Journal of Management Accounting Research	0	(0)	0
	Management Accounting Research	2	(1)	1
	Review of Accounting Studies	1	(0)	1
	The Accounting Review	3	(1)	2
	The British Accounting Review	4	(0)	4
	Subtotal of Acc journal articles	24	(7)	17
	Subtotal of general Acc (Acc/IS & Acc) articles	50	(9)	41
	Total number of journal articles in the sample	324	(81)	243

Articles that were not regular research articles, such as editorials, responses, or comments, were excluded from the sample (*Source* Authors)

the IS field, 26 in the Acc/IS field, and 24 in the Acc field. As we focused on academic research trends, we further excluded articles that were not regular research articles, such as editorials, responses, and comments. After exclusion, our final sample included 243 research articles: 202 in the IS field, 24 in the Acc/IS field, and 17 in the Acc field. Table 4.1 presents the sample selection process for each journal.

LDA Process

We performed a topical analysis of journal article abstracts to explore the research topics of DT-related studies. Specifically, we adopted LDA to categorize and identify the research topics of the articles in the sample (Blei, 2012; Blei et al., 2003). LDA assumes that a topic is a distribution of words and that a document is composed of topics based on a distribution over latent topics. As one cannot directly observe the topics but only the distribution of words in a document, LDA estimates the distribution of topics based on posterior probabilities from an observable collection of documents.

To implement LDA, we first collected the abstracts of the journal articles in our sample. The abstracts were cleaned by removing punctuations, numbers, and stop words (e.g., definite articles and pronouns), as they provided no meaningful content and increased the redundant dimensions of the document vector. We further stemmed each word to treat variations to reduce dimensions and measurement errors. After cleaning up, we vectorized each abstract, where each element in the vector represented the standardized frequency of a unique word, and performed the LDA model. In the LDA model, we set the number of topics to eight, which was the optimal number estimated according to the pre-analysis proposed by Cao et al. (2009). Finally, the LDA process identifies the topical terms for the eight topics. To label each topic, we followed Sievert and Shirley (2014) to rank the terms in each topic by a relevance ratio and used the first ranked terms to name the topic. Table 4.2 shows the eight topics identified by the LDA process, with their labels and example topical terms. The eight topics are labeled as "healthcare", "research review/Covid pandemic", "digital/social media", "blockchain/big data", "automation software", "security", "digital platform ecosystem", and "firm value". We then assigned a topic to each journal article abstract according to the highest probability estimated using the LDA process.

Results

Trends of DT Among Different Fields

First, we analyze how the discussion of digital transformation shifts among fields. Figure 4.1 demonstrates the yearly trends in the number of journal articles in our sample by research field (IS, Acc/IS, and Acc). The area chart shows the number of journal articles on DT in our sample; the fields are shown in different areas. The line chart shows the percentage change in the number of DT articles across all fields. First, Fig. 4.1 shows that the total number of DT studies has increased over the years, from 3 in 2012 to 71 in 2022. The most significant increase was in 2017, with an increasing rate of 450% (from 2 articles in 2016 to 11 articles in 2017). In addition, we observed a large increase in 2020, with an increase rate of 178.9%, from 19 articles in 2019 to 53 articles in 2020. Second, when

Table 4.2 Topic label and example terms

No	*Topic label*	*Top topical terms*
1	Healthcare	healthcar, online, health, account, offlin, particip, polici, market, inform, agenc, share, platform, manag, physician, patient
2	Research review/Covid pandemic	Research, govern, review, use, ada, chang, theory, pandem, studi, future, system, work, inform, covid
3	Digital/social media	Digit, media, afford, use, organ, technolog, analyt, social, inform, embedded, system hospit, data, posit, acquir
4	Blockchain/big data	Data, blockchain, big, busi, model, company, studi, effici, campaign, can servit, implement, perspect, audit, design
5	Automation software	Term, agil, user, autom, softwar, advertis, trust, will, need, human, interact, emarket, readmiss, develop, infrastructur
6	Security	Innov, ident institute, sourc, asset, secur, seiz, digit, rpa, bmi, cyberbully, tax, public, ontolog, transfer, breach
7	Digital platform ecosystem	Digit, transform, ecosystem, platform, product, capabl, eam, research, strategi, energy, renew, dynam, technolog, ambidexter, challeng
8	Firm value	Firm, custom, valu, ebusi, data, cloud, invest, capabl, service, develop, competit, align, stage, influenc, find

This table presents the labels and top terms of the eight topics identified by LDA. Topical terms were stemmed and ranked by the ratio proposed by Sievert and Shirley (2014). Labels were assigned based on the listed top terms (*Source* Authors)

we look into DT articles in different fields, the area chart in Fig. 4.1 shows that DT studies have been performed in the IS field since 2012, the starting year of our sample selection.[1] Starting in 2017, studies in the

[1] An additional search shows that the earliest study in the IS field following our searching process is in 2004. There are seven studies in the IS field and zero studies in the Acc field that relate to digital transformation. As we focus on the digital transformation literature in the recent decade, we do not include these seven studies in our sample.

Acc/IS field have discussed digital transformation-related issues. Finally, publications on DT research have appeared in major accounting journals (Acc) since 2019. Therefore, we observe a contagion of discussion in DT from the IS to the Acc/IS fields and eventually to the Acc field.

Keywords Analysis Among Different Fields

We next used keywords listed in the DT journal articles to provide an initial exploration of the topics in different fields, as authors are expected to list keywords that can summarize the main points of the article. To obtain the statistics, we established an auto-collection program with an RPA to collect all keywords from the authors listed in the journal articles in our sample, and we manually organized and confirmed their correctness. As words with different variations may represent similar topics (e.g., audit and auditing), we stemmed the keywords to avoid variations. We also excluded the keyword "digital transformation" because all journal articles in our sample were related to the topic. Finally, we counted the keyword frequencies and listed the top 15 keywords in Table 4.3.

In the IS field, the most listed keywords are "digit_innov" (digital innovation), "case_studi" (case study), "digit" (digital), "digit_technolog" (digital technology), and "literatur_review" (literature review). The results indicate that when addressing digital transformation, IS researchers focus on digital innovation or digital technology. The keywords also show that some studies adopted the methodology of case studies or literature reviews. In addition, the keyword "covid_19" (COVID-19) also has a high frequency, indicating that the recent pandemic may have a significant influence on digital transformation.

Table 4.3 shows that, in the general Acc field (both Acc/IS and Acc), the most frequent keywords are "audit", "blockchain", "robot_process_autom" (robotic process automation, RPA). The results indicate that, currently, Acc researchers relate DT more to auditing and process automation. Acc researchers are also interested in how blockchain technology can help digital transformation in accounting and audit processes. Regarding research methodology, several accounting studies indicate event studies ("event_studi") and market reactions ("market_reaction"). The finding about research methodology is different from that in IS research, which adopts more on case studies ("case_studi") and literature review ("literatur_review").

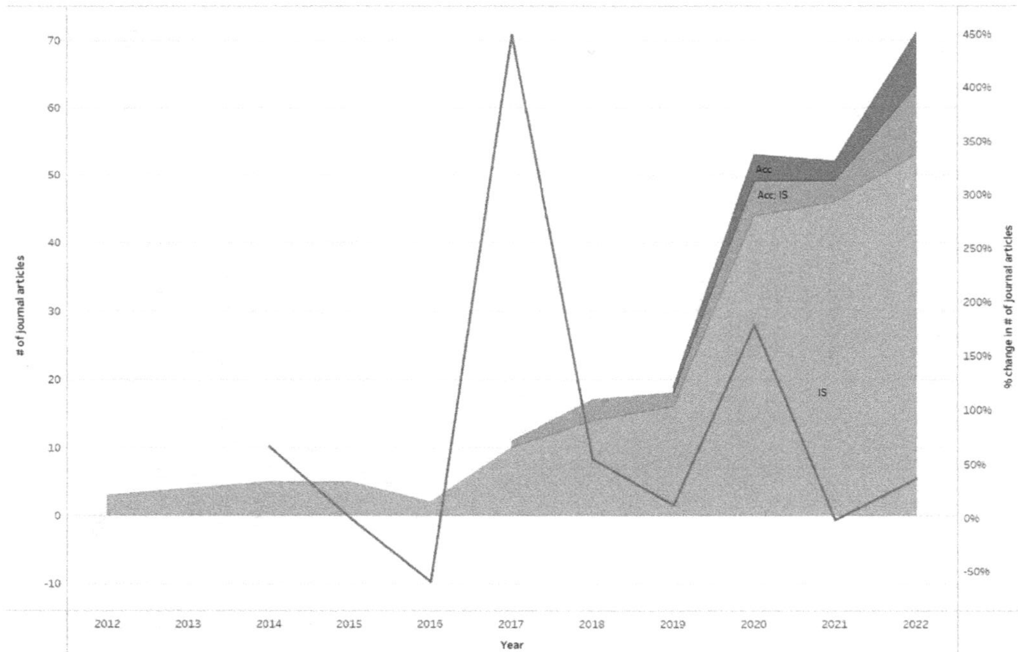

Fig. 4.1 Digital transformation literature in the IS and Accounting fields[2] (*Source* Authors)

[2] The area chart in this figure presents yearly trends in the number of journal articles in the fields of Information systems (IS), accounting information systems (Acc/IS), and accounting (Acc) from 2012 to 2022. The line represents the percentage change in the total number of journal articles on DT in our sample

Table 4.3 Top keywords of journal articles

Information systems (IS)	*Freq.*	*General accounting (Acc/IS and Acc)*	*Freq.*
digit_innov	16	audit	5
case_studi	11	blockchain	4
digit	10	robot_process_autom	4
digit_technolog	7	account	3
literatur_review	7	data_analyt	3
covid_19	6	digit	3
digit_platform	6	account_autom	2
firm_perform	6	account_digit	2
agil	5	account_innov	2
blockchain	5	artifici_intellig	2
design_scienc_research	5	audit_data_analyt	2
inform_technolog	5	big_data	2
innov	5	event_studi	2
institut_logic	5	institut_work	2
internet_of_thing	5	it_govern	2
it_govern	5	manag_account	2
platform	5	market_reaction	2
		review	2
		risk_manag	2
		robot	2
		trust	2

This table lists the top 15 keywords in the digital transformation-related journal articles in the IS and general Acc (Acc/IS and Acc) fields. The keywords stemmed from treating variations as the same. Because multiple keywords have the same frequency, we list all of them with the same frequency. Thus, we list 17 and 21 keywords in the IS and general Acc fields, respectively (*Source* Authors)

Comparing the top keywords in both fields, we find that both IS and accounting researchers have focused on the IT governance issue in digital transformation. This result demonstrates the importance of IT governance when firms devote themselves to digital transformation. Blockchain is listed as one of the top keywords in both fields, indicating that both IS and accounting researchers are interested in how blockchain can help digital transformation.

Topical Analysis of Article Abstracts and Topic Trends

To explore topic trends in different fields, we performed LDA on article abstracts in our sample. Table 4.4 summarizes the number of articles assigned to each topic. Overall, we found that DT studies in the IS field concentrated on digital platform ecosystems and research review/ covid pandemics. On the other hand, DT studies in the general Acc field address blockchain/big data and research review/Covid pandemic. Thus, we found a large difference in the focus on DT, especially in the topics of digital platform ecosystems, firm value, and security.

Figure 4.2 presents the year-by-year trends of the eight topics in both the general Acc (Acc/IS and Acc) and the IS fields. The left panel shows line graphs of the number of articles, and the right panel shows line graphs of the percentage changes in the number of articles over the years. First, for each topic, IS studies have explored DT earlier than Acc studies, consistent with our results in Fig. 4.1 that a contagion effect of DT exists from IS to Acc. Specifically, the results show that the Acc field started research on healthcare, digital platform ecosystems, and firm value. Second, both IS and Acc fields have increased their focus on DT on the topic of blockchain/big data, indicating that both fields are interested in how blockchain and big data will alter the business. Third, there is a relatively large increase in the security topic in the Acc field, showing that accounting researchers have begun to address the security issue of DT in accounting. However, the number of articles on DT in automation software is increasing in the IS field but not in the Acc field. As the application of automation software, such as RPA, is becoming popular in

Table 4.4 Topical distributions in different fields

No	*Topic label*	*# of articles in IS*	*# of articles in Acc/IS and Acc*	*Total # of articles*
1	Healthcare	15	5	20
2	Research review/ Covid pandemic	30	8	38
3	Digital/social media	27	4	31
4	Blockchain/big data	19	8	27
5	Automation software	20	7	27
6	Security	24	5	29
7	Digital platform ecosystem	36	2	38
8	Firm value	26	1	27
	Total	197	40	237

The topic assignment was based on journal abstracts. The sample excluded six articles for which abstracts could not be successfully extracted (*Source* Authors)

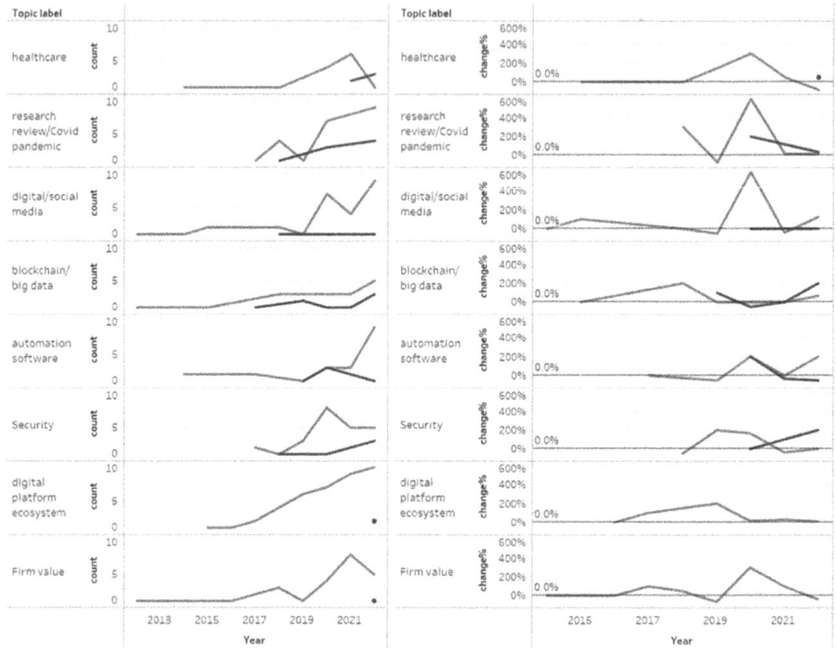

Fig. 4.2 Abstract topic trends[3] (*Source* Authors)

the accounting field, one might need to observe a longer period to see how DT, together with automation software, affects accounting practices and academic studies.

Discussion

As DT has significantly altered business models, it has become more substantial for accounting researchers and practitioners to understand how DT is going to change accounting and auditing tasks. This study fills the gap between DT and accounting by adopting a topic modeling-based

[3] This figure shows the trends of each topic based on journal article abstracts. The orange and blue lines represent IS and general Acc (Acc/IS and Acc) research, respectively. The left panel shows line graphs of the number of articles, and the right panel shows line graphs of the percentage changes in the number of articles over the years

approach to review the DT-related literature in the IS and Acc fields. Our results show that Acc researchers have started to address DT-related issues in recent years, especially in security, blockchain/big data, and the Covid pandemic. While DT has been well-developed in the IS field, Acc researchers may consider applying other topics that have been discussed in the IS field. For example, several topics shown in the IS literature are also common in accounting in the past, although not specifically about digital transformation, such as digital innovation, digital platforms, and firm performance. Digital transformation is a big concept that encompasses factors beyond technology. Acc researchers can also borrow theoretical backgrounds and research designs from IS articles in the future. We expect our findings to provide Acc researchers with a big picture of current DT applications in accounting and to illuminate potential research avenues in the future.

Our study has the following limitations. First, we selected our sample from top IS and Acc journals and ignored journals and conference proceedings in all ranks; our results may only show those DT topics that have been accepted in top journals. Second, the discussions of the LDA results might still depend on the subjectively assigned labels, although we have made every effort to make the labeling process more objective by applying the approach of Sievert and Shirley (2014).

References

Blei, D. M. (2012). Probabilistic topic models. *Communications of the ACM, 55*(4), 77–84.

Blei, D. M., Ng, A. Y., & Jordan, M. I. (2003). Latent Dirichlet allocation. *Journal of Machine Learning Research, 3*, 993–1022.

Cao, J., Xia, T., Li, J., Zhang, Y., & Tang, S. (2009). A density-based method for adaptive LDA model selection. *Neurocomputing, 72*(7), 1775–1781.

Cziesla, T. (2014). A literature review on digital transformation in the financial service industry. Bled eConference.

de Bakker, F. G. A., Rasche, A., & Ponte, S. (2019). Multi-stakeholder initiatives on sustainability: A cross-disciplinary review and research agenda for business ethics. *Business Ethics Quarterly, 29*(3), 343–383.

Feroz, A. K., Zo, H., & Chiravuri, A. (2021). Digital transformation and environmental sustainability: A review and research agenda. *Sustainability, 13*(3), 1530.

Forbes. (2021). *The future of accounting: How will digital transformation impact accountants?* Retrieved March 21, 2023, from https://www.forbes.com/sites/forbestechcouncil/2021/05/19/the-future-of-accounting-how-will-digital-transformation-impact-accountants/

Gurcan, F., Cagiltay, N. E., & Cagiltay, K. (2021). Mapping human-computer interaction research themes and trends from its existence to today: A topic-modeling-based review of past 60 years. *International Journal of Human-Computer Interaction, 37*(3), 267–280.

Han, H., Shiwakoti, R. K., Jarvis, R., Mordi, C., & Botchie, D. (2023). Accounting and auditing with blockchain technology and artificial Intelligence: A literature review. *International Journal of Accounting Information Systems, 48*, 100598.

Henriette, E., Feki, M., & Boughzala, I. (2015). The shape of digital transformation: A systematic literature review. Mediterranean Conference on Information Systems.

Kraus, S., Durst, S., Ferreira, J. J., Veiga, P., Kailer, N., & Weinmann, A. (2022). Digital transformation in business and management research: An overview of the current status quo. *International Journal of Information Management, 63*, 102466.

Liew, A., O'Leary, D. E., Perdana, A., & Wang, T. (2022). Digital transformation in accounting and auditing: 2021 International Conference of the Journal of Information Systems panel discussion. *Journal of Information Systems, 36*(3), 177–190.

Morakanyane, R., Grace, A. A., & O'Reilly, P. (2017). Conceptualizing digital transformation in business organizations: A systematic review of literature. Bled eConference.

Reis, J., Amorim, M., Melão, N., & Matos, P. (2018). Digital transformation: A literature review and guidelines for future research. In *Trends and advances in information systems and technologies.*

Sievert, C., & Shirley, K. (2014). LDAvis: A method for visualizing and interpreting topics. In *The workshop on interactive language learning, visualization, and interfaces.*

Verhoef, P. C., Broekhuizen, T., Bart, Y., Bhattacharya, A., Dong, J. Q., Fabian, N., & Haenlein, M. (2021). Digital transformation: A multidisciplinary reflection and research agenda. *Journal of Business Research, 122*, 889–901.

Vial, G. (2019). Understanding digital transformation: A review and a research agenda. *The Journal of Strategic Information Systems, 28*(2), 118–144.

PART II

Empowering Accountants: Embracing Technology Skills for Success

CHAPTER 5

Lost in Translation? The Required Vs. Actual Technology Skills of Accountants

Richard Busulwa, Jacqueline Birt, Adrian Gepp, and Grainne Oates

Introduction

Prior accounting research has investigated accountants' required and actual digital technology (DT) competencies, as well as how they are shaped by ongoing DT advancements and subsequent changes in the roles and activities expected of accountants. To this end, the literature

Research funded by the Accounting and Finance Association of Australia and New Zealand (AFAANZ grant round 2022).

R. Busulwa (✉) · G. Oates
Swinburne University, Melbourne, VIC, Australia
e-mail: rbusulwa@swin.edu.au

G. Oates
e-mail: goates@swin.edu.au

A. Perdana and T. Wang (eds.), *Digital Transformation in Accounting and Auditing*, https://doi.org/10.1007/978-3-031-46209-2_5

has identified a diverse collection of required accounting DT competencies, including information systems management, data, emerging technology, digital transformation, and digital business-related competencies. These diverse competencies compartmentalize into two broad categories: required knowledge and understanding of DTs relevant to accounting work, and required skills and abilities to use these DTs for accounting work. Focusing on the second category, we first review the relevant accounting literature from both a practitioner and academic perspective and summarize the required DT skills and abilities within these literatures. We then use survey research to investigate the extent to which accountants across different career levels, accounting functions, and accounting practice settings possess the required accounting DT skills and abilities. Understanding the gap between required and actual skills/abilities is critical to understanding the future skill/ability needs of accounting work, it is critical to improving DT skills/abilities integrated within accounting curricula, and it is critical to redesigning varied accounting curricula for increasingly digital contexts. In the remainder of this study, we interchangeably refer to skills and abilities as skills, for simplicity—but in each case we mean both skills and abilities.

Prior research has identified the accounting DT competency imperative as an ongoing and never-ending process of identifying and updating accounting DT competencies in line with ongoing DT advancements (see Birt et al., 2017; IFAC, 2001; Pincus et al., 2017; Busulwa & Evans, 2021; Wessels, 2005). It has also identified a diverse and extensive collection of emerging technologies, information systems management, data, digital transformation, and digital business-related competencies (e.g., see ACCA, 2020; Busulwa & Evans, 2021; Wessels, 2005). These studies have identified groups of related accounting DT competencies and

J. Birt
University of Western Australia, Perth, WA, Australia
e-mail: jacqueline.birt@uwa.edu.au

A. Gepp
Bond University, Gold Coast, QLD, Australia

Bangor Business School, Bangor University, Bangor, United Kingdom
e-mail: a.gepp@bangor.ac.uk

conceptualizations of their interrelationships with each other and with broader accounting competencies (e.g., see Lawson et al., 2015). Finally, some of these studies have identified different gaps in the process of translating expected and or required accounting DT competencies into accounting practices (e.g., McLarres & Oyelere, 1999; Oesterreich & Teuteberg, 2019).

Although this prior research has made important contributions to the accounting DT competence literature, some critical unresolved issues remain. First, while many accounting DT competencies have been identified, studies investigating their importance and presence across accounting services or functions, across accounting practice settings, and across accounting career levels are limited. Furthermore, the DT landscape has shifted much, whereas these studies captured data from different times and workplaces. For example, the makeup of required accounting DT competencies has expanded significantly in the last ten years—such that the priority skills today likely differ greatly from those identified prior to the last 10 years. Finally, the empirical evidence of both the importance and presence of required accounting DT competencies, as well as any discussed translation gaps, is modest.

This study investigates accountants' actual skills across accounting functions/services, across accounting career levels, and across accounting practice settings. We then explore the gap between required and actual DT accounting skills, as well as flow on implications for the profession. We conducted our study using survey research and Qualtrics software. Specifically, the research questions addressed were as follows:

RQ 1: Is there a skill gap between accountants' required and actual DT skills?

RQ 2: What is the nature of this gap across accounting functions, career levels, and practice settings?

The remainder of this paper is organized as follows. Section 5.2 provides a comprehensive literature review and development of the research questions. Section 5.3 outlines the methodology. Section 5.4 presents the results of the study. Section 5.5 discusses the results and presents the conclusions and implications of the research.

Literature Review

Unpacking Accounting DT Competencies: Knowledge vs. Skills

Digital technologies (DTs) are combinations of information, computing, communication, and connectivity technologies, such as social, mobile, analytics, cloud computing, Internet of Things, artificial intelligence, and blockchain technologies (see Bharadwaj et al., 2013; Vial, 2019). Accounting DT competencies, also referred to as accounting information communication and technology (ICT) competencies or accounting technology competencies, are the DT-related knowledge, skills, and abilities required to effectively carry out particular accounting roles, processes, or workflows (e.g., see Birt et al., 2017; IAESB, n.d.; Lawson et al., 2014). Drawing on Krathwohl (2002), we take the knowledge aspect of accounting DT competencies to refer to the remembering and understanding of factual, conceptual, procedural, and metacognitive information related to DTs. In contrast, we take the skills and abilities aspect of accounting DT competencies to refer to the ability to apply the aforementioned DT knowledge to carry out DT-related aspects of accounting work—what Krathwohl (2002) refers to as being able to effectively apply, analyze, evaluate, and create DT-related phenomena (e.g., to apply DT tools, to analyse/evaluate DT contexts, to apply/analyse/evaluate/create DT processes). Extending this definition, we conceptualize accounting DT skills and abilities as the capability to use DTs and DT knowledge to carry out accounting work. For convenience, wherever we use the term DT knowledge in isolation, we refer to it as both DT knowledge and understanding. As mentioned earlier, wherever we use the term DT skills in isolation, we mean both DT skills and abilities. Thus, accounting DT competencies can be compartmentalized into those making up accountants' DT knowledge and those making up accountants' DT skills. Particular DT knowledge may be a prerequisite to attainment of particular DT skills. And DT skills are a prerequisite for effectively carrying out digitally enhanced or dependent accounting workflows. Therefore, it is important to have a specific understanding of their makeup of required DT skills and the extent to which accountants possess these DT skills across accounting functions, career levels, and practice settings.

Current Makeup of Required Accounting DT Skills

Required accounting DT skills are manifested in different degrees of detail across the broad accounting literature, across accounting education and accreditation standards, and across professional body competency frameworks. Table 5.1 provides a summary of required DT skills identified to date, grouping them into skill groups and sub-groups. In lieu of the full list encompassing several hundred specific competencies, we provide the skill groups/subgroups and only a handful of examples specific skills that are sufficiently representative of the relevant skills and abilities for each skill group and sub-group. Where we provide one or more citations in Table 5.1 of the literature identifying each competency, these are just examples of citing sources, rather than being the only sources or the most authoritative sources. An important caveat is that no literature suggests that every accountant requires every competency. Rather, different accountants may require different subsets of these competencies depending on their particular accounting function, career level, and practice setting. For example, early career management accountants may need a different subset of these competencies in contrast to, for example, senior financial accountants or finance systems managers. And an early career management accountant in one practice setting may need different subsets of these competencies, notwithstanding that they may share some DT competency requirements common to all early career management accountants.

Translation of Required Accounting DT Skills into Practice

Prospective and current accountants develop accounting DT skills through accounting curricula, through workplace training/learning opportunities, and through other self-directed or even unintended learning experiences (e.g., see Chaffer & Webb, 2017; Lawson et al., 2014). Thus, we propose that accounting DT skills are translated into practice to the extent that they can be effectively cultivated through curricula, cultivated through workplace learning, or cultivated through self-directed or emergent learning experiences of prospective or current accountants (e.g., see Howcroft, 2017; Lawson et al., 2014; Sledgianowski et al., 2017). However, the profession's strategic leadership

Table 5.1 Groups and related subgroups of required accounting DT skills

Skill Group	*Skill Sub-groups*	*Examples of specific skills*
Working effectively in a digital context	Information and digital literacy/fluency	• Create, search for, analyse, organise, and store data (AICPA, 2020) • Identify and articulate what data/information is needed (AICPA, 2020) • Analyse and compare sources of data and critically evaluate the credibility and reliability of the sources (AICPA, 2020)
	Digital communication and collaboration	• Use relevant digital communication platforms and tools to communicate effectively (AICPA, 2020) • Evaluate and use digital tools for collaborative processes and to share information or content (AICPA, 2020)
	Digital problem solving	• Find and troubleshoot technical problems that occur when using devices or working in digital settings (AICPA, 2020)
	Digital content creation	• Create new digital content in different formats and modify or refine existing content (AICPA, 2020) • Integrate new information and content into existing information and content (AICPA, 2020)

Skill Group	*Skill Sub-groups*	*Examples of specific skills*
Business Information Systems and Accounting Information Systems	Information systems foundations	• Use the different operating system and application software of an organisation (Lawson et al., 2014) • Work with the different components of business information systems (e.g., hardware, networks, data, processes, people) (Lawson et al., 2014)
	Information systems design and development	• Document business requirements for information system design - for example, using Business Process Modelling Notation tools such as Microsoft Visio, Activiti, LucidChart (IMA, 2019) • Apply relational database concepts, including primary and secondary keys, to design reports (CPA Canada, 2019) • Apply systems design and development techniques such as E-R Diagrams, REA diagrams, flow charts, and Relational Database Models) to design relational database tables or databases (e.g. see Coyne et al., 2016; IMA, 2019)

(continued)

Table 5.1 (continued)

Skill Group	*Skill Sub-groups*	*Examples of specific skills*
	Information systems lifecycle management	• Effectively play relevant accounting roles in different information systems lifecycle stages (e.g., Systems planning, analysis, design, development, testing, implementation, and maintenance) (CPA Canada, 2019) • Lead or participate in necessary information systems change or maintenance activities and dealing with the cascading impact of changes in the integrated systems environment (CPA Canada, 2019)

Skill Group	*Skill Sub-groups*	*Examples of specific skills*
	Accounting systems, applications, and hardware	• Use ERP or other enterprise systems and modules for accounting work, to control and manage organization dataflows, and to evaluate or design workflows (e.g., see CPA Canada, 2019; IMA, 2019) • Lead and direct the definition, development, and implementation of new accounting systems/applications/ hardware or enhancements of existing ones (e.g., see CPA Canada, 2019; IMA, 2019) • Use Robotic Process Automation (RPA) tools like UiPath, Pega, and Blue Prism to automate and or optimize accounting processes and workflows (e.g. Moffitt et al., 2018)
Data and information management and governance	Data management	• Extract, transform, and load data using ETL procedures (Sledgianowski et al., 2017) • Use effective data management tools and automating data collection, validation, and reporting (AACSB, 2018; IMA, 2019) • Design data marts and data warehouses to provide access to information throughout an organisation (IMA, 2019)

(continued)

Table 5.1 (continued)

Skill Group	*Skill Sub-groups*	*Examples of specific skills*
	Data analytics and data science	• Implement analytics solutions and perform analysis using multiple query, scripted, or interpreted languages (e.g., SQL, Python, R) (e.g. IMA, 2019) • Build and use descriptive, diagnostic, predictive, and prescriptive analytics templates, dashboards, and models (e.g. CPA Canada, 2019) • Use advanced statistical and data science tools to analyse relevant datasets and reveal patterns and discover insights to achieve business outcomes (e.g. IMA, 2019)
	Data visualisation	• Evaluate, select, and apply a range of basic, intermediate, and advanced visualisations to communicate results (e.g., IMA, 2019)
	Data strategy and planning	• Develop and manage policies on data protection, privacy, intellectual property rights and ethical issues in data management (e.g., AICPA, 2020) • Define metadata using common standards and ensure data quality, accessibility, interoperability, and compliance to standards (e.g., AICPA, 2020)

Skill Group	*Skill Sub-groups*	*Examples of specific skills*
	Data governance	• Design and implement data governance systems in accordance with established frameworks such as COSO and COBIT (e.g., IMA, 2019) • Implement processes to protect the privacy of stakeholder data (e.g., IMA, 2019)
Enterprise Architecture management, technology infrastructure management, and technology services management	Digital costing and cost management in digital Systems	• Apply costing techniques to digital products / channels and analyse the structure, behaviour, drivers, and profitability of digital products / digital channels (e.g., AICPA, 2020) • Advise on the digital transformation of the organisation as a way of managing and transforming costs (e.g., AICPA, 2020)
	Effective accounting support of Enterprise architecture management (EA)	• Evaluate EA designs or configuration options (e.g., see e.g., Ballou et al., 2018; CPA Canada, 2019; O'Leary, 2021); • Devise or evaluate KPIs to enable effective EA governance (e.g., see e.g., Ballou et al., 2018; CPA Canada, 2019; O'Leary, 2021)

(continued)

Table 5.1 (continued)

Skill Group	*Skill Sub-groups*	*Examples of specific skills*
	Effective accounting support of Technology infrastructure management and technology services management	• Undertake or support technology related business case development and investment evaluation (e.g., CPA Canada, 2019) • Undertake or support technology sourcing and vendors / service provider management (e.g., CPA Canada, 2019) • Test new technology systems and manage data conversion (e.g., CPA Canada, 2019)
	Effectively collaborating with digital technology experts or specialists	• Effectively partner with digital and tech experts to ensure that the organisation has appropriate resources to implement new technology (e.g., see AICPA, 2020; IFAC, 2017) • Work with accounting firms and technology vendors to develop AI based technologies (e.g., see Kokina & Davenport, 2017)

Skill Group	*Skill Sub-groups*	*Examples of specific skills*
Accounting for digital technology assets and transactions	Accounting for new types of digital technology assets and transactions	• Measurement, recognition, and disclosure of new types of DT assets, events, and transactions (e.g., cryptographic assets) (e.g., see Leopold & Vollmann, 2018) • Audit new types of digital technology assets and services such as blockchains, blockchain services, smart contracts, and oracles (e.g., see Bible et al., 2017)
Strategic Information Systems	Maintaining awareness of the implications of specific DT advancements for organizations	• Monitor recent technology developments and recommend implementation where practical (e.g., AICPA, 2020) • Identify strategic options and opportunities to support business objectives, utilising technology, such as data analytics (e.g., ACCA, n.d)
	Effective support of business process and workflow redesign, digitalisation, automation, intelligence, and autonomy	• Recommend new systems to automate existing processes and ways to re-engineer business processes to effectively use new technology (e.g., AICPA, 2020) • Enable digital process and workflow optimisation (inc. process digitalisation) (e.g., IFAC, 2019; FSR Danish Auditors, 2018)

(continued)

Table 5.1 (continued)

Skill Group	*Skill Sub-groups*	*Examples of specific skills*
	Effective support of cybersecurity management and digital risk management	• Discharge fraud detection responsibilities (e.g., CPA Canada, 2019) • Formally test the effectiveness of an organization's cybersecurity risk management program (e.g., see Eaton et al., 2019) • Advise on and test the readiness of an organization for a formal assurance engagement (e.g., see Eaton et al., 2019)
	Effectively supporting the building, maintenance, and optimisation of digital business capabilities	• Effectively support digital business transformation strategy (e.g., Busulwa & Evans, 2021) • Effectively support digital innovation (e.g., Busulwa & Evans, 2021)

Source Authors

entities (e.g., International Federation of Accountants/IFAC), the profession's education and accreditation standard-setting entities (e.g., International Accounting Education Standards Board/IAESB), the profession's professional bodies (e.g., American Institute of Certified Public Accountants, Association of Chartered Certified Accountants, Chartered Institute of Management Accountants), as well as accounting researchers and employing organizations can influence or shape curricula makeup or delivery, influence or shape workplace learning, and influence or shape accountants' self-directed or emergent learning experiences (e.g., see Chaffer & Webb, 2017; Wessels, 2005). For example, accounting researchers can identify competency needs through explorations or investigations of employer and societal competence needs. Education and accreditation entities can validate, curate, and translate validated competency needs into formal competency requirements within the education and accreditation standards. And professional bodies can draw on education and accreditation standards requirements, as well as broad accounting research, to translate them into specific skill requirements within their professional body competency frameworks (e.g., see Wessels, 2005). These frameworks can subsequently feed into professional body curricula, qualification standards for admission into professional body memberships, and continuing professional development requirements during accountants' careers (e.g., see Wessels, 2005).

Education entities can subsequently draw on the skill requirements of education and accreditation standards entities, as well as the requirements of professional bodies and broad accounting research, to integrate DT skill requirements into accounting curricula (e.g., see Coyne et al., 2016; Lawson et al., 2015; Sledgianowski et al., 2017; Wessels, 2005). Through their communication and incentivization activities, the profession's strategic leadership and advocacy, accreditation, professional bodies, professional service firms, and other key entities can influence the type of learning that occurs in the workplace, as well as the self-directed or emergent learning activities of prospective or current accountants. For example, such communication and incentivization activities can motivate both current and prospective accountants to undertake relevant self-directed learning activities. Employers can also be motivated or incentivised to invest in professional development opportunities for accountants. Finally, the profession's strategic leadership and advocacy entities can fund various research, consultation, and curricula integration initiatives undertaken by other entities within the profession, thus influencing the impact of those initiatives on the translation of required accounting DT skills into practice.

Overview of Studies Investigating the Accounting DT Skills Gap

Studies investigating the actual DT skills of accountants, and thus informing an understanding of the accounting DT skills gap, have largely focused on recent accounting graduates (e.g., Bui & Porter, 2010; Daff, 2021; McLarres & Oyelere, 1999) or on more senior accountants in a particular accounting function, such as management accountants and auditors (e.g., Greenstein & McKee, 2004; Oesterreich & Teuteberg, 2019). Apart from Daff (2021) and Oesterreich and Teuteberg (2019) being relatively recent, most of these tudies are in the main quite aged. And the composition of required accounting DT skills has evolved significantly since most of these studies were conducted. Thus, their usefulness in understanding accountants' actual DT skills today is very limited. However, although Daff (2021) and Oesterreich and Teuteberg (2019) are recent studies, their focus is limited to only a subset of the skills identified in Table 5.1. For example, Daff (2021) limited her focus on the extent to which recent graduates used particular software programs (accounting software packages or systems, Microsoft Excel/Word/PowerPoint/Outlook, and the Internet); and on employers' expectations of accounting graduate ICT skills. Similarly, Oesterreich and Teuteberg (2019) focused on particular business analytics skills (e.g., proficiency with particular business analytics methods/techniques), and on IT systems/applications proficiency (e.g., proficiency with ERP systems, CRM applications, Microsoft Office suite, SQL, and data warehouses).

Methodologically, these studies have either employed analysis of online information, employed case study methods (e.g., Oesterreich & Teuteberg, 2019), employed survey methods (e.g., Greenstein & McKee, 2004; McLarres & Oyelere, 1999), or employed mixed-methods studies consisting of case interviews and surveys (e.g., see Daff, 2021). To determine accountants' actual DT skill levels, the studies either analyzed accountants' online professional profiles/resume equivalents (e.g., Oesterreich & Teuteberg, 2019), or captured and analyzed employers/line managers' perceptions of the DT skills possessed by accountants (e.g., Bui & Porter, 2010; Daff, 2021), or captured accountants' self-rated proficiency levels across required accounting DT skills (Greenstein & McKee, 2004; McLarres & Oyelere, 1999).

There are a range of interesting findings from these studies, notwithstanding the broad need for further empirical support and inclusion of vastly expanded required skills. In relation to these interesting findings, Oesterreich and Teuteberg (2019) found that the business analytics skills they investigated were present in only 14% of management accountants' online competency profiles. And the presence of these business analytics skills in management accountants' profiles differed significantly across organization sizes, age, work experience, and gender. Focusing on early career accountants, Daff (2021) found that a significant proportion of employers were concerned that graduates did not have sufficient skills in accounting software and frequently used office software such as Microsoft Excel. In relation to accounting DT skills gaps, some of these studies point to the existence of a gap between employer expectations of accounting DT skills and actual accounting DT skills—that is, they found that employers expect better skills than those accountants actually have (e.g., Bui & Porter, 2010; Daff, 2021). These studies also point to the potential existence of a gap between DT skill requirements within education/accreditation standards vs. professional body frameworks vs. the actual DT skills of accountants (e.g., McLarres & Oyelere, 1999; Wessels, 2005). The studies also point to the potential existance of a gap between the skills that accounting curricula should develop vs. those actually developed (e.g., Daff, 2021; Oesterreich & Teuteberg, 2019; Wessels, 2005).

In line with these findings, various studies have called for better integration of the DT skill requirements contained within accounting education/accreditation standards and professional body frameworks into accounting curricula (e.g., Coyne et al., 2016; Lawson et al., 2015; Sledgianowski et al., 2017; Wessels, 2005). Although some studies have pointed to specific DT skills for which there is a gap between expected or required competencies vs. the actual competencies of accountants (e.g., Daff, 2021; Greenstein & McKee, 2004; Oesterreich & Teuteberg, 2019), in general, the studies do not investigate the gap for most of the skills listed in Table 5.1. Nor do they investigate the gap across accounting services/functions, career levels, and practice settings. As a result, this understanding is lacking within the literature. Finally, various studies point out that some of the potential moderators of the gap between expected or required skills vs. the actual skills of accountants may include organizational context, type of tertiary study/curricula makeup, gender, job experience, age, and the national or geographic settings of accountants (e.g., see McLarres & Oyelere, 1999; Oesterreich & Teuteberg, 2019).

The literature discussed in this section indicates that further research is warranted to provide a more specific understanding of the gap between accountants' required and actual skills. Such research and understanding may, in turn, feed into a better understanding of the barriers to the effective translation of required accounting DT skills into accounting practice.

Methodology

To answer our two research questions: (1) *Is there a skills gap between required and actual DT skills of accountants*? and (2) *What is the nature of this gap?*, we adopted a qualitative survey approach. The survey was administered using Qualtrics in late 2021, and a strict set of criteria was applied to select accountants.[1] The selected respondents had to have an accounting role and qualification, and were working in Australia or New Zealand. We also ensured representation across various accounting functions, career levels, and types of accounting practices. After deleting incomplete responses, we were left with a final sample of 119 responses.

We asked the survey respondents a number of questions, including demographic questions such as accounting role, accounting workplace, number of years in role, industry, and accounting qualifications. Next, we asked respondents to self-assess their self-rated DT ability using Likert scales (ranging from 1 (strongly disagree) to 5 (strongly agree)). For example, we asked them questions such as: *how they would rate their level of competency (knowledge, skills, abilities) in the following competency areas;* then we would proceed to list skill groups and subgroups, along with corresponding specific skills (see skill groups/subgroups and specific skills in Table 5.1).

Table 5.2 summarizes the positions held by each of the study respondents. The table shows a broad coverage of roles, with a strong representation of senior leaders. There is also extensive coverage of work types, with consulting and advisory being the least represented—as evidenced by Table 5.3 summarizing the answers to the question: *Which of the*

[1] Ethics was applied for and granted at two of the authors' higher education institution.

following best describes the nature of the work you mainly perform?[2] (participants were presented with a selection of common work activities mapping to each accounting function or area of work listed in Table 5.3). In terms of the types organizations that study participants worked at, 59% were public practice accounting firms and 41% were non-accounting firm organisations.

Results and Discussion

Table 5.4 presents accountants' self-rated DT skill and ability levels across accounting functions, career levels, and practice settings in reference to the following question—*How would you rate your level of competency (knowledge, skills, abilities) in the following competency areas?* The respondents recorded their answers using a 5-point Likert scale (1-not at all competent to 5-Very competent).

As shown in Table 5.4, the overall skill group averages for the surveyed respondents range from 2.3 to a maximum of 3.3 out of 5, with the majority of averages being below 3. Accountants are most confident of their skill levels relating to working effectively in a digital context and relating to using Business Information Systems and Accounting Information Systems—for these skill groups they mostly rated themselves at 3 or above (i.e average or a bit above average). This is consistent across most accounting functions, career levels, and practice settings. However, in general, Junior/Trainee accountants consistently have lower self ratings than other career levels (about 10% lower self-ratings).

The lowest skill group average self rated competence level is for the skill group *Enterprise Architecture Management, technology infrastructure management, and technology services management*. This skill group had a mean of 2.24 for all accounting functions, with tax recording the lowest mean of 2.04, and financial accounting recording the highest mean of 2.34. The highest skill group average self rated competence level is for the skill group *Working effectively in a digital context* with a mean of 3.35 for all accounting functions. The competencies of senior leaders, experts or junior leaders/managers, and trainees are very similar for some skill groups; for example, it is reasonably low for the skill group's *ability to learn and keep up with digital technologies* (2.8 mean). In contrast,

[2] Note that multiple answers can be selected in answering this question and so the totals do not sum to the sample size, and the percentages do not sum to 100% (Table 5.3).

Table 5.2 Career Level and Roles of survey respondents

Career Level	*Frequency (Percentage)*	*Roles included*
Senior Leader	65 (56%)	CFO or other executive, Owner, Partner, Senior Manager
Expert or Junior Leader/Manager	27 (23%)	Middle Manager, Team Leader, Senior Accountant
Junior/Trainee	19 (16%)	Junior Accountant, Graduate, Trainee Accountant
Support/Other	6 (5%)	Support Services Employee Other

Source Authors

Table 5.3 Accounting Function or nature of main work done by survey respondents

Accounting Function or Nature of work (Q4)	*Frequency (Percentage)*
Financial accounting	54 (46%)
Tax	32 (27%)
Consulting & advisory	20 (17%)
Management accounting & AIS	65 (56%)
Audit, forensic & other	64 (55%)

Source Authors

Table 5.4 Accountants' mean self-rated DT skill/ability levels across accounting functions, career levels, practice settings

Skill Group	*Skill Sub-group*	*All*	*Nature of Work of Respondent*					*Role of Respondent*			*Practice Type*	
			Financial Acc.	*Tax*	*Consult & Advisory*	*Mgmt Acc. & AIS*	*Audit, Forensic, Other*	*Senior Leader*	*Expert or Junior Leader/Manager*	*Junior/Trainee*	*Public*	*Private*
Working effectively in a digital context	**Skill Group Average**	**3.335**	**3.49**	**3.23**	**3.20**	**3.38**	**3.29**	**3.35**	**3.32**	**3.30**	**3.35**	**3.32**
	Information and digital literacy/fluency	3.786	3.96	3.66	3.80	3.88	3.81	3.80	3.89	3.58	3.81	3.75
	Digital communication and collaboration	3.547	3.72	3.44	3.40	3.57	3.52	3.55	3.59	3.53	3.54	3.56
	Digital problem solving	3.333	3.54	3.19	3.35	3.35	3.30	3.37	3.30	3.32	3.33	3.33
	Digital content creation	2.675	2.74	2.66	2.25	2.72	2.55	2.69	2.52	2.79	2.71	2.63
Business Information Systems and Accounting Information Systems	**Skill Group Average**	**3.27**	**3.43**	**3.17**	**3.13**	**3.39**	**3.26**	**3.34**	**3.30**	**3.05**	**3.37**	**3.13**
	Information systems foundations	3.718	3.81	3.63	3.50	3.75	3.72	3.77	3.81	3.47	3.75	3.67
	Information systems design and development	2.932	3.04	2.88	2.85	3.08	2.97	2.98	2.85	2.79	2.94	2.92
	Information systems lifecycle management	3.051	3.20	2.78	2.80	3.20	3.05	3.18	3.04	2.74	3.25	2.77
	Accounting systems, applications, and hardware	3.624	4.00	3.72	3.60	3.85	3.48	3.68	3.70	3.42	3.80	3.38
	Strategic information systems	2.778	2.93	2.70	2.93	2.96	2.64	2.85	2.94	2.38	2.93	2.54

Skill Group	*Skill Sub-group*	*All*	*Nature of Work of Respondent*					*Role of Respondent*			*Practice Type*	
			Financial Acc.	*Tax*	*Consult & Advisory*	*Mgmt Acc. & AIS*	*Audit, Forensic, Other*	*Senior Leader*	*Expert or Junior Leader/ Manager*	*Junior/ Trainee*	*Public*	*Private*
Data and information management and governance	**Skill Group Average**	**2.703**	**2.74**	**2.52**	**2.52**	**2.78**	**2.69**	**2.76**	**2.64**	**2.65**	**2.77**	**2.60**
	Data management	3.06	3.20	2.88	2.90	3.17	3.13	3.17	3.00	2.84	3.20	2.85
	Data analytics and data science	2.624	2.63	2.38	2.35	2.69	2.58	2.78	2.37	2.47	2.71	2.50
	Data visualisation	3.026	3.15	2.88	2.95	3.15	2.89	3.12	2.89	2.95	3.16	2.83
	Data strategy and planning	2.513	2.52	2.47	2.35	2.51	2.59	2.51	2.52	2.63	2.45	2.60
	Data governance	2.291	2.20	2.00	2.05	2.40	2.28	2.23	2.44	2.37	2.35	2.21
Enterprise Architecture management, technology infrastructure management, and technology services management	**Skill Group Average**	**2.29**	**2.34**	**2.04**	**2.29**	**2.33**	**2.31**	**2.33**	**2.28**	**2.20**	**2.40**	**2.13**
	Digital costing and cost management in digital Systems	2.385	2.46	2.09	2.40	2.43	2.45	2.43	2.19	2.58	2.45	2.29
	Enterprise architecture management (EA)	2.017	2.04	1.81	1.80	2.06	2.08	2.02	2.04	2.05	2.10	1.90
	Technology infrastructure management and technology services management	2.291	2.37	2.09	2.30	2.32	2.33	2.32	2.30	2.16	2.41	2.13
	Effectively collaborating with digital technology experts or specialists	2.462	2.48	2.16	2.65	2.52	2.39	2.54	2.59	2.00	2.65	2.19

(continued)

Table 5.4 (continued)

Skill Group	*Skill Sub-group*	*All*	*Nature of Work of Respondent*					*Role of Respondent*			*Practice Type*	
			Financial Acc.	*Tax*	*Consult & Advisory*	*Mgmt Acc. & AIS*	*Audit, Forensic, Other*	*Senior Leader*	*Expert or Junior Leader/ Manager*	*Junior/ Trainee*	*Public*	*Private*
Accounting for digital technology assets and transactions	**Skill Group Average**	**2.316**	**2.24**	**2.16**	**1.75**	**2.18**	**2.36**	**2.28**	**2.15**	**2.58**	**2.30**	**2.33**
Learning and Keeping up with digital technologies	**Skill Group Average**	**2.795**	**2.89**	**2.59**	**2.60**	**2.75**	**2.78**	**2.80**	**2.78**	**2.79**	**2.74**	**2.88**

Source Authors

there are DT skills for which the highest competence level is possessed by senior leaders (e.g., *Data analytics and data science* with a mean of 2.8) or the competence level is posessed to the same degree by both senior leaders as well as experts and junior leaders/managers (for example, *Business Information Systems and Accounting Information Systems* with a mean of 3.3, and *effectively collaborating with digital technology experts or specialists* with a mean of 2.5–2.6. Juniors/trainees also possess slightly better competency in *Digital content creation* (2.8 mean), *Data planning and strategy* (2.6 mean), and *Digital costing and Cost management in digital systems* (2.6 mean).

Respondents from public and private firms record similar results across most DT skills and abilities, but accountants in public practice accounting firms rated their skill levels higher than other accountants for some skill groups/subgroups. For example, in the *information systems life-cycle management*, *accounting systems, applications and hardware* and *effectively collaborating with digital technology experts or specialists* skill groups/subgroups, accountants working at public practice accounting firms had a mean self rating that was 0.4 than other accountants.

Overall, most results are reasonably consistent across the different accounting functions and types of accounting work that respondents do. Specific pairwise differences can be observed by analyzing the table.

Conclusions and Implications

Nature of the Skills Gap Across Accounting Functions, Career Levels, and Practice Settings

The findings reported in Sect. 5.4 highlight that most accountants rate themselves below average on most skills requirements identified within the broad accounting literature. This is consistent across accounting functions, career levels, and practice settings. The highest mean self rated skill level is 4.0 by accountants working in financial accounting for the skills sub-groups of *Business Information Systems and Accounting Information Systems.* And the lowest self rated competence level was 1.8 by accountants working in consulting and advisory for the skills sub-groups of *Enterprise Architecture management* and *Accounting for digital technology assets and transactions*.

In terms of the career level of respondents, junior accountants generally rated their DT skill levels the lowest (about 10% lower than other career levels). The highest mean self rated skill level reported by Expert or Junior Leader/Manager accountants (3.89) was or the skills group *Working effectively in a digital context* and, more specifically the skill subgroup, *Information and digital literacy/fluency*. The lowest mean self rated skill level reported by Senior Leaders (2.02) was for the skills group *Enterprise Architecture management (EA)*.

In terms of practice setting, the highest mean self rated competence level was reported by Public Practice (3.81) was for the skills group of *Working effectively in a digital context* and, more specifically for the skills subgroup *Information and digital literacy/fluency*. The lowest mean self rated comptence level was reported by non accounting firm organisations (1.9) for the skills sub-group of *Enterprise Architecture management (EA)*.

Potential Moderators/Mediators of the Skills Gap

While the breadth and depth of the skills gap may be surprising, the individual skill areas lacking the most and least are probably not as surprising. Traditional skills groups, such *as working effectively in a digital context* and *business information systems and accounting information systems* were rated more highly than less newer and less familiar skills groups, such as *Enterprise Architecture management, technology infrastructure management, Technology services management* and *Accounting for digital technology assets and transactions*. So newness of the requited skills to accounting practice is a potential moderator and or mediator of the skills gap.

In terms of the roles of respondents, not surprisingly, Senior Leaders rated themselves the highest in nearly all skills groups compared to Expert or Junior Leader/Manager and Junior accountants. Although less senior accountants rated themselves higher on skill groups/subgroups such as: *Information and digital literacy/fluency*, *Digital communication and collaboration*, *Information systems foundations*, *Accounting systems, applications, and hardware*; *strategic information systems*; *Data strategy and Data governance*; *Enterprise Architecture Management* and *effectively collaborating with digital technology experts or specialists*. This suggest that career level is also a potential moderator and or mediator of the skills gap. Not surprisingly, in almost all skills groups, junior/trainees rated lower than Senior Leaders and Experts or Junior Leaders/Managers (i.e except for the skill groups/subgroups of *Digital content creation; Data strategy and planning*, and *Accounting for digital technology assets and transactions)*. This suggests that skills/abilities cultivated in accounting curricula/early career workplace training may be a potential moderator and or mediator of the skills gap.

Implications for Accounting Education and for Accreditation/ Governance Bodies

Our study investigating the required vs. actual DT skills of accountants makes a number of important contributions to the accounting literature. First, our study is a recent investigation of encompansing the latest DT skills and data collected during the pandemic. This is an interesting time period to investigate required vs. actual DT skills, as many accounting firms, practices, and companies have increased their use of technology during the pandemic and are likely to be more concious of required vs. actual DT skills. Similarly, many accountants are likely to be more conscious of the DT skills they have and do not have. As we know, there has been much more use of DTs to enable working from home practices and to increase the efficiency of accounting workloads during the pandemic.

Second, we investigate the perceptions of accountants working in a broad range of accounting functions, in accounting firms versus non accounting firms, as well as at different accounting career levels (including Junior Accountant, Expert or Junior Leader/Manager, and Senior Leaders). Investigating perceptions across different accounting functions, accounting practice settings, and career levels provides interesting insights into perceptions of DT competence. Our findings highlight the differences in competence levels across all DT skill types, across accounting functions, and across career levels.

Third, our findings provide important insights for a range of stakeholders, including educators, accounting practitioners, and professional bodies. For educators, our findings suggest a need to better embed the right DT skills in curricula to improve junior accountants' lower DT competence and perhaps confidence levels. Our findings also offer an avenue for educators to have an emphasised focus on particular skills that accountants at different career levels rated themselves as deficient in. While there are skills gaps in a number of areas, the gaps in some areas stant out more (e.g., *accounting for digital assets and transactions* and *enteprise architecture management*). We suggest that it is important that educators undertake their own professional development in such areas to be more DT competent in the classroom. Understandably, this will have limitations, and we suggest that education institutions consider expanding technology vendor/academic and employer/academic partnerships as a parallel skills cultivation avenue. Through these partnerships, they could provide students with the opportunity to practice using relevant DT tools in the classroom (e.g., RPA, XBRL, machine learning tools), and to apply what they learn to real workplace issues (e.g., through industry internships). We suggest that organisations/workplaces also need to provide better professional development opportunities for their employees in relevant DT competence areas, whether this be done formally (e.g., online external training/certifications) or informally (e.g. through the workplace training/experiences). We suggest that professional bodies note the DT competence gaps we have identified and explore ways to better embed relevant skill areas into their professional programs (e.g., while many of these skills are recently a part of professional body programs, it was surprising that more early career accountants did not rate their competence in them highly). Finally, we suggest that key accounting entities pay particular attention to compartmentalising the vast and overwhelming competence requirements of the profession into those required by each accounting function, those required by each accounting career level, and perhaps even those required in particular practice settings. Doing so would go a long way toward addressing warranted scepticism about the vast DT competence requirements. It would also aid accounting curricula by providing guidance about what DT competencies need to be integrated into what curricula (e.g. what DT competence requirements need to be integrated in management accounting curricula vs. AIS curricula vs. Tax curricula, and what DT competence requirements need to be cultivated in undergraduate vs. postgraduate curricula).

References

AACSB. (2018). *2018 Accounting Accreditation Standards*. Association to Advance Collegiate Schools of Business. Tampa. Florida.

ACCA. (2020). *Future ready: accountancy careers in the 2020s. Association of Chartered Certified Accountants*. Available at: https://www.accaglobal.com/in/en/professional-insights/pro-accountants-the-future/future_ready_2020s.html. Accessed 3 December 2021.

AICPA. (2020). *The CGMA competency framework guide and tool*. Association of International Certified Professional Accountants.

Ballou, B., Heitger, D. L., & Stoel, D. (2018). Data-driven decision-making and its impact on accounting undergraduate curriculum. *Journal of Accounting Education, 44*, 14–24.

Birt, J., Wells,P., Kavanagh,M., Robb, A., & Bir, P. (2017). *ICT literature review*. Available at: https://www.iaesb.org/system/files/meetings/files/6-2-ICT-Literature-Review.pdf.

Bharadwaj, A., El Sawy, O. A., Pavlou, P. A., & Venkatraman, N. (2013). Digital business strategy: Towards a next generation of insights. *Management Information Systems Quarterly, 37*(2), 471–482.

Bible, W., Raphael, J., Taylor, P., & Valiente, I. (2017). *Blockchain Technology and its potential impact on the audit and assurance profession*. Deloitte & Touche LLC.

Bui, B., & Porter, B. (2010). The expectation-performance gap in accounting education: An exploratory study. *Accounting Education: An International Journal, 19*(1–2), 23–50.

Busulwa, R., & Evans, N. (2021). *Digital transformation in accounting*. Routledge.

Chaffer, C., & Webb, J. (2017). An evaluation of competency development in accounting trainees. *Accounting Education, 26*(5–6), 431–458. https://doi.org/10.1080/09639284.2017.1286602

Coyne, J. G., Coyne, E. M., & Walker, K. B. (2016). A model to update accounting curricula for emerging technologies. *Journal of Emerging Technologies in Accounting, 13*(1), 161–169.

CPA Canada. (2019). *The chartered professional accountant competency map: Understanding the competencies a candidate must demonstrate to become a CPA*. Available at: https://www.cpacanada.ca/-/media/site/become-a-cpa/docs/competencymap.pdf. Accessed 3 December 2021.

Daff, L. (2021). Employers' perspectives of accounting graduates and their world of work: Software use and ICT competencies. *Accounting Education, 30*(5), 495–524.

Eaton, T. V., Grenier, J. H., & Layman, D. (2019). Accounting and cybersecurity risk management. *Current Issues in Auditing, 13*(2), C1–C9.

FSR Danish Auditors. (2018). *Digital Transformation—Impact of new technologies on the accounting industry*. Available at: https://pub.publify.dk/catalogues/digital-transformation-accounting-industry/#page/1. Accessed 3 December 2021.

Greenstein, M., & McKee, T. E. (2004). Assurance practitioners' and educators' self-perceived IT knowledge level: An empirical assessment. *International Journal of Accounting Information Systems, 5*(2), 213–243.

Howcroft, D. (2017). Graduates' vocational skills for the management accountancy profession: Exploring the accounting education expectation-performance gap. *Accounting Education, 26*(5–6), 459–481.

IAESB. (n.d.). *Glossary of terms (Revised)*. International Federation of Accountants.

IMA. (2019). *IMA management accounting competency framework*. Institute of Management Accountants. Available at: https://www.imanet.org/-/media/bc3871509fb5418a8488b848e6aa0ff4.ashx. Accessed 16 December 2021.

International Federation of Accountants (IFAC). (2001). Education Committee. *Exposure Draft IEG-11*.

International Federation of Accountants (IFAC). (2017). *Developing a future ready profession*. Available at: https://www.ifac.org/system/files/publications/files/Developing-a-Future-Ready-Profession.pdf. Accessed 16 December 2021.

International Federation of Accountants (IFAC). (2019). *Future—Fit Accountants: CFO and Finance Function Roles for the Next Decade*. International Federation of Accountants. Available at: https://www.ifac.org/system/files/publications/files/IFAC-Future-Fit-Accountant-ROLES-V5-Singles.pdf. Accessed 16 December 2021.

Kokina, J., & Davenport, T. H. (2017). The emergence of artificial intelligence: How automation is changing auditing. *Journal of Emerging Technologies in Accounting, 14*(1), 115–122.

Krathwohl, D. (2002). A revision of bloom's taxonomy: An overview. *Theory into Practice, 41*(4), 212–218.

Lawson, R. A., Blocher, E. J., Brewer, P. C., Cokins, G., Sorensen, J. E., Stout, D. E., Sundem, G. L., Wolcott, S. K., & Wouters, M. J. (2014). Focusing accounting curricula on students' long-run careers: Recommendations for an integrated competency-based framework for accounting education. *Issues in Accounting Education, 29*(2), 295–317.

Lawson, R. A., Blocher, E. J., Brewer, P. C., Morris, J. T., Stocks, K. D., Sorensen, J. E., Stout, D. E., & Wouters, M. J. (2015). Thoughts on competency integration in accounting education. *Issues in Accounting Education, 30*(3), 149–171.

Leopold, R., & Vollmann, P. (2018). *Cryptographic assets and related transactions: accounting considerations under IFRS*. PWC.

McLarres & Oyelere. (1999). A critical analysis of self-assessed entry-level personal computer skills among newly-qualified Irish chartered accountants. *Accounting Education, 8*(3), 203–216.

Moffitt, K. C., Rozario, A. M., & Vasarhelyi, M. A. (2018). Robotic process automation for auditing. *Journal of Emerging Technologies in Accounting, 15*(1), 1–10.

Oesterreich, T. D., & Teuteberg, F. (2019). The role of business analytics in the controllers and management accountants' competence profiles: An exploratory study on individual-level data. *Journal of Accounting & Organizational Change., 15*(2), 330–356.

O'Leary, D. E. (2021). Enterprise architecture for accounting and finance transformation: Using strategy maps to develop high-performance finance. *Journal of Emerging Technologies in Accounting, 18*(1), 61–76.

Pincus, K. V., Stout, D. E., Sorensen, J. E., Stocks, K. D., & Lawson, R. A. (2017). Forces for change in higher education and implications for the accounting academy. *Journal of Accounting Education, 40*, 1–18.

Sledgianowski, D., Gomaa, M., & Tan, C. (2017). Toward integration of Big Data, technology and information systems competencies into the accounting curriculum. *Journal of Accounting Education, 38*, 81–93.

Vial, G. (2019). Understanding digital transformation: A review and a research agenda. *Journal of Strategic Information Systems, 28*, 118–144.

Wessels, P. L. (2005). Critical information and communication technology (ICT) skills for professional accountants. *Meditari: Research Journal of the School of Accounting Sciences, 13*(1), 87–103.

CHAPTER 6

Accountants' Attitudes to Digital Technology: A Barrier to the Digital Transformation of Accounting?

Richard Busulwa, Jacqueline Birt, Adrian Gepp, and Grainne Oates

Introduction

Accounting researchers have long been interested in effectively cultivating the required accounting technology competencies in the face of accelerating digital technology advancements. More recently, they have also been interested in understanding how accountants' attitudes impact

This research is partly funded by Accounting and Finance Association of Australia and New Zealand (AFAANZ).

R. Busulwa (✉) · G. Oates
Swinburne University, Melbourne, VIC, Australia
e-mail: rbusulwa@swin.edu.au

G. Oates
e-mail: goates@swin.edu.au

A. Perdana and T. Wang (eds.), *Digital Transformation in Accounting and Auditing*, https://doi.org/10.1007/978-3-031-46209-2_6

various accounting-related phenomena, such as corporate social responsibility reporting, ethics, and accounting education (e.g., see Bebbington et al., 1994; Emerson et al., 2007; Husam & Sulieman, 2009). However, the nexus issue, the nature of accountants' attitudes toward digital technology (DT), and its subsequent effect on the cultivation of accounting DT competencies has received little attention to date. This is despite researchers in the adjacent areas of information systems and learning science proposing or inferring that attitudes toward technology play a critical role in technology learning, or the cultivation of technology competencies (e.g., see Mao et al., 2021; Rong & Grover, 2009). One reason for this limited attention from the accounting literature may be that, while DT competencies have long been important to accounting (e.g., see Berkeley, 1950; Jones & McNamara, 1988; Mathews, 1967), until the advent of accelerating digital disruption and digital transformation of accounting practice, they have not enjoyed the center stage they now increasingly occupy within the literature (e.g., see Busulwa & Evans, 2021; IFAC, 2017, 2019).

Given the current and growing importance of DT competencies in accounting practice, and the proposed link between the impact of attitudes toward DTs on the development of accounting DT competencies, an enhanced understanding of the nature of accounting attitudes to DTs and their impacts is needed. For example, related research has argued that attitudes toward accounting impact tertiary academic performance (Bui & Porter, 2010; Wooten, 1998), that accountants tend to have more lenient attitudes toward legal but ethically questionable practices and are therefore more accepting of them (Emerson et al., 2007), that accounting educators' attitudes toward technology impact its use in curricula (Shapka & Ferrari, 2003; Yushau, 2006), and that educators'

J. Birt
University of Western Australia, Perth, WA, Australia
e-mail: jacqueline.birt@uwa.edu.au

A. Gepp
Bond University, Gold Coast, QLD, Australia

Bangor Business School, Bangor University, Bangor, United Kingdom
e-mail: a.gepp@bangor.ac.uk

attitudes toward technology impact students' attitudes toward and use of technology (Teo, 2011). It may then follow that accountants' attitudes toward DTs impact their ability to cultivate DT competencies. If so, it would also follow that understanding the nature of accountants' attitudes toward DTs is important. This understanding may enable policy-makers, accreditation bodies, curricula designers, and accounting practice settings to shape, mitigate, or catalyze relevant attitudes to optimize DT competency development. Given the need for and potential importance of such an understanding, contributing to more specificity in such an understanding is the aim of this study. That is, this study aims to provide a more specific understanding of the nature of accounting attitudes toward technology and their impacts on the cultivation of accounting DT competencies.

The term attitudes have been defined and operationalized in diverse ways across research disciplines, and often even within the same disciplines. Based on our review of relevant literature, we have adopted the Osborne et al. (2003) definition, which suggests that accountants' attitudes toward DTs are the feelings, beliefs, and values they have about DTs. Following this, we adopted Savelsbergh et al's. (2016) attitude sub-constructs of interest, societal relevance, and self-efficacy, which we reframe as DT interest, DT job relevance, and DT learning self-efficacy. Subsequently, we operationalize the reframed constructs as follows: DT interest (operationalized as accountants' stated interest in DTs and/or in learning DTs), DT job relevance (operationalized as the proportion of DTs and the specific DTs accountants perceive to be important to their current and future job performance), and DT learning self-efficacy (operationalized as accountants' self-rated ability to learn and to keep up with DTs, the reasons for their self-rated understanding of DTs, and their perceived barriers to understanding and using DTs).

We conducted this research using a cross-sectional survey and content analysis of open-ended responses within the survey. Cross-sectional surveys have been shown to be useful for identifying the characteristics of a focal population, examining phenomena across varied settings, and exploring potential variables that may influence phenomena (Pinsonneault & Kraemer, 1993). Content analysis is a well-established method for drawing credible inferences from textual data (e.g., see Krippendorff, 2018; Morris, 1994). Using cross-sectional surveys and content analysis, we seek to enhance our understanding of the nature of accountants' attitudes toward DTs and their likely effect on the development of accounting DT competencies. Thus, our two guiding research questions are: (1) What are accountants' attitudes toward digital technology, and (2) are these attitudes a barrier to the digital transformation of accounting through inhibition of digital technology competency attainment?

The remainder of this paper is organized as follows. Section 6.2 provides the background to our research, focusing on digital technology advancements and digital disruption, digital transformation of accounting practice, and the relationship between attitudes toward a phenomenon and learning outcomes in relation to that phenomenon. Section 6.3 outlines our research methodology. Section 6.4 summarizes the results of this study. Section 6.5 discusses the results and the implications of the findings. Finally, Sect. 6.6 concludes the study.

Background

Digital Technology Advancements and Digital Disruption of Accounting

Digital technologies (DTs) combine information, computing, communication, and connectivity technologies such as mobile computing, cloud computing, the Internet of Things, and social media technologies (e.g., see Bharadwaj et al., 2013; Vial, 2019). Therefore, DT advancements refer to the introduction of new DTs or breakthroughs in existing DTs. Digital disruption refers to the DT-induced prevention of processes, routines, or activities from occuring the way they have always occurred (e.g., see Busulwa & Evans, 2021; Vial, 2019). In the accounting context, digital disruption refers to the DT-induced prevention of accounting processes, routines, or activities from being done as they have always been done. Digital technology advancements drive the digital disruption of accounting practice in several ways. First, they disrupt accounting stakeholders' expectations of accountants. More specifically, accounting stakeholders expect accountants to play new and or enhanced roles in helping organizations to guard against or navigate digital disruption, and to safely undertake digital business transformation (e.g., see IFAC, 2017, 2019). Second, DT advancements disrupt the data available to accountants by introducing much more diverse and voluminous data, such as video data, mobile data, social media data, big data, machine data, and sensor data (e.g., see Janvrin & Watson, 2017; Vial, 2019). Third, DT advancements disrupt the tools used to perform accounting work, introducing tools such as drones and sensors for automated stock-takes, XBRL for personalisable reporting, and machine learning for more reliable audits (e.g., see Busulwa & Evans, 2021). Fourth, DT advancements disrupt the optimal ways to carry out accounting processes or activities. For example, although auditors may have previously provided assurance using a sample of data, they can now leverage machine learning to examine the whole population and potentially do this in less time, leading to more optimal assurance. Fifth, DT advancements drive disruption in the type of value accountants can create. For example, by leveraging DTs that automate particular accounting activities, accountants can create new and/or enhanced types of value.

Digital Transformation of Accounting Roles and Competencies

These disruptions drive or necessitate the digital transformation of accounting. Drawing on Vial's (2019) definition of digital transformation, we consider the digital transformation of accounting to be the change process involved in effectively responding to digital disruption of accounting processes or activities, as well as to the effective leveraging of DTs to live up to or to exceed stakeholder expectations of accountants. At the individual accountant level, such transformation manifests itself as required and or effected changes in accounting roles and competencies. More specifically, it manifests itself as a new or enhanced accounting roles and competencies. For example, IFAC (2017) and IFAC (2019) have provided examples of such new accounting roles; and researchers have started to explore the required enhancements in specific accounting roles (e.g., see Andreassen, 2020; Marrone & Hazelton, 2019; Moll & Yigitbasioglu, 2019). Digital technology advancements drive changes in the DT competencies required to effectively fulfill new digital and digitally enhanced accounting roles and activities. Researchers have identified a diverse collection of required data, emerging technologies, digital transformation, and digital business-related competencies required by accountants (e.g., see ACCA, 2020; Busulwa & Evans, 2021; Wessels, 2005). These competencies continue to expand rapidly with the advancement of DTs. A logical emerging issue, therefore, is how accountants can efficiently and effectively cultivate the DT competencies required to effectively use new DT tools and to perform new digital and digitally enhanced roles and activities. Further compounding this issue, information systems and learning science researchers have noted that addressing such an issue can be challenging and beset with the risks of likely overwhelm and ultimate capitulation (e.g., Rong & Grover, 2009; Soucek & Moser, 2010; Zerr et al., 2018).

Attitudes to New Technology and Their Impact on Technology Learning

Research on the impact of attitudes to learning has occurred mostly in the learning science, information systems, education, and profession-related disciplines. These studies provide conceptual and empirical evidence of a positive association between learner attitudes to phenomenon and that phenomenon's learning efficiency/effectiveness measures. For example, in a meta-analysis of 37 studies across more than 1 million participants, Mao et al. (2021) provided evidence of a positive association between attitudes toward science and learning achievement in science. The authors noted that learning self-efficacy had the strongest impact on science learning our of the three attitude subcontracts of science relevance, interest in science, and learning self-efficacy.

Echoing these findings, other learning science researchers have linked curiosity and constructive self-talk to learning efficiency and effectiveness. Thus, inferring that interest in DTs and self-confident beliefs in relation to one's ability to learn and use DTs positively impacts DT competence (e.g., see Andersen, 2016). These researchers have also linked attention control and learning strategies to learning efficiency and effectiveness (e.g., see Zerr et al., 2018). Thus, inferring that attitude sub-constructs that negatively impact the amount of attention paid to DT advancements and the ability to choose strategies for learning DTs may negatively impact the development of DT competence.

Similarly, within the IS research on technological knowledge renewal effectiveness, researchers have identified attitudes toward DTs as a key driver of the ability to learn DTs and to keep up with DT changes. In particular, this research identified the driving attitude subcontracts of: perceived need for DT competencies, sufficient appreciation of the DT learning challenge, and tolerance for ambiguity (e.g. see Rong & Grover, 2009).

Education and accounting research has, in general, also echoed the aforementioned findings. For example, Edmunds et al. (2012) found that students' expected usefulness of DTs plays a strong role in their willingness to develop DT skills. Interestingly, in relation to tertiary students, some studies have noted that tertiary educators tend to have negative attitudes toward DTs, which in turn tend to be contagious to their students, thus impeding the development of student DT competencies that educators may be required to or seek to develop (e.g., see Edmunds et al., 2012; Watty et al., 2016).

Methodology

In this study, a qualitative approach was undertaken to investigate accountants' attitudes toward digital technology, and whether these attitudes are barriers to the digital transformation of accounting. The qualitative approach involved thematic coding of open-ended questions within a cross-sectional survey. The survey was administered using Qualtrics in late 2021, and we applied a strict set of criteria to select our accountants.[1] The selected respondents had to have an accounting role, an accounting qualification, and work in Australia or New Zealand. We also purposively sampled to ensure representation across various accounting functions, career levels, and accounting practice settings. After removing incomplete responses, we were left with a final sample of 119 responses.

A number of questions were asked, including demographic questions and career information, such as accounting role, accounting workplace, industry, and accounting qualifications. Next, respondents self-rated their DT competence using Likert scales ranging from 1 (strongly disagree) to 5 (strongly agree), including their ability to learn digital technologies and to keep up with digital technology advancements. We also asked respondents to reflect on the reasons for their DT competence, and to identify any barriers they faced to better understand and use digital technologies. The survey also featured questions on the proportion of digital technologies seen as important, and the digital technology topics and digital technology products perceived as most important to current and future job performance.

[1] Ethics was applied for and granted at the authors higher education institution (University of Western.

Australia Ref: 2021/ET000863 and Swinburne University of Technology Ref: 20,216,107–8666).

Results

The results of this study are organized into four sections. The first section provides an overview of the characteristics of the study participants to enable better contextualization of the findings and their generalizability. The second, third, and fourth parts present the findings in relation to accountants' perceived DT job relevance, DT interest, and DT learning self-efficacy, respectively. The results relating to each subconstruct are discussed under the subconstruct heading. The various tables provide data that typically relate to two or more attitude sub-constructs; however, in the discussion, we focus on the aspects of each table relevant to the focal subconstruct being discussed. This approach has enabled us to present more data, so readers can reach their own broader conclusions, and to better triangulate data across tables for more reliable insights.

Sample Characteristics

Our final participant cohort had a broad representation of accountants from a diverse range of sectors and industries (e.g., primary industries, manufacturing, services), and practicing in Australia and New Zealand. More importantly, the cohort had a balanced representation of accountants across accounting functions, career levels, and practice settings. In relation to accounting functions, Table 6.1 shows that while financial accounting, management accounting and AIS, and Audit, Forensic & Other were the most represented (at 45%, 56%, and 55%, respectively), each of the other accounting functions still had sufficient representation (between 17% and 27%). Thus, although generalizability for the most represented functions is the most meaningful, it is also meaningful for the remaining functions. Table 6.2 shows that although most study participants were at the strategic leadership career level (the career level at which they are part of the dominant ownership or management/ leadership coalition), mid-career accountants (23%) and junior accountants (16%) were also suitably represented, such that relevant findings can reasonably be generalized to those career levels. In relation to accounting practice settings, the study had a nearly 50/50 representation of accountants in public practice settings versus private practice settings (see Table 6.3). Thus, the relevant study findings are equally generalizable to both the groups. Approximately one-third of accountants worked either in a DT-intensive industry (e.g., Information Technology,

Table 6.1 Nature of main work undertaken by study participants and accounting function corresponding to that work

Nature of work and corresponding accounting function	*Frequency (Percentage)*
Financial Accounting	54 (46%)
Tax	32 (27%)
Consulting & Advisory	20 (17%)
Management Accounting & AIS	65 (56%)
Audit, Forensic & Other	64 (55%)

Source Author

Table 6.2 Career levels of study participants

Career level	*Frequency (Percentage)*	*Roles included*
Strategic Leader	65 (56%)	CFO or other executive, Owner, Partner, Senior Manager
Expert or Leader or Manager	27 (23%)	Middle Manager, Team Leader, Senior Accountant
Junior/Trainee	19 (16%)	Junior Accountant, Graduate, Trainee Accountant
Support/Other	6 (5%)	Support Services Employee Other

Source Author

FinTech, Telecommunications) or serving clients in such an industry—the remainder worked outside of such industries, as Table 6.4 shows. Nevertheless, DT-intensive industries were sufficiently represented to enable meaningful generalizations about the attitudes of accountants in DT-intensive industries.

DT Job Relevance

As noted earlier, DT job relevance was operationalized in two ways. First, it was operationalized as the proportion of DTs accountants rated as important to their current job performance. Second, it was operationalized as the specific DTs, specific DT topics, and specific DT products

Table 6.3 Proportion of participants employed in public practice firms vs within the accounting function of an organization (i.e a non-accounting firm organisation)

Employer / practice setting	*Frequency (Percentage)*
Public practice setting	53 (45%)
Non-public practice setting	66 (55%)

Source Author

Table 6.4 Proportion of participants employed in DT intensive industries or serving DT intensive industry clients

Employing industry or client industry type	*Frequency (Percentage)*
DT intensive industry	31 (26%)
Non-DT intensive industry	66 (74%)

Source Author

that accountants proposed were important to their current and future job performance. Together, the aim of these two operationalizations was to show whether accountants see the growing number and diversity of DT advancements as relevant to their current and future work, and to show which specific DTs/DT topics/DT products they perceive as most important. It was reasoned that if they do not perceive DTs as important to their current or future job performance, this may result in a negative attitude toward learning DTs and therefore poor proficiency in the use of DTs. The full results are presented in three tables: Table 6.5 (shows the proportion of DTs that accountants see as job relevant), Table 6.6 (shows perceived job relevance of each specific DT), and Table 6.7 (shows the DT topics and vendor products perceived as most relevant).

Some standout insights from the aforementioned table include:

1. Table 6.5 presents the **proportion of DTs seen as relevant to accountants' current jobs**, suggesting that most accountants (72%) perceive that up to half or less of the required DTs are relevant to their current jobs. This perception was consistent across career levels and practice settings. About 30% of accountants perceive that most technologies are relevant to their current jobs. Almost 60% of

Table 6.5 Accountants' perception of the proportion of DTs that are important to their current job performance and percentage of accountants citing each proportion across career levels and practice settings

Likert Scale: proportion of DTs relevant to current job	*All accountants*	*Junior/ Trainee*	*Expert/ Manager/ Leader*	*Strategic leader*	*Hi-tech or hi-tech facing industries*	*Non-high tech*	*public practice*	*Private practice*
1 (None of the technologies)	5%	21%	3%	0%	0%	7%	6%	4%
2	32%	37%	34%	29%	42%	29%	40%	28%
3	35%	16%	32%	52%	36%	35%	29%	39%
4	25%	21%	29%	15%	19%	27%	21%	28%
5 (All of the technologies)	3%	5%	2%	4%	3%	2%	4%	1%
Mean	2.872	2.526	2.923	2.926	2.839	2.884	2.771	2.942

Source Author

junior/trainee-level accountants perceived that almost none of the DTs are relevant to their current job performance.

2. Table 6.6 compares the perceived **job relevance of established vs emerging DTs**, showing that established DTs are perceived as much more relevant to current job performance than emerging DTs (by a factor of 10 or more). However, in terms of future job performance, emerging DTs are almost equally relevant. This finding is more apparent if Table 6.6 is considered without the "*accounting systems, applications, and hardware*" category, which is likely to always be core to current and future accounting work. Table 6.6 also suggests that these two findings are consistent across accounting career levels and accounting practice settings, i.e., across public practice (i.e., accounting firms) vs. non-public practice (i.e., non-accounting firms), and across DT-intensive and non-DT-intensive industries.
3. Table 6.6 presents what are perceived as the **most job relevant emerging technologies**. *Artificial intelligence* is perceived as the most job relevant emerging technology for both current and future job performance. Artificial intelligence is closely followed by

Table 6.6 Accountants' perception of the importance of different types of DTs to their current job performance and percentage of accountants citing them across career levels and practice settings

	Important to current job role (%)	*Important to future job roles (%)*	*Junior/ Trainee (%)*	*Expert/ Manager/ Leader (%)*	*Strategic leader (%)*	*Public practice (%)*	*Non-public practice (%)*	*Hi-tech or hi-tech facing industries (%)*	*Non-high tech (%)*
Established Technologies									
Accounting Systems, applications, and hardware	45	29	30	31	30	30	27	26	30
Business systems, applications, and hardware	26	14	15	15	15	17	12	19	13
Data analytics and data science systems and applications	21	26	20	29	19	22	28	26	26
Process and workflow digitalization and optimization systems and applications	12	11	10	10	11	13	9	16	9
Data visualization systems and applications	10	12	15	13	7	11	12	10	13
Cloud computing services, service types, and service levels	8	7	15	5	7	6	7	6	7
Data management technologies	4	5	10	6	0	6	4	0	7

	Important to current job role (%)	*Important to future job roles (%)*	*Junior/ Trainee (%)*	*Expert/ Manager/ Leader (%)*	*Strategic leader (%)*	*Public practice (%)*	*Non-public practice (%)*	*Hi-tech or hi-tech facing industries (%)*	*Non-high tech (%)*
Programming languages used in accounting workflows	1	3	5	3	0	2	3	3	2
Emerging Technologies									
Artificial Intelligence	4	10	0	11	15	9	10	13	9
Blockchain and other distributed ledgers and databases	3	3	5	3	0	4	1	3	2
Internet of things and edge computing	1	3	0	3	4	2	3	3	2
Robotics and drone technologies	1	1	0	0	4	0	1	0	1
Virtual/Augmented/ Mixed Reality technologies	0	1	0	0	4	0	1	0	1
Video content analytics and computer vision technologies	0	1	0	0	0	0	1	0	1

Source Author

Table 6.7 The specific DT topics and vendor products perceived as most important to accountants' current and future job roles

	Important to current Job (%)	*Important to future job (%)*	*Junior/ Trainee (%)*	*Expert/ Manager/ Leader (%)*	*Strategic Leader (%)*	*Public practice (%)*	*Non-public practice (%)*	*Hi-tech or hi-tech facing industry (%)*	*Non-high tech (%)*
Specific topics identified									
ERP Systems	16	8	10	3	4	7	1	6	3
Cloud Accounting systems/platforms	6	6	15	3	7	6	6	6	6
Robotic Process Automation (RPA)	2	2	0	2	4	0	3	0	2
Cryptocurrencies	2	1	0	0	4	2	0	3	0
Cybersecurity applications	1	1	5	0	0	0	1	0	1
Modeling technologies	1	1	0	0	0	2	0	3	0
Subscription management software	1	0	0	0	0	0	0	0	0
Big Data	1	1	0	2	0	0	1	0	1
Q2C digital channels	1	0	0	0	0	0	0	0	0
Enterprise systems and applications	1	0	0	0	0	0	0	0	0
Enterprise tax software	1	0	0	0	0	0	0	0	0
Financial Management Information Systems (FMIS)	1	1	0	2	0	2	0	3	0

	Important to current Job (%)	*Important to future job (%)*	*Junior/ Trainee (%)*	*Expert/ Manager/ Leader (%)*	*Strategic Leader (%)*	*Public practice (%)*	*Non-public practice (%)*	*Hi-tech or hi-tech facing industry (%)*	*Non-high tech (%)*
CRM systems	1	1	0	0	4	2	0	3	0
Big Data	1	1	0	2	0	0	1	0	1
Q2C digital channels	1	0	0	0	0	0	0	0	0
Computing networks	0	1	0	2	0	2	0	0	1
Machine Learning	0	1	0	2	0	2	0	3	0
Audit analytics software	0	1	0	0	0	2	0	0	1
Apps and App marketplaces	0	2	0	0	7	4	0	3	1
Specific Vendor Systems/applications Identified									
Tableau	3	2	0	3	0	2	1	0	2
Xero	3	0	0	0	0	0	0	0	0
Microsoft Excel	3	3	5	2	4	4	1	0	3
Microsoft Power BI	1	2	0	2	4	2	1	3	1
IBM Power Systems	1	0	0	0	0	0	0	0	0
Microsoft Word	1	0	0	0	0	0	0	0	0
Alteryx	1	0	0	0	0	0	0	0	0

Source Author

blockchain/other distributed ledgers and the *Internet of Things (IoT)*. Each of these three emerging technologies is more often cited as important to future job performance, except for blockchain/other distributed ledgers, which are considered important both now and in the future. This finding also holds true across accounting practice settings and career levels.

4. Table 6.6 presents the perceived **job relevance of emerging technologies across career levels and practice settings**. In general, emerging technologies are more often perceived as relevant to current job performance by strategic leaders, accountants in public practice firms, and accountants in high-tech industries.
5. Table 6.7 presents perceptions of the **most job relevant DT topics and vendor products**. The DT topics perceived as most job relentant include ERP systems, cloud accounting systems/platforms, Robotic Process Automation (RPA), and cryptocurrencies. The vendor products perceived as most job relevant included the Tableau data visualization platform, Xero cloud accounting platform, and Microsoft Excel spreadsheet application. The job-relevant DT topics perceived as most important to future job performance are surprisingly the same as those for current job performance. However, the specific DT products perceived as most important for future job performance are Microsoft Excel, Microsoft Power BI (for data visualization), and Tableau (for data visualization).

DT Interest

DT interest was operationalized as the extent to which accountants identified interest in DTs or in learning DTs as the reason for their current DT competence. To effect this operationalization, we asked accountants for the reasons behind their current level of competence with DTs. The content analyzed responses and the resultant themes/categories of responses are presented in Table 6.8.

Some standout insights from the aforementioned table include:

1. Table 6.8 shows the **interest of accountants in DTs** across career levels and practice settings. Just over 15% of all accountants have an interest in DTs, which is consistent across most career levels and practice settings. DT interest is worst among junior/trainee

Table 6.8 Accountants' stated reasons for their current DT competence level and percentage of accountants citing each reason across career levels and practice settings

Reason Classification	*Reason for current competence*	*All accountants (%)*	*Junior/ Trainee (%)*	*Expert/ Manager/ Leader (%)*	*Strategic leader (%)*	*Public practice (%)*	*Non-public practice (%)*	*Hi-tech industry (%)*	*Non-Hi-Tech (%)*
Positive Internal Locus of Control	Interest in DTs	16	10	15	22	20	12	26	13
Positive Internal Locus of Control	Self-directed learning	17	15	11	26	15	18	16	17
Positive Internal Locus of Control	Natural ability to learn DTs	1	0	2	0	0	1	0	1
Positive External Locus of Control	Occupy a Technology-oriented role	3	0	3	4	4	3	3	3
Positive External Locus of Control	Exposure to DTs during study or work	30	25	35	33	28	31	26	32
Positive External Locus of Control	Access to appropriate DT education/ training	11	10	11	7	6	15	6	13
Negative External Locus of Control	Lack of access to appropriate DT education/ training	9	10	10	7	4	13	3	11

(continued)

Table 6.8 (continued)

Reason Classification	*Reason for current competence*	*All accountants (%)*	*Junior/ Trainee (%)*	*Expert/ Manager/ Leader (%)*	*Strategic leader (%)*	*Public practice (%)*	*Non-public practice (%)*	*Hi-tech industry (%)*	*Non-Hi-Tech (%)*
Negative External Locus of Control	Lack of Exposure or opportunity to use DTs	31	50	27	19	31	30	29	32
Negative External Locus of Control	Lack of time to learn DTs	6	5	10	0	4	7	3	7
Negative External Locus of Control	Overwhelmed by scope and speed of DT changes	5	0	3	11	4	6	3	6
Other	No need/no incentive to learn DTs	8	5	10	7	9	7	16	6
Other	Threat to current job so not embracing	1	0	0	4	2	0	3	0

Source Author

accountants (with only 10% interest) and accountants in non-public practice settings (only 12% interest). DT interest is strongest among strategic leaders (22% interest) and among accountants in high-tech industries (26% interest).

2. Table 6.8 shows the **interest of accountants in learning DTs** across career levels and practice settings. Just over 15% of accountants are interested in learning DTs (as evidenced by their self - directed learning activity), which is consistent across most career levels and practice settings. Interest in learning DTs is the worst among the expert/manager/leader career levels (11%) and about the same (approx 16%) across practice settings.

DT Learning Self-efficacy

DT learning self-efficacy was operationalized in three ways. First, it was operationalized as accountants' self-rated ability to learn DTs (see Table 6.9). It was then operationalized as accountants' stated reasons for their current DT competence (see Table 6.8). Finally, it was operationalized as accountants' perceived barriers to understanding DTs (see Table 6.10). The aim of our three operationalizations was to quantify the levels of DT learning self-efficacy and to identify accountants' attributions of their DT learning self-efficacy.

Some standout insights from the aforementioned tables include:

1. Table 6.8 also shows what accountants attribute to their DT competency levels. The majority of accountants (approximately 80%) have an **external locus of control**, attributing their strong or weak DT competency level to external factors (e.g. employer not providing sufficient opportunities to learn, prohibitive organisation culture, low workplace or client adoption). In the table, a positive locus of control refers to external attributions for strong DT competency, whereas a negative locus of control refers to external attributions for weak DT competency.
2. As shown in Table 6.8, most accountants with strong DT competencies attribute this competency to an **exposure to DTs during study or work** (approximately 30% of accountants). Surprisingly, most accountants with weak DT competency attribute this competency

Table 6.9 Accountants' self-rated ability to learn DTs and to keep up with DT advancements and percentage of accountants citing them across career levels and practice settings

Likert Scale: ability to learn and keep up with DTs	*All accountants*	*Junior/ Trainee*	*Expert/ Manager/ Leader*	*Strategic Leader*	*Hi-tech or hi-tech facing industries*	*Non- High Tech*
1 (Not at all Competent)	9%	11%	9%	11%	10%	9%
2	28%	26%	31%	26%	26%	29%
3	38%	37%	32%	41%	32%	40%
4	23%	26%	26%	18%	29%	21%
5 (Very Competent)	2%	0	2%	4%	3%	1%
Mean	2.8	2.79	2.8	2.78	2.9	2.76

Source Author

to a lack of exposure to DTs during work or study (approximately 30% of accountants).

3. As Table 6.8 shows, almost 10% of accountants attributed their weak DT competency to a **perceived lack of need to use DTs**. Surprisingly, this attribution was more pronounced among accountants in high-tech industries—although we did have fewer of them in the study, this would discount this finding somewhat.
4. As shown in Table 6.9, 75% of accountants rated their **ability to learn DTs and to keep up with DT changes** as below average, with almost 40% rating themselves as barely or not at all competent in this area. About 25% of the accountants rated themselves as above-average or very competent. These three findings were consistent across career levels and practice settings.
5. As per Table 6.10, most accountants attribute their DT competency shortcomings to **lack of time to learn DTs** and to **employer or job-related shortcomings**.

Table 6.10 Accountants' perceived barriers to understanding digital technologies and percentage of accountants citing them across career levels and practice settings

Response Group	*Barriers*	*All accountants (%)*	*Junior/ Trainee (%)*	*Expert/ Manager/ Leader (%)*	*Strategic Leader (%)*	*Public Practice (%)*	*Non-Public Practice (%)*	*Hi-tech or hi-tech facing industries (%)*	*Non-High Tech (%)*
Mixed attribution	Lack of time to learn technology	45	25	47	52	38	50	55	41
Employer attribution	Insufficient exposure/ Opportunity to use technology	20	25	19	15	17	23	16	22
Employer attribution	Lack of access to appropriate education/ training	12	10	16	4	13	11	13	11
	Low workplace or client adoption	11	25	8	7	15	8	10	11
Employer attribution	Prohibitive Organization Culture/ Attitude to Adoption	4	0	3	7	4	5	3	5
Employer attribution	Lack of management/ organization support	4	0	3	7	4	5	6	3

(continued)

Table 6.10 (continued)

Response Group	*Barriers*	*All accountants (%)*	*Junior/ Trainee (%)*	*Expert/ Manager/ Leader (%)*	*Strategic Leader (%)*	*Public Practice (%)*	*Non-Public Practice (%)*	*Hi-tech or hi-tech facing industries (%)*	*Non-High Tech (%)*
Employer attribution	Likely risk of use	1	0	0	0	0	2	3	0
Employer attribution	Accounting role overloaded	2	0	3	0	0	3	6	0
Self-attribution	No need/Not Relevant	18	30	18	15	23	14	13	19
Self-attribution	Lack of interest/ motivation	4	15	2	4	8	2	3	5
Self-attribution	Overwhelmed by pace of change/ Amount to learn	5	0	3	11	2	8	3	6
Education attribution	Lack of formal education background	6	5	6	7	4	8	0	8
Education attribution	Cost of education	8	0	11	4	4	11	13	6

Source Author

Discussion

Our research investigating the nature and prevalence of accountants' attitudes toward digital technology yielded interesting and somewhat surprising results, with important implications for a broad range of stakeholders. Our discussion of the potential meaning, implications, and required stakeholder actions are organized as follows. First, we discuss standout findings in relation to each attitude subconstruct (i.e., DT job relevance, DT interest, and DT learning self-efficacy) and their potential meaning and implications for required stakeholder actions. We then discuss the implications of the overall results for the digital transformation of accounting.

Accountants' Interest in New Technology

A surprising and key finding in relation to the attitude subconstruct of DT interest was that accountants' interest in DTs appears to be very low in general, yet particularly low in junior/trainee accountants. More specifically, the results show that only 15% of accountants have an interest in DTs, with this interest being weakest among junior/trainee accountants (10%) and strongest among strategic leaders (22%) and high-tech industries (26%). This result is counterintuitive, as it seems more logital that junior/trainee accountants, as digital natives, should have more interest in DTs than more senior career levels. For example, we expected this result for more senior accountants, as that group would contain more digital immigrants—who have been noted to fear or resist adoption of DTs (e.g., see Schmidt et al., 2020; Soja & Soja, 2020; Watty et al., 2016). Based on this finding, we suggest that the professions' strategic leadership and education entities ought to explore reasons for early career accountants' lack of interest in DTs, as well as optimal policies and initiatives to shape positive interest in DTs among prospective and early career accountants. Further, we suggest that these entities invest time and resources to help accountants cultivate an optimal locus of control, as opposed to the currently detrimental external locus of control of a majority of accountants.

Relevance of DTs to Accountants' Current and Future Job Roles

Another surprising finding was that 72% of accountants perceived that only about half or less of the required DTs were relevant to their current job. In relation to early career accountants, approximately 60% of junior/trainee-level accountants perceive that almost none of the DTs are relevant to their current job performance. This finding raises important professional issues, depending on the meaning attributed to it. For example, it might mean that early career accountants who attempt to use new DTs for accounting work are being sidelined or not taken seriously, and thus are disincentivized to use DTs—so that they are more akin to seeing them as not relevant/not wanted by their line managers. This may stem from more senior accountants distrusting DTs, or having more incentives to maintain the status quo of limited DT use. Alternatively, it could be that effective integration of DTs into accounting curricula has been lacking, so that early career accountants are yet to understand why new technologies have anything to do with their current and future job roles (i.e., they may be oblivious to the digital transformation of accounting that is under way). Or, it may be that throughout students' education experiences, accounting educators have ignored or trivialized the importance of DTs, and thus early career accountants mirror their faculties' attitudes toward DTs (e.g., see Blin & Munroe, 2008; Keller, 2005). Whatever the reason for early career accountants' views that almost none of DTs are relevant to their current or future work, we propose that this is a very important perception for the profession's strategic leadership and educational institutions to reverse. We suggest that it can be reversed through policies and initiatives that educate prospective and early career accountants of how important DTs are to their current and future job roles; as well as policies and initiatives that support early career accountants to overcome the influences of potentially outdated but strongly undermining attitudes of educators, workplace colleagues, or even line managers. Further, we suggest that the profession's strategic leadership and educational institutions invest time and resources to further compartmentalize the extensive and likely overwhelming collection of required DT competencies into the accounting functions and career levels in which they are needed. This would help accountants in specific accounting functions, job roles, and career levels to better see and understand the DT's relevant to their. In addition, we suggest that educational institutions find an optimal balance between curricula that equip students with DT competencies relevant to current vs. future job requirements. A biased focus on future job relevance may result in students not clearly seeing job relevance now, whereas a biased focus on current job relevance may result in students clearly seeing job relevance now but not effectively cultivating required future DT competencies.

Accountants' Confidence in Their Ability to Learn DTs

Another surprising finding is that 75% of accountants rated their ability to learn DTs and to keep up with DT changes as below average, with almost 40% rating themselves as barely or not at all competent in this area. This finding suggests that there may be two shortcomings in accounting education. First, accountants may not be being educated on how challenging it is to continuously lean and keep up with rapidly advancing and increasingly more diverse DT changes. Second, accountants may not be being taught how to effectively learn new DTs, or may not be being equipped with effective strategies for keeping up with DT changes. These shortcomings are likely to undermine accountants' confidence with DTs in two ways. First, they are likely to find that most of their efforts to learn DTs and to keep up with DT changes are ineffective, undermining their resilience and efforts to keep trying in the face of rapid changes and continued frustration. Second, even when they have some success, they are likely to see that their success is limited and potentially not impactful in a meaningful way. We suggest that the professions' strategic leadership and education entities invest in teaching prospective and early career accountants what we consider to be the most important skill in the digital era: learning how to effectively learn DTs and learning/instituting effective strategies for keeping up with DT changes.

Further, in relation to DT learning self-efficacy, we found that 80% of accountants identified external factors (workplace exposure to DTs, access to appropriate training programs) as determining their DT competence rather than internal factors (e.g., self-motivation, self-directed learning). This finding has implications for both professional development programs and university curricula that incorporate digital technology. We propose that both types of educators invest more time and resources in cultivating accountants' interest in DTs, in building accountants' DT learning self-efficacy, and in helping accountants have an optimal locus of control. We also suggest that such programs focus on cultivating and assessing accountants' self-directed DT learning activities, as opposed to encouraging them to wait to be spoon-fed through the "perfect" curricula delivered by the right accounting institution.

Implications of Findings for the Digital Transformation of Accounting

There is alingment in our study findings the extant literature on the relationship between attitudes toward a skill area and competence in that skill area. Specifically, both converge to support the logic that negative attitudes toward DTs (e.g., in our case, this includes lack of interest in DTs, lack of perceived job relevance of DTs, and lack of confidence to effectively lean DTs and to keep up with DTs) negatively impact the development of accounting DT competencies. For example, negative attitudes to DTs likely do this by limiting attention to important DT changes and DT learning opportunities, by negatively impacting motivation to learn DTs, by limiting the scope and nature of self-directed DT learning activities, by negatively impacting prioritization of time to learn DTs, and by negatively impacting resilience in the face of DT learning setbacks. Irrespective of the various ways in which the negative impact manifests itself, the eventual outcome is to thwart self-directed, profession-led, and employer-led efforts to develop accounting DT competencies.

This is a significant risk for the profession as, even without such thwarting, the profession already faces a serious challenge keeping accountants' competency development efforts aligned with exponential changes in DT advancements. As noted earlier, DT advancements are driving the digital transformation imperative. Thus, accountants' competence in these DTs is critical, as the digital transformation of accounting occurs at the accountant level. That is, since the digital transformation of accounting manifests itself as required and actual changes in accounting roles, processes, workflows, and work tools, it cannot occur without accountants having sufficient DT competencies to perform digitally transformed roles/processes/workflows, and to use new DT work tools. We propose that, absent meaningful interventions from the professions' strategic leadership and education entities to bring about changes in accountants' interest in DTs, perceived job relevance of DTs, and DT learning self-efficacy, accountants' DT competencies will become an increasingly significant barrier to the digital transformation of accounting. However, the digital transformation of accounting can be accelerated and be less disruptive if the profession's strategic leadership, accreditation, and professional body entities work in concert with educators to improve accountants' interest in DTs, DT learning self-efficacy, and locus of control.

Conclusion

In this study, we investigated accountants' attitudes toward DTs through operationalizations of accountants' perceived job relevance of DTs, accountants' interest in DTs, and accountants' DT learning self-efficacy. We found that most accountants do not perceive the majority of DTs as being relevant to their current or future work, are not interested in using or learning DTs, do not feel confident in their ability to learn DTs, and attribute their low DT competency to external—rather than internal factors or a balance of internal and external factors. These findings provide evidence of an overall negative attitude toward DTs. Given the evidence in the extant literature on such negative DT attitudes impeding DT competence development, we suggest that, absent meaningful intervention of the profession's strategic leadership and educational institutions, accountants' attitudes toward DTs will become an increasingly significant barrier to the digital transformation of accounting. Our study provides important implications for accounting practitioners, employers, professional and accreditation bodies, and educational institutions.

References

ACCA. (2020). *Future ready: Accountancy careers in the 2020s*. Association of Chartered Certified Accountants. https://www.accaglobal.com/in/en/professional-insights/pro-accountants-the-future/future_ready_2020s.html. Accessed 3 August 2021.

Andersen, E. (2016). Learning to learn. *Harvard Business Review*. Retrieved June 15, 2020, from Harvard Business. https://hbr.org/2016/03/learning-to-learn

Andreassen, R. I. (2020). Digital technology and changing roles: A management accountant's dream or nightmare? *Journal of Management Control, 31*(3), 209–238.

Bebbington, J., Gray, R., Thomson, I., & Walters, D. (1994). Accountants' attitudes and environmentally-sensitive accounting. *Accounting and Business Research, 24*(94), 109–120.

Berkeley, E. C. (1950). The uses of automatic computers in financial and accounting operations. *Journal of Accountancy (pre-1986), 90*(000004), 306.

Bharadwaj, A., El Sawy, O. A., Pavlou, P. A., & Venkatraman, N. (2013). Digital business strategy: Toward a next generation of insights. *MIS Quarterly, 37*(2), 471–482.

Blin, F., & Munro, M. (2008). Why hasn't technology disrupted academics' teaching practices? Understanding resistance to change through the lens of activity theory. *Computers & Education, 50*(2), 475–490.

Bui, B., & Porter, B. (2010). The expectation-performance gap in accounting education: An exploratory study. *Accounting Education: An International Journal, 19*(1–2), 23–50.

Busulwa, R., & Evans, N. (2021). *Digital transformation in accounting*. Routledge.

Edmunds, R., Thorpe, M., & Conole, G. (2012). Student attitudes towards and use of ICT in course study, work and social activity: A technology acceptance model approach. *British Journal of Educational Technology, 43*(1), 71–84.

Emerson, T. L., Conroy, S. J., & Stanley, C. W. (2007). Ethical attitudes of accountants: Recent evidence from a practitioners' survey. *Journal of Business Ethics, 71*(1), 73–87.

Husam, A. A. K., & Sulieman, A. B. (2009). Attitudes toward learning accounting by computers: The impact on perceived skills. *Journal of Accounting and Taxation, 1*(1), 001–007.

International Federation of Accountants (IFAC). (2017). *Developing a future ready profession*. https://www.ifac.org/system/files/publications/files/Developing-a-Future-Ready-Profession.pdf. Accessed 16 December 2021.

International Federation of Accountants (IFAC). (2019). *Future-Fit accountants: CFO and finance function roles for the next decade*. International Federation of Accountants. https://www.ifac.org/system/files/publications/files/IFAC-Future-Fit-Accountant-ROLES-V5-Singles.pdf. Accessed 16 December 2021.

Janvrin, D. J., & Watson, M. W. (2017). "Big Data": A new twist to accounting. *Journal of Accounting Education, 38*, 3–8.

Jones, G., & McNamara, T. (1988). *Information technology and the new accounting*. McGraw-Hill.

Keller, C. (2005). Virtual learning environments: Three implementation perspectives. *Learning, media and technology, 30*(3), 299–311.

Krippendorff, K. (2018). *Content analysis: An introduction to its methodology* (pp. 81–87). Sage publications.

Mao, P., Cai, Z., He, J., Chen, X., & Fan, X. (2021). The Relationship between attitude toward science and academic achievement in science: A three-level meta-analysis. *Frontiers in Psychology, 12*, 784068.

Marrone, M., & Hazelton, J. (2019). The disruptive and transformative potential of new technologies for accounting, accountants and accountability: A review of current literature and call for further research. *Meditari Accountancy Research, 27*(5), 677–694.

Mathews, R. L. (1967). A computer programming approach to the design of accounting systems. *Abacus, 3*(2), 133–152.

Moll, J., & Yigitbasioglu, O. (2019). The role of internet-related technologies in shaping the work of accountants: New directions for accounting research. *The British Accounting Review, 51*(6), 100833.

Morris, R. (1994). Computerized content analysis in management research: A demonstration of advantages & limitations. *Journal of Management, 20*(4), 903–931.

Osborne, J., Simon, S., & Collins, S. (2003). Attitudes towards science: A review of the literature and its implications. *International Journal of Science Education., 25*, 1049–1079. https://doi.org/10.1080/0950069032000032199

Pinsonneault, A., & Kraemer, K. L. (1993). Survey research methodology in management information systems: An assessment. *Journal of Management Information Systems, 10*(2), 75–85.

Rong, G., & Grover, V. (2009). Keeping up-to-date with information technology: Testing a model of technological knowledge renewal effectiveness for it professionals. *Information & Management, 46*(7), 376–387.

Savelsbergh, E. R., Prins, G. T., Rietbergen, C., Fechner, S., Vaessen, B. E., Draijer, J. M., & Bakker, A. (2016). Effects of innovative science and mathematics teaching on student attitudes and achievement: A meta-analytic study. *Educational Research Review, 19*, 158–172.

Schmidt, P. J., Church, K. S., & Riley, J. (2020). Clinging to excel as a security blanket: Investigating accountants' resistance to emerging data analytics technology. *Journal of Emerging Technologies in Accounting, 17*(1), 33–39.

Shapka, J. D., & Ferrari, M. (2003). Computer-related attitudes and actions of teacher candidates. *Computers in Human Behavior, 19*(3), 319–334.

Soja, E., & Soja, P. (2020). Fostering ICT use by older workers: Lessons from perceptions of barriers to enterprise system adoption. *Journal of Enterprise Information Management, 33*(2), 407–434.

Soucek, R., & Moser, K. (2010). Coping with information overload in email communication: Evaluation of a training intervention. *Computers in Human Behavior, 26*(6), 1458–1466.

Teo, T. (2011). Factors influencing teachers' intention to use technology: Model development and test. *Computers & Education, 57*(4), 2432–2440.

Vial, G. (2019). Understanding digital transformation: A review and a research agenda. *The Journal of Strategic Information Systems, 28*(2), 118–144.

Watty, K., McKay, J., & Ngo, L. (2016). Innovators or inhibitors? Accounting faculty resistance to new educational technologies in higher education. *Journal of Accounting Education, 36*, 1–15.

Wessels, P. L. (2005). Critical information and communication technology (ICT) skills for professional accountants. *Meditari: Research Journal of the School of Accounting Sciences, 13*(1), 87–103.

Wooten, T. C. (1998). Factors influencing student learning in introductory accounting classes: A comparison of traditional and non-traditional students. *Issues in Accounting Education, 13*(2), 357–373.

Yushau, B. (2006). Computer attitude, use, experience, software familiarity and perceived pedagogical usefulness: The case of mathematics professors. *Eurasia Journal of Mathematics, Science and Technology Education, 2*(3), 1–17.

Zerr, C. L., Berg, J. J., Nelson, S. M., Fishell, A. K., Savalia, N. K., & McDermott, K. B. (2018b). Learning efficiency: Identifying individual differences in learning rate and retention in healthy adults. *Psychological Science, 29*(9), 1436–1450. https://doi.org/10.1177/0956797618772540

PART III

The Technological Frontier: Transforming Accounting and Auditing Practices

CHAPTER 7

How Accountants Can Drive Digital Transformation

Clarence Goh and Kevin Ow Yong

State of Digital Transformation in the Accounting Sector in Singapore

The Singapore Accountancy Commission launched the Accountancy Industry Digital Plan with the mission to digitally transform the accountancy sector (Accountancy IDP, 2019). This plan focuses on three strategies: enhancing digital skills and knowledge; promoting the adoption of technology; and developing accounting technology and innovation. The plan was jointly developed by Singapore Accountancy Commission (SAC), the Institute of Singapore Chartered Accountants (ISCA), and the Infocomm Media Development Authority (IMDA). It is also part of

C. Goh
Singapore Management University, Singapore, Singapore
e-mail: clarencegoh@smu.edu.sg

K. O. Yong (✉)
Singapore Institute of Technology, Singapore, Singapore
e-mail: kevin.owyong@singaporetech.edu.sg

A. Perdana and T. Wang (eds.), *Digital Transformation in Accounting and Auditing*, https://doi.org/10.1007/978-3-031-46209-2_7

IMDA's SMEs Go Digital programme that aims to make going digital simple for small medium accounting practices.

A recent Singapore Accountancy Commission Accounting Entity Census showed that there are approximately 700 accounting entities (AEs) operating in Singapore (AEcensus, 2021). These are firms registered under the Accountants Act (Chapter 2) and companies that provide accounting-related services. They employed more than 20,000 accounting professionals and generated more than $2 billion in revenue. The Singapore Accountancy Commission conducts a national census on the accountancy sector in Singapore to gather data on revenue, productivity, job creation, employment outlook, professionally qualified workforce, diversity of services, and volume of work performed overseas. Given that small- and medium-sized practices (SMPs) account for 98% of the accountancy industry in Singapore, the focus of the Accountancy Industry Digital Plan is to help these firms adopt technology for greater productivity and competitiveness.

In relation to the digital transformation of the accountancy sector in Singapore, the roadmap spells out three distinct stages that showcase different digital solutions for each stage of digital readiness. The first stage aims to provide digital solutions to enable digital economic readiness. The second stage seeks to utilize various digital solutions to create growth in the digital economy. The third stage encompasses digital solutions for developing innovative and intelligent business services.

In the first stage, the emphasis is on streamlining operations and optimizing resources to enhance productivity. Digital solutions included in this first stage of digital transformation in the Accountancy Industry Digital Plan include: (1) Audit Management, (2) Cloud Accounting, (3) data analytics for audit, (4) Document Management, (5) Practice Management, and (6) Taxation Management.

Audit management is a digital solution that seeks to enable better audit planning with customizable work steps based on risk assessments and reports. A digital dashboard within the audit management software module provides navigation for various audit tasks and steps. A key strength of this digital solution is that data are interconnected to enable the digital documentation of supporting documents throughout the audit workflow process. Properly implemented, this digital tool will allow for real-time collaboration among various audit teams and will also help streamline the audit review process. Overall, this digital solution can enhance audit quality and facilitate compliance compared with manual audit management processes. It also allows auditors to review and manage their audit engagements with greater ease and efficiency.

Cloud accounting is a cloud-based solution that enables multiple users to simultaneously access real-time accounting information from multiple locations. This software can include e-invoicing capabilities for the efficient billing of customers. The main advantage of the cloud accounting software solution is that it helps to improve the accessibility of real-time information for the firm. In addition, it allows automatic software updates and data backups through the cloud. Data security is managed and maintained through restricted access rights to authorized users.

Data analytics for audits uses big data analysis to detect anomalies and fraudulent activities. It provides a more focused risk approach by determining certain high-risk areas that warrant further investigation by the auditor or accountant. It is also important that this digital solution retains an audit trail to ensure compliance and documentation.

Document management optimized for the digital world will digitalize hardcopy documents and enable digital sharing of these documents across virtual spaces between users. There should also be search capabilities within the digital archive of documents for the ease of file retrieval and search functionality. In addition, these digital documents should provide access to authorized users and facilitate the e-signing of documents. Such digital capabilities provide security over the handling of sensitive and confidential information.

Digital solutions for practice management aim to manage the onboarding process more efficiently for clients. It will also monitor the progress over the invoicing status and utilize scheduling tools to optimize staff planning needs, utilization rates, and billing contributions. Good digital practice management software can provide efficient monitoring of audit engagements, optimize staff allocation effectively to save costs, and enhance the client service delivery process.

Finally, the taxation management module seeks to integrate the tax preparation process using customizable templates that can be auto-filled from financial statements. The software module should have the ability to input notes and explanations, link attachments, and supporting documents, and provide references to computations. Integrated taxation management software should ultimately reduce unnecessary human errors and manual duplication. It can also facilitate ease of review through the provision of review comments, notes, and references in the tracking system.

In the second stage of the Accountancy Industry Digital Plan, emphasis is placed on growing and connecting businesses in a digital ecosystem. Two digital solutions that underpin this digital transformation that are covered in the Accountancy Industry Digital Plan are (1) e-payment capabilities and (2) an integrated e-platform for seamless transactions.

With e-payment capabilities, manual payment options that might be inefficient or time-consuming can be minimized. There will be a cost reduction gained through economies of scale in the payment processes, especially for large organizations. The e-payment digital solution is a streamlined, paperless payment function that, coupled with e-invoicing functionality, seeks to achieve higher office productivity for back-end processing work.

Another digital solution to promote a thriving digital ecosystem among connected businesses and enterprises is for the government to establish an integrated e-platform that connects various systems through application programming interfaces (APIs) to allow seamless transactions among businesses and government agencies (or with other enterprises). Such a platform will reduce the duplication of work, as a single submission can be simultaneously transmitted to various government agencies. It is envisaged that this platform will provide a one-stop business-friendly portal to facilitate transactions and submissions between businesses and various government bodies.

In the third stage of the digital transformation of the accountancy sector, there will be enhanced use of artificial intelligence (AI) in both audits and accounting processes. AI for audits enables audit staff to make informed decisions for audit planning and execution. An AI-enabled digital solution can suggest high-risk areas based on prior data or industry-specific patterns for further investigation. AI for accounting seeks to increase the efficiency and accuracy of information in routine accounting processes so that accounting staff can better allocate their time and resources to higher-value work. Such digital tools include AI-empowered accounts payable (AP)/accounts receivable (AR) processing tools for reconciliation and checks. AI-enabled chatbots can also be utilized to help staff better cope with queries relating to account balances, status of payments, delivery status, billing processes, and other types of questions from customers or vendors.

Figure 7.1 suggests that there is an increase in the adoption of eight out of 12 digital solutions listed in the census of audit firms that were carried out in 2021. The rate of adoption of these technologies varies differently across various software solutions. For example, technologies such as tax software and cloud accounting software saw the highest increase in adoption, with adoption of tax software increasing from 19 to 27% and cloud accounting software increasing from 22 to 30% among the accounting entities (AEs) surveyed. Overall, the census found that 91% of AEs have adopted at least one or more technological solutions, while 66% of AEs have adopted at least two or more technological solutions.

A major issue underpinning technological advancement and automation is accountants' involvement in these technologies. Will these technological solutions make accountants redundant? Alternatively, would these technological solutions help enhance the accountant's job scope? In the

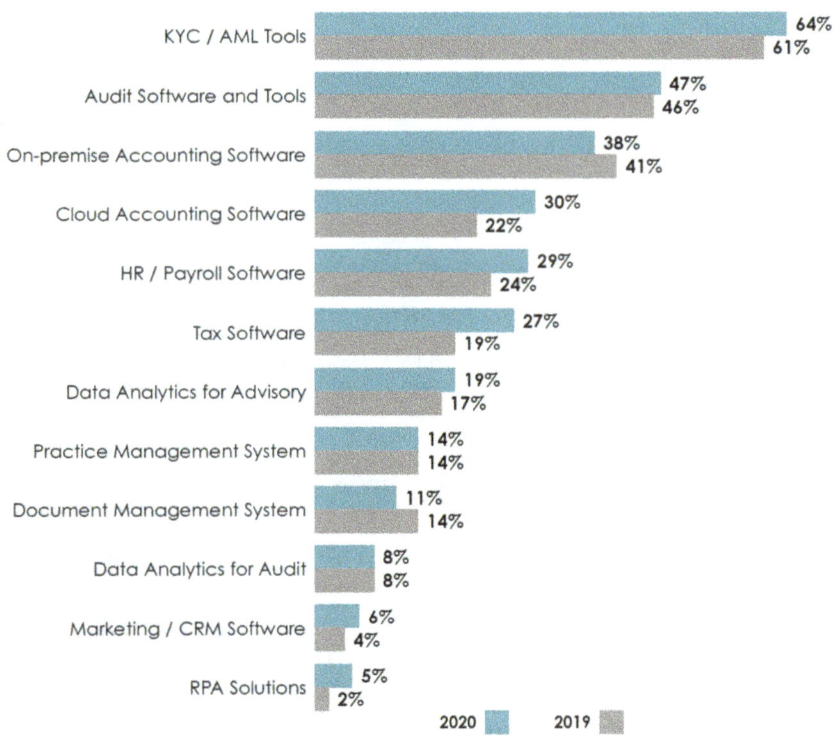

Fig. 7.1 Technology adoption rates of the accountancy sector in Singapore (*Source* AEcensus, 2021)

next section, we explore five perspectives on how the role of accountants changes with the implementation of various types of accounting technological solutions.

Five Perspectives in Adapting to Technological Advancement and Automation

In a recent article titled *Beyond Automation* published in the Harvard Business Review, Davenport & Kirby (2015) identified five perspectives that employees can adopt to add value to their organizations in an environment of rapid technological advancement and automation. Table 7.1 summarizes how accountants can add value to their organizations in the context of each of these perspectives.

The five perspectives highlighted in the table allow accountants to continue to add value to their organizations in the following ways.

- Accountants who possess relevant experience, skills, and domain knowledge can *step up* to perform higher-level tasks that cannot

Table 7.1 Five perspectives that accountants can adopt

Perspective	*How accountants can add value*
Step up	The employee is senior manager material and better than any computer at considering the big picture and making strategic decisions. He/she can *step up* to perform higher-level tasks that computers may not be able to
Step aside	The employee brings strengths to the table that aren't about purely rational, codifiable cognition. He/she can *step aside* from tasks that can be performed or automated by computers to focus on other aspects of his/her job which cannot easily be automated
Step narrowly	The employee specializes in something for which no computer program has yet been developed. He/she *steps narrowly* by working in an area which computers cannot yet play a role
Step in	The employee understands how software makes decisions and is able to monitor and modify its functions and outputs. He/she can *step in* to work alongside computers
Step forward	The employee builds the next generation or application of smart machines. He/she encourages the organization to *step forward* by adopting newer emerging technologies

Adapted from: Davenport, T., Kirby, J. (2015), Beyond Automation, *Harvard Business Review*, June 2015: 58–65 be performed by computers. This is especially pertinent in the accounting context. Although computers today are capable of handling straightforward (and often mundane) bookkeeping and accounting tasks, such as record keeping and data entry, it is unlikely that they will ever develop the capabilities to perform tasks that involve higher levels of abstraction, which senior accountants undertake regularly. Such tasks can include strategy and planning work, which often involve a high level of professional accounting judgments and interpersonal interactions involving senior managers within the organization.

- Senior accountants typically undertake higher-level strategies and plan work. Therefore, not every accountant has the opportunity to adopt a *step-up* strategy. Regardless, our view is that it is possible for all accountants to identify tasks within their existing job areas that cannot be performed by technology and automation. This can include tasks related to stakeholder management and advisory work, which typically involve substantial interpersonal interactions, or aspects such as valuation, which typically involves the application of professional accounting judgment. Accountants should focus their time and effort on these tasks while *stepping aside* to allow the technology to perform tasks that can be automated.
- Accountants can adopt the *step narrow* perspective to develop their careers in these niche areas, which are shielded from possible displacement due to the implementation of technology and automation. For example, mastering XBRL, a popular financial programming language, could help accountants develop a niche in the growing area of financial reporting.
- Technological advancements have enabled computers to play a growing role in accounting. Today, many tasks performed by accountants are aided by computers. To leverage the productivity gains offered by technological advances, accountants need to *step in* to work alongside such technology. Accountants can play a key role in facilitating the implementation of technology in accounting, thereby enhancing the efficiency of accounting processes in their organizations.
- Rapid technological advancements have created opportunities for accountants to develop new tools. Accountants who possess relevant knowledge can help the industry *step forward* by developing the next

generation of computing and automation tools that enable them to increase the value they bring to their organizations.

While the first three perspectives highlighted in the table (*step up*, *step aside*, and *step narrowly*) allow accountants to add value to their organizations amidst the introduction of technology and automation, they do not contribute directly to their organizations' digital transformation efforts because they do not require accountants to play a role in the implementation or adoption of technology.

In contrast, the next two perspectives highlighted in the table (i.e., *step in* and *step forward*) not only allow accountants to add value to their organizations amidst the introduction of technology and automation but also enable them to contribute to the digital transformation efforts of their organization by facilitating the adoption and implementation of technology and automation processes.

Accountants must also be cognizant of the potential risks that can arise from the implementation of *step-in* and *step-forward* strategies. One aspect that can derail an organization's digital transformation effects relates to the misalignment between an organization's business strategy and its digital transformation efforts. Managers must ensure that the organization's efforts to implement step-in and step-forward strategies are guided by its broader business strategy. Another aspect relates to cultural and behavioral factors that involve key organizational stakeholders. For example, while driving digital transformation via *step-in* and *step-forward* strategies can provide an organization with important insights that allow it to solve problems and make better decisions, the value of such insights can be blunted if organizational stakeholders are resistant to implementing them. Accordingly, organizations need to take steps to address this risk by clearly addressing the concerns that organizational stakeholders may have about their digital transformation efforts.

Overall, our discussion highlights that accountants should focus particularly on implementing step-in-and-step-forward strategies to drive digital transformation within their organizations, accountants should focus particularly on implementing *step-in* and *step-forward* strategies. In the following three sections, we discuss how accountants can effectively implement *step-in* and *step-forward* strategies in areas such as management reporting, continuous auditing, and forensic accounting.

Implementing the Step-in Strategy: Decision-Making in Management Accounting

Management accountants play a key role in supporting strategic decision-making within an organization. For instance, they are regularly asked to provide an analysis of alternative courses of action that managers contemplate in areas such as capital budgeting, outsourcing, product mix, and the addition or dropping of specific product lines. Such analysis frequently requires management accountants to recommend specific courses of action that an organization should adopt, which would lead to an optimal outcome (e.g., maximizing profits or minimizing costs) given a limited set of resources (e.g., limited production inputs such as labor, time, raw material, and capital). Such an analysis is also expected to be conducted under uncertain conditions, which can increase the difficulty associated with such an analysis.

To perform such an analysis appropriately, management accountants not only require broad knowledge of their organizations' activities but also an intimate understanding of how such activities interact with and relate to one another. However, as the operating environment of organizations around the world continues to grow in complexity and uncertainty, it is becoming particularly challenging for management accountants to provide accurate analysis that senior managers can rely on in decision-making.

In this regard, it is crucial that management accountants consider how they can adopt the *step-in* strategy of working with technological tools that can enhance their ability to perform the required analysis. Common analytical techniques that can be useful include optimization and simulation.

- Optimization: This is a mathematical technique that approaches problem-solving by seeking to mirror real-world business problems by representing unique business processes and problems in a computer model. An optimization model mathematically represents the following three aspects of a business problem:
  - Decision variable: the decisions that have to be made.
  - Constraints: the business rules that have to be adhered to.
  - Objectives: the business objectives that the decision maker hopes to achieve.

- Simulation: This is a mathematical technique that approaches problem-solving by performing a large number of trial runs (called simulations) and inferring a solution from the collective results of the trial runs. Simulation is a particularly useful tool for analyzing decision-making under conditions of uncertainty in a business situation because it explicitly incorporates uncertainty into the simulation model using random variables.

While management accountants typically possess expertise in their domain areas of business and accounting, they often lack the technological skills to *step in* to develop computer models that can aid them in decision-making. For example, to the extent that the optimization and simulation analytical techniques described above require extensive use of data and the development of sophisticated analytical models, management accountants would need to develop skillsets in database management and programming. To the extent that management accountants need to disseminate the results from these analyses to other senior managers within their organizations, they would need to develop skillsets in data visualization to more effectively present their findings.

However, given the rapidly changing business environment and the increasing availability of technology tools that can aid decision-making, it is important to ensure that management accountants seek to develop the relevant technology skills that can allow them to continue to add value to their organizations, thereby providing additional momentum to their organizations' digital transformation efforts.

Implementing the Step-in Strategy: Continuous Auditing

In recent years, rapid technological developments have dramatically changed business operations. One example of such a change can be seen in the widespread adoption of enterprise resource planning (ERP) systems, which enable a business to generate financial information in real time and allow different functional areas within the business to share data.

These developments present both challenges and opportunities to auditors. Broadly speaking, audit methods have not kept up with technological developments in the accounting sector. In particular, a significant proportion of audit procedures regularly employed in audit engagements today involve high degrees of manual work and are often costly in terms of both time and money. Many of these audit procedures also involve audit sampling, which refers to the application of audit procedures to less than 100% of items within a population of audit relevance, which can introduce sampling risk, where the auditor's conclusions based on a sample may be different from the conclusion if the entire population is the subject of the same audit procedure. In this regard, the International Standards on Auditing 530 highlight that sampling risk can lead to two types of erroneous conclusions (IFAC, 2009). First, the auditor may conclude that controls operate effectively when they are not. For example, the auditor may conclude that a material misstatement does not exist when it does. Such erroneous conclusions can lead to incorrect opinions being formed by an auditor. Second, the auditor may conclude that controls do not operate effectively. For example, an auditor may conclude that a material misstatement exists when it does not. Such erroneous conclusions can lead to additional work for auditors, which would otherwise be unnecessary.

In recent years, continuous audits have gained prominence in the audit industry as a concept that can improve the effectiveness and efficiency of audit processes via automation. According to the American Institute of Certified Public Accountants (AICPA) and Canadian Institute of Chartered Accountants (CICA), a continuous audit is "a methodology that enables independent auditors to provide written assurance on a subject matter for which an entity's management is responsible, using a series of auditors' reports issued virtually simultaneously with, or a short period of time after, the occurrence of events underlying the subject matter." Continuous auditing processes can drive digital transformation within an organization by introducing well-defined automated audit procedures that can run smoothly without any human intervention. According to the professional services firm PwC (2022), a continuous auditing program typically includes the following components:

- Continuous risk monitoring, including the monitoring of key performance indicators (KPIs).
- Continuous control monitoring.
- Continuous transaction or activity monitoring.
- Investigation of potentially inappropriate activities that have been detected.
- Continuous reporting to stakeholders.

In addition, employing continuous auditing processes involves the analysis of all transactions, as opposed to a sampling method, thus reducing the sampling risk in the audit.

Although the concept of a continuous audit was first introduced about 20 years ago and is not new, auditors have been largely prevented from effectively implementing such processes due to technological limitations. However, recent developments, including rapid advancements in information technology, the growth of big data, and the increasing adoption of ERP systems and data analytics by business, have prompted both internal and external auditors to seriously consider the potential for widespread implementation of continuous auditing processes within their organizations.

A recent article by Shilts (2017), published in the Journal of Accountancy, introduced an implementation plan that organizations can adopt in the implementation of continuous auditing. The implementation plan consisted of the following seven steps:

- Establish priority areas.
- Identify audit rules.
- Determine process frequency.
- Configure parameters and execute.
- Manage results and follow up.
- Report results.
- Assess emerging risk and add to register.

These seven steps introduce ample opportunities for auditors to implement the *step-in* strategy to work with technology to implement and execute continuous auditing procedures. For example, a report published by the professional services firm KPMG (2016) highlights that auditors' continuous auditing and data analytical procedures can be integrated via the macro-analytic, control, and transaction dimensions. First, the macro-analytic dimension provides a broad perspective for the effective analysis of business issues across organizations. Here, the auditor can employ relevant data analytical techniques to identify and recognize unusual trends, patterns, or results that may signal a larger macro-issue that deserves a closer look. To the extent that this can involve the extensive use of data and development of complex data models, auditors need to develop relevant skill sets in data management and data modeling. Second, the control dimension incorporates rules related to financial control management and segregation of duties. The auditor can implement technological tools that automate the implementation and enforcement of these rules. To the extent that this can involve the automation of predefined rules in the audit process, the auditor must develop relevant skills in areas such as robotic process automation (RPA) and programming. Third, the transaction dimension includes transaction-based exception analysis and business rule management. This dimension focuses on the effectiveness of the controls in place as well as identifying the control gaps that may be exploited. The auditor can apply relevant data analytics techniques to granular transaction data and account balances to monitor and test for exceptions in a continuous auditing environment. To the extent that it can involve constant monitoring of the continuous audit environment and the flagging of exceptions, the auditor needs to develop relevant skills in areas such as data visualization, which can facilitate this aspect of the task by clearly presenting the state of the continuous auditing environment.

Like all aspects of business, the audit function must constantly evolve and progress to keep up with the growing complexity of the business environment. Continuous audits represent a growing area that can potentially allow audits to leverage technology and automation to improve the effectiveness and efficiency of the auditing process. However, the successful implementation of continuous auditing hinges on auditors possessing relevant technology skillsets and being able to *step in* to work with the available technology to implement and execute continuous auditing processes and procedures.

Implementing the Step-Forward Strategy: Forensic Accounting

A recent report published by the Association of Certified Fraud Examiners highlights that fraud accounts for approximately US$6.3 billion in losses globally, with the typical firm losing up to 5% of its revenues to fraud annually. In addition, the 2018 Global Economic Crime and Fraud survey conducted by PwC (2018) across 123 territories finds that 49% of organizations have fallen victim to fraud and economic crime, with 64% of these organizations further estimating that their losses from such fraud could total US$1 million.

Given the growing risk of loss from fraud faced by organizations, there has been a focus on forensic accounting, which is a branch of accounting that focuses on the investigation of fraud or financial manipulation. In this regard, data analytics represents one of the most effective tools that organizations can leverage, as they redouble their efforts to combat fraud. In discussing how data analytics can be a valuable tool for forensic accountants in a recent commentary, Lawrence Lai and Sidarth Khashu from the accounting firm Ernst and Young suggest that data analytics can provide "insights that drive you to see what you would otherwise never expect to see. It helps organizations scan each data point within enormous data sets in an effective and efficient manner to generate meaningful information, which is easy to comprehend and valuable for decision-making." However, evidence suggests that there remains considerable scope to increase the extent to which they employ such tools. For example, the PwC survey reports that only 4% of companies' most disruptive fraud is detected using data analytics.

Data analytics involves the use of data, information technology, statistical analysis, quantitative models, and computer-based models to help organizations gain insights and make better fact-based decisions. When applied to the forensic accounting context, data analytics enables forensic investigators to more effectively comb voluminous datasets to identify anomalies or patterns that may be indicative of fraudulent activity. Beyond detecting fraudulent activity that has already occurred, data analytics can also identify red flags in areas where fraud has the potential to occur, thereby allowing organizations to take preventive measures to ensure that fraudulent activity does not take place. Accordingly, employing data analytics in forensic accounting can play a key role in fostering digital transformation within an organization.

A recent book titled Fraud Analytics by Spann (2014) highlights five common categories of analytical approaches that forensic investigators can employ to detect fraud. They include:

- Rule-based: Detection of fraud based on known behaviors or relationships. For example, this can involve looking at correlations between variables to examine their behavior.
- Anomaly detection: The identification of abnormal behavior in data that do not conform to "normal" behavior. For instance, Benford's law, which defines logical patterns in which digits occur in randomly generated numbers, is a commonly used technique to identify abnormal duplications of digits in a set of transactions.

- Predictive modeling: Statistical analysis of current and historical data to forecast future (fraudulent) behavior (using techniques such as regression analysis and time-series analysis).
- Neural networks: unsupervised learning based on historical data for identifying unknown patterns that may be indicative of fraud.
- Visual analytics: Graphical representation of relationships found within data to gain insights into possible fraudulent activities.

In this regard, there are opportunities for accountants to employ a *step-forward* strategy to develop the next generation of data analytical tools that enhance organizations' ability to detect fraud. For instance, accountants can develop neural networks that can effectively predict the occurrence of fraud. According to Investopedia, neural networks are a set of algorithms that seek to recognize underlying relationships within a dataset through a process that mimics the manner in which the human brain functions. Neural networks can dynamically adapt to changing inputs such that they can generate optimal results without the need for human intervention to redesign the output criteria. Neural networks can be deployed in a diverse range of settings, including financial operations, enterprise planning, trading, risk assessment, and fraud detection. With the technology underpinning neural networks predicted to improve significantly in the coming years, it is clear that the technology holds the potential to accurately predict and uncover fraud. Accordingly, it presents an opportunity for accountants who possess domain knowledge in forensic accounting to help their organizations *step forward* by leveraging neural networks to develop the next generation of analytical tools that their organizations can use to predict and detect fraud more reliably.

Another emerging area, where forensic accountants can employ a *step-forward* strategy with respect to fraud detection and prevention, relates to blockchain technology. Blockchain refers to a distributed database of records of all digital events (or transactions) that have been executed and shared among the participating parties (Gerrard & Ong, 2021). "Blocks" on the blockchain are made up of digital pieces of information, including transaction and participant details, which are recorded using a unique "digital signature."

Blockchain technology can play a critical role in resolving many of the challenges that organizations face with respect to fraud detection and prevention. For example, blockchain can provide a decentralized data repository that provides a complete view of an organization's underlying transaction history, thereby allowing forensic accountants to independently verify the integrity of specific aspects of the transactions (e.g., customer details), which can help detect and prevent fraud.

How Accountants Can Develop the Skillsets for Digital Transformation

Step-in strategies (such as continuous auditing) and step-forward strategies (such as forensic accounting and blockchain technology) represent exciting areas of growth for which accountants and auditors can innovate and harness these technologies in their workplaces. This is especially so if they need to execute these strategies to drive digital transformation in these areas.

To facilitate digital transformation in their organizations, accountants must acquire a set of digital skills to ensure digital literacy. In this regard, digital skills can be classified into two general categories: (1) digital skills that serve to inculcate a broad-based innovation mindset and a general sense of digital awareness ("tech basics" skills), and (2) digital skills that require a higher proficiency level of digital competency ("tech advanced" skills). These digital skills can be viewed as complementing the current skills that the accountant has already acquired in joining the profession. This is important because digital skills are not to be learned in isolation but rather to leverage what the accountant already possesses (e.g., auditing technical expertise, financial acumen, etc.).

The digital roadmap on training envisaged in the Accountancy Industry Digital Plan highlighted some examples of the various types of courses that an accounting professional can embark on his or her digitalization journey. For the "tech basics" courses, the emphasis is on giving accounting professionals an introduction to the various technologies available, and how these technologies might be implemented by the organization. These courses also explain the impact of these technologies on the accountants. With greater digital awareness, it becomes possible for accounting professionals to venture into the "tech advanced" courses. These courses differ from the "tech basics" courses in that they typically entail greater technical content and complexity. Some of these courses required programming skills. In addition, "tech advanced" courses tend to be of longer duration relative to the "tech basic" courses that are being offered (Fig. 7.2).

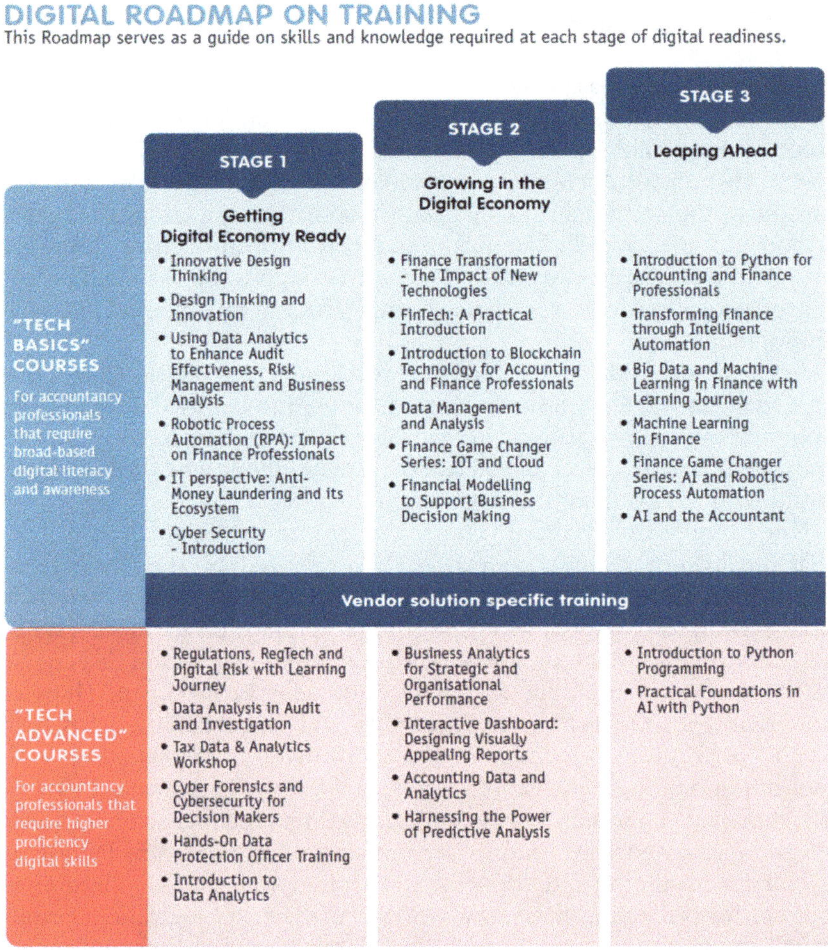

Fig. 7.2 Digital roadmap to build digital skills (*Source* Accountancy Industry Digital Plan, 2019)

To provide the relevant training courses, there are curated courses for each pathway that are developed by various universities and educational institutes or with an accountancy professional body (e.g., Institute of Singapore Chartered Accountants, n.d.). As an illustration, we examine one area of interest (e.g., artificial intelligence) and explore the various types of training courses that are available to build skills competency in this area.

Under the "tech basics" courses, an example of an artificial intelligence training course that is organized by the Institute of Singapore Chartered Accountants would be an introductory AI course ("IT072: Introduction to Python for Accounting and Finance Professionals"). This course introduces the accountant to Python, a popular programming language. Python is a user-friendly language taught as an introductory computer science course that is powerful and flexible enough to be used in a variety of professional settings (e.g., data science, artificial intelligence, and web development).

As the course is delivered in a context relevant to professional accountants, trainees will learn how Python can be used to consolidate data from reports of varying templates. They will also be shown how to compare and contrast the use of Excel spreadsheets versus Python, when to use each, and how to complement one another.

Under the "tech advanced" courses, a comparative example of an artificial intelligence training course that is organized by the Institute of Singapore Chartered Accountants would be an AI course ("DGT043: Basic Python for Financial Modelling") that requires programming skills.

Unlike the introductory course, the training participants in this course will be immersed in an Integrated Development Environment (Jupyter Notebook for Python) to manage code and share results. They will have to perform financial calculations with variables and operations with booleans and strings, and store, access, and manipulate financial data in lists, dictionaries and sets, and wrangle data using functions, control flows, and the Numpy package. NumPy, which stands for Numerical Python, is a library consisting of multidimensional array objects and a collection of routines for processing these arrays. Mathematical and logical operations on the arrays can be performed using NumPy. As a real-life simulation exercise, training participants will also perform a case study involving financial analysis by calculating and comparing the price-earnings ratios of S&P companies.

If the accountant wishes to venture further into this field, there are professional certificates through which they can acquire further skills and knowledge and become an associate AI Engineer. In this instance, the accountant must demonstrate programming proficiency in four ways: code readability, code reusability, self-explanatory code, and exception handling.

Code readability means that the coding is organized in a clean and readable format. It is also important that the code layout style, such as indentation and maximum line length, be consistent with industry conventions such as PEP8. Code reusability implies that the accountant can code in a manner that minimizes repeated code (e.g., using functions). The coding should also be prepared in such a manner that it is self-explanatory for another user. This is achieved through the proper naming of conventions for variables, functions, and classes. It also includes documentation with online comments in the source code, and the intent of Functions and Classes is clearly stated. Finally, there should be a demonstration of the competency in exception handling. This skillset allows a good programmer to include codes to catch and handle exceptions, such as insufficient data, empty datasets, or incorrect data types.

Apart from training to develop useful digital skill sets, it is also imperative that accountants remain cognizant of the role of the accounting profession in an organization and their key contributions. While technical skills are important in digital transformation, it is vital that accountants are aware of and able to add value by understanding the connections between their business operations and strategic priorities. To that extent, other skills (e.g., soft skills such as communication and collaboration, business knowledge, and acumen) should also not be neglected, as these non-technical skills play a role in accounting professionals' effective performance of various functions.

Conclusion

Digital transformation journeys impact both the organization and people in the organization. Properly executed digital transformation initiatives can lead to a stronger and more resilient organization. To achieve this, it is important for the organization to carefully consider how best to leverage its workforce (e.g., step-in, step-up, step aside, step narrowly, or step-forward strategies) with respect to the types of digital transformation processes that management is planning to execute. With the digital transformation strategies put in place by the organization, it is also vital for individuals to consider how they can respond and prepare themselves to acquire various digital skills to support these digital transformation initiatives.

Accountants should also be mindful of the potential opportunities and limitations related to these technologies. While a data scientist will be keen to utilize cutting-edge technologies or to accumulate large amounts of data to make inferences and employ various analytics to detect patterns or relationships in their data sets, the accountant's competitive advantage is to utilize their financial knowledge and analytical mindset to consider how these technologies can significantly improve their organizational capabilities. In that context, cost–benefit exercises that are conducted prior to the implementation of new technologies can also help the organization articulate the potential risks and rewards of bringing these digital solutions on board to drive cost efficiencies or to achieve better financial insights regarding their operations.

References

Accountancy Industry Digital Plan. (2019). https://www.sac.gov.sg/corporate-support/accountancy-industry-digital-plan

AEcensus. (2021). https://www.sac.gov.sg/accounting-entity-surveys

Davenport, T., & Kirby, J. (2015, June). Beyond automation. *Harvard Business Review, 93*, 58–65.

Gerrard, A., & Ong, J. (2021). How blockchain can enable digital transformation in financial services. In P. S. Seow, C. Goh, G. Pan, M. Yong, & J. Chek (Eds.), *Embracing digital transformation in accounting & finance* (pp. 47–59). https://www.cpaaustralia.com.au/-/media/project/cpa/corporate/documents/tools-and-resources/business-management/embracing-digital-transformation-in-accounting-report.pdf?rev=79569e37637e4576b7ed49e0dcd5cf75

International Federation of Accountants (IFAC). (2009). *International standard of auditing 530*. https://www.ifac.org/system/files/downloads/a027-2010-iaasb-handbook-isa-530.pdf

Institute of Singapore Chartered Accountants. (n.d.). *Full course listing*. https://isca.org.sg/learn-connect/cpe-courses

KPMG. (2016). *Leveraging data analytics and continuous auditing processes for improved audit planning, effectiveness, and efficiency*. https://assets.kpmg/content/dam/kpmg/pdf/2016/05/Leveraging-Data-Analytics.pdf

PwC. (2018). *PwC global economic crime and fraud survey 2018*. https://isca.org.sg/media/2240376/gecs-2018-slide-presentation.pdf

PwC. (2022). *Continuous auditing and monitoring*. https://www.pwc.com/vn/en/services/consulting/continuous-audit-monitoring.html

Shilts, J. (2017). A framework for continuous auditing: Why companies don't need to spend big money. *Journal of Accountancy*. https://www.journalofaccountancy.com/issues/2017/mar/continuous-auditing.html

Spann, D. (2014). *Fraud analytics*. Wiley.

CHAPTER 8

The Role of Artificial Intelligence in Management Accounting: An Exploratory Case Study

Silvana Secinaro, Davide Calandra, Federico Lanzalonga, and Paolo Biancone

Introduction

Artificial intelligence (AI) has increased innovative pressure in several areas (Coles, 1977; Dal Mas et al., 2019). Accounting is no exception and has witnessed numerous disruptions in recent years. Today, technology can solve old problems by supporting activities in the accounting processes

S. Secinaro · D. Calandra (✉) · F. Lanzalonga · P. Biancone
Department of Management "Valter Cantino", University of Turin, Turin, Italy
e-mail: davide.calandra@unito.it

S. Secinaro
e-mail: silvana.secinaro@unito.it

F. Lanzalonga
e-mail: federico.lanzalonga@unito.it

P. Biancone
e-mail: paolo.biancone@unito.it

A. Perdana and T. Wang (eds.), *Digital Transformation in Accounting and Auditing*, https://doi.org/10.1007/978-3-031-46209-2_8

(Baldwin et al., 2006). AI can automate the most repetitive accounting tasks while avoiding human errors by reducing the cost of individual transactions (Kolbjørnsrud et al., 2016). In addition, AI can perform repetitive operations by fully managing the entire process of daily and continuous item accounting and illustrating an economic, patrimonial, and financial situation to stakeholders (Shahsahebi et al., 2020). Because intelligent algorithms still underlie ex-ante human control, this reduces the cost of processing repetitive tasks by allowing accountants and bookkeepers to perform other higher value-added tasks (Faccia et al., 2019). For example, less time from day-to-day bookkeeping can be spent on consulting or management control activities critical to business variables. Makridakis (2017) described the AI-appropriate challenges faced in the future. On the one hand, the author considers exploiting the advantages of using AI; on the other hand, AI will reduce its effect on unemployment and, more specifically, inequalities.

Scientific literature is launching an interesting debate in this area to investigate the impact and implications of AI on accounting activities. However, starting from this strand of the literature, several authors have called for further research. For example, Sutton et al. (2016) call for further studies to understand the relationship between technology and accounting. The results of Moll and Yigitbasioglu (2019) are critical for researchers admitting a gap in research concerning technologies and their daily use by accountants. Therefore, the same authors called for new research to determine new capabilities, activities, and skills that can add value to the role of accountants. Finally, even the primary findings in the literature of Bakarich and O'Brien (2020) demonstrate a developing area of research with non-extensive use by accountants that requires further investigation.

In this vibrant, interdisciplinary context (Li et al., 2021), research has focused on the capabilities of emerging technologies, rather than the impact of AI on social change dictated by this disruptive technology (Bonsón et al., 2021; Di Vaio et al., 2022). Although some studies have focused on the extent to which AI can replace humans or its possible impact on economic growth (Haefner et al., 2021; Kopka & Grashof, 2021), less emphasis has been placed on the evolving capabilities of practitioners. Thus, while it appears clear that entrepreneurs choose to take advantage of AI investment opportunities in countries with stable economic governance that provide high standards of education, health, social capital, and a safe natural environment (Jabeur et al., 2022), there is no equal evidence regarding the role of accountants. This is also claimed by Sutton et al. (2016), who call for more research on the usability and general use of artificial intelligence techniques in accounting.

Based on these premises, we investigate a case study to understand how AI may affect management accounting using the theoretical lens of contingency theory (Cunningham & Kwakkel, 2011). According to a traditional interpretation, contingency theory considers contextual factors that influence the administrative control of accounting systems (Hayes, 1977). This approach clarifies the technological implications of management accounting, leaving room for technological and social factors (Bruun et al., 2002; Tortorella et al., 2020). Considering AI as a disruptive technology exogenous to the management accounting context, the phenomena appear suitable for observation through the theoretical lens of contingency theory (Fisher, 1995). Our analysis uses two well-established traditional management accounting models. It exploits Kaplan and Norton's (1992) model to identify business areas in which the effect of introducing AI can be observed in accounting processes. On the other hand, it bases the consequences of disruptive technological introduction on three traditional planes of management accounting: controlling, assessment, and planning (Cokins, 2001). Accordingly, the authors identified the following research question:

RQ: How can artificial intelligence affect management accounting?

Employing a rigorous qualitative research method (Yin, 2009), we conducted seven interviews with business managers and experts in AI (Biancone et al., 2021). This case study relates to an innovative startup formed in 2019 with a vision to automate current accounting and payment operations.

Our study presents substantial theoretical and practical implications. This research adds value and confirms the results of Gulin et al. (2019), showing how AI can add value to accounting. We also confirm Drum and Pulvermacher's (2016) theory of accounting accuracy. From a theoretical perspective and considering the case study, we argue that AI will not altogether remove accountants, but will provide opportunities to act more quickly and efficiently (Azudin & Mansor, 2018; Bhattacharya, 2018).

Finally, this study uses the theoretical lens of contingency theory to investigate the new role of accountants. Because technology, culture, and the external environment are influential in changing organizations, this approach has interesting implications related to the changing responsibilities of the accountant to be elaborated (Islam & Hu, 2012). Thus, this chapter extends the scope of application of the theory to AI, highlighting efficient routine practices and reducing the risk of human error, resulting in more time being spent on value-added activities (Chukwudi et al., 2018; Gotthardt et al., 2019). This represents a societal shift in the role of accountants and their relationship with firm managers. From a practical point of view, our contribution focuses on accountants, corporate accountants, and managers. The investigation shows that AI is a new paradigm that allows automation and, at the same time, rethinking their business models. On the one hand, accountants run external software, incurring additional costs. However, they have the possibility of filling in daily accounting ledgers. Indeed, a change will occur as a direct consequence of this development, reducing the accountant's marginality in day-to-day operations and encouraging new activities such as auditing and management control, which will require new skills.

The remainder of this paper is organized as follows. Section "Literature Review and Case Study Description" presents a literature review, considering management accounting theory and business models for accountants. Section "Methodology" focuses on the methods adopted by researchers. Section "Findings" will show the results of the analysis. Section Discussion will discuss our results by drawing inspiration from the theoretical background. Finally, section "Conclusion" will conclude the study.

Literature Review and Case Study Description

Artificial Intelligence and Management Accounting

Although several authors have defined management accounting, it seems difficult to accept unified theorization. According to Lavia López and Hiebl (2015), this concept summarizes various practices used by managers to meet their information needs. From a modern perspective, management accounting techniques involve budgeting, performance and cost evaluation, communication, and strategic analysis (Chand & Dahiya, 2010). However, it has been conceived as a valuable tool for managers to plan, control, and improve the company (see Howorth & Westhead, 2003). One forecast argues that the introduction of automation will increase the value of services rather than decrease it (Gulin et al., 2019). Thus, essential accountant services will be provided even more efficiently and will save time invested in future customer demand (Gulin et al., 2019). According to the authors, software development and technologies such as clouds, AI, and blockchain will enhance the role of accountants and the entire financial sector by reducing manual data entry and improving data speed, quality, and accuracy. Decentralization resulting from new technologies provides companies with a continuous flow of information, allowing for increased transparency and trust among stakeholders (Secinaro et al., 2021). Furthermore, it is well recognized that the spreadsheets currently used tend to favor uncertainty owing to the involvement of manual processes and the introduction of a high potential for errors and outdated data (Drum & Pulvermacher, 2016). From the perspective of accounting process automation, new technologies will enable rethinking the role of intermediation (Cong & Klotz, 2018), and accountants will be required to develop critical thinking and problem-solving, a high level of adaptability, flexibility, and interpersonal interaction (David, 2015; Marcello et al., 2017).

Nevertheless, Schrage (2017) identified four paths through which AI can participate in the business decision-making process: (i) autonomous consultants, where AI algorithms are seen as the best strategic consultants; (ii) autonomous outsourcers, owners determine the allocation of resources and whether automation should lead to more significant innovation and optimization; (iii) challenging autonomy employees, intelligent software is integrated into the company, allowing them to train through the best algorithms effectively; and (iv) all autonomously, organizations are fully committed to letting algorithmic automation lead the company to innovations.

According to Cokins (2001), managerial accounting can be divided into two sections: cost measurement and cost use (Fig. 8.1). AI can potentially affect each of the processes constituting the entire process.

Several researchers have addressed the impact of disruptive technologies on cost measurements (e.g., Chen et al., 2022; Yu, 2019). In particular, the role of artificial intelligence in cost measurements related to virtuous business paradigms such as the circular economy has been explored (Chen et al., 2022). In addition, blockchain applications represent an improvement in the quality of data collection in cost measurements (Yu, 2019).

The effects of introducing AI on the cost-use side were less intense. Although it is not clear whether digitization and automation can be useful tools for control, assessment, and planning (Moudud-Ul-Huq, 2014;

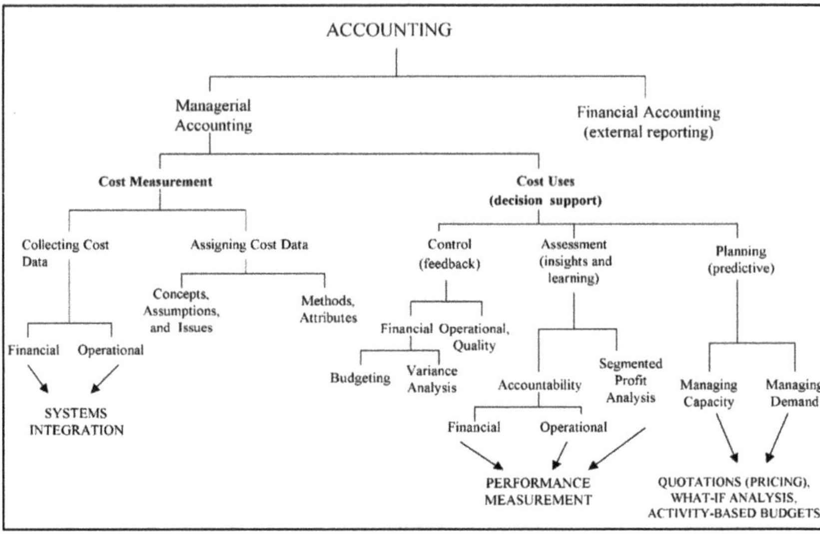

Fig. 8.1 Managerial accounting framework (Based on Cokins [2001])

Rikhardsson & Yigitbasioglu, 2018), the introduction of these technologies in accounting cannot replace the central role of the manager. The application of AI can eliminate or reduce routine and repetitive activities (Herbert et al., 2016), it cannot replace the accountant in interpreting and analyzing information at this stage (Plastino & Purdy, 2018). AI can change financial institutions' management through cost savings and operational efficiency (Chukwudi et al., 2018). However, the technological transformation of accounting is inevitable. In this sense, business intelligence tools that leverage big data technology and artificial intelligence can help improve the quality and depth of financial analysis (Sun et al., 2018). Therefore, the application of AI can improve conditions from both qualitative and quantitative points of view by allowing accountants better access to information almost in real time and enabling them to obtain information from a more significant number of sources (Tredinnick, 2017). However, human skills must be applied to make decisions that require judgment (Gotthardt et al., 2019; Noriega, 2020).

In the assessment field, Gulin et al. (2019) identified areas of digitization and automation applications, such as AI, Blockchain, continuous accounting, and Big Data. For example, continuous accounting is a decline in this technological innovation that no longer aims at a periodic analysis of financial information but offers the possibility of providing new information daily (Gao & Jiang, 2020; Schmitz & Leoni, 2019). Technological developments that can lead to accountability have also been explored (Vărzaru, 2022). To date, state-of-the-art methods appear to be less significant for understanding the accountant's role in overseeing the process.

Finally, planning benefits from disruptive technologies as it enables more qualitative data processing and frees the manager from computation time (Corazza & Zanin, 2020). Although it appears inevitable that AI will have a significant impact on professional jobs, we have not yet reached a stage where the deployment of this technology can compromise it (Azudin & Mansor, 2018; Gurstein, 1985). Currently, implementing this feature reproduces existing functions; therefore, the entire transformative process begins when AI starts to alter the business environment within which it is applied (Plastino & Purdy, 2018). Thus far, the literature has focused on how AI within management accounting can be implemented or what role an accountant can play in the transformation process.

Theoretical Framework

Modern definitions of managerial accounting offered on the topic result from the evolution of this concept over time. In the 1990s, the debate on management accounting focused on planning, controlling, and reducing waste to include a more strategic understanding of value creation. This stage is characterized by the introduction of new accounting techniques, such as the balanced scorecard (Kaplan & Norton, 1992) and strategic management accounting systems capable of providing information and forecasts on strategic uncertainty (Simons, 1991). During the 1980s, interest centered on reducing waste in business processes due to the increasing implementation of quality management programs and the introduction of new cost allocation systems. Previously, the spotlight was on planning and management control, namely, the process used to ensure effective and efficient use in achieving objectives (Anthony, 1965). At the same time, several authors (Gordon & Miller, 1976; Hayes, 1977) have emphasized the value of Contingency Theory in establishing that contextual factors could affect the administrative control of accounting information systems and other supervisory mechanics.

Consequently, this assumes that organizational structure is not universally applicable since effectiveness depends on adaptation to contingent forces. The introduction of contingent elements marked a break from the previous activities. Thus, until the twentieth century, activities focused on costing and financial control through budgeting and cost accounting systems (Ittner & Larcker, 2001). Contingency theory allows us to consider the implications of technology on management accounting. Fisher (1995) suggested contingent factors, among which are the external environment, technology, competitive strategy and mission, the characteristics of the business unit and industry, and knowledge and observability factors. Specifically, for the paper's aim, technology is considered that improves performance. Integrating innovative activity translates into introducing new processes (Frishammar & Åke Hörte, 2005).

Based on these assumptions, AI affects the managerial accounting dimension linked to the traditional control, assessment, and planning components of cost use to support managers in decision-making (Cokins, 2001) (Fig. 8.2).

Concerning control, two determinant dimensions were noted: financial and operational. This section considers how AI can improve and simplify the depth of financial analysis (Friedlob & Schleifer, 2003). Assessment is evaluated in the dimension of accountability to assess how transparency in the accounting registration process changes (Mattli & Büthe, 2005).

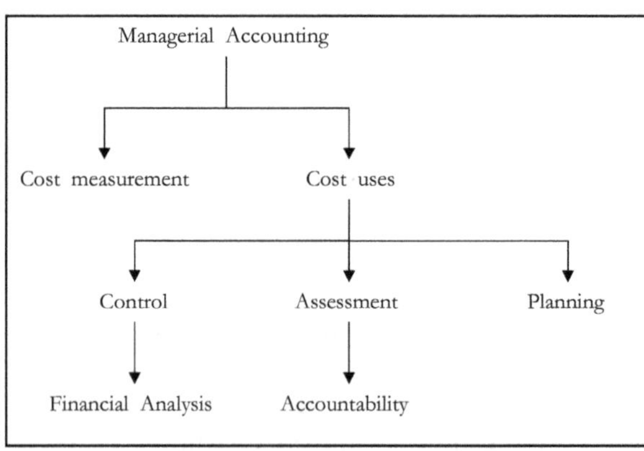

Fig. 8.2 The research framework (Based on Authors' elaboration on Cokins [2001])

Table 8.1 Assessment areas under observation

Focus area	*Elements under observation*	*Source*
Financial area	Efficiency	Chukwudi et al. (2018)
Customer area	Accountability (Transparency)	Secinaro et al. (2021)
Operations area	Routine operations	Drum and Pulvermacher (2016)
Organizational area	Accountant's responsibility	Plastino and Purdy (2018)

Source Authors

The assessment dimension was further explored using a balanced scorecard framework. In the present context, the areas already identified by Kaplan and Norton (1992) in implementing the balanced scorecard can be used to assess the effects of AI on organizational behaviors. Therefore, this study aimed to evaluate the effects of introducing AI in accounting. Thus, the amount will be measured (i) from a financial point of view by assessing the impact on cost efficiency, (ii) from the customers' perspective through transparency, (iii) from the angle of internal processes through the reduction of routine operations, and (iv) from the organizational capacity viewpoint by considering the changes in the accountant's responsibility (Table 8.1). Finally, the framework considers the effects of AI on planning and how the role of the accountant may be changed by the introduction of AI (Frezatti et al., 2011).

Case Study Description

This study explores the impact of AI in management accounting and assesses contingency theory in the context of a case study. According to Yin (2009), a case study is an empirical investigation that allows the analysis of a contemporary phenomenon in which theory and researchers do not yet have complete control. Furthermore, according to Vaivio (2008), qualitative methods and field research allow for theory development and practicality by providing scientific evidence. Therefore, considering the primary basis of our article, the case study method is appropriate for exploring management accounting and contingency theory in a specific research context characterized by new technologies such as AI (Carbonell et al., 2016; Kokina & Davenport, 2017; Zemánková, 2019).

To conduct this research, the authors initiated a specific analysis of the Italian market for AI applications in management accounting. The adopted approach enabled the selection of BookForAccounting (a fictitious name to ensure anonymity), a European company based in Italy that provides a decentralized accounting protocol. The company was founded in 2019 and was positioned as one of the first companies to apply AI to accounting. The company's roots originate from two practical market problems: the need for transparency in accounting numbers and repetitive requirements that force accounting human resources to focus on low value-added activities.

The company's mission is to automate accounting processes, payments, and creation of accounting documents by translating human rules of practice into algorithms. The underlying logic of entrepreneurial projects is to alleviate some of the repetitive operations of the accounting profession by prioritizing management control activities.

Today, the company provides advanced software solutions based on AI to small and medium enterprises and accountants applying a diversified business model. In the first years of activity, the company developed a strong knowledge of accounting rules in Italy, translating human know-how in the accounting field into machine learning models and creating algorithms based on past behavior patterns. The company's vision is to provide stakeholders with up-to-date numbers of automated accounting operations. The firm, continuing its research and development efforts, has recently integrated treasury management, providing accountant-client and real-time financial reconciliation, and planning tools. Approximately a year ago, the company obtained a license for automated bank reconciliation.

Undoubtedly, the features described here introduce disruptive elements within management accounting and contingency theory, including the decentralization of activities with the concept of trust, reduction of costs for performing manual actions, and the removal of the risk of repetitive human activities by promoting accountants' modification of their core activities.

Based on the characteristics described above, the authors claim that BookForAccounting is a unique case study that can meet the research hypothesis we formulated. Indeed, it is possible to discern individual elements in this company and detect changes in management accounting (Lamberton, 2000; Yin, 2004).

Methodology

Considering the literature gap and theoretical framework, the authors employ a qualitative and exploratory approach to investigate a single case to examine the effects of AI on management accounting (Yin, 2009). Qualitative management research allows researchers to capture several intangible factors that create value in the literature (Gummesson, 2006). According to Cascante et al. (2022), the research is structured into four phases to ensure the reliability of the results. In the first phase, the research design and research question are defined based on a literature review (Eisenhardt, 1989; Massaro et al., 2020). A transparent and rigorous process was used in the second stage to determine the case study selection methods (Massaro et al., 2019). Notably, the authors set up a specific analysis of AI applications in management accounting in Italy. The selection process was developed using AIDA, a database that collects financial information on Italian companies (Lotti & Marin, 2013). The snowball sampling technique was employed for case study selection. According to Noy (2008), this technique allows researchers to access information through the contact inputs provided by other informants.

Furthermore, the snowball effect allows unknown cases to be searched for through auxiliary and informal systems (Hendriks et al., 1992). The third phase involved collecting primary data and conducting semi-structured interviews with company management and five independent experts (Meng et al., 2019). Finally, the authors analyzed the data in an iterative cycle of inductive reasoning through an inductive research approach known as the Gioia methodology (Gioia et al., 2013). This technique allows us to explain the phenomena of interest by identifying relevant connections between information flows and theory (Fig. 8.3).

Data Collection and Analysis

As Yin (2009) suggested, the authors used multiple sources to construct a holistic case study by implementing data triangulation. To explore the phenomenon comprehensively, the authors used the company's website, the published white paper, interviews with the company's Chief Executive Officer (CEO) and Chief Technology Officer (CTO), and the viewing of multiple videos in which the business group presented their business ideas to customers. The researchers analyzed all qualitative data collected using ATLAS.TI version 9 software to ensure transparency and reliability among

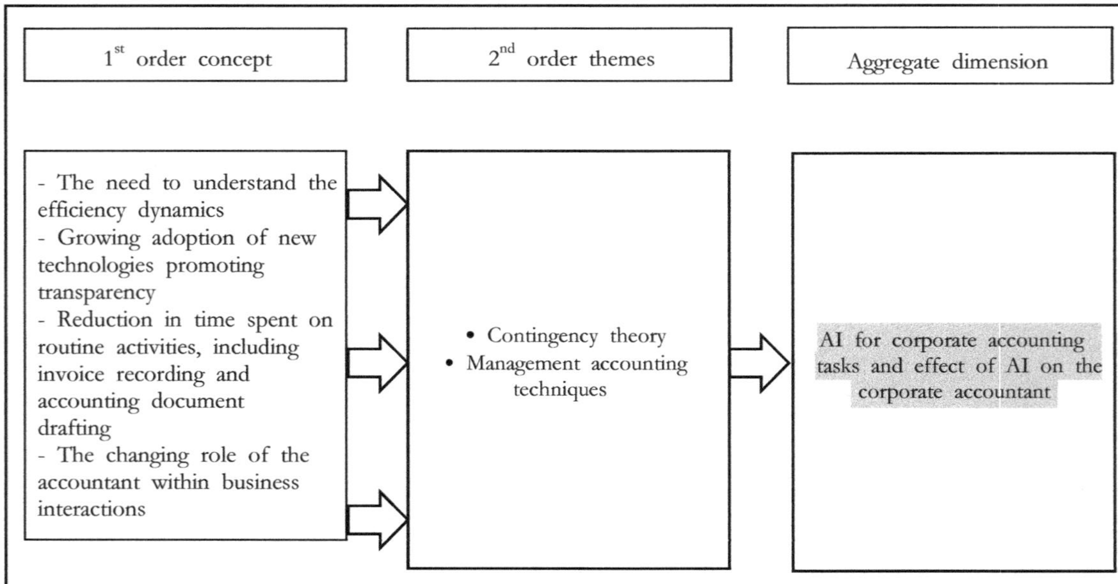

Fig. 8.3 Summary of the analysis (Modified from Gioia et al. [2013])

Table 8.2 Data used in the analysis

Data	*Description*
Internal documents	Company's white paper
Interviews of the founders	Interviews with CEO and CTO
Other publicly available interviews	Five interviews with experts in the field of Artificial Intelligence discussing the company

Source Authors' elaboration

the group of authors (Hwang, 2008). The results were obtained through interviews with five independent experts in AI and accounting (Biancone et al., 2021) (Table 8.2).

Data collection for the present research follows a protocol of source triangulation that provides observations of the phenomenon from different points of view (Flick, 1998). In traditional qualitative research, source identification through this method allows data from different sources at different times, in different places, or from different people to be combined, and the subjective influences of individuals to be balanced (Flick, 2004). In addition to the interviews conducted with the CEO and corporate CTO, the present study takes advantage of the validation of five experts from outside the facility to ensure the veracity of the information. All interviews were conducted in a virtual room using Webex software, and the composition of the minutes was subsequently analyzed as described above (Smith et al., 1994). The interviews lasted two hours for the CTO and one-and-a-half hours for the CEO (Table 8.3). The authors conducted the remaining interviews in parallel to implement and validate the results obtained, with a total duration of 6 hours and 15 minutes (Balasubramanian et al., 2021). The company's website and whitepaper were used as official sources of communication to combine the methods within a single research approach (Blaikie, 1991). Specifically, the authors used the website to look at examples of the implementation of the system implemented by the company and the section of the whitepaper on business development related to planned further developments.

Table 8.3 Interview duration

Case study	*Number of interviews*	*Duration*
1. BookForAccounting	2 (CTO and CEO)	1 hours and 30 minutes
2. Expert in the field	5	6 hours and 15 minutes

Source Author's elaboration

FINDINGS

The following section identifies and illustrates the results of this analysis. The first block describes the accounting process implemented by BookForAccounting. The second section presents how the BookForAccounting case study provides new factors and perspectives on process automation. The last section analyzes the new role of the accountant and the emerging responsibility. This section considers the aggregate size of the results, as discussed in the previous section.

AI Effect on Corporate Accounting Tasks

Several authors have highlighted saving resources as the main effect of introducing AI in management accounting (Chukwudi et al., 2018). According to Plastino and Purdy (2018), the automation of accounting processes reduces time commitment. Furthermore, the literature argues that introducing AI will also lead to cost savings (Kolbjørnsrud et al., 2016). Moreover, the current manual approach comprises numerous activities that make it prone to human error and can lead to complex judgments (Gotthardt et al., 2019).

BookForAccounting operates to fit the manual accounting process through the introduction of AI, specifically Optical Character Recognition (OCR) technology. Therefore, the software will be able to automatically detect and read invoices, and store and archive them by the due date through learning over time. Practically speaking, users can scan financial records, save time (an estimated 72%), and eliminate the possibility of human error. Subsequently, a machine learning system called Intelligent Document Recognition (IDR) identifies the metadata that qualifies a document as a purchase, supplier, seller, etc. Specifically, the CTO shared the effect of technology on the accounting process:

A business owner can simply scan invoices, receipts, and other financial documents to have the documents automatically entered into the bookkeeping software, saving the user hours performing data entry tasks.

However, the service can be categorized into four sections: (1) automated identification of relevant data from accounting documents, (2) generation of information about financial and economic events from account records, (3) customer support, and (4) analysis of financial and economic data. To reduce the total operational risk of human error, the first step involves the application of text analysis (Semantic Engine) assisted by machine learning models, such as Convolutional Neural Networks (CNN), together with the Layout Engine, allowing the recognition of accounting documents. Regarding the second point, the aim is to provide a record from the accounts of financial/economic events. Specifically, it will apply the categorization of costs and revenues in the accounts identified under the current regulations, open credit or debit notes from the customer or supplier, adjust the entries of accruals and deferrals, and categorize VAT according to the regulations and any other necessary activity. The third aspect of the AI system is to identify user problems that occur to find automated solutions without the assistance of Customer Care. This will be possible through a machine learning-based mechanism that can provide resolutions depending on the experiences provided by Customer Care. Finally, the last application is the most challenging and is intended to structure algorithms that study a company's patterns and habits. Therefore, costs, invoices, payment times, purchase preferences, and other actions may belong to this field. The output of this application includes various functions such as predictive analysis and indicators useful to the company to improve supplies and optimal markets for business growth.

As a result of what has just been described, it is clear that automation will allow the disintermediation of the accountant's role in promoting transparency and accessibility to information. Indeed, BookForAccounting applications take advantage of the technology in the market to validate accounts using the highest possible level of automation. Therefore, the company's purpose is readable on white paper.

BookForAccounting is a next-generation accounting protocol that provides transparency, accountability and bookkeeping services to cryptocurrency and traditional businesses.

AI Effect on the Corporate Accountant

The traditional accountant's role does not apply to new conditions, and the practitioner is expected to find new responsibilities. The reason for this is the replacement of manual data processing by automation, making the function a disintermediated process. The aforementioned represents a real paradigm shift in terms of achieving transparency, which becomes feasible as human involvement is minimized. Moreover, the booking mechanism intended by BookForAccounting avoids alterations in recurring statements, allowing stakeholders to inquire efficiently about the company's financial situation.

On the topic, the company's CTO stated:

> *BookForAccounting is the new standard for financial integrity, promoting continuity and accountability using blockchain technology. BookForAccounting is a universal protocol that allows transaction rules and all payments to be recorded, all written within the blockchain. The service offered to the end-user will be a multi-functional dashboard that includes reviewing detailed business financial records. Book for Accounting integrates accounting, payments, and a corporate wallet for traditional and blockchain companies.*

Indeed, this is possible because blockchain technology allows companies to securely store financial statement information on a decentralized ledger. Accessibility ensures that a trustless mechanism is established that provides the highest levels of transparency.

For example, Company A may wish to examine Company B. Traditionally, Company B employed an accounting firm to track expenses, budgets, and generate reports. If A were interested in investigating B, after it was granted, it would be possible to view the financial records and perform analysis and evaluation. The first problem A might run into is that the data format cannot match its own. Furthermore, A would be forced to depend on the accuracy and reliability of Company B's accountants. This lack of uniformity and consistency is an obstacle. The development of blockchain in bookkeeping is a solution for the accounting world to achieve decentralized accounting.

Hence, BookForAccounting can change its business model by relying on new technologies such as AI. Rather than spending time in the recording process, the new model will involve the accountant as the guarantor of success. According to the company's CEO,

> *When discussing accounts, it is necessary to remember that it is a process that cannot always be standardized and involves thousands of different records and a wide range of rules. For this reason, BookForAccounting is designed to include various types of users in the process to guarantee the quality of service while gradually reducing the need for human intervention.*

Therefore, it considers three types of users who will have their place in the accounting process of firms that use BookForAccounting applications. First, the non-qualified user is able to validate and integrate the metadata identified by the Optical Reader. Second, a qualified accountant can validate and integrate the information generated by the AI system. Finally, the accountant will be able to use the results of the process to analyze and assess performance indicators, providing the client with a customized consulting service.

Thus, according to the literature review, it is possible to assert that BookForAccounting introduced a new Business Model built on AI, which can affect time, human error, and transparency. The results and answers to the RQ will be deepened in the following section.

Discussion

This case study illustrates how the impact of AI within a traditional accounting system can be evaluated in different dimensions. In particular, the study allows us to observe evidence from a control, assessment, and planning perspective, as declined within the business dimensions were evaluated concerning the areas identified by Kaplan and Norton's management system (1992). First, the impact was evaluated regarding financial costs. Second, the effect on accountability transparency was measured within the customer area. Human error was also considered as an element under observation inside the operation area. Finally, the influence of AI deployment on the role of accountants was observed (Table 8.4).

BookForAccounting showed that the implementation of AI increases the value of the service rather than decreasing it (Campo Gulin et al., 2019) and allows for the development of additional features. Moreover, according to Moudud-Ul-Huq (2014), automation can be useful in strategic evaluations related to accounting; however, the impact in this area is not only associated with the implementation of algorithms. The decreased cost and time spent produce greater efficiency (Chukwudi et al.,

Table 8.4 Finding evidence for discussion

Focus area	*Elements under observation*	*Results*	*Source*	*Support statements*
Financial area	Efficiency	Decreasing in terms of time and cost	White Paper	Time dedicated to the administrative aspects of business represents an unnecessary cost for the company that can today be significantly reduced by applying relevant technology such as OCR, AI, and blockchain
			CTO interview	BookForAccounting will help them save over 70% of their accounting time and costs compared to traditional software
Customer area	Accountability (transparency)	Disintermediation	White Paper	AI-based information tagging of transactions for accountancy purposes as well as OCR-technology for invoice/receipt scanning are applied for maximum transparency while minimizing the time spent for bookkeeping
			Interviews with five experts	No intermediaries provide real-time transparency that is lacking in traditional business, allowing traditional companies to access peer-to-peer financing in the future, which is typical of the blockchain environment
Operations area	Routine operations	Reduction of risk for human error	White paper	BookForAccounting aims to help reduce the total operational risk of human error

(continued)

Table 8.4 (continued)

Focus area	*Elements under observation*	*Results*	*Source*	*Support statements*
			CEO Interview	The user can leverage artificial intelligence to make sure that the data extracted in an automated manner is accurate, thus reducing routine operations
Organizational area	Accountant's responsibility	Increase time for strategic activities	Interviews with five experts	The time saved by accountants in the process of bookkeeping can be spent on analyzing the performance of the company. Therefore, strategic business activity can be implemented
			CTO Interview	The deployment of artificial intelligence is not aimed at replacing human work. Depending on their qualifications, each accountant will be able to validate and integrate the metadata or information generated by the BookForAccounting system

Source Authors' elaboration

2018). Therefore, the results extend the validity of the efficiency of AI technology in accounting and management accounting.

As argued by Herbert et al. (2016), AI can reduce or eliminate routine tasks. The findings section revealed an impact on efficiency, measured by the time saved in using AI over traditional management systems. This is one of two elements already recognized in the literature that identifies time and cost as involved in the change, which AI will positively affect in a positive way (Kolbjørnsrud et al., 2016), as confirmed by the results.

The present study demonstrated that in addition to high time savings, the management system implemented by the algorithms also decreases the risk of human error. This is argued by previous evidence in the literature, namely, that currently used approaches tend to favor uncertainty due to the implication of manual processes and the introduction of a significant potential for errors and outdated data (Drum & Pulvermacher, 2016).

Additionally, the system ensures specific processing and secure preservation of accounting data through collaboration and blockchain technology. According to Dal Mas et al. (2020), the implementation of blockchain within a system provides an opportunity to improve efficiency, increase transparency, reduce costs, improve customer experience, improve data quality, increase trust between parties, and support verifiability, among other benefits. Therefore, clarity is provided by the absence of intermediaries, which is no longer necessary and contradictory to the pursuit of the goal of increasing traceability and transparency (Cong & Klotz, 2018; Secinaro et al., 2021).

Considering these results, we can argue that the aim of continuing accounting (Gulin et al., 2019) cannot be deemed to be achieved; indeed, at this stage, AI will be able to perform administrative tasks that consume the resources of managers (Kolbjørnsrud et al., 2016), but not to compromise the professional role of accountants (Azudin & Mansor, 2018).

Although modified in its functions, the analysis confirmed the relevance of the accountant's role, on the one hand, as a validator of the process; on the other hand, with a strategic role as an analyst of the data generated by the implemented strategy. As already assumed by (Schrage, 2017), the four areas of decision-making that may be affected by the implementation of AI are:

i. The autonomous advisor, where AI algorithms are considered the best strategic advisors.
ii. The autonomous outsourcer, where owners determine resource allocation and whether automation should lead to more significant innovation and optimization.
iii. The demanding autonomous employee intelligent software is integrated into the enterprise, allowing it to train effectively through the best algorithms.
iv. All autonomous organizations are fully committed to allowing algorithmic automation to lead the company to innovate.

Our analysis contradicts this assumption by allowing the accountant to play a role in a company's strategic planning. However, this is also confirmed by what is already present in the literature; thus, AI is proficient in making routine, structured business decisions, but it is still in an evolutionary phase in the area of unstructured strategic decisions (Bhattacharya, 2018).

The impact of implementing a system that includes AI can be identified to assess the appropriateness of the tool. To answer RQ, it is necessary to emphasize that, owing to increasing data, soaring computing power at decreasing costs, and technological advances, AI can be adopted as a productivity enhancer (Plastino & Purdy, 2018). Therefore, we can consider the effects of AI from four perspectives. Moreover, measurements may be carried out based on four results, which are decreasing in terms of time and cost, disintermediation, reduction in risk of human error, and increased time for strategic activities. Indeed, the automated system significantly affects these elements, which has positive implications for management accounting. In particular, AI can increase the speed of data processing. This dimension affects the control side (Cokins, 2001). In this sense, the new role described for the accountant is determined by his or her ability to analyze and implement a business intelligence system (Sun et al., 2018). Thus, there is a change in the role of the manager in charge of control, who will not only have to manage costs but also the digital skills required for data interpretation. The assessment side appeared to be significantly affected by artificial intelligence. In particular, the use of disruptive technologies improves accountability and transparency (Secinaro et al., 2021). In this sense, the role of AI is to remove much of the human interaction in daily tasks by suggesting a closed system with no possibility of human error. From the perspective of planning, AI works to enable the qualitative improvement of information. Therefore, implementing AI enables managers to make more accurate forecasts and budgets and achieve more accurate forecasting.

Contingency Theory supports the study of contextual factors that influence the administrative control of accounting information systems (Hayes, 1977). In this sense, theory encourages flexibility in choosing and adapting strategies to accommodate changing circumstances (Gordon & Miller, 1976). Therefore, the reduction of time due to the introduction of AI invested by accountants in the management of routine operations (Herbert et al., 2016), can be invested in activities that require judgment

(Gotthardt et al., 2019) and the development of critical thinking (Bhattacharya, 2018). Professionals benefitting the most from the inclusion of AI will increase their value within the business system. Based on these assumptions, the inclusion of AI will not challenge the accountant's role; instead, it will stimulate professional improvement. BookForAccounting showed that there is still a place for accountants, not only as a validator of the automated process's success, but also as a strategic resource for analyzing outcomes.

Theoretical and Practical Implications

The results of this study have several theoretical implications. According to Gulin et al. (2019), the implementation of AI in traditional operations has increased its value. On this basis, our results confirm what has been stated for the impact on costs and transparency, as well as empowering the accountant with a new role to redefine the profession as traditionally known by providing a strategic dimension to it. Furthermore, it has been shown that automation can reduce the risks associated with repetitive tasks (Herbert et al., 2016). Specifically, the study shows that the automated process can provide higher accuracy in the data and in the subsequent indexes based on it. This finding supports the arguments of Drum and Pulvermacher (2016), detailing the accounting dimension. According to Bhattacharya (2018), our work verifies that AI does not entirely replace the accountant, but portrays a new role that interests unstructured strategic decisions. In addition, it shows that for now, the implementation does not compromise the accountant profession (Azudin & Mansor, 2018), because the transition advocated by Schrage (2017) has not yet been initiated. Even when automation occurs, the human role as a validator of the various steps remains necessary, and it also confirms that strategic positions requiring critical skills (Bhattacharya, 2018), judgment (Gotthardt et al., 2019), empathy, and knowledge of corporate culture remain prerogative of the traditional accountant. Finally, our results from Moll and Yigitbasioglu (2019) show how accountants can use new skills in challenging activities. Finally, this study contributes to the ongoing debate on contingency theory. This theory emphasizes that contingency factors influence the administrative control of accounting information systems. Technology, culture, and the external environment are influential elements in the operation of organizations (Islam & Hu, 2012). Contingency theory allows for consideration of the implications of technology in management accounting. Specifically, this study uses this theoretical approach to observe the new role of accountants. Increased efficiency in performing repetitive tasks increases the time required for higher value-added activities (Bhattacharya, 2018; Gotthardt et al., 2019). Therefore, professionals will see their social role change, leading them to a more penetrating strategic value and less operational role. According to Frishammar and Åke Hörte (2005), new technological developments have led to changes in social interaction. Therefore, including AI in the accounting process stimulates new scenarios for accounting roles.

Technology decisively changes the current paradigm, and consequently, practical implications are also present. Blockchain technology ensures transparency maximization. The findings describe the desired characteristics and new role of accountants based on their competencies. Three levels of engagement are proposed based on skills: the process validator only, the results integrator, and the accountant who operates strategically based on process results. Notably, our study addresses all professionals working in the field of management accounting: accountants, auditors, and administrative practitioners.

Research Limitations and Future Research

Our study had some limitations. The embryonic, undeveloped state of the topic could alter current findings. Although supported by the literature (Yin, 2009), this case study alone does not allow for a uniform perspective. Most notably, the case analyzed refers to only a single geographic area in Italy. Moreover, this implies the validity of the case only with applications of Italian accounting rules or those internationally recognized; therefore, we cannot know the feasibility of the application where different accounting standards are present. Although the case study identifies the areas affected by AI implementation, it does not measure the economic impact that could be achieved.

These limitations provide a flourishing ground for future research. Studies that consider a larger number of cases may be beneficial. Furthermore, this should include various geographic areas to validate or contradict the results of our study. It would be of particular interest to conduct an analysis of countries that apply different accounting standards. Finally, research should be conducted to quantify the observed economic benefits.

Conclusion

This study explores how the impact of AI can be assessed through management accounting. The main results revealed the impact within four dimensions (Kaplan & Norton, 1992): financial, customer, operations, and organizational areas. Concerning the first point, we consider the reduction in time and cost as a significant consequence of implementing technology. Indeed, this allows a considerable saving of time, which BookForAccounting itself quantifies at 72% compared to the application of traditional management software. As far as the customer area is concerned, a considerable increase in accountability and transparency using blockchain technology is considered significant. Furthermore, the resulting decrease in intermediation supports enhanced transparency and data traceability, a topic we showed to be noticeable in the literature (Cong & Klotz, 2018; Secinaro et al., 2021). The reduction of risk in routine operations through the minimization of human error is of primary importance. This is part of BookForAccounting's business model, which operates under the assumption of providing accurate automated extraction to mitigate human errors. Finally, our findings revealed that the new paradigm would not exclude accountants from the business, although it is expected to improve their skills to develop critical thinking to provide the company with insight through data analysis. Furthermore, the increased available time will allow accountants to acquire the skills required for the new role. To conclude, AI fundamentally alters the current paradigm, and the findings describe the accountant's desired characteristics and new competency-based role. Indeed, three levels of engagement based on skills have been proposed: process validator only, results integrator, and accountant, who operate strategically based on process results. Notably, this chapter aims to involve all professionals in management accounting, including accountants, auditors, and administrative practitioners.

Acknowledgements The authors thank the CEO, the CTO, and all experts for their availability.

Funding This research did not receive any specific grants from funding agencies in the public, commercial, or not-for-profit sectors.

References

Anthony, R. N. (1965). *Planning and control systems: A framework for analysis [By]*. Division of Research, Graduate School of Business Administration, Harvard.

Azudin, A., & Mansor, N. (2018). Management accounting practices of SMEs: The impact of organizational DNA, business potential and operational technology. *Asia Pacific Management Review, 23*(3), 222–226.

Bakarich, K. M., & O'Brien, P. (2020). The robots are coming...but aren't here yet: The use of artificial intelligence technologies in the public accounting profession. *Journal of Emerging Technologies in Accounting*, No. JETA-19-11-20-47. https://doi.org/10.2308/JETA-19-11-20-47

Balasubramanian, S., Shukla, V., Sethi, J. S., Islam, N., & Saloum, R. (2021). A readiness assessment framework for blockchain adoption: A healthcare case study. *Technological Forecasting and Social Change, 165*, 120536.

Baldwin, A. A., Brown, C. E., & Trinkle, B. S. (2006). Opportunities for artificial intelligence development in the accounting domain: The case for auditing. *Intelligent Systems in Accounting, Finance and Management, 14*(3), 77–86.

Bhattacharya, P. (2018). Artificial intelligence in the boardroom: Enabling 'machines' to 'learn' to make strategic business decisions. In *2018 fifth HCT information technology trends (ITT)* (pp. 170–174). IEEE, Dubai, United Arab Emirates.

Biancone, P., Secinaro, S., Marseglia, R., & Calandra, D. (2021). E-health for the future: Managerial perspectives using a multiple case study approach. *Technovation*, 102406.

Blaikie, N. (1991). A critique of the use of triangulation in social research. *Quality & Quantity: International Journal of Methodology, 25*(2), 115–136.

Bonsón, E., Lavorato, D., Lamboglia, R., & Mancini, D. (2021). Artificial intelligence activities and ethical approaches in leading listed companies in the European Union. *International Journal of Accounting Information Systems, 43*, 100535.

Bruun, H., Hukkinen, J., & Eklund, E. (2002). Scenarios for coping with contingency: The case of aquaculture in the Finnish Archipelago Sea. *Technological Forecasting and Social Change, 69*(2), 107–127.

Carbonell, J., Sánchez-Esguevillas, A., & Carro, B. (2016). The role of metaphors in the development of technologies: The case of the artificial intelligence. *Futures, 84*, 145–153.

Cascante, M. Q., García, N. A., & Fold, N. (2022). The role of external forces in the adoption of aquaculture innovations: An ex-ante case study of fish farming in Colombia's southern Amazonian region. *Technological Forecasting and Social Change, 174*, 121185.

Chand, M., & Dahiya, A. (2010). Application of management accounting techniques in Indian small and medium hospitality enterprises: An empirical study. *International Journal of Entrepreneurship and Small Business, 11*(1), 25–41.

Chen, M., Liu, Q., Huang, S., & Dang, C. (2022). Environmental cost control system of manufacturing enterprises using artificial intelligence based on value chain of circular economy. *Enterprise Information Systems, 16*(8–9), 1856422.

Chukwudi, O. L., Echefu, S. C., Boniface, U. U., & Victoria, C. N. (2018). Effect of artificial intelligence on the performance of accounting operations among accounting firms in South East Nigeria. *Asian Journal of Economics, Business and Accounting*, 1–11.

Cokins, G. (2001). A management accounting framework. *Journal of Corporate Accounting & Finance, 13*(1), 73–82.

Coles, L. S. (1977). The application of artificial intelligence to medicine. *Futures, 9*(4), 315–323.

Cong, L., & Klotz, F. (2018). *Navigating the next wave of blockchain innovation: Smart contracts*. MIT Sloan Management Review.

Corazza, G., & Zanin, F. (2020). Impact of artificial intelligence on managerial accounting systems. In *Handbook of research on IT applications for strategic competitive advantage and decision making* (pp. 17–35). IGI Global.

Cunningham, S. W., & Kwakkel, J. (2011). Innovation forecasting: A case study of the management of engineering and technology literature. *Technological Forecasting and Social Change, 78*(2), 346–357.

Dal Mas, F., Dicuonzo, G., Massaro, M., & Dell'Atti, V. (2020). Smart contracts to enable sustainable business models: A case study. *Management Decision, 58*(8), 1601–1619.

Dal Mas, F., Piccolo, D., Cobianchi, L., Edvinsson, L., Presch, G., Massaro, M., Skrap, M., Ferrario di Tor Vajana, A., D'Auria, S., & Bagnoli, C. (2019). *The effects of artificial intelligence, robotics, and industry 4.0 technologies: Insights from the healthcare sector*. https://doi.org/10.34190/ECIAIR.19.015

David, H. (2015). Why are there still so many jobs? The history and future of workplace automation. *Journal of Economic Perspectives, 29*(3), 3–30.

Di Vaio, A., Hassan, R., & Alavoine, C. (2022). Data intelligence and analytics: A bibliometric analysis of human–artificial intelligence in public sector decision-making effectiveness. *Technological Forecasting and Social Change, 174*, 121201.

Drum, D. M., & Pulvermacher, A. (2016). Accounting automation and insight at the speed of thought. *Journal of Emerging Technologies in Accounting, 13*(1), 181–186.

Eisenhardt, K. M. (1989). Building theories from case study research. *Academy of Management Review, 14*(4), 532–550.

Faccia, A., Al Naqbi, M. Y. K., & Lootah, S. A. (2019). Integrated cloud financial accounting cycle: How artificial intelligence, blockchain, and XBRL will change the accounting, fiscal and auditing practices. In *Proceedings of the 2019 3rd international conference on cloud and big data computing* (pp. 31–37). Association for Computing Machinery, New York, NY, USA.

Fisher, J. (1995). Contingency-based research on management control systems: Categorization by level of complexity. *Journal of Accounting Literature, 14*, 24.

Flick, U. (1998). *The psychology of the social*. Cambridge University Press.

Flick, U. (2004). Triangulation in qualitative research. *A Companion to Qualitative Research, 3*, 178–183.

Frezatti, F., Aguiar, A. B., Guerreiro, R., & Gouvea, M. A. (2011). Does management accounting play role in planning process? *Journal of Business Research, 64*(3), 242–249.

Friedlob, G. T., & Schleifer, L. L. (2003). *Essentials of financial analysis* (Vol. 23). Wiley.

Frishammar, J., & Åke Hörte, S. (2005). Managing external information in manufacturing firms: The impact on innovation performance. *Journal of Product Innovation Management, 22*(3), 251–266.

Gao, P., & Jiang, X. (2020). The economic consequences of discrete recognition and continuous measurement. *Journal of Accounting and Economics, 69*(1), 101250.

Gioia, D. A., Corley, K. G., & Hamilton, A. L. (2013). Seeking qualitative rigor in inductive research: Notes on the Gioia methodology. *Organizational Research Methods, 16*(1), 15–31.

Gordon, L. A., & Miller, D. (1976). A contingency framework for the design of accounting information systems. In *Readings in accounting for management control* (pp. 569–585). Springer.

Gotthardt, M., Koivulaakso, D., Paksoy, O., Saramo, C., Martikainen, M., & Lehner, O. M. (2019). Current state and challenges in the implementation of robotic process automation and artificial intelligence in accounting and auditing. *ACRN Oxford Journal of Finance Risk Perspectives, 8*, 31–46.

Gulin, D., Hladika, M., & Valenta, I. (2019). *Digitalization and the challenges for the accounting profession*. Available at SSRN 3492237.

Gummesson, E. (2006). Qualitative research in management: Addressing complexity, context and persona. *Management Decision*. https://doi.org/10.1108/00251740610650175

Gurstein, M. (1985). Social impacts of selected artificial intelligence applications: The Canadian context. *Futures, 17*(6), 652–671.

Haefner, N., Wincent, J., Parida, V., & Gassmann, O. (2021). Artificial intelligence and innovation management: A review, framework, and research agenda✰. *Technological Forecasting and Social Change, 162*, 120392.

Hayes, D. C. (1977). The contingency theory of managerial accounting. *Accounting Review*, 22–39.

Hendriks, V. M., Blanken, P., Adriaans, N. F. P., & Hartnoll, R. (1992). *Snowball sampling: A pilot study on cocaine use*. IVO, Instituut voor Verslavingsonderzoek, Erasmus Universiteit Rotterdam.

Herbert, I., Dhayalan, A., & Scott, A. (2016). The future of professional work: Will you be replaced, or will you be sitting next to a robot. *Management Services Journal, 2016*, 22–27.

Howorth, C., & Westhead, P. (2003). The focus of working capital management in UK small firms. *Management Accounting Research, 14*(2), 94–111.

Hwang, S. (2008). Utilizing qualitative data analysis software: A review of Atlas.ti. *Social Science Computer Review, 26*(4), 519–527.

Islam, J., & Hu, H. (2012). A review of literature on contingency theory in managerial accounting. *African Journal of Business Management, 6*(15), 5159–5164.

Ittner, C. D., & Larcker, D. F. (2001). Assessing empirical research in managerial accounting: A value-based management perspective. *Journal of Accounting and Economics, 32*(1–3), 349–410.

Jabeur, S. B., Ballouk, H., Mefteh-Wali, S., & Omri, A. (2022). Forecasting the macrolevel determinants of entrepreneurial opportunities using artificial intelligence models. *Technological Forecasting and Social Change, 175*, 121353.

Kaplan, R. S., & Norton, D. P. (1992). The balanced scorecard: Measures that drive performance. *Harvard Business Review, 83*(7), 172.

Kokina, J., & Davenport, T. H. (2017). The emergence of artificial intelligence: How automation is changing auditing. *Journal of Emerging Technologies in Accounting, 14*(1), 115–122.

Kolbjørnsrud, V., Amico, R., & Thomas, R. J. (2016). How artificial intelligence will redefine management. *Harvard Business Review*, 6.

Kopka, A., & Grashof, N. (2021). Artificial intelligence: Catalyst or barrier on the path to sustainability? *Technological Forecasting and Social Change, 175*, 121318.

Lamberton, G. (2000). Accounting for sustainable development—A case study of city farm. *Critical Perspectives on Accounting, 11*(5), 583–605.

Lavia López, O., & Hiebl, M. R. (2015). Management accounting in small and medium-sized enterprises: Current knowledge and avenues for further research. *Journal of Management Accounting Research, 27*(1), 81–119.

Li, M., Wang, W., & Zhou, K. (2021). Exploring the technology emergence related to artificial intelligence: A perspective of coupling analyses. *Technological Forecasting and Social Change, 172*, 121064.

Lotti, F., & Marin, G. (2013). *Matching of PATSTAT applications to AIDA firms: Discussion of the methodology and results, No. 166, Questioni Di Economia e*

Finanza (Occasional Papers). Bank of Italy, Economic Research and International Relations Area. https://ideas.repec.org/p/bdi/opques/qef_166_13.html. Accessed 21 May 2020.

Makridakis, S. (2017). The forthcoming Artificial Intelligence (AI) revolution: Its impact on society and firms. *Futures, 90*, 46–60.

Marcello, S., Ray, T., Carmichael, D., Peterson, J., Ramamoorti, S., Collemi, S., & Nearon, B. (2017). The future of auditing: A roundtable discussion. *The CPA Journal*, 39.

Massaro, M., Dal Mas, F., Chiappetta Jabbour, C. J., & Bagnoli, C. (2020). Crypto-economy and new sustainable business models: Reflections and projections using a case study analysis. *Corporate Social Responsibility and Environmental Management, 27*(5), 2150–2160.

Massaro, M., Dumay, J., & Bagnoli, C. (2019). Transparency and the rhetorical use of citations to Robert Yin in case study research. *Meditari Accountancy Research, 27*(1), 44–71.

Mattli, W., & Büthe, T. (2005). Accountability in accounting? The politics of private rule-making in the public interest. *Governance, 18*(3), 399–429.

Meng, D., Li, X., & Rong, K. (2019). Industry-to-university knowledge transfer in ecosystem-based academic entrepreneurship: Case study of automotive dynamics & control group in Tsinghua University. *Technological Forecasting and Social Change, 141*, 249–262.

Moll, J., & Yigitbasioglu, O. (2019). The role of internet-related technologies in shaping the work of accountants: New directions for accounting research. *The British Accounting Review, 51*(6), 100833.

Moudud-Ul-Huq, S. (2014). The role of artificial intelligence in the development of accounting systems: A review. *IUP Journal of Accounting Research & Audit Practices, 13*(2).

Noriega, M. (2020). The application of artificial intelligence in police interrogations: An analysis addressing the proposed effect AI has on racial and gender bias, cooperation, and false confessions. *Futures, 117*, 102510.

Noy, C. (2008). Sampling knowledge: The hermeneutics of snowball sampling in qualitative research. *International Journal of Social Research Methodology, 11*(4), 327–344.

Plastino, E., & Purdy, M. (2018). Game changing value from artificial intelligence: Eight strategies. *Strategy & Leadership, 46*(1), 16–22.

Rikhardsson, P., & Yigitbasioglu, O. (2018). Business intelligence & analytics in management accounting research: Status and future focus. *International Journal of Accounting Information Systems, 29*, 37–58.

Schmitz, J., & Leoni, G. (2019). Accounting and auditing at the time of blockchain technology: A research agenda. *Australian Accounting Review, 29*(2), 331–342.

Schrage, M. (2017). Models for using AI to make decisions. *Harvard Business Review*.

Secinaro, S., Dal Mas, F., Brescia, V., & Calandra, D. (2021). Blockchain in the accounting, auditing and accountability fields: A bibliometric and coding analysis. *Accounting, Auditing & Accountability Journal, 35*(9), 168–203. https://doi.org/10.1108/AAAJ-10-2020-4987

Shahsahebi, S. M., Darabi, R., & Hamidian, M. (2020). Artificial intelligence approach analyzing management ability based on accounting and corporate governance criteria. *International Journal of Finance & Managerial Accounting, 5*(17), 67–83.

Simons, R. (1991). Strategic orientation and top management attention to control systems. *Strategic Management Journal, 12*(1), 49–62.

Smith, L. M., Denzin, N., & Lincoln, Y. (1994). *Biographical method*. Sage.

Sun, Z., Sun, L., & Strang, K. (2018). Big data analytics services for enhancing business intelligence. *Journal of Computer Information Systems, 58*(2), 162–169.

Sutton, S. G., Holt, M., & Arnold, V. (2016). 'The reports of my death are greatly exaggerated'—Artificial intelligence research in accounting. *International Journal of Accounting Information Systems, 22*, 60–73.

Tortorella, G. L., Fogliatto, F. S., Espôsto, K. F., Vergara, A. M. C., Vassolo, R., Mendoza, D. T., & Narayanamurthy, G. (2020). Effects of contingencies on healthcare 4.0 technologies adoption and barriers in emerging economies. *Technological Forecasting and Social Change, 156*, 120048.

Tredinnick, L. (2017). Artificial intelligence and professional roles. *Business Information Review, 34*(1), 37–41.

Vaivio, J. (2008). Qualitative management accounting research: Rationale, pitfalls and potential. *Qualitative Research in Accounting & Management, 5*(1), 64–86.

Vărzaru, A. A. (2022). Assessing artificial intelligence technology acceptance in managerial accounting. *Electronics, 11*(14), 2256.

Yin, R. K. (2004). *The case study anthology*. Sage.

Yin, R. K. (2009). *Case study research: Design and methods*. Sage.

Yu, T. (2019). Accounting information quality optimization of the listed company based on blockchain. *Academic Journal of Business & Management, 1*(3), 49–59.

Zemánková, A. (2019). Artificial intelligence and blockchain in audit and accounting: Literature review. *WSEAS Transactions on Business and Economics, 16*, 568–581.

CHAPTER 9

Blockchain and the Future of Accountancy: A Review on Policies and Regulations

Ridoan Karim

Introduction: Background and Driving Forces

The creation, preservation, and modification of financial data have fundamentally changed because of blockchain. Blockchain innovation ensures the deployment of a sophisticated consensus and verification system in which each participant receives an identical copy of a single entry that is shared forever (Bonsón & Bednárová, 2019). This is also known as "universal entry bookkeeping" (ICAEW, 2017). Any future user can access a blockchain without permission in a permissionless blockchain. For instance, the Bitcoin blockchain is a public or permissionless blockchain; anybody may join the chain as a node and access the authenticated network for cryptotransactions. In general, downloading the software and Bitcoin ledger from the Internet is required to join the blockchain. It

R. Karim (✉)
Department of Business Law & Taxation, School of Business, Monash University Malaysia, Selangor Darul Ehsan, Subang Jaya, Malaysia
e-mail: ridoan.karim@monash.edu

A. Perdana and T. Wang (eds.), *Digital Transformation in Accounting and Auditing*, https://doi.org/10.1007/978-3-031-46209-2_9

represents the entire transaction history and account balances of all participants because the blockchain keeps track of every transaction that has ever been made into the system.

This feature of blockchain technology influences several sectors. According to several financial services industry analysts, the financial services sector is about to be disrupted by innovations in cutting-edge technologies, such as blockchain, which are anticipated to alter the sector and its workforce by automating many of the tasks now carried out by humans (Cai, 2018). In addition to the financial industries, accounting and auditing scenarios are also impacted by technology (Bonsón & Bednárová, 2019).

The general public expects auditors to increase their confidence in the audited data of the firms they audit and support a multi-trillion-dollar capital market system (Griffin, 2014). Auditors are independent of the organizations they audit and need to follow stringent rules, professional codes of conduct, and auditing standards in the process. They use impartiality and professional care to offer reasonable assurance of financial statements, depending on the efficiency of an organization's internal controls over financial reporting. According to some studies, blockchain technology may completely replace the requirement for auditors to audit financial statements (De Oliveira et al., 2017; Sargent, 2021; Tan & Low, 2019). What remains for an auditor if all transactions are recorded on an immutable blockchain? Verifying the existence of a transaction is simply one of the crucial components of a financial statement audit. An audit determines whether the supporting documentation for recorded transactions is pertinent, trustworthy, impartial, accurate, and verifiable.

Accepting a transaction in a blockchain might provide enough audit proof for a financial statement of a transaction's occurrence (e.g., an asset recorded on the blockchain has transferred from a seller to a buyer). A Bitcoin transaction for a product may record its transfer to the blockchain. However, based purely on analysing data from the Bitcoin blockchain, the auditor might or might not be able to identify the goods provided. Therefore, depending on the nature of the transaction, storing it in a blockchain may offer sufficient audit-proof. In addition, many transactions in financial statements have anticipated values that differ from their historical costs. Despite the fact that underlying transactions are documented in a blockchain, auditors still need to carry out audit processes on management's estimates (ICAEW, 2017). With the widespread use of blockchain technology, it may be possible to collect audit data from centralized sites, and auditors may create processes to obtain audit evidence directly from blockchains.

Nevertheless, auditors must consider the possibility of fraud or errors, even in blockchain transactions (Bonsón & Bednárová, 2019). Data from the blockchain will need to be extracted by the auditor, who will also need to evaluate its reliability. General information technology controls (GITCs), relevant to blockchain ecosystems may be considered throughout this procedure (White et al., 2020). It is also necessary for the auditor to comprehend and evaluate the dependability of the consensus protocol for a particular blockchain (White et al., 2020).

Hence, although blockchain may disrupt the auditing process, it will not remove the jobs of auditors. Nevertheless, auditors must be aware of the possible effects of using private or public blockchains may have on their audits as a new source of information for financial statements. This is because an increasing number of firms are exploring the use of these systems. In addition, as neither international financial reporting standards nor generally accepted accounting principles specifically address digital assets and liabilities, they also need to assess managerial accounting practices in this area. They need to consider how to modify audit processes to take full use of blockchain's advantages and handle escalating dangers.

Apart from these technical issues, technological development in a specific industry requires both regulatory and policy reforms. In line with this, this chapter examines internationally functional models of blockchain technology in the accounting and auditing industry. The analysis of these models has been helpful in recommending the utilization of blockchain technology in the financial industry. This eventually paves the way towards appropriate governance frameworks to ensure a decentralized, transparent, and sustainable auditing process in the digital era. This study had two main objectives. First, it explores the regulatory and policy applications of blockchain technology in the accounting and auditing industries. Second, the study analyses policy and regulatory models that have been helpful in recommending the utilization of blockchain technology in the industry.

Characteristics of Blockchain

With the introduction of Satoshi Nakamoto's Bitcoin or cryptocurrency in 2008, blockchain became a ledger system that can store data and transactions in real-time scenarios (Elommal & Manita, 2022). Direct private-to-private transactions without an intermediary are achievable using this technology. Several scholars describe blockchain as "a network of nodes (i.e., users' computers) working together as peers to produce an immutable transaction history that can be made viewable to the public" (Elommal & Manita, 2022; Sheldon, 2019).

Every newly completed transaction is automatically recorded in a block. A blockchain is created by connecting several blocks in a chain, each of which is a separate block. As a result, blockchain enables users to deal with each other directly without requiring a reliable third party (Gruber, 2013; Singh, 2015). This technology is also compared to a vast notepad or open book that anybody can peruse for free and without restriction, but no one can be held accountable (Elommal & Manita, 2022).

Transparency and traceability are the fundamental characteristics of a blockchain. Users may exchange information on the blockchain that cannot be changed or removed. Another aspect of this technology is data security. The requirement of the technology for validation by a group of nodes decreases the danger of hacking or data tempering. Without a central network, the chain verifies the operations recorded and transacted between two parties without intermediaries through smart contracts. Thus, removing intermediaries would allow for increased production and efficiency and decrease transaction expenses such as inspection and verification fees. These features make blockchain technology a groundbreaking innovation that may inspire businesses to create innovative processes and new business models.

According to Beck and Müller-Bloch (2017), blockchain represents a radical innovation because it has established new functionalities that go beyond existing technologies and practices rather than being an incremental technology (consisting of adding some functionalities to current technology) (Utterback & Acee, 2021). Businesses may save time and considerably reduce human errors and fraud by using this approach instead of inputting and recording transactions in various databases. This technology may undoubtedly provide businesses with a competitive edge. However, it comes with risks because it calls for significant organizational changes, new talents, tools, and working ways that could replace outdated conventions. Given its enormous potential to bring about fundamental changes in several industries, the development of blockchain is sometimes likened to that of the internet (Shoker, 2021).

Prospects of Blockchain Technology in Accounting Profession

Blockchain is an accounting-based technology (Centobelli et al., 2022). It focuses on transferring ownership of assets and keeping a record of precise financial data. The collection, reporting, and analysis of financial information fall under the broad purview of the accounting profession. Planning how to effectively use financial resources or determine or quantify rights and duties regarding property constitutes a large portion of the profession. By providing accountants with clarity over every transaction, blockchain technology has the potential to increase productivity significantly. Blockchain can improve the efficiency of the accounting profession by lowering the expense of maintaining and reconciling ledgers and providing complete clarity on the ownership and history of assets (Abdennadher et al., 2022). Blockchain will also help increase the amount of transactional-level accounting in conjunction with other automation trends such as machine learning (Griguta et al., 2021).

Blockchain will not only change audit procedures but it also has strategic value in advancing the overall accounting profession (Demirkan et al., 2020). Overall, blockchain technology will enable audit firms to save time and improve audit effectiveness, prefer an audit covering the entire population over an audit covering a sample, concentrate the audit on testing controls rather than testing transactions, set up a continuous audit process, foster a more strategic audit role, and develop new advisory services (see Fig. 9.1). These consequences boost audit quality and provide the accounting profession with new opportunities to modify its operational procedures, services, and delivery models.

Time-Saving Audit

Blockchain promises to represent unique information to each organization into a shared and collectively validated information system. Additionally, this process secures broadcasting to stakeholders regarding concurrent transactions. Without the need for time-consuming data collection, the auditor can see and extract a range of trustworthy information from the client's blockchain system. The auditor will be able to

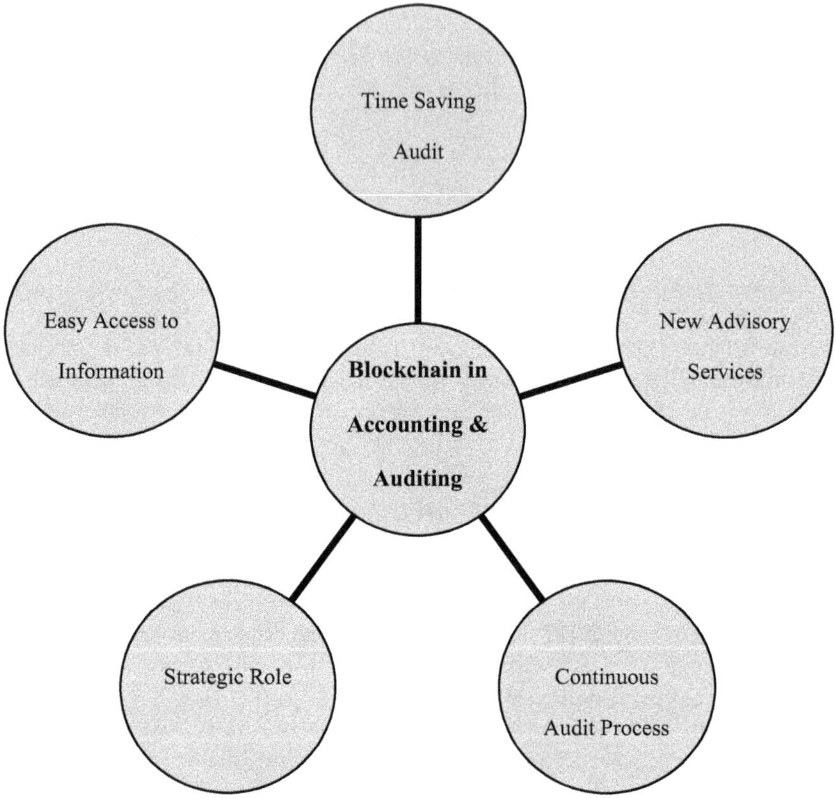

Fig. 9.1 Prospects of blockchain technology in Accounting profession (*Source* Author)

save time not only in data gathering and comprehension of the client's operations but also in validating the transactions. Because the complete transaction history and accompanying data would be stored and broadcast immediately as a block in the blockchain, the auditor might, for instance, avoid the manual correspondence test conducted on numerous samples (Elommal & Manita, 2022). This feature enables auditors to concentrate on tasks that add value to the client, such as examining accounting estimations at the end of the financial year, assessing blockchain-level control systems, and quantifying risk areas. Consequently, the effectiveness of audits will increase, leading to an improvement in audit quality.

Continuous Audit Process

Direct access to transaction history is another benefit of blockchain technology that makes the auditor's job easier. This will be made more feasible by the incorporation of other technologies such as big data and analytics. The auditing methodology will change as blockchain is increasingly being used in commercial transactions (Tseng & Shang, 2021).

Blockchain allows the audit profession to alter the audit process by building a stock of accessible and encrypted information accepted by an unchangeable consensus (owing to the timestamp functionality and the distinct hash ID issued to information blocks) (McCallig et al., 2019). The auditor will be able to build a continuous audit process using blockchain, allowing the validation of information continuously and consistently (Schmitz & Leoni, 2019). Auditors will not need to ask or wait for information and papers from their clients because all the information recorded on a blockchain is accessible.

Additionally, the blockchain enables us to securely store large amounts of financial and non-financial data, giving the auditor more opportunities to widen the scope of their audits and make them more pertinent (Roszkowska, 2021). A continual audit is encouraged by the range of information that the blockchain instantaneously makes available and stored. If these data are maintained and accessible on a blockchain, some information verifications that are part of the conventional audit procedure will no longer be required. With blockchain, the former manual inventory count may be carried out swiftly and continually. This is also true of confirmations, which are no longer necessary because the blocks of information produced instantly verify all the information. Finally, blockchain enables reconciliation to be automated, particularly when transactions occur between parties inside a single blockchain network (Schmitz & Leoni, 2019). An auditor should be able to save time and improve the effectiveness and quality of his audit by performing procedures that are not feasible with the traditional audit.

Additionally, blockchain promotes the growth of smart contracts, which has an impact on the auditing process. Blockchain automatically carries out these contracts, which incorporate contractual rights and duties into the network. These agreements should lower the prices of transactions, arbitration, and fraud. Additionally, this should make it easier to set up ongoing audits and reduce mistakes (De Andrés & Lorca, 2021). Nevertheless, with a continuous audit process, auditors must create new control strategies that accommodate the changing technological landscape. Blockchain does, in fact, provide auditors with the chance to develop their audit process by allowing them to examine specific transactions, confirm the existence of digital assets, and assess the consistency between the data on a blockchain and the outside world. Verifying the code and structure of a blockchain is a new audit process. Auditors can create novel techniques to establish ownership using their experience in auditing IT systems. In this situation, future auditors should be trained in technical auditing.

Easy Access to Audit Information

As mentioned previously, the validation and recording of information via the blockchain enables all users to track real-time information. This tamper-proof technology creates a method for restoring information that impacts auditing. Auditors generally use sampling techniques for inspections. In this instance, the auditor may complete his audit by utilizing cumulative data because blockchain technology provides rapid access to all information. When blockchain is combined with other current technologies, such as big data, automation, and analytics, it is highly likely that information processing will be much easier for future auditors (Kend & Nguyen, 2020).

Strategic Role

The function of audit firms would change more into a strategic role if blockchain technology was included and used more widely (Nowiński & Kozma, 2017). The auditor will be able to study the data collected from the blockchain, interpret it to provide significance, and make it valuable for the management decision-making process. In this situation, the auditor might transform from a straightforward overseer of the accuracy of information to his client's strategic counsellor to develop his management and control systems (Nowiński & Kozma, 2017).

New Advisory Services

By introducing new services, blockchain allows auditors to grow their business services. They can help their clients select the most acceptable technique to use and install. Audit firms may advise customers to use blockchain to strengthen their internal controls and risk management systems based on their evaluation of the systems already in place (Dyball & Seethamraju, 2021).

Additionally, audit firms may create new consultancy assignments on best practices for blockchain usage protocols by using their sectoral knowledge. They can also provide novel services as planners and coordinators for future blockchain players. Finally, audit companies may provide new services related to blockchain audit internal controls, such as data integrity and security, change management, and blockchain governance. For auditors, blockchain technology has specific potential. These potentials, meanwhile, necessitate budgeting for expenses, such as hiring staff and purchasing suitable IT solutions. These expenses, which may be high, are long-term investments for market adaptation.

Blockchain Technology in Auditing: Anticipated Practices and Unanswered Questions

Auditors may utilize the maximum number of blockchain platforms to standardize transaction processing across numerous sectors. Nevertheless, considerable obstacles remain that may still need to be overcome, and the forthcoming sections of this chapter briefly discuss these challenges.

The First Mile and the Last Mile Problem

Without placing blockchains within the business context that connects the database to actual transactions, it is impossible to debate them as a practical solution for auditing. The first-mile difficulty of blockchain entails that the initial recordings in the distributed ledger and the corresponding at the transaction layer reflect the same, which indicates that the information on the blockchain is identical to the information it claims to reflect in the real world (Alles & Gray, 2020).

Auditors and accountants may use a technical instrument (such as an RFID tag) to trace the physical transaction of an item to overcome the first-mile problem (Alles & Gray, 2020). However, regulatory quality control is necessary in addition to technological control to solve the first-mile challenge. In general, the first-mile problem will benefit auditors because there will be a growth in demand for third-party auditing to address the issue, which entails determining whether the blockchain's data correspond correctly with the actual item (Alles & Gray, 2020). Nevertheless, the auditing body must have sufficient confidence in competence and independence to be accepted by end users. This makes it possible for conventional auditing businesses to promote new services. To deal with the first-mile issue, however, this new role for auditors demands significant training in professional skepticism. However, there is still no assurance that traditional financial auditors will be able to meet the increasing need for blockchain auditing.

In contrast, "last mile" challenges in blockchain auditing might arise when unforeseen events occur during system processing and require the auditor's skill and discretion to handle (Saripalli, 2021). Explicitly stating how a blockchain-based auditing system would produce solutions is one thing, and another is the actual delivery of a digital and technical system. The size of the auditing management system is the first factor in the transformation and resolution of the last-mile problem because working on a smaller scale is simpler. The entrepreneurship theory states that implementing a disruptive idea does not necessarily follow a disruptive model (Christensen et al., 2018). Carefully chosen collaborations are sometimes more successful in bringing about changes. The main challenge is to integrate a crucial new technology into an established value chain through discreet and cautious commercial relationships. Therefore, a small-scale test of the blockchain-based accounting and auditing system is recommended. This approach may be applied to larger commodities and services once the "small" blockchain-driven auditing is operational, eventually leading to a fully-fledged blockchain system for auditing.

Challenges of Auditing the Smart Contracts and Oracles

Blockchains can incorporate smart contracts to automate their commercial operations. Contracting parties may wish to work with assurance services to ensure that smart contracts are executed with proper business logic. Nevertheless, auditors should evaluate how smart contracts interact with other data sources that lead to business events. Users of blockchain technology face the possibility of undetected flaws or vulnerabilities in the absence of third-party examinations (Guo & Yu, 2022). Auditors need new skills, such as a grasp of technical programming languages and the workings of blockchain, to take on this new position.

For the auditing profession, this type of employment also poses crucial questions, such as: What skill sets do the field require to be relevant?

What variables affect the risk of assurance engagement? What would a supplier of an assurance's ongoing obligations be once a smart contract is published on a blockchain? Management will be in charge of setting up controls to check that the smart contract source code adheres to the desired business logic in the context of an audit of financial statements. Management controls over the smart contract code are likely to be considered by an independent auditor evaluating a firm using blockchain/smart contracts. However, many businesses can decide to use smart contracts created by other organizations already operating on a blockchain. Future auditing guidelines and standards may need to consider this technology to clarify the function of the auditor in certain instances.

Technicalities Relating to Service Auditing for the Consortium Blockchains

Users of a blockchain system may require independent assurance of the stability and robustness of its architecture before launching a new application on an existing blockchain platform or subscribing to an existing blockchain product (Werbach, 2019). Sophisticated General IT Controls (GITCs) that offer ongoing protection for sensitive data should be incorporated into the design of essential blockchain components such as cryptographic key management to ensure data security, integrity, and privacy (Swammy et al., 2018). GITCs play a crucial role in corporate operations and control over financial information. They lay the groundwork for relying on information, reports, automated checks, and other system features to support business operations. Adequate access, change management, and operational controls are necessary to ensure the security, integrity, and dependability of financial information.

Nevertheless, a reliable and impartial third party may require continued assurance of the efficacy of controls over a private blockchain. When implementing service auditing in blockchains, the following important questions still need to be addressed: who is the client when offering assurance through a blockchain? How would an auditor evaluate the risk of an autonomous system's engagement?

Understanding the Administrator's Function

A dependable, impartial, and unbiased third party performing the duties of a central access-granting administrator may be beneficial for permissioned blockchain systems (CPA, 2017). This function could be in charge of conducting further background checks on participants before allowing them access to a blockchain or verifying their identity. This central administrator could certify that the blockchain protocols were being followed and enforced. If a user or node of the blockchain performs this role, an unfair advantage may exist and the trust of consortium members may be compromised (Swammy et al., 2018). Due diligence will be required when creating this role's purpose and its legal obligations because it would be created with the intention of building confidence for the blockchain as a whole. An independent auditor can handle this duty as a professional. However, this position brings up one unanswered question for the industry: Is the auditor separate from the blockchain participants while playing such a crucial role?

Implementing Arbitration Function

Even the most well-intentioned parties can get into conflict over business agreements because they are complicated. In the future, an arbitration mechanism for blockchain could be required to resolve conflicts among consortium-blockchain members (Xu et al., 2020). This duty is comparable to that of an estate executor, often performed by certified individuals, including auditors. When the spirit of a smart contract deviates from the language or spirit of a legal document, contract, or letter, blockchain participants may require this function to enforce the conditions of the contract. Nevertheless, several factors must be investigated to establish an arbitration function. The questions that remain to be considered are: What legal framework should be utilized to settle disputes? What qualifications would an auditor require? Could the independent nature of an auditor's work be unintentionally affected by this role?

Association of Digital Assets with Non-fungible Tokens (NFTs)

Non-Fungible Tokens (NFTs) are cryptographic assets on the blockchain that include unique information and identify unique codes (Bamakan et al., 2022). The primary difference between NFTs and cryptocurrencies is that cryptocurrencies can be exchanged or traded at equivalency, whereas NFTs cannot (Chalmers et al., 2022). Each NFT is built in such a way that it can be utilized in a variety of applications. NFTs, for instance, are best suited for digitally embodying tangible things, such as artwork and real estate. NFTs are also being developed as a type of blockchain, making it feasible to use them to eliminate intermediaries and simpler for participants to interact. Furthermore, non-fungible tokens may be used for identity management, and NFTs can therefore be used to open new markets and streamline transactions.

Non-fungible tokens (NFTs), which include identifying information stored in smart contracts, are regarded as digital assets. These tokens cannot be substituted for each other because of the distinctive identification data included in each NFT. Despite having the same value, NFTs cannot be switched because they are distinct from one another. Because banknotes of the same value may be readily stolen from one another, they vary greatly from banknote trades. On the other hand, NFTs are tied to a certain asset and the underlying asset has a significant impact on their value. Their main objective was to establish ownership of particular digital assets. The immutability, as a powerful attribute of NFTs, makes them incredibly important for digital ownership and beneficial development in the rapidly evolving digital world (Joshua Fairfield, 2021). Hence, there are no simpler NFT exchanges in daily accounting.

The creation of new, more effective tools for managing and generating NFTs is the second major problem faced in NFTs trading because many individuals still find it difficult to grasp NFTs. Additionally, smart contracts and NFTs protocols are still being developed; therefore, several difficult situations arise when trading NFTs. This phenomenon can also be attributed to the fragmentation of blockchain advancement. Because different developers have different opinions about what needs to be changed, they are divided in their efforts to create a platform that is more efficient for the everyday trading of NFTs.

Regulatory Reporting and Compliance

Regulators constantly expect auditing firms to have large volumes of data that can be evaluated to identify noncompliance with legal and regulatory requirements. Collecting and analysing the necessary data is a significant challenge. There is also a substantial danger of the data falling into the wrong hands and being misused, exposing confidential business information and placing a company at a strategic disadvantage.

Blockchain could theoretically solve many of these problems, facilitating accountability, encouraging regulators to access safe, transparent data at source, and encouraging businesses to maintain tight control over what information is accessible and who can access it. A significant advantage of having such a forum to exchange knowledge with regulators is that it will establish an industry-standard data format, which is currently impossible.

Legal and Regulatory Challenges

Blockchain poses a range of legal concerns, just like every other dramatic transition in new technologies. Legal concerns vary from private to public international law and financial to privacy laws and regulations based on the nature and scope of blockchain applications. Some of the legal concerns regarding blockchain related to the accounting and auditing industries are highlighted here:

Regulation of Crypto-assets

Crypto assets are not covered by any accounting rules or regulations, which makes it difficult to categorize and quantify them. The lack of a standard also means that crypto assets are hard to categorize as intangible or financial (Procházka, 2018; Smith et al., 2019). The creation of appropriate legislation is hampered by the ambiguity surrounding the valuation of crypto assets because this problem impacts the core qualitative elements of financial accounting, such as relevance and faithful representation (Garanina et al., 2022). Additionally, the concepts of prudence, neutrality, and conservatism continue to make it difficult to accurately portray crypto-assets in financial statements, as outlined in the Conceptual Framework for Financial Reporting (Financial Reporting Council [FRC], 2018). Researchers claim that a new regulatory framework must be developed to minimize the risk of fraud concerning crypto assets (Garanina et al., 2022). For instance, ICOs are prone to fraud and manipulation because investor protection is less than in the stock market (Clayton, 2017).

Regulators now deal with the cryptocurrency asset market on a case-by-case basis, but not in a way that allows investors to increase confidence in cryptocurrency assets (Garanina et al., 2022). Additionally, given their volatility, only some market players are keen to classify crypto-assets as securities, making it challenging to determine an acceptable value to record income statements and balance sheet reasons (Clayton, 2017; Dumay & Guthrie, 2019). Consequently, the ambiguity surrounding the measurement of crypto assets is a challenge in the adoption of standard regulations for the global market. A regulatory framework that is proactive rather than passively responding to the concerns of crypto-assets is the answer to this challenge.

Applicable Law

The topic of applicable law is the first issue to be posed in the blockchain. In a blockchain, jurisdiction is important because the parties of each transaction will be in separate countries. Hence, determining an applicable law is challenging. For each transnational transaction in the blockchain, all parties to the smart contract feel the necessity to understand the applicable/governing law. This problem only does not arise in situations where the parties to the agreement reside within the EU, as the legislation applicable to contractual obligations remains the same which is the "Regulation of the European Parliament and of the Council on the law applicable to contractual obligations (Rome I58)" (Giancaspro, 2017). However, what happens if contracting parties are not in the EU?

The matter should then be dealt with either under private international law or under the applicable law mentioned in the contract (Governatori et al., 2018). A possible solution to this may be to provide a range of alternative options to choose the applicable law in a smart contract by clicking on the preferred country or region. In the case of imposing blockchain applications in the financial industry, selecting a proper governing law for each transaction may lead to complex legal and regulatory situations in which tech giants, auditing firms, and the government should consider a more profound and holistic approach.

Identity Within a Blockchain

To date, most blockchain applications have been held in public blockchains. All transactions in public blockchain are easily accessible. Nevertheless, transactions in public blockchains do not always indicate that the identity of the parties is understandable. For example, parties involved in a Bitcoin transaction can participate anonymously. This, therefore, can be an added advantage for cryptocurrency situations;

nevertheless, it contributes to difficulties in auditing, both politically and philosophically. Unidentifiability leads to a situation in which auditors cannot identify the real problem or hold any authority responsible for a wrong, which stands against the core philosophy of introducing blockchain in the financial industry.

This will affect the integrity of the relevant traditional economy, except for implementing blockchain applications that can identify parties in financial transactions. Therefore, a range of regulatory reforms has been developed for blockchain applications, especially in the financial sector. While there are expert arguments on blockchain recognition/identification of electronic profiles (Caytas, 2017), such access to identity remains unanswered due to technical and regulatory barriers.

Liability and Responsibility

The perfect blockchain paradigm allows for a mechanism that operates without central authority (Radziwill, 2018). This means that legal personality is not defined in blockchain applications (Kshetri, 2017). If any damage arises, existing liability laws and regimes are not sufficient to deal with compensation (Corrales Compagnucci et al., 2020). This constitutes a series of legal problems. Hence, specific liability laws related to blockchain in financial industries are needed to guarantee the legal responsibilities of the parties involved. Specific laws are needed to administer liability principles in payment defaults, technological breakdowns, or deliberate non-performance.

Personal Data

One of the basic features of the blockchain is that it contradicts personal data laws. Most of the laws relating to data protection state that personal data must be deleted after they have served their purpose. Many practitioners and academic observers have argued that blockchain technology is incompatible with privacy laws such as the EU General Data Protection Regulation (GDPR) (Feng et al., 2019). The original goal of the blockchain was to allow peer-to-peer transactions without the need for a central data possessor. No party is responsible for the availability or protection of a specific blockchain network in a permissionless public blockchain system.

Challenges with the Financial Market Regulation

As finance transactions move from banks to a peer-to-peer system, the question arises as to who is accountable for securing each financial transaction's settlement. Such a duty of care can not only be levied on technology users and providers. Instead, an individual body or network operator should be formed to conform to the requirements of financial services, in compliance with banking laws and regulations.

Ownership

Blockchain, in general, creates different legal issues, including the potential for money laundering, the sale of drugs and weapons, and the financing of terrorism, all of which are well-known (Whyte, 2018). Nevertheless, the ownership issue is something that the world of finance is struggling with blockchain (Ehrenberg & King, 2020). Particularly, in property law, the processes through which ownership may be transferred from one party to another are carefully listed. It sets certain requirements, such as an agreement between the current owner and the potential new owner. Blockchain does not mandate or guarantee the existence of such contracts. It only requires the proper usage of private and public keys, which is a technological prerequisite. Thus, the outcomes of blockchain can conflict with those of traditional private law. A more challenging issue is determining which national law will apply to the transfer, as in traditional cases, there must be national governing legislation determined for each transaction.

Because blockchain is a virtual and global ledger, it is difficult to pinpoint the national law behind every transaction. The fundamental problem is that although legislation is primarily created at the national level, technology, such as blockchain, is entirely delocalized and international (Lehmann, 2019). Therefore, determining the legal framework governing blockchain feels like trying to fit a square peg into a round hole. On the other hand, it is important to recognize the uniqueness of blockchain, which theoretically generates irreversible transactions in a decentralized manner independent of any one state. This makes it difficult to apply traditional private law principles.

The Way Forward

The transition to a financial system with a significant blockchain component opens several prospects for the accounting industry. Accountants are regarded as authorities in standard settings, business logic, complicated rule applications, and record-keeping. They have the opportunity to shape how blockchain is integrated and utilized in the future and create blockchain-powered products and services. Blockchain must be developed, standardized, and optimized as a true component of the financial system (Yoo, 2017). Because there is still much to be done, and it has already been nine years since the inception of Bitcoin, this process is likely to take more years.

Several blockchain applications and start-ups are working towards this, but only a few have advanced with pilot studies or testing (Garanina et al., 2022). Leading accounting companies and authorities may contribute their experience to developing regulations and standards to encompass blockchain, which will require a lot of work. Accountants may also serve as consultants for businesses thinking about utilizing blockchain technology, helping them analyse the benefits and drawbacks of the new technology. Due to their combination of business and financial expertise, accountants and auditors will be in a prime position to advice companies wishing to capitalize on these emerging technologies.

The use of blockchain technology and smart contracts will revolutionize the areas of accounting that deal with transactional assurance and the transfer of property rights. The accounting function will become more effective and valuable by using blockchain and other cutting-edge technologies, such as data analytics or machine learning, to optimize many current accounting department operations. While specific tasks such as provenance assurance and reconciliation will be scaled back or abolished, others, such as technology consulting services, will be expanded. Accountants will not need to have an in-depth understanding of blockchain technology such as engineers; however, they will need to be able to offer advice on blockchain adoption and consider how blockchain will affect their clients and businesses. They must also have the communication skills to serve as a bridge between business stakeholders and technology. Since blockchain is already covered in the ICAEW's ACA, ACCA, and CPA curricula, accountants' skill sets will need to be expanded to incorporate knowledge of its key features and operations.

Additionally, policymakers need to collaborate with the industry and ensure regulatory enforcement to benefit from blockchain technologies. In some instances, policymakers cannot implement comprehensive, prescriptive, and detailed guidelines as the technology itself in the embryo stage. Policymakers must promote technology through flexible laws to cover a wide spectrum of technical applications. In all cases, regulators should collaborate with stakeholders to ensure that the implemented laws, rules, and regulations are well-reasoned for the industry.

Among the proposed remedies, regulatory sandboxes represent a highly promising one pertaining to distributed ledger technology (Ahl et al., 2020). This allows an opportunity for program testing in isolated and highly regulated environments with real people and bona fide consumers. The entire process is also free from the threats of regulatory intervention or retaliation. Furthermore, policymakers may achieve an opportunity to better understand the underlying technology and work closely with industry stakeholders to further refine and fine-tune the enforcement procedure. The final result is the formulation of a regulatory framework that encourages and nurtures innovation without compromising security, privacy, accountability, or forward-thinking solutions (Yeoh, 2017).

One challenge of regulatory sandboxes is ensuring that the financial sector is appealing to them. Sandboxes should promote innovation to expand rather than merely offering legal value. The proliferation of decentralized systems affords regulators discretionary powers that can be misused or misapplied. For instance, participants may inadvertently fall into the liability of a compliance breach trap. The delicate handling of these matters is complicated by the lack of precedents in legal materials.

Hence, governance of blockchain systems is a critical issue; however, that is often overlooked. The governance of a blockchain defines its success and adoption in many ways. Interestingly, different aspects of blockchain governance are analogous to how an organization, consortium, or organization distributes responsibilities among themselves. Each organization/industry must understand this before deciding to adopt blockchain as a solution. This calls for a new governance model, which may be challenging.

A regulatory framework surrounding any novel technology instils confidence in adopters. In contrast, the lack of such a framework creates uncertainties. Therefore, a blockchain-friendly regulatory framework can be an effective tool to overcome many challenges in the financial industry.

It is evident that law and enforcement would work as significant determinants of either open blockchain implementations or closing them for good. The rapid development of proactive regulations remains a challenge for regulators.

Conclusion

Recent policy actions concerning blockchain technologies have focused on digital currencies and financial applications. Nevertheless, in addition to fintech, blockchain has great potential in the accounting and auditing profession. It is imperative to use the potential of every new technology to achieve maximal growth and welfare in all countries. Blockchain has the power to unite various fragmented systems to generate insights and properly assess the value of care. In the long haul, blockchain in accounting will ensure efficiency and bolster a better record-keeping mechanism. However, blockchain technology has not reached the maturity stage, nor is it a silver bullet or an instant solution. Several organizational, technical, and behavioural economic challenges must be overcome before adopting blockchain. Therefore, although this technology has tremendous potential, it is very important to note that it should be dealt with cautiously and with sincerity.

References

Abdennadher, S., Grassa, R., Abdulla, H., & Alfalasi, A. (2022). The effects of blockchain technology on the accounting and assurance profession in the UAE: An exploratory study. *Journal of Financial Reporting and Accounting, 20*(1), 53–71. https://doi.org/10.1108/JFRA-05-2020-0151

Ahl, A., Yarime, M., Goto, M., Chopra, S. S., Kumar, N. M., Tanaka, K., & Sagawa, D. (2020). Exploring blockchain for the energy transition: Opportunities and challenges based on a case study in Japan. *Renewable and Sustainable Energy Reviews*. https://doi.org/10.1016/j.rser.2019.109488

Alles, M., & Gray, G. L. (2020). "The first mile problem": Deriving an endogenous demand for auditing in blockchain-based business processes. *International Journal of Accounting Information Systems, 38*,. https://doi.org/10.1016/j.accinf.2020.100465

Bamakan, S. M. H., Nezhadsistani, N., Bodaghi, O., & Qu, Q. (2022). Patents and intellectual property assets as non-fungible tokens; key technologies and challenges. *Scientific Reports, 12*(1). https://doi.org/10.1038/s41598-022-05920-6

Beck, R., & Müller-Bloch, C. (2017). Blockchain as radical innovation: A framework for engaging with distributed ledgers. *Proceedings of the Annual Hawaii International Conference on System Sciences, 2017-January*.

Bonsón, E., & Bednárová, M. (2019). Blockchain and its implications for accounting and auditing. *Meditari Accountancy Research, 27*(5), 725–740. https://doi.org/10.1108/MEDAR-11-2018-0406

Cai, C. W. (2018). Disruption of financial intermediation by FinTech: A review on crowdfunding and blockchain. *Accounting and Finance, 58*(4), 965–992. https://doi.org/10.1111/acfi.12405

Caytas, J. (2017). Blockchain in the US regulatory setting: Evidentiary use in Vermont, Delaware, and elsewhere. *The Columbia Science and Technology Law Review*.

Centobelli, P., Cerchione, R., Del Vecchio, P., Oropallo, E., & Secundo, G. (2022). Blockchain technology design in accounting: Game changer to tackle fraud or technological fairy tale? *Accounting, Auditing and Accountability Journal, 35*(7), 1566–1597. https://doi.org/10.1108/AAAJ-10-2020-4994

Chalmers, D., Fisch, C., Matthews, R., Quinn, W., & Recker, J. (2022). Beyond the bubble: Will NFTs and digital proof of ownership empower creative industry entrepreneurs? *Journal of Business Venturing Insights, 17*,. https://doi.org/10.1016/j.jbvi.2022.e00309

Christensen, C. M., McDonald, R., Altman, E. J., & Palmer, J. E. (2018). Disruptive innovation: An intellectual history and directions for future research. *Journal of Management Studies*, *55*(7). https://doi.org/10.1111/joms.12349

Clayton, J. (2017). *Statement on cryptocurrencies and initial coin offerings*. https://www.sec.gov/news/public-statement/statement-clayton-2017-12-11

Corrales Compagnucci, M., Kono, T., & Teramoto, S. (2020). Legal aspects of decentralized and platform-driven economies. *Perspectives in Law, Business and Innovation*. https://doi.org/10.1007/978-981-15-1350-3_1

CPA. (2017). *Blockchain technology and its potential impact on the audit and assurance profession*. https://us.aicpa.org/content/dam/aicpa/interestareas/frc/assuranceadvisoryservices/downloadabledocuments/blockchain-technology-and-its-potential-impact-on-the-audit-and-assurance-profession.pdf

De Andrés, J., & Lorca, P. (2021). On the impact of smart contracts on auditing. *International Journal of Digital Accounting Research, 21*, 155–181. https://doi.org/10.4192/1577-8517-v21_6

De Oliveira, L. C., Simoyama, F. D. O., Grigg, I., & Bueno, R. L. P. (2017). Triple entry ledgers with blockchain for auditing. *International Journal of Auditing Technology, 3*(3), 163–183. https://doi.org/10.1504/ijaudit.2017.10007789

Demirkan, S., Demirkan, I., & McKee, A. (2020). Blockchain technology in the future of business cyber security and accounting. *Journal of Management Analytics, 7*(2), 189–208. https://doi.org/10.1080/23270012.2020.1731721

Dumay, J., & Guthrie, J. (2019). Reflections on interdisciplinary critical intellectual capital accounting research: Multidisciplinary propositions for a new future. *Accounting, Auditing and Accountability Journal, 32*(8). https://doi.org/10.1108/AAAJ-08-2018-3636

Dyball, M. C., & Seethamraju, R. (2021). The impact of client use of blockchain technology on audit risk and audit approach—An exploratory study. *International Journal of Auditing, 25*(2), 602–615. https://doi.org/10.1111/ijau.12238

Ehrenberg, A. J., & King, J. L. (2020). Blockchain in Context. *Information Systems Frontiers, 22*(1). https://doi.org/10.1007/s10796-019-09946-6

Elommal, N., & Manita, R. (2022). How blockchain innovation could affect the audit profession: A qualitative study. *Journal of Innovation Economics & Management, 37*(1), 37–63. https://doi.org/10.3917/jie.pr1.0103

Feng, Q., He, D., Zeadally, S., Khan, M. K., & Kumar, N. (2019). A survey on privacy protection in blockchain system. *Journal of Network and Computer Applications*. https://doi.org/10.1016/j.jnca.2018.10.020

Financial Reporting Council (FRC). (2018). *FRC submission to the treasury select committee digital currencies inquiry*. https://www.frc.org.uk/getattachment/52cdb6cb-7498-4a92-9e67-c1f4f8fbb3f7/130418-FRC-response-Treasury-Select-Committee-Digital-Currencies-Inquiry.pdf

Garanina, T., Ranta, M., & Dumay, J. (2022). Blockchain in accounting research: Current trends and emerging topics. *Accounting, Auditing and Accountability Journal, 35*(7), 1507–1533. https://doi.org/10.1108/AAAJ-10-2020-4991

Giancaspro, M. (2017). Is a 'smart contract' really a smart idea? Insights from a legal perspective. *Computer Law and Security Review*. https://doi.org/10.1016/j.clsr.2017.05.007

Governatori, G., Idelberger, F., Milosevic, Z., Riveret, R., Sartor, G., & Xu, X. (2018). On legal contracts, imperative and declarative smart contracts, and blockchain systems. *Artificial Intelligence and Law*. https://doi.org/10.1007/s10506-018-9223-3

Griffin, P. A. (2014). The market for credit default swaps: New insights into investors' use of accounting information? *Accounting and Finance, 54*(3), 847–883. https://doi.org/10.1111/acfi.12092

Griguta, V. M., Gerber, L., Slater-Petty, H., Crocket, K., & Fry, J. (2021). Automated data processing of bank statements for cash balance forecasting. *Intelligent Computing—Proceedings of the 2021 Computing Conference*. https://doi.org/10.1007/978-3-030-80126-7_5

Gruber, S. (2013). Trust, identity, and disclosure: Are bitcoin exchanges the virtual havens for money laundering and tax evasion? *Quinnipiac Law Review*, *32*(1).

Guo, H., & Yu, X. (2022). A survey on blockchain technology and its security. *Blockchain: Research and Applications*, *3*(2). https://doi.org/10.1016/j.bcra.2022.100067

ICAEW. (2017). *Blockchain and the future of accountancy*. ICAEW. https://www.icaew.com/-/media/corporate/files/technical/technology/thought-leadership/blockchain-and-the-future-of-accountancy.ashx

Joshua Fairfield. (2021). Tokenized: The law of non-fungible tokens and unique digital property. *Indiana Law Journal*.

Kend, M., & Nguyen, L. A. (2020). Big data analytics and other emerging technologies: The impact on the Australian audit and assurance profession. *Australian Accounting Review, 30*(4), 269–282. https://doi.org/10.1111/auar.12305

Kshetri, N. (2017). Blockchain's roles in strengthening cybersecurity and protecting privacy. *Telecommunications Policy*. https://doi.org/10.1016/j.telpol.2017.09.003

Lehmann, M. (2019). Who owns bitcoin? Private law facing the blockchain. *Minnesota Journal of Law, Science & Technology, 21*, 93. https://doi.org/10.2139/ssrn.3402678

McCallig, J., Robb, A., & Rohde, F. (2019). Establishing the representational faithfulness of financial accounting information using multiparty security, network analysis and a blockchain. *International Journal of Accounting Information Systems, 33*, 47–58. https://doi.org/10.1016/j.accinf.2019.03.004

Nowiński, W., & Kozma, M. (2017). How can blockchain technology disrupt the existing business models? *Entrepreneurial Business and Economics Review*, *5*(3), 174–188. https://doi.org/10.15678/EBER.2017.050309

Procházka, D. (2018). Accounting for bitcoin and other cryptocurrencies under IFRS: A comparison and assessment of competing models. *International Journal of Digital Accounting Research, 18*(24), 161–188. https://doi.org/10.4192/1577-8517-v18_7

Radziwill, N. (2018). Blockchain revolution: How the technology behind bitcoin is changing money, business, and the world. *Quality Management Journal*. https://doi.org/10.1080/10686967.2018.1404373

Roszkowska, P. (2021). Fintech in financial reporting and audit for fraud prevention and safeguarding equity investments. *Journal of Accounting and Organizational Change, 17*(2), 164–196. https://doi.org/10.1108/JAOC-09-2019-0098

Sargent, C. S. (2021). Replacing financial audits with blockchain: The verification issue. *Journal of Computer Information Systems*. https://doi.org/10.1080/08874417.2021.1992805

Saripalli, S. H. (2021). Transforming Government banking by leveraging the potential of blockchain technology. *Journal of Banking and Financial Technology*, *5*(2). https://doi.org/10.1007/s42786-021-00035-4

Schmitz, J., & Leoni, G. (2019). Accounting and auditing at the time of blockchain technology: A research agenda. *Australian Accounting Review*, *29*(2), 331–342. https://doi.org/10.1111/auar.12286

Sheldon, M. D. (2019). A primer for information technology general control considerations on a private and permissioned blockchain audit. *Current Issues in Auditing*, *13*(1), 15–29. https://doi.org/10.2308/ciia-52356

Shoker, A. (2021). Blockchain technology as a means of sustainable development. *One Earth*, *4*(6). https://doi.org/10.1016/j.oneear.2021.05.014

Singh, K. (2015). The New Wild West: Preventing money laundering in the bitcoin network. *Northwestern Journal of Technology and Intellectual Property*, *13*(1).

Smith, S. S., Petkov, R., & Lahijani, R. (2019). Blockchain and cryptocurrencies—Considerations for treatment and reporting for financial services professionals. *International Journal of Digital Accounting Research*, *19*, 59–78. https://doi.org/10.4192/1577-8517-v19_3

Swammy, S., Thompson, R., & Loh, M. (2018). ICO regulatory and reporting framework. In *Crypto uncovered* (pp. 149–168). Palgrave Macmillan. https://doi.org/10.1007/978-3-030-00135-3_8

Tan, B. S., & Low, K. Y. (2019). Blockchain as the database engine in the accounting system. *Australian Accounting Review*, *29*(2), 312–318. https://doi.org/10.1111/auar.12278

Tseng, C. Te, & Shang, S. S. C. (2021). Exploring the sustainability of the intermediary role in blockchain. *Sustainability (Switzerland)*, *13*(4). https://doi.org/10.3390/su13041936

Utterback, J. M., & Acee, H. J. (2021). Disruptive technologies: An expanded view. *Digital Disruptive Innovation*. https://doi.org/10.1142/s1363919605001162

Werbach, K. (2019). The blockchain and the new architecture of trust. *The Blockchain and the New Architecture of Trust*. https://doi.org/10.7551/mitpress/11449.001.0001

White, B. S., King, C. G., & Holladay, J. (2020). Blockchain security risk assessment and the auditor. *Journal of Corporate Accounting and Finance*, *31*(2), 47–53. https://doi.org/10.1002/jcaf.22433

Whyte, C. (2018). Cryptoterrorism: Assessing the utility of blockchain technologies for terrorist enterprise. *Studies in Conflict and Terrorism*. https://doi.org/10.1080/1057610X.2018.1531565

Xu, Y., Ren, J., Zhang, Y., Zhang, C., Shen, B., & Zhang, Y. (2020). Blockchain empowered arbitrable data auditing scheme for network storage as a service.

IEEE Transactions on Services Computing, *13*(2). https://doi.org/10.1109/TSC.2019.2953033

Yeoh, P. (2017). Regulatory issues in blockchain technology. *Journal of Financial Regulation and Compliance*. https://doi.org/10.1108/JFRC-08-2016-0068

Yoo, S. (2017). Blockchain based financial case analysis and its implications. *Asia Pacific Journal of Innovation and Entrepreneurship*, *11*(3), 312–321. https://doi.org/10.1108/apjie-12-2017-036

PART IV

Innovation in Practice: Applying Technology to Accounting and Auditing

CHAPTER 10

Blockchain Technology in Accounting and Auditing: A Comprehensive Analysis and Review of Feasible Applications

Sheng-Feng Hsieh and Po-Lin Li

Introduction

Blockchains are highly innovative and disruptive information technology that has begun to cause drastic transformations in the business models of several industries (Dai & Vasarhelyi, 2017; Yen & Wang, 2021). Blockchain has several features that make it compatible with accounting information technology, including tamper resistance, high transparency, and automatic verification capabilities (Tyma et al., 2022). Therefore, blockchains are expected to strongly affect accounting and auditing (AICPA, 2018).

S.-F. Hsieh (✉)
Department and Graduate Institute of Accounting, College of Management, National Taiwan University, Taipei, Taiwan
e-mail: sfhsieh@ntu.edu.tw

P.-L. Li
Deloitte & Touche Taiwan, Taipei, Taiwan
e-mail: lli13@deloitte.com.tw

A. Perdana and T. Wang (eds.), *Digital Transformation in Accounting and Auditing*, https://doi.org/10.1007/978-3-031-46209-2_10

Studies have explored how blockchain can be applied to various domains such as supply chains (Liu et al., 2021), fintech (Cai, 2018), initial coin offering (ICO) (Zhang et al., 2021), cryptocurrency (Zhang et al., 2019), and other emerging technologies (Appelbaum & Nehmer, 2020; Church et al., 2020). With the rapid development of blockchain, the amount of research on blockchain in accounting has grown considerably (Lombardi et al., 2021). However, the large volume of information on blockchains prevents scholars from closely monitoring their development. Therefore, literature reviews are useful for surveying information regarding blockchain in accounting and auditing (Garanina et al., 2021). In addition, literature reviews should be conducted to explore the uncertainty surrounding the effects of blockchain and the accompanying digital transformation on accounting and auditing.

In such reviews, motivation and rationale should be explicitly stated (Snyder, 2019). Several studies explore the effects of blockchain on accounting and auditing. In addition, enterprises have increasingly integrated blockchain into their business operations (Guo et al., 2021) in the form of distributed ledgers, smart contracts, and cryptocurrency, representing the motivation for this literature review on how blockchain has evolved and advanced in accounting and auditing. According to Snyder (2019), the findings of studies must be clearly described and related to the research questions (RQs) of a literature review.

The studies included in this review were collected from the top 60 international accounting journals, as identified by Chin et al. (2012). These studies are comprehensively reviewed to determine the effects of blockchain technology on accounting and auditing. Because blockchain technology has not yet been widely adopted (Karajovic et al., 2019), we focus on concepts that may be applied to accounting and auditing in the future. Determining how blockchain disrupts accounting and auditing can benefit these domains. We also propose constructive suggestions and directions for future research.

The remainder of this paper is organized as follows. In Section "Background", we describe the concept and characteristics of blockchain. Section "Methodology" presents the research methods and workflow of this review. Section "Results" presents a comprehensive analysis of the selected studies and interpretation of the results. Section "Directions for Future Research" proposes directions for future research and offers suggestions. Section "Conclusion" presents a summary of the results and implications of blockchain technology for accounting information systems (AISs). This review can serve as a reference for professionals, practitioners, and scholars in accounting and auditing.

Background

Nakamoto (2008) explored the use of blockchain technology for Bitcoin, a well-known and widely traded cryptocurrency. Since then, the applicability of blockchain technology in numerous fields has increased. Blockchains have considerably changed various industries (Deloitte, 2016), such as finance and logistics. Blockchains have also transitioned from being a secure means of monetary trading to being part of an ecosystem of disruptive technology, including the Internet of Things (IoT) (Albizri & Appelbaum, 2021), artificial intelligence (AI), robotic process automation (RPA), and machine learning (ML) (Zhang, 2019). Although applications of blockchain technology are still being explored, the focus has gradually shifted from cryptocurrency to business applications (Stratopoulos et al., 2022); this shift indicates that blockchain technology has evolved into a fundamental technology in contemporary business ecosystems. Professionals, practitioners, and scholars in accounting have highlighted the decentralized and distributed nature of blockchains and expect them to become key components of next-generation AISs (Dai & Vasarhelyi, 2017).

Types of Blockchain

Blockchains can be operated publicly, privately, or by consortiums. In public blockchains, also called permissionless blockchains, all participants receive the same records of transaction data, and no central authority controls the entire chain or approves transactions (Wang & Kogan, 2018). Therefore, the advantage of the public blockchain is that every node has equal authority to maintain the operations of public blockchains. However, one difficulty in implementing public blockchains in business is that transaction data can be leaked, which affects companies (Vincent et al., 2020).

Private blockchains restrict membership, thereby creating a closed environment in which the activity in the system is monitored (Liu et al., 2019). They lack data transparency and public participation because a centralized agency controls the chain. As a result, private blockchains are more conducive to maintaining privacy and meeting business needs than public blockchains (Carrasco & Romi, 2021).

Consortium blockchains combine the characteristics of both public and private blockchains. In consortium blockchains, members are selected in advance and certain participants have authority over the network, as in a private blockchain (Tyma et al., 2022). Private and consortium blockchains are also known as permissioned blockchains. However, consortium blockchains afford more flexibility to engage in activities in the network because approval of a single central authority is not required, as in public blockchains (Tyma et al., 2022). Consortium blockchains are partially decentralized because each participant is authorized to have different levels of access (Liu et al., 2019). Thus, each form of blockchain has a distinct function.

Decentralization and Consensus Mechanisms

Without a central authority approving transactions, members cannot tamper arbitrarily with the system arbitrarily (Tan & Low, 2019). Transactional information is recorded through a globally distributed network of computers based on a mechanism in which each coordinate node shares identical copies of transactional data without control of the central authority. Nodes, usually called miners, are incentivized to create and verify blocks. (Kokina et al., 2017). The block verification process involves numerous mechanisms such as proof of work (PoW), proof of stake (PoS), delegated proof of stake (DPoS), proof of authority (PoA), and proof of capacity (PoC).

In PoW, miners use their computers' processing power to solve a mathematical puzzle involving the hash of a set of transactions and the hash of a prior block as quickly as possible (Kokina et al., 2017). This protocol depends on the power of miners' computers, and the one who solves the puzzle first receives a reward.

PoS requires less computational power, and those who possess cryptocurrency verify transactions based on their account balances (Coyne & McMickle, 2017). Those who hold more assets have more opportunities to verify their transactions. Thus, members holding more units of cryptocurrency have greater potential to sustain the system and preserve the value of their assets.

The DPoS is a popular method that represents a more democratic version of the PoS. Members of a blockchain network vote to elect delegates to validate new blocks. PoA is a specialized consensus mechanism for permissioned blockchains; nodes must pass a preliminary authentication to obtain the right to generate a new block. The PoC depends on the available memory or hard disk space of miners' devices to determine mining rights and validate transactions. Several other mechanisms of consensus exist; however, they are not covered in this literature review.

Through these mechanisms, network members reach consensus and establish trust only if they can solve mathematical problems or receive verification from an authority. The key advantage of using blockchains is that, once a transaction is verified by nodes in the network, modification of the sequence of blocks becomes nearly impossible (Moll & Yigitbasioglu, 2019).

Immutability and Confidentiality

A blockchain is a distributed ledger that provides a secure database of transactions that cannot be altered, which is the so-called immutability. When nodes reach a consensus, valid blocks are chronologically added to the blockchain to form a series of records (Kokina et al., 2017). Thus, blockchain is a distributed and tamper-resistant system that ensures that all members have accurate and identical records and that the integrity of the network is maintained (Zhang et al., 2017). The network is equipped with a robust authentication process in which all nodes are connected by trust. To maintain records, a hash function is used to ensure that transaction data remain private. A hash function is a mathematical algorithm that processes a transaction and generates a fixed value known as a hash value (Lee et al., 2022; Stratopoulos, 2020). Each block generates a unique hash value in which considering the hash value of the previous block (Dunn et al., 2021). Any change to a block creates a new hash value, and tampering with a block requires modification of the previous block. As a result, tampering is nearly impossible because modifying records is extremely difficult and time-consuming.

Another aspect of blockchain technology is asymmetric cryptography, which enables every member to access transactional data to be verified (Harrast et al., 2021). Asymmetric cryptography involves public and private keys that enable encryption and decryption, respectively (Pimentel et al., 2021). A public key can generate a cryptographic number that can be shared with other users, releasing information or receiving cryptoassets (Dunn et al., 2021). A private key is a secret code that enables users to access information or claim ownership of assets (Harrast et al., 2021).

Digital signatures involve the encryption of information using senders' private keys, and whoever knows the sender's public key can decrypt a message and access its information. The purpose of this process is to verify the senders' identities and prevent information from being modified. When the sender's information is modified, those who know the sender's public key cannot access it. The sender can also use the receiver's public key to encrypt information, which the receiver can decrypt using their private key. This maintains the confidentiality of the information and ensures that only those who have the private key can decrypt it. This cryptography mechanism is crucial for protecting private keys that prevent information leaks in blockchain systems (Lineros, 2021). Failure to secure private keys can threaten the integrity and confidentiality of transaction data in blockchain systems.

Transparency and Real-Time Updates

Because a blockchain is a peer-to-peer and distributed network, all transactions recorded in the blocks are shared, and any change to a ledger becomes visible to all parties (Centobelli et al., 2021). Owing to the use of shared ledgers, every node has the same level of authority, resulting in decentralization. Hence, distributed ledgers can increase a company's transparency and ensure that its information is trusted (Garanina et al., 2021). Transparency in internal operations and transaction data can help companies establish trust among market participants and help key entities to understand their business models. Building robust trust among trading partners creates opportunities for cooperation, and strengthens companies' competitive advantages and market positions.

Transactions are posted on the blockchain as they occur and undergo a consensus mechanism (Sheldon, 2019). Thus, every node in a blockchain network can receive information in real time (Cho et al., 2019), accelerating operational procedures. Yermack (2017) explores real-time accounting. Firms can achieve real-time accounting by posting their transaction records on a blockchain system and using tokenization, as discussed by Dai and Vasarhelyi (2017). In such a system, management can provide financial reports to authorities immediately and shareholders can obtain financial statements at any time and evaluate a company's status. Auditors can also access and inspect clients' transaction records at any time; transparency in these records and their ability to be accessed in real time substantially reduces audit risks.

Challenges and Opportunities

Blockchains entail several challenges, including contractual provisions that are difficult to translate into programmable codes, high energy demands, low scalability, and privacy issues (Garanina et al., 2021). Blockchains are also limited by the lack of strict regulations. Concerns regarding regulatory uncertainties and deficiencies have arisen because these factors increase risk and are associated with immoral behavior (Lineros, 2021). However, the regulation of blockchain networks threatens their decentralized nature. Thus, research on blockchain must continue to identify its advantages and disadvantages.

The integration of blockchains into business operations and financial reporting means that AISs and audit procedures must be refined (Kocsis, 2019). According to Dai and Vasarhelyi (2017), blockchains are expected to strongly affect accounting and improve the associated information systems, auditing, and assurance. Therefore, a review of the literature on blockchain in accounting and auditing would be worthwhile.

Methodology

This study was a semi-systematic literature review following the methods prescribed by Snyder (2019), which involved (a) designing the review, specifying the requirement for a review, and selecting a search strategy; (b) searching the literature and documenting the sample selection process; (c) abstracting the selected studies for analysis; and (d) presenting the related results and contributions.

Designing the Review

Although blockchain technology is in the early adoption phase, developments in triple-entry accounting and smart contracts have highlighted its disruptive potential. In addition, with the growing number of studies on blockchain technology in accounting and auditing, the Big Four accounting firms have begun to adopt blockchain to meet clients' needs.

Blockchain technology has significantly affected both accounting and auditing research and practice. Thus, the literature should be reviewed to clearly define the purpose and scope of blockchain applications in accounting and auditing, and to develop questions for further research.

According to Snyder (2019), semi-systematic reviews usually focus on how research in a field has developed and how certain topics have progressed. This review was conducted to identify and synthesize the results of studies that investigated the implications of blockchain for auditing and accounting. We developed standards and detailed plans to ensure that key studies would be included in the review and followed the methods of Snyder (2019); therefore, this study is a semi-systematic literature review.

The search strategy involved the use of searchable terms, databases, and the inclusion and exclusion criteria. As cryptocurrencies, smart contracts, and triple-entry accounting are based on blockchain technology, studies on these topics usually discuss blockchain technology. For this reason, we used the term "blockchain" to search the literature. In addition, studies have been limited to accounting and auditing in international accounting journals. The detailed sample selection process is discussed in the next section.

Conducting the Review

We selected the top 60 international accounting journals identified by Chin et al. (2012) to ensure the quality and reliability of the literature. Table 10.1 lists the journals and their respective rankings. We searched the EBSCO database for studies in these journals from 2016 to 2021 using the keyword "blockchain." The initial search returned a total of 112 studies. We then searched each journal's website following the same process to ensure that the search covered all academic studies on accounting and auditing. After searching each journal's website, 194 studies were obtained.

We then determined the relevance of the studies to the effects and applications of blockchain technology in accounting and auditing by skimming abstracts before reading the full text. Through this process, we eliminated three types of studies: (a) those on blockchain technology that did not relate to accounting or auditing; (b) those that discussed blockchain technology in reference to possibilities for future research or noted it as an emerging technology but did not cover its applications in

Table 10.1 Top 60 international accounting journals

Ranking	*International accounting journals*
1	The Accounting Review
2	Journal of Accounting and Economics
3	Journal of Accounting Research
4	Review of Accounting Studies
5	Accounting, Organizations and Society
6	Contemporary Accounting Research
7	Auditing: A Journal of Practice and Theory
8	Journal of Management Accounting Research
9	Journal of Accounting and Public Policy
10	Journal of the American Taxation Association
11	Journal of Accounting, Auditing and Finance
12	Journal of Business Finance and Accounting
13	Accounting Horizons
14	European Accounting Review
15	National Tax Journal
16	Accounting and Business Research
17	Behavioral Research in Accounting
18	Abacus
19	Journal of Accounting Literature
20	International Journal of Accounting
21	Review of Quantitative Finance and Accounting
22	Journal of Information Systems
23	Asia Pacific Journal of Accounting and Economics
24	Management Accounting Research
25	Issues in Accounting Education
26	British Accounting Review
27	Advances in Accounting
28	Accounting and Finance
29	Journal of Contemporary Accounting & Economics
30	Journal of International Accounting Research
31	International Journal of Accounting Information Systems
32	Critical Perspectives on Accounting
33	Journal of Accounting Education
34	Accounting, Auditing & Accountability Journal
35	Financial Accountability and Management in Governments, Public Services & Charities
36	International Journal of Auditing
37	Accounting and the Public Interest
38	Advances in Quantitative Analysis of Finance and Accounting
39	Journal of International Financial Management and Accounting

(continued)

Table 10.1 (continued)

Ranking	*International accounting journals*
40	Research on Accounting Ethics
41	Pacific Accounting Review
42	Research in Governmental and Non-profit Accounting
43	Advances in Public Interest Accounting
44	Accounting Historians
45	Journal of International Accounting, Auditing and Taxation
46	Advances in Management Accounting
47	Journal of Taxation
48	The ATA Journal of Legal Tax Research
49	Journal of Forensic Accounting
50	Australian Accounting Review
51	Research in Accounting Regulation
52	Accounting Educators' Journal
53	Current Issues in Auditing
54	Journal of Emerging Technologies in Accounting
55	Accounting in Europe
56	Accounting Enquiries
57	The Government Accountants Journal
58	Qualitative Research in Accounting & Management
59	Accounting Forum
60	Accounting, Business and Financial History

and effects on accounting and auditing; and (c) those for which the term "blockchain" only appeared in the names of papers in the reference. After the selection process, and 80 studies remained. Table 10.2 presents the sample selection process.

Results

These studies were comprehensively analyzed to map the development of blockchain technology in accounting and auditing. Table 10.3 presents the distribution of 80 studies in the relevant journals. Table 10.4 presents essential information from each paper, such as author(s), year, research methodology, and area of accounting involved.

Table 10.2 Process of sample selection

Preliminary search results:	
Studies from 2016 to 2021 in the EBSCO database are from the top 60 international accounting journals and contain the keyword "blockchain"	112
Studies from each journal's website	82
Subtotal	194
Excluded:	
Those about blockchain that did not relate to accounting or auditing	(9)
Those that discussed blockchain technology in reference to possibilities for future research or noted it as an emerging technology but did not cover its applications in and effects on accounting and auditing	(83)
Those for which the term "blockchain" only appeared in the references	(22)
Final sample	80

Source Author

Table 10.3 Distribution of studies

Accounting journals	*Number of studies*
Journal of Accounting and Public Policy	2
Journal of Accounting, Auditing and Finance	1
Accounting Horizons	4
Journal of Information Systems	8
Issues in Accounting Education	4
British Accounting Review	2
Accounting and Finance	2
International Journal of Accounting Information Systems	7
Journal of Accounting Education	1
Accounting, Auditing & Accountability Journal	8
International Journal of Auditing	1
Journal of International Accounting, Auditing and Taxation	1
The ATA Journal of Legal Tax Research	2
Australian Accounting Review	6
Accounting Educators' Journal	1
Current Issues in Auditing	7
Journal of Emerging Technologies in Accounting	23

Source Author

Table 10.4 Overview of selected articles

Accounting journals	*Authors*	*Year*	*Articles*	*Main research method*	*Accounting areas*
Journal of Accounting and Public Policy	Miles Gietzmann Francesco Grossetti	2021	Blockchain and other distributed ledger technologies: Where is the accounting?	Conceptual	AIS
	Ashley A. Austin L. Tyler Williams	2021	Evaluating company adoptions of blockchain technology: How do management and auditor communications affect nonprofessional investor judgments?	Empirical	Audit
Journal of Accounting, Auditing and Finance	Eyal Beigman Gerard Brennan Sheng-Feng Hsieh Alexander J. Sannella	2021	Dynamic Principal Market Determination: Fair Value Measurement of Cryptocurrency	Analytical	FA
Accounting Horizons *Accounting Horizons*	Deniz Appelbaum D. Scott Showalter Ting Sun Miklos A. Vasarhelyi	2021	A Framework for Auditor Data Literacy: A Normative Position	Conceptual	Audit AIS
	Vernon J. Richardson Marcia Weidenmier Watson	2021	Act or Be Acted Upon: Revolutionizing Accounting Curriculums with Data Analytics	Conceptual	Audit
	Nikola Kostić Tomaz Sedej	2021	Blockchain technology, inter-organizational relationships and management accounting: A synthesis and a research agenda[a]	Literature Review	MA
	Theophanis C. Stratopoulos Victor Xiaoqi Wang Hua (Jonathan) Ye	2021	Use of Corporate Disclosures to Identify the Stage of Blockchain Adoption[a]	Analytical	Audit

(continued)

Table 10.4 (continued)

Accounting journals	*Authors*	*Year*	*Articles*	*Main research method*	*Accounting areas*
Journal of Information Systems Journal of Information Systems	Feng Guo Stephanie Walton Patrick R. Wheeler Yiyang (Ian) Zhang	2021	Early Disruptors: Examining the Determinants and Consequences of Blockchain Early Adoption	Empirical	MA
	Abdullah Albizri Deniz Appelbaum	2021	Trust but Verify: The Oracle Paradox of Blockchain Smart Contract	DSR	Audit AIS
	Erica Pimentel Emilio Boulianne Shayan Eskandari Jeremy Clark	2021	Systemizing the Challenges of Auditing Blockchain-Based Assets	Interviews	FA Audit AIS
	Mark D. Sheldon	2021	Auditing the Blockchain Oracle Problem	Conceptual	Audit AIS
	Deniz Appelbaum Robert A. Nehmer	2020	Auditing Cloud-Based Blockchain Accounting Systems	DSR	Audit AIS
	Jun Dai Miklos A. Vasarhelyi	2017	Toward Blockchain-Based Accounting and Assurance	Conceptual	Audit AIS
	Kimberly Swanson Church Pamela J SchmidtKemi Ajayi	2020	Forecast Cloudy—Fair or Stormy Weather: Cloud Computing Insights and Issues	Conceptual	AIS
	Chi-Chun Chou Nen-Chen Richard Hwang Gary P. Schneider Tawei Wang Chang-Wei Li William Wei	2021	Using Smart Contracts to Establish Decentralized Accounting Contracts: An Example of Revenue Recognition	Conceptual	FA Audit AIS

(continued)

Table 10.4 (continued)

Accounting journals	*Authors*	*Year*	*Articles*	*Main research method*	*Accounting areas*
Issues in Accounting Education	Stacey R. Kaden Jeff W. Lingwall Trevor T. Shonhiwa	2021	Teaching Blockchain through Coding: Educating the Future Accounting Professional	Conceptual	AIS
	Ryan T. Dunn J. Gregory Jenkins Mark D. Sheldon	2021	Bitcoin and Blockchain: Audit Implications of the Killer Bs	Case Study	FA Audit AIS
	Kerry K. Inger Mollie Mathis	2021	Taxes: Taking a Bite out of Bitcoin	Case Study	Taxation
	Michael E. Ozlanski Eric M. Negangard Rebecca G. Fay	2020	Kabbage: A Fresh Approach to Understanding Fundamental Auditing Concepts and the Effects of Disruptive Technology	Case Study	FA Audit AIS
British Accounting Review *British Accounting Review*	Jodie Moll Ogan Yigitbasioglu	2019	The role of internet-related technologies in shaping the work of accountants: New directions for accounting research	Literature Review	FA MA Audit AIS
	Niamh M. Brennan Nava Subramaniam Chris J. van Staden	2019	Corporate governance implications of disruptive technology: An overview	Commentary	FA MA Audit AIS
Accounting and Finance	Cynthia Weiyi Cai	2021	Triple-entry accounting with blockchain: How far have we come?	Case Study	Audit AIS
	Cynthia Weiyi Cai	2018	Disruption of financial intermediation by FinTech: a review on crowdfunding and blockchain	Literature Review	FA MA AIS

(continued)

Table 10.4 (continued)

Accounting journals	*Authors*	*Year*	*Articles*	*Main research method*	*Accounting areas*
International Journal of Accounting Information Systems	Jonas Sveistrup Søgaard	2021	A Blockchain-enabled Platform for VAT settlement	DSR	AIS Taxation
	Ju-Chun Yen Tawei Wang	2021	Stock price relevance of voluntary disclosures about blockchain technology and cryptocurrencies	Empirical	FA
	Yunsen Wang Alexander Kogan	2018	Designing confidentiality-preserving Blockchain-based transaction processing systems	Conceptual	Audit AIS
	John McCallig Alastair Robb Fiona Rohde	2019	Establishing the representational faithfulness of financial accounting information using multiparty security, network analysis, and a blockchain	Conceptual	FA Audit AIS
International Journal of Accounting Information Systems	Nishani Edirisinghe Vincent Anthony Skjellum Sai Medury	2020	Blockchain architecture: A design that helps CPA firms leverage the technology	Conceptual	Audit AIS
	Michael Alles Glen L. Gray	2020	"The first mile problem": Deriving an endogenous demand for auditing in blockchain-based business processes	Conceptual	Audit AIS
	David Kocsis	2019	A conceptual foundation of design and implementation research in accounting information systems	Literature Review	AIS
Journal of Accounting Education	Myles Stern Alan Reinstein	2021	A blockchain course for accounting and other business students	Conceptual	FA MA Audit AIS Taxation

(continued)

Table 10.4 (continued)

Accounting journals	*Authors*	*Year*	*Articles*	*Main research method*	*Accounting areas*
Accounting, Auditing & Accountability Journal	Bridget Tyma Rina Dhillon Prabhu Sivabalan Bernhard Wieder	2021	Understanding accountability in blockchain systems	Interviews	MA Audit AIS
Accounting, Auditing & Accountability Journal	Piera Centobelli Roberto Cerchione Pasquale Del Vecchio Eugenio Oropallo Giustina Secundo	2021	Blockchain technology design in accounting: Game changer to tackle fraud or technological fairy tale?	DSR	MA Audit AIS
	Heather Carrasco Andrea M. Romi	2021	Toward an omniopticon: the potential of blockchain technology toward influencing vulnerable populations in contested markets	Conceptual	MA Audit AIS
	Tatiana Garanina Mikko Ranta John Dumay	2021	Blockchain in accounting research: current trends and emerging topics	Literature Review	FA MA Audit AIS
	Maria Cadiz Dyball Ravi Seethamraju	2021	Client use of blockchain technology: exploring its (potential) impact on financial statement audits of Australian accounting firms	Interviews	Audit AIS

(continued)

Table 10.4 (continued)

Accounting journals	*Authors*	*Year*	*Articles*	*Main research method*	*Accounting areas*
	Silvana Secinaro Francesca Dal Mas Valerio Brescia Davide Calandra	2021	Blockchain in the accounting, auditing and accountability fields: a bibliometric and coding analysis	Literature Review	FA MA Audit AIS
	Rosa Lombardi Charl de Villiers Nicola Moscariello Michele Pizzo	2021	The disruption of blockchain in auditing—a systematic literature review and an agenda for future research	Literature Review	FA MA Audit AIS
	Paola Ramassa Giulia Leoni	2021	Standard setting in times of technological change: accounting for cryptocurrency holdings	Conceptual	FA
International Journal of Auditing	Maria Cadiz Dyball Ravi Seethamraju	2021	The impact of client use of blockchain technology on audit risk and audit approach—An exploratory study	Interviews	Audit AIS
Journal of International Accounting, Auditing and Taxation	Victor Tiberiusa Stefanie Hirth	2019	Impacts of digitization on auditing: A Delphi study for Germany	Interviews	Audit AIS
The ATA Journal of Legal Tax Research	William D. Terando Bryan Cataldi	2017	Impact of the IRC Section 475 Mark-to-Market Election on Bitcoin Taxation	Conceptual	Taxation

(continued)

Table 10.4 (continued)

Accounting journals	*Authors*	*Year*	*Articles*	*Main research method*	*Accounting areas*
	Mollie T. Adams William A. Bailey	2021	Emerging Cryptocurrencies and IRS Summons Power: Striking the Proper Balance between IRS Audit Authority and Taxpayer Privacy	Conceptual	Taxation
Australian Accounting Review	Michael Kend Lan Anh Nguyen	2020	Big Data Analytics and Other Emerging Technologies: The Impact on the Australian Audit and Assurance Profession	Interviews	Audit AIS
	Jana Schmitz Giulia Leoni	2019	Accounting and Auditing at the Time of Blockchain Technology: A Research Agenda	Literature Review	MA Audit AIS
	Maria Karajovic Marek Laskowski Henry M. Kim	2019	Thinking Outside the Block: Projected Phases of Blockchain Integration in the Accounting Industry	Conceptual	MA Audit AIS
	Boon Seng Tan Kin Yew Low	2019	Blockchain as the Database Engine in the Accounting System	Conceptual	Audit AIS
Australian Accounting Review	TyroneCarlin	2019	Blockchain and the Journey Beyond Double Entry	Conceptual	AIS
	Filip Hampl Lucie Gyönyörová	2021	Can Fiat-backed Stablecoins Be Considered Cash or Cash Equivalents Under International Financial Reporting Standards Rules?	Conceptual	FA
Accounting Educators' Journal	Elizabeth A. Felski Tyson B. Empey	2020	Should Blockchain be added to the Accounting Curriculum? Evidence from a Survey of Students, Professionals and Academics	Survey	Audit AIS

(continued)

Table 10.4 (continued)

Accounting journals	*Authors*	*Year*	*Articles*	*Main research method*	*Accounting areas*
Current Issues in Auditing	Nishani Edirisinghe Vincent Reza Barkhi	2021	Evaluating Blockchain Using COSO	Conceptual	MA Audit AIS
	Manlu Liu Kean Wu Jennifer Jie Xu	2019	How Will Blockchain Technology Impact Auditing and Accounting: Permissionless versus Permissioned Blockchain	Conceptual	MA Audit AIS
	Mark D. Sheldon	2019	A Primer for Information Technology General Control Considerations on a Private and Permissioned Blockchain Audit	Conceptual	Audit AIS
	Mark D. Sheldon	2018	Using Blockchain to Aggregate and Share Misconduct Issues across the Accounting Profession	Conceptual	Audit
	Nishani Edirisinghe Vincent Anne M. Wilkins	2020	Challenges when Auditing Cryptocurrencies	Conceptual	FA Audit
Current Issues in Auditing	Mark D. Sheldon	2021	Preparing Auditors for the Blockchain Oracle Problem	Commentary	Audit AIS
	Steven A. Harrast Debra Mcgilsky Yan (Tricia) Sun	2021	Determining the Inherent Risks of Cryptocurrency: A Survey Analysis[a]	Survey	FA Audit
Journal of Emerging Technologies in Accounting	Stanton Heister Matthew Kaufman Kristi Yuthas	2021	Blockchain and the Future of Business Data Analytics	Case Study	Audit AIS
	Kimberly Swanson Church Sean Stein Smith Ethan Kinory	2021	Accounting Implications of Blockchain: A Hyperledger Composer Use Case for Intangible Assets	Case Study	MA Audit AIS

(continued)

Table 10.4 (continued)

Accounting journals	*Authors*	*Year*	*Articles*	*Main research method*	*Accounting areas*
	Jose Victor Lineros	2021	IT Governance Considerations for Permissioned Blockchains	Conceptual	MA Audit AIS
	Theophanis C. Stratopoulos	2020	Teaching Blockchain to Accounting Students	Conceptual	Audit AIS
	Sean Stein Smith John "Jack" Castonguay	2020	Blockchain and Accounting Governance: Emerging Issues and Considerations for Accounting and Assurance Professionals	Conceptual	MA Audit AIS
	Ethan Kinory Sean Stein Smith Kimberly Swanson Church	2020	Exploring the Playground: Blockchain Prototype Use Cases with Hyperledger Composer	Case Study	AIS
Journal of Emerging Technologies in Accounting	Amer Qasim Faten F. Kharbat	2020	Blockchain Technology, Business Data Analytics, and Artificial Intelligence: Use in the Accounting Profession and Ideas for Inclusion into the Accounting Curriculum	Conceptual	FA MA Audit AIS
	Irfan Bora Huijue Kelly Duan Miklos A. Vasarhelyi Chanyuan (Abigail) Zhang Jun Dai	2021	The Transformation of Government Accountability and Reporting	Commentary	MA Audit AIS
	Andrea M. Rozario Chanta Thomas	2019	Reengineering the Audit with Blockchain and Smart Contracts	DSR	Audit AIS

(continued)

Table 10.4 (continued)

Accounting journals	*Authors*	*Year*	*Articles*	*Main research method*	*Accounting areas*
	Ahmed A. Gomaa Mohamed I. Gomaa Ashley Stampone	2019	A Transaction on the Blockchain: An AIS Perspective, Intro Case to Explain Transactions on the ERP and the Role of the Internal and External Auditor	Case Study	Audit AIS
	Jun Dai Na He Haizong Yu	2019	Utilizing Blockchain and Smart Contracts to Enable Audit 4.0: From the Perspective of Accountability Audit of Air Pollution Control in China	Conceptual	MA Audit AIS
	Julia Kokina Ruben Mancha Dessislava Pachamanova	2017	Blockchain: Emergent Industry Adoption and Implications for Accounting	Conceptual	MA Audit AIS
Journal of Emerging Technologies in Accounting *Journal of Emerging Technologies in Accounting*	Joshua G. Coyne Peter L. McMickle	2017	Can Blockchains Serve an Accounting Purpose?	Conceptual	Audit AIS
	Lazarus Elad Fotoh Johan Ingemar Lorentzon	2021	The Impact of Digitalization on Future Audits	Literature Review	Audit
	Robert H. Herz Duo Pei	2021	Advancing Financial Reporting in the Age of Technology: An Interview with Robert H. Herz	Interviews	Audit AIS
	Soohyun Cho Miklos A. Vasarhelyi Chanyuan (Abigail) Zhang	2019	The Forthcoming Data Ecosystem for Business Measurement and Assurance	Commentary	Audit AIS
	Yu Cong Hui Du Miklos A. Vasarhelyi	2018	Technological Disruption in Accounting and Auditing	Commentary	Audit AIS

(continued)

Table 10.4 (continued)

Accounting journals	*Authors*	*Year*	*Articles*	*Main research method*	*Accounting areas*
	Qingliang Tang Lie Ming Tang	2019	Toward a Distributed Carbon Ledger for Carbon Emissions Trading and Accounting for Corporate Carbon Management	Conceptual	MA Audit AIS
	Michael G. Alles Jun Dai Miklos A. Vasarhelyi	2021	Reporting 4.0: Business Reporting for the Age of Mass Customization	Commentary	Audit AIS
	Li Zhang Duo Pei Miklos A. Vasarhelyi	2017	Toward a New Business Reporting Model	Commentary	Audit AIS
	Manlu Liu Ashok Robin Kean Wu Jennifer Xu	2021	Blockchain's Impact on Accounting and Auditing: A Use Case on Supply Chain Traceability[a]	Case Study	MA Audit AIS
	Lorraine S. Lee Deniz Appelbaum Richard D. Mautz III	2021	Blockchains: An Experiential Accounting Learning Activity[a]	Conceptual	Audit AIS
	Nishani Edirisinghe Vincent Stephan A. Davenport	2021	Accounting Research Opportunities for Cryptocurrencies[a]	Conceptual	FA MA Audit AIS Taxation

[a]Online early paper
[b]AIS: accounting information system; MA: management accounting; FA: financial accounting
[c]The sorting criteria are followed by the ranking of international accounting journals

Comprehensive Analysis

The studies were analyzed to determine the year in which the most studies were published, the research methodology they used, and the implications of their results. We also analyzed themes among the studies to understand the influence of blockchain on accounting and auditing.

Trends in Practice and Academia

Blockchain technology can increase the transparency, traceability, confidentiality, and integrity of financial data and transaction records owing to its distributed and cryptographical information-sharing mechanism (Albizri & Appelbaum, 2021). For this reason, blockchain technology can benefit AISs by eliminating repetition and the need for reconciliation by enabling entire databases rather than samples to be tested and by preventing human error (Dai & Vasarhelyi, 2017). Thus, blockchains can streamline numerous redundant tasks in accounting and auditing, enabling accountants and auditors to focus on tasks that require human judgment (Karajovic et al., 2019).

To maintain relationships with their clients, Big Four accounting firms have begun to provide blockchain services to enterprises. For example, Deloitte created "Deloitte Blockchain Labs"[1] in 2017 to provide consultation services to companies adopting blockchain technology. PwC created the "Crypto Center"[2] to help inform consumers about cryptocurrency and provide digital asset strategies, accounting and auditing of digital assets, and risk management and control. In addition, KPMG Blockchain Services[3] collaborated with Microsoft to develop a range of professional services related to blockchain technology. EY Blockchain Solutions[4] support contracting, ordering, fulfilling, invoicing,

[1] "Deloitte Blockchain Labs", available at: https://www2.deloitte.com/us/en/pages/consulting/solutions/blockchain-labs.html.

[2] "Crypto Center", available at: https://www.pwc.com/gx/en/about/new-ventures/crypto-center.html.

[3] "KPMG Blockchain Services", available at: https://home.kpmg/xx/en/home/insights/2017/02/digital-ledger-services-at-kpmg-fs.html.

[4] "Blockchain solutions", available at: https://www.ey.com/en_gl/blockchain-platforms.

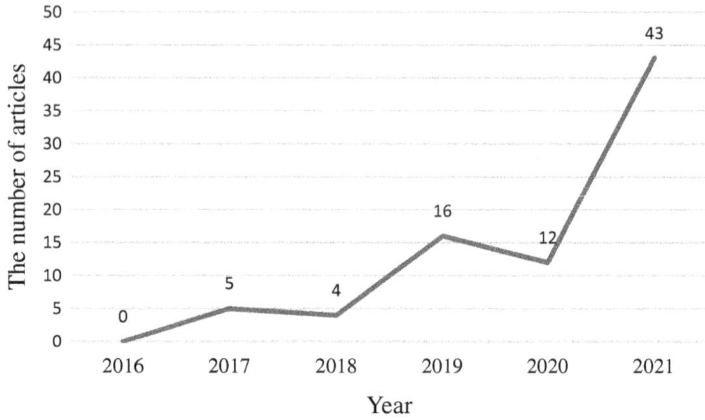

Fig. 10.1 Number of studies by year (*Source* Author)

and payment and manage audit requirements for blockchain-based transactions. These services demonstrate the proactiveness and openness of Big Four accounting firms to blockchain technology.

According to practitioners and scholars, auditors must develop new skills and knowledge related to blockchain technology to satisfy their clients (Felski & Empey, 2020). Scholars are increasingly interested in how blockchain technology affects accounting and auditing, as revealed by the considerable increase in the number of studies in 2021 (see Fig. 10.1). Most relevant studies explore how blockchain technology has progressed and how it can be applied to accounting and auditing. Once blockchain technology is widely adopted in accounting and auditing, studies will begin to investigate its effects in detail and the number of related studies in international accounting journals will increase substantially.

Methodology of Selected Articles Adopted

To categorize the research methods, we refer to Moll and Yigitbasioglu (2019). As shown in Fig. 10.2, most of the relevant studies used conceptual methods (approximately 45%). Others have used literature reviews and case studies. Only three studies involved empirical research.

One study examined the determinants of the early adoption of blockchain technology among public companies, namely the number of

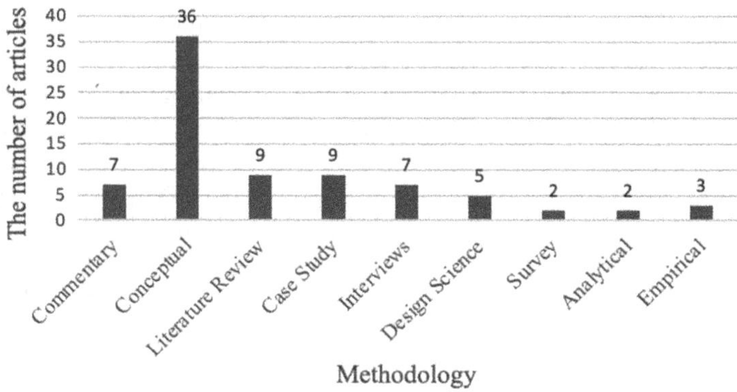

Fig. 10.2 Number of studies by methodology (*Source* Author)

patents, agency costs (managerial discretion), complexity, and degree of external monitoring through the release of financial statements and online business news (Guo et al., 2021). The study revealed that several early adopters were in high-tech industries and that companies with more patents had more opportunities to implement blockchain technology earlier. In addition, the study indicated that managers with the authority to make risky decisions can encourage early adoption, whereas strong external monitoring discourages early adoption.

Another study explored the stock price relevance of voluntary disclosure of information regarding blockchain technology and cryptocurrency (Yen & Wang, 2021). This study revealed that the release of information regarding blockchain has positive stock price relevance, but cryptocurrency does not. The study also involved a thematic analysis of relevant information: information regarding blockchain solutions and risk factors has positive stock price relevance, whereas information regarding Bitcoin transactions has negative stock price relevance.

Another study investigated how communication among managers and auditors regarding companies' adoption of blockchain technology affects nonprofessional investors (Austin & Williams, 2021). The study demonstrated that investor evaluations are generally unfavorable when auditor reports include critical audit matters related to companies' adoption of advanced technology and when Form 10-K specifically references blockchain technology. However, that study also revealed that specific mentions of blockchain technology in managers' descriptions of advanced technology did not affect investors' judgments when audit reports did not note companies' use of advanced technology.

Each of these studies analyzed the release of financial reporting, noting blockchains. Few studies have focused on the effects of blockchain technology on accounting and auditing as an immature and rarely adopted technology, resulting in a lack of empirical data. Despite this lack of data, several studies have proposed novel ideas and made substantive contributions to the literature. Dai and Vasarhelyi (2017) proposed the concept of triple-entry AISs. Centobelli et al. (2021) designed a conceptual framework for a blockchain-based accounting ecosystem comprising a technological infrastructure layer, control layer, and business application layer. Liu et al. (2021) conducted a case study to illustrate how a blockchain system traces transaction flows and records the transaction data. Thus, the results of these studies have contributed to the development of blockchain technology for accounting and auditing.

Aspects of Accounting

Following Qasim and Kharbat (2020), we subdivided accounting into financial accounting (FA), management accounting (MA), auditing, AISs, and taxation. Figure 10.3 presents the number of studies related to each subdivision. Because a single study can cover multiple areas of accounting, the total number exceeds 80.

Blockchain technology can serve as a disruptive AIS and transform audit procedures. Most of the related studies involved AISs and auditing topics such as smart contracts, triple-entry accounting, and continuous auditing. Blockchain technology can improve AISs because it ensures the integrity of data and enables the immediate sharing of transaction information and programming and automatization of procedures. A total of 64 studies proposed blockchain-based AISs and investigated how blockchain technology can improve AISs. For example, Cai (2021) used three case studies to explore a triple-entry AIS and discovered that it increases trust and transparency. Tan and Low (2019) examined how blockchain technology can transform accounting by digitizing AIS databases. In brief, AIS is an important and crucial domain for observing the development of a blockchain.

The number of studies on auditing is similar to that on AISs. As it automatizes certain audit procedures through smart contracts, continuous auditing is used to examine companies' transaction data and internal controls at any time, rather than at the end of quarters or years (Carlin,

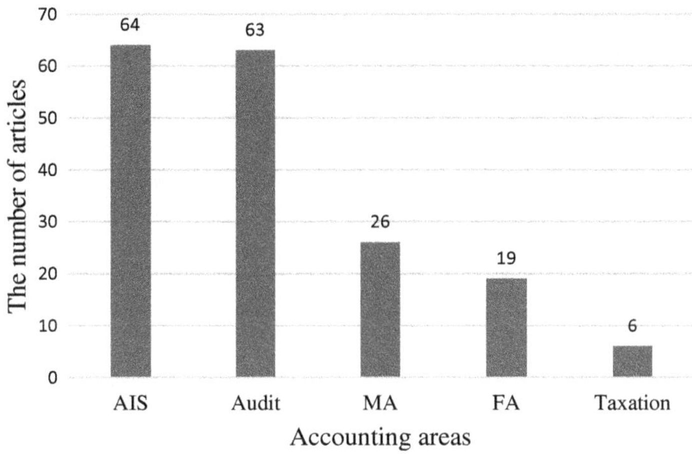

Fig. 10.3 Number of studies by accounting field (*Because a single study can cover multiple areas of accounting, the total number of exceeds 80. *Source* Author)

2019). The transaction records recorded in a blockchain system enable real-time auditing and help auditors understand their clients. Rozario and Thomas (2019) suggested that smart contracts can enable auditors to automatize audit procedures using predetermined parameters in a blockchain network, thereby increasing efficiency and preventing human error. Moreover, Cong et al. (2018) noted that continuous auditing can enable real-time detection of misstatements and automatic correction, thereby ensuring that companies provide financial reports in real time.

One-third of the studies included MA. In MA, blockchain technology is usually related to inter-organizational relations, accountability, and corporate governance. The ability of blockchain technology to enable instantaneous, high-fidelity, low-cost reporting can facilitate inter-organizational communication and collaboration (Heister et al., 2021). Kostić and Sedej (2021) showed that inter-organizational cooperation can reduce monitoring costs, which may improve cost structures. Tyma et al. (2022) explored various accountability mechanisms in blockchain technology and revealed that even immature applications of blockchain technology can ensure accountability. Besides Brennan et al. (2019) indicated that blockchain-based corporate governance is decentralized, with decisions being made through consensus mechanisms. Therefore, management must consider the degree of decentralization and the appropriate consensus mechanism to implement. Management must also determine an appropriate response to the transformation of MA caused by the use of blockchain technology. Liu et al. (2019) suggest that permissioned blockchains can satisfy the need for corporate governance because they entail robust authority and accountability mechanisms.

The FA involves the classification and evaluation of cryptocurrencies. As Ramassa and Leoni (2021) indicated, the International Financial Reporting Standards Interpretation Committee (IFRSIC) indicated that cryptocurrency matches its definition of an asset. According to IAS 2, inventories are assets held for sale in normal business practices. Some enterprises that hold cryptocurrencies for sale can treat cryptocurrencies as inventory in accounting (Hampl & Gyönyörová, 2021; IASB, 2019; Ramassa & Leoni, 2021). Furthermore, cryptocurrencies meet the definition of IAS 38 (IASB, 2014), which defines intangible assets as assets that are identifiable, controlled by an entity, and have future economic benefits. Therefore, in some cases, they can be considered intangible assets in some cases (Hampl & Gyönyörová, 2021; IASB, 2019; Ramassa & Leoni, 2021).

Under the U.S. generally accepted accounting principles (U.S. GAAP), AICPA (2022) indicated that cryptocurrencies are not tangible assets and therefore do not satisfy the definition of inventory for general companies. However, in light of a broker-dealer's business practice, the AICPA regarded cryptocurrencies as inventories that are held for trading. AICPA (2022) also indicated that cryptocurrencies meet the definition of intangible assets and would generally be accounted for under U.S. GAAP.

Whether cryptocurrencies should be treated as inventory or intangible assets depends on the situation. Beigman et al. (2021) developed an approach to dynamically specify principal markets and evaluate the fair value of cryptocurrency for financial reporting. The real-time fair value derived from this approach is expected to enhance the quality and representativeness of financial reporting. After the decision made by the Financial Accounting Standards Board (FASB) that cryptocurrencies meeting the criteria should be measured at fair value on companies' financial statements (FASB, 2022),[5] an approach that consistently complies

[5] In August 2022, the FASB defined the criteria for the scope of its crypto asset project as follows:

with fair value accounting standards (ASC 820) would become more relevant and bring benefits to the practice.

Few studies have covered taxation and several topics remain to be investigated. Søgaard (2021) proposed a blockchain-based platform to increase the efficiency and transparency of value-added tax settlements and reduce the heavy administrative burden imposed by governments. This platform can also strengthen the relationship between companies' AISs and government agencies. Søgaard (2021) conducted a case study to demonstrate how governments lighten the administrative burdens on small and medium-sized companies while maintaining the flow of tax revenue. With the popularity of virtual currencies, several taxation-related problems have emerged. The Internal Revenue Service's Notice 2014–21 indicates that virtual currencies, including Bitcoin, should be treated as property rather than as currency for federal tax purposes, and that the tax principles applicable to property transactions also apply to virtual currency transactions (Adams & Bailey, 2021; IRS, 2014; Terando et al., 2017). Inger and Mathis (2021) conducted a case study to introduce students to problems related to taxation on virtual currency for miners and short- and long-term investors and indicated that 95% of the students believed or strongly believed that they had gained knowledge of this topic. Thus, a case study is an efficient way to strengthen students' comprehension of virtual currencies and related tax issues.

Each accounting domain presents a unique challenge. As Albizri and Appelbaum (2021) indicated, the ability of blockchain technology to store records that accurately represent physical transactions still requires independent verification. Coyne and McMickle (2017) identified several factors impeding the adoption of blockchains to support financial reporting, namely, concerns regarding confidentiality, 51% attacks, and the lack of a transaction verification mechanism. Therefore, the development of blockchains in each field must be further investigated.

- *Meet the definition of intangible asset as defined in the Codification Master Glossary.*
- *Do not provide the asset holder with enforceable rights to, or claims on, underlying goods, services, or other assets.*
- *Are created* or *reside on a distributed ledger or "blockchain.".*
- *Are* secured *through cryptography.*
- *Are* fungible.

The board meeting minutes are available at: https://www.fasb.org/document/blob?fileName=CRYPTO-MIN-20220831.pdf.

Finally, we selected keywords from the studies to create a word cloud (see Fig. 10.4) and identified key themes. Because nine studies did not provide keywords, the word cloud only contained keywords from 71 studies. The three most frequently used keywords were blockchain (60 times), accounting (28 times), and audit (23 times).

Triple-entry bookkeeping, smart contracts, continuous auditing, accountability, and governance are the key topics. Although the authors of the studies did not use triple-entry bookkeeping or "triple-entry bookkeeping" or "continuous auditing" as keywords, 20 and 37 studies, respectively, covered (or at least mentioned) these terms. Therefore,

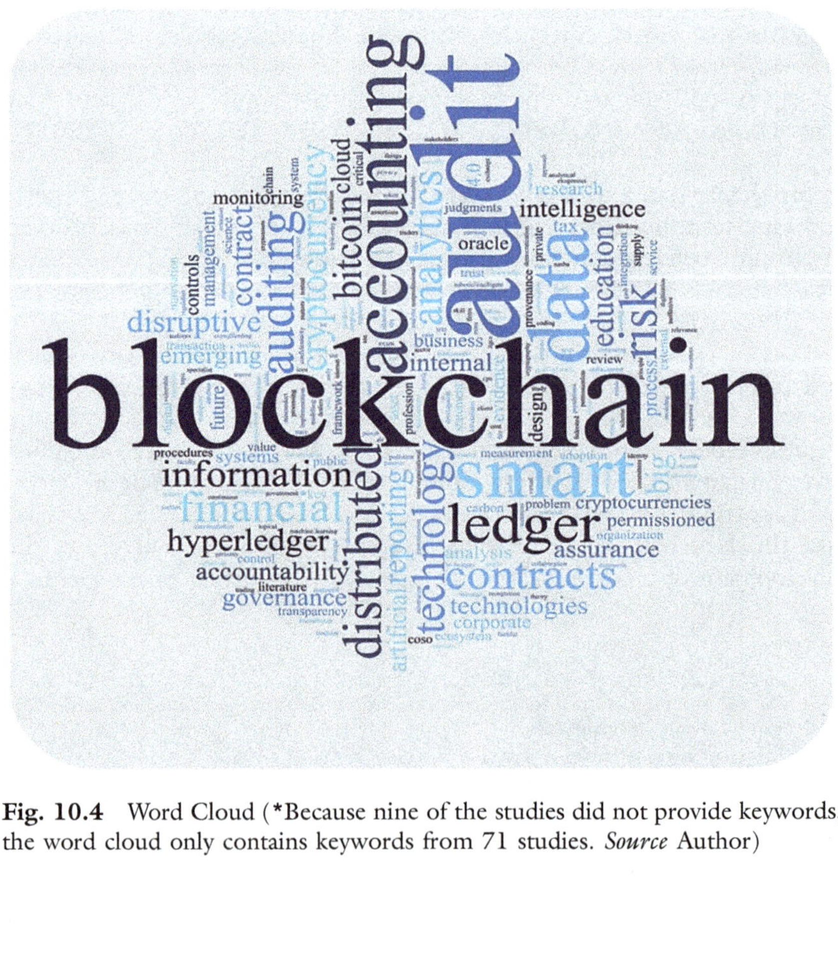

Fig. 10.4 Word Cloud (*Because nine of the studies did not provide keywords, the word cloud only contains keywords from 71 studies. *Source* Author)

triple-entry bookkeeping and continuous auditing are also key concepts that can help scholars and practitioners understand blockchain applications in accounting and auditing.

Feasible Concepts and Applications

Triple-Entry Bookkeeping

Blockchain enables triple-entry bookkeeping to serve as an AIS in which every transaction is recorded in debit and credit accounts and then encoded in the blockchain as a third accounting entry (Cai, 2021). Thus, blockchains can enhance traditional double-entry systems such as enterprise resource planning (ERP). Smart contracts can also accelerate bookkeeping in triple-entry AISs by enabling the encoding of accounting standards and predetermined conditions (Dai & Vasarhelyi, 2017). In such an AIS, each account in the ERP system has a corresponding blockchain account. Figure 10.5 presents a possible framework for a triple-entry AIS proposed by Dai and Vasarhelyi (2017).

The third entry is recorded by tokens, indicates transaction flows, and acts as a credential to verify the rights to or ownership of assets among trading partners (Gomaa et al., 2019). In traditional AISs, when companies sell products or provide services to customers on credit, they debit

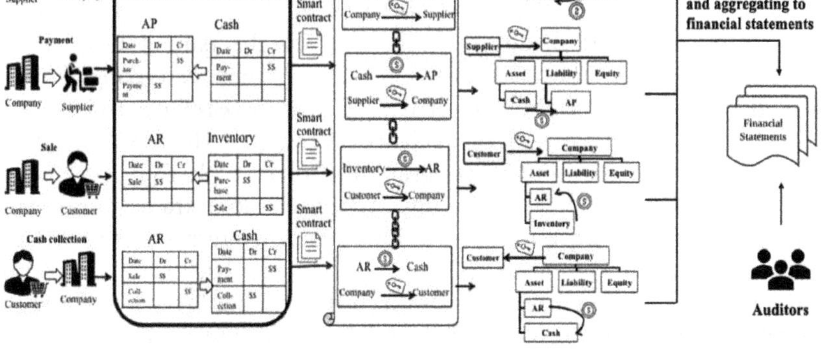

Fig. 10.5 A triple-entry AIS (*Source* Modified from Dai and Vasarhelyi [2017])

accounts receivable, credit sales revenue, and service revenue. Companies also debit the cost of goods sold and credit inventory. With blockchains, companies can then post these transactions in a blockchain ledger using smart contracts, thereby accomplishing triple-entry bookkeeping. Dai and Vasarhelyi (2017) described one notable advantage of this process: "*Accounts in the blockchain ledger would be organized in a hierarchical to aggregate data at various levels, which enables both instant balancing of accounting equation and different views of information for different users.*" This hierarchical structure facilitates balance reconciliation and reduces costs considerably.

Encrypting information is crucial for enabling companies to maintain confidentiality. Blockchains provide several solutions to ensure that problems related to confidentiality and privacy do not create a substantial risk to triple-entry bookkeeping for accounting and auditing (Coyne & McMickle, 2017). Examples of such solutions include cryptographic functions involving hash values and private and public keys that encrypt transaction data. Companies can use this function to ensure security among trading partners and confidentiality of transactions (Dai & Vasarhelyi, 2017).

Another solution is to create a permissioned blockchain network in which a limited number of members are authorized to access internal data. In a permissioned blockchain, only trusted members such as business partners have authority over access control, which enables companies to allow certain members to record or verify transactions, with the other members only having read access (Rozario & Thomas, 2019). Permissionless blockchains are more vulnerable to 51% of attacks than permissioned blockchains. In 51% of attacks, because each block is added to a blockchain through a consensus mechanism, if more than half of the members of a blockchain collude, they can considerably modify data (Coyne & McMickle, 2017). Companies prefer permissioned blockchains to permissionless blockchains because of their privacy. The increased confidentiality and cryptographic nature of blockchains ensure the security of triple-entry bookkeeping and trust among trading partners.

The third accounting entry in the blockchain ledgers can be used to track transaction flows and detect errors. As Cai (2021) and Dai and Vasarhelyi (2017) indicate transactions in blockchain ledgers are stored in the form of tokens and recorded in chronological order in a triple-entry AIS. These records were also connected to the internal records of the ERP system. Companies can allow read-only access to auditors to verify transaction data in permissioned blockchains. Thus, triple-entry AISs make transactions easily observable and verifiable, leaving a transparent audit trial. Although using a blockchain's distributed ledgers as infrastructure for accounting entails risk and requires considerable investment, it would ensure a transparent, automatically verifiable, and error-less AIS. In addition, using a blockchain's distributed ledgers as AIS reduces operating costs, prevents fraud, facilitates bookkeeping, and increases the operational efficiency and auditability of transactions. Blockchain technology has transformed accounting and auditing technologies. As secure and distributed platforms, triple-entry AISs would increase accounting efficiency and improve the auditing process.

Smart Contracts

Another popular blockchain-based feature is smart contracts. In smart contracts, contractual parties transform covenant clauses into computer program codes to execute transactions (Chou et al., 2021). Smart contracts are event-oriented digital contracts, the terms of which are specified by users that automatically execute conditions (Rozario & Thomas, 2019). Because blockchain data cannot be modified, the provisions in smart contracts cannot be changed arbitrarily by any party (Cai, 2021). Once certain situations arise, smart contracts automatically initiate predetermined functions, as shown in Fig. 10.6 demonstrates this process. For example, a company and its suppliers can set the conditions for a purchase by using smart contracts. Once the company receives goods it orders on credit, the smart contract will automatically become active, settle the accounts payable, and write off the accounts receivable of the supplier when payment is received. Thus, transactions are managed in real time, which accelerates the flow of information and bookkeeping.

As blockchain technology offers real-time data sharing, each node can monitor the activities and breaches of smart contracts at any time. Centobelli et al. (2021) indicated that smart contracts enable nodes to monitor transactions, accelerate processes, and ensure automatization and decentralization. Smart contracts in blockchain technology can also eliminate the requirement for balance reconciliation among the trading parties. As agreed-upon requirements are encoded in smart contracts, trading partners can avoid disputes and prevent deceit (Vincent & Barkhi, 2021). Thus, smart contracts are advantageous tools that can transform businesses by increasing efficiency, eliminating transaction costs,

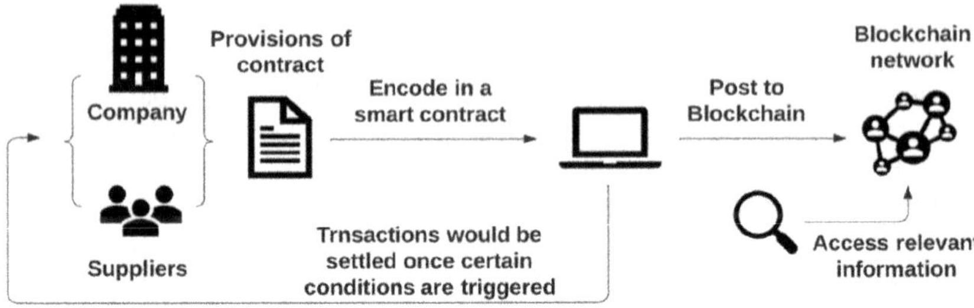

Fig. 10.6 A demonstration of smart contract (*Source* Author)

and preventing fraud and human error, particularly in accounting and auditing.

In addition to covenant provisions, smart contracts can encode conditions for specific procedures to assign tasks in accordance with established rules such as accounting standards, audit procedures, and operational routines (Dai & Vasarhelyi, 2017). As discussed in the previous section, Cai (2021) demonstrates that smart contracts can be applied to triple-entry AISs. This framework increases operational efficiency and creates audit trails, thus enabling auditors to collect evidence with little effort. Chou et al. (2021) developed a model of decentralized accounting contracts and used five case studies involving revenue recognition to demonstrate how accounting principles are embedded in smart contracts. Their results revealed that smart contracts can solve numerous accounting issues. Smart contracts also enable action on a real-time basis and considerably reduce transaction costs considerably (Vincent & Barkhi, 2021). Therefore, smart contracts can increase the efficiency and automation of accounting.

Auditors can determine whether the predetermined conditions of smart contracts have been upheld. Dai et al. (2019) explored how smart contracts can facilitate Auditing 4.0, by enabling the monitoring of companies' operations and warning auditors when quantitative indicators of critical audit issues exceed predetermined numeric thresholds. For example, auditors can encode prespecified thresholds for account balances in financial statements into a smart contract. The smart contract then automatically reviews the account balance and alerts auditors when the balance exceeds a relevant threshold. Accounting firms should adopt smart contracts because completely automated audit procedures prevent human error and improve audit quality (Tiberius & Hirth, 2019). The process of translating audit procedures into computer programs using smart contracts is called "smart auditing" (Alles et al., 2021; Rozario & Thomas, 2019). As Rozario and Thomas (2019) indicate, smart auditing enables audits to be performed automatically without auditors' professional judgment. This leaves time for auditors to address other problems and thus improve audit quality and reporting.

Smart contracts increase the efficiency of triple-entry bookkeeping and enable auditors to obtain synchronous and accurate financial data to present more precise opinions for financial statements. In addition, smart contracts can be used to detect abnormal transactions and irregular activity that would compromise the integrity of the smart audit process in real time on the basis of prespecified numeric thresholds. Thus, the automated audit procedures of smart contracts facilitate the testing of control and substantive tests, and increase the quality and efficiency of auditing (Appelbaum et al., 2021). Users of financial statements and investors can also acquire more transparent and reliable information in real time to make informed decisions.

Continuous Auditing

Most audit practices and procedures are labor intensive. However, blockchain's distributed nature and smart contracts may simplify and streamline several accounting and auditing procedures. In addition, blockchains can enhance financial reporting processes by providing reliable and timely evidence to improve management assertions in relation to transactions (Brennan et al., 2019). Consequently, auditing can potentially be shifted from periodic or annual to continuous (Schmitz & Leoni, 2019).

The evidence collected from audit procedures should be relevant, sufficient, and reliable. Alles et al. (2021) indicated that auditors can use rule-based auditing and monitoring paradigms to provide adequate assurance for financial reporting through smart contracts in blockchain networks. Thus, auditors can translate audit procedures into computer programming codes to test transaction data, which would support management assertions. Because blockchains are shared databases, auditors can access clients' transaction records with little effort, which enables auditors to examine entire populations in real time rather than select samples periodically (Kokina et al., 2017; Rozario & Thomas, 2019). This mechanism can help auditors collect sufficient evidence from their clients to make informed decisions. Rozario and Thomas (2019) demonstrated that administrators of permissioned blockchain networks can authorize write-and-read access for clients' blockchains. Auditors can thus participate in clients' permissioned blockchain systems as read-only nodes, without engaging in their clients' business operations, and acquire transaction data to increase the reliability and authenticity of audit evidence. In addition, auditors can automatically execute procedures using blockchain and smart contracts. These emerging technologies also enable auditors to instantaneously determine the validity of transaction data and identify material misstatements in clients' financial statements rather than at the end of the reporting period (Schmitz & Leoni, 2019).

In blockchain networks, the occurrence and bookkeeping of transactions are almost simultaneous. This facilitates balance reconciliation and creates a detailed transaction trail that auditors can track easily (Kokina et al., 2017). Because of the efficiency of continuous auditing, auditors can save considerable time and refine their audit procedures. Appelbaum and Nehmer (2020) identified tasks that auditors should perform to continuously collect evidence in permissioned blockchains, namely, observation, inquiry, confirmation, inspection, recalculation, and analysis. They also suggested that auditors should determine whether clients' blockchains are connected to data flows and transactions with trading partners during the confirmation step. Unlike traditional auditing, continuous auditing helps auditors understand their clients' businesses at any time, rather than at the end of financial reporting periods (Cong et al., 2018; Schmitz & Leoni, 2019).

With the convenient and automated nature of blockchain systems, auditors can avoid tedious procedures and concentrate on high-risk matters (Rozario & Thomas, 2019). Continuous auditing enabled by blockchain also increases the efficiency and quality of audits, because auditors have more time to address risky material misstatements, malicious fraud, and other financial statement problems. Wang and Kogan (2018) developed a prototype of a blockchain-based transaction-processing system for continuous auditing that deters fraud through blockchain, zero-knowledge proof, and homomorphic encryption. This system helps auditors access transaction data and continuously monitor firms' transaction activities. Continuous auditing and monitoring help prevent earnings manipulation and other illegal management activities.

Because blockchain technology increases auditing efficiency and facilitates automation, ERP systems and auditors may be replaced by blockchain technology (Church et al., 2021; Vincent et al., 2020). However, to replace ERP systems with blockchain-related distributed ledgers, companies must invest considerable capital to establish new AISs. The application of blockchain technology remains immature and under-adopted and using it to create a new system entails risks (Vincent et al., 2020). Whether the information encoded in blockchains accurately represents transaction data is difficult to determine (Alles & Gray, 2020), and the differences between the records in the blockchain and actual transactions must be identified for auditing. To reduce the gap between the physical and digital worlds, Albizri and Appelbaum (2021) developed a model by introducing IoT as a node in a blockchain, thereby enabling peer-to-peer traceability and transparent provenance. Miners' verification processes aim to check whether a block submitted by an authorized blockchain user is valid, rather than examining the authenticity of information (Richardson & Watson, 2021). Miners do not always know the details and authenticity of transactions, and transactions on blockchain can be unauthorized or fraudulent. Concerns that ERP systems and auditors may be replaced by blockchains are unjustified, because some procedures still require auditors to determine the authenticity of transactions. Once blockchains become prevalent in business, new demand for auditing will arise to bridge the gap between the digital and physical worlds (Fotoh & Lorentzon, 2021; Sheldon, 2021a, 2021b). Moreover, if auditors can participate in clients' blockchains with read-only authority to acquire data directly (Rozario & Thomas, 2019), audit quality will improve considerably and help auditors and users of financial statements meet others' expectations.

Accountability and Governance

Accountability refers to an entity's responsibilities (Tyma et al., 2022). Increasing attention to blockchain has led to several studies on accountability and governance in accounting literature. Secinaro et al. (2021) conducted a literature review to explore accountability as it relates to accounting and auditing. Because decentralization eliminates the need for an intermediary or trusted third party to process and verify transactions among trading partners, accountability is distributed to each node in blockchain systems. Tyma et al. (2022) explored accountability in public, private, and consortium blockchains. Each type of blockchain system requires different accountability mechanisms. Because public blockchains do not have a central authority, users are incentivized to verify blocks that depend on consensus mechanisms. Therefore, consensus mechanisms help align members' incentives to maintain a public blockchain's operation and accountability. However, private blockchains' accountability is mainly driven by trust in a central authority, which plays a key role in the operations of private blockchains.

Blockchain-based AISs can strengthen the trust among network members. Thus, blockchain-based accounting platforms compensate for the lack of transparency and accountability by automatically recording, verifying, and tracing transactions (Carrasco & Romi, 2021). Although blockchain systems optimize accounting and auditing, they do not fully eliminate the responsibilities of accountants and auditors. To communicate the information of the (misconduct) behavior of certified public accountants' (CPAs) among all states of the U.S., Sheldon (2018) proposed using blockchains to aggregate and share information regarding negligence and misconduct in real time. Specifically, he suggested that CPAs and constituents such as the AICPA, the National Association of State Boards of Accountancy, and the Public Company Accounting Oversight Board (PCAOB) create accounts in blockchains. These constituents then assign endorsements to CPAs' accounts, including those for passing the CPA exam, state licenses, and records of misconduct. Because CPAs in the US are state-based registrations, this approach may facilitate interstate information sharing and communication and help accounting authorities review practitioners' accounts and oversee their activity at any moment, thus ensuring that accounting practitioners uphold their responsibilities.

Brennan et al. (2019) and Smith and Castonguay (2020) suggested that the blockchain-based corporate governance structure depends on the degree of decentralization. Each type of blockchain creates different organizational structures; therefore, management should consider the degree of decentralization when determining firms' corporate governance structures, strategies, internal control procedures, and risk assessment procedures with regard to blockchain. Auditors should also consider their clients' governance processes in peer-to-peer ecosystems such as blockchains to understand their internal control mechanisms and develop audit plans and control objectives. (Appelbaum & Nehmer, 2020; Dyball & Seethamraju, 2021b). Smith and Castonguay (2020) suggested that auditors should assess policies for internal control and the operational effectiveness of controls in blockchains. They also advised auditors to understand the underlying code embedded in blockchains for internal control audits if auditors want to depend on blockchain information.

Auditors should thus investigate how various entities establish corporate governance mechanisms and refine the accountability mechanisms of their management and employees in blockchains.

Under the situation of air pollution control in China, Dai et al. (2019) considered accountability essential for monitoring government officials' performance and reporting. If monitoring authorities and regulatory agencies can obtain evidence and original transaction records from a blockchain system in real time, monitoring costs can be considerably reduced (Gietzmann & Grossetti, 2021). Thus, authorities should use the traceability afforded by blockchain networks to strengthen accountability mechanisms and monitor officials to release information (Bora et al., 2021). Tang and Tang (2019) also considered blockchains to be emerging tools for increasing the efficiency of governance because blockchains are integrated networks that create direct connections between each other.

In sum, accounting practitioners and government officials must acquire blockchain-related knowledge and skills related to adapting to blockchain ecosystems. For internal control and corporate governance, management needs to refine companies' organizational and operational models to adopt blockchain as their new system. Moreover, accountants and auditors should explore ways to uphold their responsibilities and maintain neutrality in the blockchain environment.

Directions for Future Research

This section presents possible implications related to blockchains and specific RQs for accounting and auditing studies based on a literature review. Table 10.5 summarizes the RQs.

Opportunities and Challenges for Accounting Practitioners

Oracles operate outside blockchains, collect external data, and transform them into a format that can be transferred to blockchains (Sheldon, 2021a). The external data provided by oracles are essential for the operation of smart contracts to confirm whether the specific conditions of smart contracts are met. Once the agreed-upon conditions are met, smart contracts automatically execute the predefined subsequent actions. However, the consensus mechanism of blockchain ensures data reliability only for transactions that occur within a blockchain system. As

Table 10.5 A summary of the RQs for future research

Category	*RQs*
Opportunities and challenges for accounting practitioners	1. How have accounting practitioners solved the problem of oracles in blockchain technology? 2. What audit procedures are necessary to reconcile on-chain and off-chain data? 3. What are the benefits of blockchain-related services for accounting firms? 4. How does adopting blockchain technology affect companies' business operations? 5. Which audit procedures can be encoded into smart contracts? 6. How does blockchain technology affect the quality of audit reports? 7. Which audit procedures should be reformulated to ensure the collection of reliable evidence in the context of blockchain technology? 8. How can blockchain technology and smart contracts be combined with traditional AISs? 9. Does triple-entry bookkeeping improve financial reports? 10. How do companies and accounting firms control their operating and human resource costs by using blockchain technology? 11. How would auditors view the impact of blockchain governance on their works?
Compelling empirical studies and practical case studies	12. What are the effects of blockchain technology on accounting and auditing? 13. What are the outcomes of collaboration between accounting firms and companies implementing blockchain technology in auditing? 14. Does blockchain technology ensure real-time monitoring, high transparency, and immutability?

Category	*RQs*
	15. How do companies balance the transparency and privacy of transaction data in blockchain technology?
	16. Is the quality of financial reporting enhanced after the implementation of the fair value accounting for cryptocurrencies (FASB 2022)?
	17. What are the accounting treatments that companies select to use if they are holding cryptocurrencies, NFTs, and/or CBDCs?
	18. How do auditors examine the ownership of cryptocurrencies, NFTs, and/or CBDCs of companies and track transactions of cryptocurrencies, NFTs, and/or CBDCs and activities in DeFi?
Monitoring and Regulations	19. What official regulations on the accounting and auditing of digital assets have accounting authorities established?
	20. What legally binding regulations on companies have regulators developed for the context of blockchain technology?
	21. What guidelines have accounting authorities developed to manage auditing in the context of blockchain technology?
Education	22. How can blockchain technology be introduced in accounting curricula?
	23. What skills related to blockchain technology should accounting students develop?
	24. What courses related to blockchain technology should accounting faculty create?

Source Author

oracles are regarded as intermediaries that operate outside blockchains, the external data provided by oracles may threaten the authenticity and reliability of transaction data[6] recorded in blockchains (Sheldon, 2021a). Therefore, on-chain and off-chain data must be reconciled, and accountants and auditors must determine the authenticity of the transaction data (Alles & Gray, 2020; Church et al., 2021). Studies should explore solutions to this problem and determine the audit procedures required for management assertions in financial reporting by interviewing auditors of companies that have adopted the blockchain technology. We also expect that blockchain will create a range of multifaceted jobs for accounting practitioners. As Dyball and Seethamraju (2021a) indicate, numerous Australian accounting firms have begun to engage with clients who have implemented blockchain systems in their businesses. Thus, studies should explore whether blockchain-related services provided by accounting firms are beneficial and assess the results of companies adopting blockchain in their business operations.

RQ 1: How have accounting practitioners solved the problem of oracles in the blockchain technology?
RQ 2: What audit procedures are necessary to reconcile on- and off-chain data?
RQ 3: What are the benefits of blockchain-related services to accounting firms?
RQ 4: How does adopting blockchain technology affect companies' business operations?

The use of smart contracts to develop automated audit procedures is a key topic for future research, because smart contracts facilitate continuous auditing. In addition to the authenticity and reliability of transaction data, studies should explore the quality of audit reports in relation to blockchain. Audit procedures must be reformulated to ensure the collection of relevant, sufficient, and reliable evidence from clients in the blockchain context. If auditors can obtain reliable information through blockchain-related applications without errors, the quality of audit reports will improve considerably.

[6] Liu, Szalachowski, and Zhou (2021) inspected and provided empirical evidence that there was a (significant) price deviation by using price data extracted from various oracles, including AmpleForth, Synthetix, MakerDAO, and Compound.

RQ 5: Which audit procedures can be encoded into smart contracts?
RQ 6: How do blockchains affect the quality of audit reports?
RQ 7: Which audit procedures should be reformulated to ensure the collection of reliable evidence in the blockchain context?

Triple-entry AISs, as secure and distributed platforms, can increase bookkeeping efficiency and financial reporting quality through blockchains and smart contracts. McCallig et al. (2019) proposed a new AIS model to increase the reliability of financial reports, enabling companies to secure their transaction data and share information with trading parties. How blockchains and smart contracts can be combined with traditional AISs to accomplish triple-entry bookkeeping is a critical topic requiring further investigation. Studies can explore this topic by investigating companies that use blockchains to create new AISs and evaluating the effects of triple-entry bookkeeping.

RQ 8: How can blockchains and smart contracts be combined with traditional AISs?
RQ 9: Does triple-entry bookkeeping improve financial reports?

Blockchain technology is an energy-consuming and complicated technology that can increase the operating and human resource costs for companies and related accounting firms. Whether accounting practitioners view blockchains as sustainable or disruptive remains unclear (Kend & Nguyen, 2020). Researchers should explore the sustainability of blockchains and investigate how accounting firms can limit their operating and human resource costs by implementing blockchain.

RQ 10: How do companies and accounting firms control their operating and human resource costs by using blockchains?

Blockchain governance is different from traditional governance, contractual governance,[7] and relational governance[8] in terms of regulatory principles, mode of enforcement, and forms (Lumineau et al., 2021). Lumineau et al. (2021) elaborated how blockchain works as a governance mechanism to facilitate cooperation and coordination among different stakeholders effectively and efficiently. Moreover, Ziolkowski et al. (2020) conducted expert interviews to understand how 14 practitioners implemented blockchain governance in practice and dealt with six major problems (demand management, data management, system architecture design and development, membership, ownership disputes, and transaction reversals.) when they were doing so. We recommend that scholars understand how blockchain governance impacts auditors' work from various perspectives using a survey approach.

RQ 11: How do auditors view the impact of blockchain governance on their work?

Compelling Empirical Studies and Practical Case Studies

Given the lack of empirical results regarding these topics, additional empirical studies should be conducted, especially given the large body of conceptual literature. Existing case studies, such as those in Gomaa et al. (2019), Kinory et al. (2020), and Liu et al. (2021), can serve as resources to familiarize accounting students with blockchains and strengthen their technical skills. Additional case studies must be conducted to determine how blockchains can transform accounting and auditing (Garanina et al., 2021).

RQ 12: What are the effects of blockchains on accounting and auditing?

As Karajovic et al. (2019) and Kokina et al. (2017) have demonstrated, Big 4 accounting firms have collaborated with companies to implement

[7] "Contractual governance relates to a legally binding promise defining the rights and obligations of the parties" (Lumineau et al., 2021).

[8] "Relational governance is based on the patterns of behavior to which parties are expected to conform" (Lumineau et al., 2021).

blockchains and provide new services; however, no study has analyzed the results of this process. Scholars should thus interview accountants, auditors, and business practitioners to understand their perspectives on blockchains and the results of this collaboration, and thereby move toward a methodology based on empirical evidence.

RQ 13: What are the outcomes of collaboration between accounting firms and companies implementing blockchain technology in auditing?

Because blockchains have developed rapidly, additional practical applications in business are likely to emerge; studies should continue to investigate the effects of these applications. The implementation of blockchain technology requires a balance between the transparency and privacy of transaction data (Herz & Pei, 2021). Studies should analyze how companies address this balance, how accounting firms help companies with blockchain-related services, and the advantages and disadvantages thereof.

RQ 14: Do blockchains ensure real-time monitoring, high transparency, and immutability?

RQ 15: How do companies balance the transparency and privacy of transaction data in blockchain?

With the emerging development and involvement of cryptocurrencies, non-fungible tokens (NFTs), decentralized finance (DeFi), and central bank digital currencies (CBDCs), there are important research questions that accounting and auditing scholars should address, for example:

RQ 16: Is the quality of financial reporting enhanced after the implementation of fair value accounting for cryptocurrencies (FASB, 2022)?

RQ 17: What accounting treatments do companies select to use if they hold cryptocurrencies, NFTs, and/or CBDCs?

RQ 18: How do auditors examine the ownership of cryptocurrencies, NFTs, and/or CBDCs of companies, and track transactions of cryptocurrencies, NFTs, and/or CBDCs and activities in DeFi?

Monitoring and Regulations

Cryptocurrency transactions remain ambiguous and lack legally binding regulations (Vincent & Wilkins, 2020). This creates audit risk and other accounting problems that should be considered during audits and client interactions. Several problems in accounting and auditing, such as those affecting asset classification, revenue recognition, and financial disclosure, remain unsolved (Vincent & Davenport, 2021).

AICPA (2022) has proposed guidelines for the accounting and auditing of digital assets, and PCAOB (2020) has released an advisory report that describes procedures for auditing certain digital assets, both of which provide non-binding guidelines that help those preparing financial statements and auditors account for and audit digital assets. The AICPA (2022) indicated that digital assets should be considered intangible assets with indefinite lives and that auditors should determine a cutoff for digital asset transactions; few studies have explored these topics. The requirements for official regulations on digital assets for accountants and auditors remain, and studies should explore the process of their development by investigating, for example, whether audit risk is lower after official regulations on digital assets are established.

RQ 19: What official regulations on accounting and the auditing of digital assets have accounting authorities established?

As digital assets are prevalent, accounting authorities such as the International Accounting Standards Board (IASB), FASB, and PCAOB should develop explicit guidelines and standards for accountants and auditors to report and inspect them accordingly. Legal institutions, monitoring authorities, and regulators should develop legally binding regulations for companies and trading partners. Studies should track the development and effects of such regulations.

RQ 20: What legally binding regulations have regulators developed in the context of blockchains?

RQ 21: What guidelines have accounting authorities developed to manage auditing in the blockchain context?

Education

As the number of accounting aspects affected by blockchain increases, scholars have begun to encourage the addition of blockchain technology to accounting curricula (Qasim & Kharbat, 2020). Stern and Reinstein (2021) described how blockchain technology should be taught in an independent course or added to existing courses. They designed a series of courses and materials for guided readings and group-based and individual assignments. Furthermore, they recorded lectures and helped students apply what they learned. In addition, a questionnaire revealed that students rated class 4.1 on a 5-point scale. Kaden et al. (2021) demonstrated that coding exercises can deepen accounting students' understanding of blockchain technology. They introduced blockchain technology in a data analytics class and developed exercises to teach students how to write blockchain code in the R programming language. The results of the study were promising: 82% of the students demonstrated that they understood the roles of transactions and blocks in blockchains, and 79% of them comprehended the concept of PoW after the lectures and coding exercises.

RQ 22: How can blockchain technology be introduced in accounting curricula?

RQ 23: What skills related to blockchain technology should accounting students develop?

Several scholars have used case studies of blockchain technology as an instructional resource. Dunn et al. (2021) investigated the implications of Bitcoin and blockchain for auditing, by having students audit an online retailer using Bitcoin. The study revealed that 95% of students considered the learning experience to be positive. Ozlanski et al. (2020) illustrated the imminent transformation of auditing for students by demonstrating how an online lending company disrupted lending in non-traditional businesses. After the case study, the students rated the experience highly, with every item on the questionnaire receiving 4 points or more on a 5-point scale, and the students provided positive feedback.

Instructors and students indicated that case studies help them understand blockchain and its effects on accounting and auditing. Therefore, accounting curricula should introduce blockchain-related case studies to equip students with new skills and prepare them for a future in which they can work with blockchain technology. Thus, studies should explore the effects of introducing blockchain technology into accounting curricula and the development of courses on blockchain technology.

RQ 24: What courses related to blockchain technology should accounting faculty create?

Conclusion

This literature review investigates how blockchain technology can affect accounting and auditing, especially in terms of practice. It also explores how blockchain technology has evolved in accounting by reviewing 80 studies from 2016 to 2021 selected from the top 60 international accounting journals. Additionally, this study provides a survey of the literature on blockchain technology in accounting and auditing. The number of studies has increased considerably, and most have been conceptual in nature (see Fig. 10.2), whereas few have been empirical. This may be ascribed to the fact that blockchain technology is not mature and widely adopted, resulting in a lack of data indicating the effects of blockchain technology on accounting. Given that blockchain technology could serve as a disruptive AIS and drastically transform audit procedures, the AIS and auditing, in which the final 80 studies are involved. Instructors and practitioners have increasingly expressed that introducing blockchain technology to accounting courses can equip students with the necessary skills for their future careers. Some studies indicate that blockchain technology can replace accountants and auditors. However, most studies have noted that these professions will change rather than be fully automated and that a demand for accounting practitioners' professional judgment will remain (Garanina et al., 2021).

This literature review explores several key concepts related to blockchains in accounting and auditing, namely, triple-entry bookkeeping, smart contracts, continuous auditing, accountability, and governance. Triple-entry bookkeeping is a new method of representing transaction flows through tokens, in which accounts in blockchain ledgers function as layered aggregations of data. Smart contracts can be embedded into triple-entry AISs to automatically record the transaction data. Triple-entry AISs can benefit companies and auditors by increasing their operational procedure efficiency. Smart contracts encode contractual provisions and specific procedures to ensure that tasks are accomplished in accordance with the established rules, standards, procedures, and routines. The use of smart contracts to automatically execute audits and processes can help reduce human errors and improve auditing. Auditors can continuously acquire transaction data from clients in real time using shared blockchain databases. This also enables auditors to extract data from entire populations, rather than from selected samples. Continuous auditing helps auditors collect evidence from their clients to make informed decisions regarding financial reports. Additionally, the decentralized nature of blockchains eliminates the need for intermediaries and trusted third parties, and accountability is distributed to each node in a blockchain system. As described by Tyma et al. (2022), each blockchain system should use a mechanism of accountability that suits the operating model. Therefore, accountants and auditors should investigate how various entities use accountability mechanisms and establish new corporate governance systems using blockchain. They should also maintain their professionalism, sense of responsibility, and neutrality as they address the transformations caused by blockchain technology.

This literature review can help researchers to understand the key resources and topics related to blockchain technology in accounting and auditing. The results can also help accountants, auditors, and business practitioners understand the effects of blockchain technology, the opportunities it has created, its key characteristics, and its practical application. However, this study has several limitations. For example, the dataset comprises only studies from the top 60 international accounting journals identified by Chin et al. (2012); several other journals were not considered. In addition, the validity of the results depends on the timing of the study. Additional studies should be conducted to provide new insights into blockchain technology for accounting and auditing.

References

Adams, M. T., & Bailey, W. A. (2021). Emerging cryptocurrencies and IRS summons power: Striking the proper balance between IRS audit authority and taxpayer privacy. *ATA Journal of Legal Tax Research, 19*(1), 61–81.

AICPA. (2018). *Accounting firm leaders and innovators gather for strategic discussions on blockchain technology*. https://www.aicpa.org/news/article/accounting-leaders-innovators-hold-strategic-discussions-on-blockchain-technology

AICPA. (2022). *Accounting for and auditing of digital assets*. https://www.aicpa.org/resources/download/accounting-for-and-auditing-of-digital-assets-practice-aid-pdf

Albizri, A., & Appelbaum, D. (2021). Trust but verify: The oracle paradox of blockchain smart contracts. *Journal of Information Systems, 35*(2), 1–16.

Alles, M., & Gray, G. L. (2020). "The first mile problem": Deriving an endogenous demand for auditing in blockchain-based business processes. *International Journal of Accounting Information Systems, 38*, 100465.

Alles, M. G., Dai, J., & Vasarhelyi, M. A. (2021). Reporting 4.0: Business reporting for the age of mass customization. *Journal of Emerging Technologies in Accounting, 18*(1), 1–15.

Appelbaum, D., & Nehmer, R. A. (2020). Auditing cloud-based blockchain accounting systems. *Journal of Information Systems, 34*(2), 5–21.

Appelbaum, D., Showalter, D. S., Sun, T., & Vasarhelyi, M. A. (2021). A framework for auditor data literacy: A normative position. *Accounting Horizons, 35*(2), 5–25.

Austin, A. A., & Williams, L. T. (2021). Evaluating company adoptions of blockchain technology: How do management and auditor communications affect nonprofessional investor judgments? *Journal of Accounting and Public Policy, 40*(5), 106882.

Beigman, E., Brennan, G., Hsieh, S.-F., & Sannella, A. J. (2021). Dynamic principal market determination: Fair value measurement of cryptocurrency. *Journal of Accounting, Auditing & Finance, 38*(4), 731–748. https://doi.org/10.1177/0148558X211004134.

Bora, I., Duan, H. K., Vasarhelyi, M. A., Zhang, C., & Dai, J. (2021). The transformation of government accountability and reporting. *Journal of Emerging Technologies in Accounting, 18*(2), 1–21.

Brennan, N. M., Subramaniam, N., & Van Staden, C. J. (2019). Corporate governance implications of disruptive technology: An overview. *The British Accounting Review, 51*(6), 100860.

Cai, C. W. (2018). Disruption of financial intermediation by FinTech: A review on crowdfunding and blockchain. *Accounting & Finance, 58*(4), 965–992.

Cai, C. W. (2021). Triple-entry accounting with blockchain: How far have we come? *Accounting & Finance, 61*(1), 71–93.

Carlin, T. (2019). Blockchain and the journey beyond double entry. *Australian Accounting Review, 29*(2), 305–311.

Carrasco, H., & Romi, A. M. (2021). Toward an omniopticon: the potential of blockchain technology toward influencing vulnerable populations in contested markets. *Accounting, Auditing & Accountability Journal, 35*(7), 1685–1713.

Centobelli, P., Cerchione, R., Del Vecchio, P., Oropallo, E., & Secundo, G. (2021). Blockchain technology design in accounting: Game changer to tackle fraud or technological fairy tale? *Accounting, Auditing & Accountability Journal, 35*(7), 1566–1597.

Chin, C.-L., Wang, T.-C., Lee, C.-L., Wu, T.-Z., Lin, H.-W., & Yu, H.-C. (2012). *Preparation of NSC project reports—The updated schedule for the classification and ranking of international accounting journals in the field of accounting and finance.* https://www.most.gov.tw/most/attachments/ae148faa-2b2a-4de0-916e-33b4e27bc5b1

Cho, S., Vasarhelyi, M. A., & Zhang, C. (2019). The forthcoming data ecosystem for business measurement and assurance. *Journal of Emerging Technologies in Accounting, 16*(2), 1–21.

Chou, C.-C., Hwang, N.-C.R., Schneider, G. P., Wang, T., Li, C.-W., & Wei, W. (2021). Using smart contracts to establish decentralized accounting contracts: An example of revenue recognition. *Journal of Information Systems, 35*(3), 17–52.

Church, K. S., Schmidt, P. J., & Ajayi, K. (2020). Forecast cloudy—Fair or stormy weather: Cloud computing insights and issues. *Journal of Information Systems, 34*(2), 23–46.

Church, K. S., Smith, S. S., & Kinory, E. (2021). Accounting implications of blockchain: A hyperledger composer use case for intangible assets. *Journal of Emerging Technologies in Accounting, 18*(2), 23–52.

Cong, Y., Du, H., & Vasarhelyi, M. A. (2018). Technological disruption in accounting and auditing. *Journal of Emerging Technologies in Accounting, 15*(2), 1–10.

Coyne, J. G., & McMickle, P. L. (2017). Can blockchains serve an accounting purpose? *Journal of Emerging Technologies in Accounting, 14*(2), 101–111.

Dai, J., He, N., & Yu, H. (2019). Utilizing blockchain and smart contracts to enable audit 4.0: From the perspective of accountability audit of air pollution control in China. *Journal of Emerging Technologies in Accounting, 16*(2), 23–41.

Dai, J., & Vasarhelyi, M. A. (2017). Toward blockchain-based accounting and assurance. *Journal of Information Systems, 31*(3), 5–21.

Deloitte. (2016). Blockchain_A game-changer in accounting.pdf.

Dunn, R. T., Jenkins, J. G., & Sheldon, M. D. (2021). Bitcoin and blockchain: Audit implications of the killer Bs. *Issues in Accounting Education, 36*(1), 43–56.

Dyball, M. C., & Seethamraju, R. (2021a). Client use of blockchain technology: Exploring its (potential) impact on financial statement audits of Australian accounting firms. *Accounting, Auditing & Accountability Journal, 35*(7), 1656–1684.

Dyball, M. C., & Seethamraju, R. (2021b). The impact of client use of blockchain technology on audit risk and audit approach—An exploratory study. *International Journal of Auditing, 25*(2), 602–615.

Financial Accounting Standards Board (FASB). (2022). Tentative board decisions (October 12, 2022). https://fasb.org/Page/PageContent?pageId=/meetings/pastmeetings/10-12-22.html&bcpath=tff

Felski, E. A., & Empey, T. B. (2020). Should blockchain be added to the accounting curriculum? Evidence forma survey of students, professionals and academics. *The Accounting Educators' Journal, 30*.

Fotoh, L. E., & Lorentzon, J. I. (2021). The impact of digitalization on future audits. *Journal of Emerging Technologies in Accounting, 18*(2), 77–97.

Garanina, T., Ranta, M., & Dumay, J. (2021). Blockchain in accounting research: Current trends and emerging topics. *Accounting, Auditing & Accountability Journal, 35*(7), 1507–1533.

Gietzmann, M., & Grossetti, F. (2021). Blockchain and other distributed ledger technologies: Where is the accounting? *Journal of Accounting and Public Policy, 40*(5), 106881.

Gomaa, A. A., Gomaa, M. I., & Stampone, A. (2019). A transaction on the blockchain: An AIS perspective, intro case to explain transactions on the ERP and the role of the internal and external auditor. *Journal of Emerging Technologies in Accounting, 16*(1), 47–64.

Guo, F., Walton, S., Wheeler, P. R., & Zhang, Y. (2021). Early disruptors: Examining the determinants and consequences of blockchain early adoption. *Journal of Information Systems, 35*(2), 219–242.

Hampl, F., & Gyönyörová, L. (2021). Can fiat-backed stablecoins be considered cash or cash equivalents under international financial reporting standards rules? *Australian Accounting Review, 31*(3), 233–255.

Harrast, S. A., Mcgilsky, D., & Sun, Y. (2021). Determining the inherent risks of cryptocurrency: A survey analysis. *Current Issues in Auditing, 16*(2), A10–A17.

Heister, S., Kaufman, M., & Yuthas, K. (2021). Blockchain and the future of business data analytics. *Journal of Emerging Technologies in Accounting, 18*(1), 87–98.

Herz, R. H., & Pei, D. (2021). Advancing financial reporting in the age of technology: An interview with Robert H. Herz. *Journal of Emerging Technologies in Accounting, 18*(2), 117–124.

International Accounting Standards Board (IASB). (2014). International accounting standard 38 *intangible assets*. https://www.ifrs.org/content/dam/ifrs/publications/pdf-standards/english/2021/issued/part-a/ias-38-intangible-assets.pdf

International Accounting Standards Board (IASB). (2019). *IFRSIC update June 2019*. https://www.ifrs.org/news-and-events/updates/ifric/2019/ifric-update-june-2019/

Inger, K. K., & Mathis, M. (2021). Taxes: Taking a bite out of bitcoin. *Issues in Accounting Education Teaching Notes, 36*(1), 41–53.

Internal Revenue Service (IRS). (2014). *IRS notice 2014–21*. https://www.irs.gov/pub/irs-drop/n-14-21.pdf

Kaden, S. R., Lingwall, J. W., & Shonhiwa, T. T. (2021). Teaching Blockchain through coding: Educating the future accounting professional. *Issues in Accounting Education, 36*(4), 281–290.

Karajovic, M., Kim, H. M., & Laskowski, M. (2019). Thinking outside the block: Projected phases of blockchain integration in the accounting industry. *Australian Accounting Review, 29*(2), 319–330.

Kend, M., & Nguyen, L. A. (2020). Big data analytics and other emerging technologies: The impact on the Australian audit and assurance profession. *Australian Accounting Review, 30*(4), 269–282.

Kinory, E., Smith, S. S., & Church, K. S. (2020). Exploring the playground: Blockchain prototype use cases with hyperledger composer. *Journal of Emerging Technologies in Accounting, 17*(1), 77–88.

Kocsis, D. (2019). A conceptual foundation of design and implementation research in accounting information systems. *International Journal of Accounting Information Systems, 34*, 100420.

Kokina, J., Mancha, R., & Pachamanova, D. (2017). Blockchain: Emergent industry adoption and implications for accounting. *Journal of Emerging Technologies in Accounting, 14*(2), 91–100.

Kostić, N., & Sedej, T. (2021). Blockchain technology, inter-organizational relationships and management accounting: A synthesis and a research agenda. *Accounting Horizons, 36*(2), 123–141.

Lee, L. S., Appelbaum, D., & Mautz III, R. (2022). Blockchains: An experiential accounting learning activity blockchains: An experiential accounting learning activity. *Journal of Emerging Technologies in Accounting, 19*(1), 181–197.

Lineros, J. V. (2021). IT governance considerations for permissioned blockchains. *Journal of Emerging Technologies in Accounting, 18*(1), 45–59.

Liu, M., Robin, A., Wu, K., & Xu, J. (2021). Blockchain's impact on accounting and auditing: A use case on supply chain traceability. *Journal of Emerging Technologies in Accounting, 19*(2), 105–119.

Liu, M., Wu, K., & Xu, J. J. (2019). How will blockchain technology impact auditing and accounting: Permissionless versus permissioned blockchain. *Current Issues in Auditing, 13*(2), A19–A29.

Lombardi, R., de Villiers, C., Moscariello, N., & Pizzo, M. (2021). The disruption of blockchain in auditing—A systematic literature review and an agenda for future research. *Accounting, Auditing & Accountability Journal*.

Lumineau, F., Wang, W., & Schilke, O. (2021). Blockchain governance—A new way of organizing collaborations? *Organization Science, 32*(2), 257–525.

McCallig, J., Robb, A., & Rohde, F. (2019). Establishing the representational faithfulness of financial accounting information using multiparty security, network analysis and a blockchain. *International Journal of Accounting Information Systems, 33*, 47–58.

Moll, J., & Yigitbasioglu, O. (2019). The role of internet-related technologies in shaping the work of accountants: New directions for accounting research. *The British Accounting Review, 51*(6), 100833.

Nakamoto, S. (2008). Bitcoin: A peer-to-peer electronic cash system. *Decentralized Business Review*, 21260.

Ozlanski, M. E., Negangard, E. M., & Fay, R. G. (2020). Kabbage: A fresh approach to understanding fundamental auditing concepts and the effects of disruptive technology. *Issues in Accounting Education Teaching Notes, 35*(2), 26–38.

PCAOB. (2020). *Audits involving cryptoassets—Information for auditors and audit committees*. https://pcaobus.org/Documents/Audits-Involving-Cryptoassets-Spotlight.pdf.

Pimentel, E., Boulianne, E., Eskandari, S., & Clark, J. (2021). Systemizing the challenges of auditing blockchain-based assets. *Journal of Information Systems, 35*(2), 61–75.

Qasim, A., & Kharbat, F. F. (2020). Blockchain technology, business data analytics, and artificial intelligence: Use in the accounting profession and ideas for inclusion into the accounting curriculum. *Journal of Emerging Technologies in Accounting, 17*(1), 107–117.

Ramassa, P., & Leoni, G. (2021). Standard setting in times of technological change: Accounting for cryptocurrency holdings. *Accounting, Auditing & Accountability Journal, 35*(7), 1598–1624.

Richardson, V. J., & Watson, M. W. (2021). Act or be acted upon: Revolutionizing accounting curriculums with data analytics. *Accounting Horizons, 35*(2), 129–144.

Rozario, A. M., & Thomas, C. (2019). Reengineering the audit with blockchain and smart contracts. *Journal of Emerging Technologies in Accounting, 16*(1), 21–35.

Schmitz, J., & Leoni, G. (2019). Accounting and auditing at the time of blockchain technology: A research agenda. *Australian Accounting Review, 29*(2), 331–342.

Secinaro, S., Dal Mas, F., Brescia, V., & Calandra, D. (2021). Blockchain in the accounting, auditing and accountability fields: A bibliometric and coding analysis. *Accounting, Auditing & Accountability Journal, 35*(9), 168–203.

Sheldon, M. D. (2018). Using blockchain to aggregate and share misconduct issues across the accounting profession. *Current Issues in Auditing, 12*(2), A27–A35.

Sheldon, M. D. (2019). A primer for information technology general control considerations on a private and permissioned blockchain audit. *Current Issues in Auditing, 13*(1), A15–A29.

Sheldon, M. D. (2021a). Auditing the blockchain oracle problem. *Journal of Information Systems, 35*(1), 121–133.

Sheldon, M. D. (2021b). Preparing auditors for the blockchain oracle problem. *Current Issues in Auditing, 15*(2), P27–P39.

Smith, S. S., & Castonguay, J. J. (2020). Blockchain and accounting governance: Emerging issues and considerations for accounting and assurance professionals. *Journal of Emerging Technologies in Accounting, 17*(1), 119–131.

Snyder, H. (2019). Literature review as a research methodology: An overview and guidelines. *Journal of Business Research, 104*, 333–339.

Søgaard, J. S. (2021). A blockchain-enabled platform for VAT settlement. *International Journal of Accounting Information Systems, 40*, 100502.

Stern, M., & Reinstein, A. (2021). A blockchain course for accounting and other business students. *Journal of Accounting Education, 56*, 100742.

Stratopoulos, T. C. (2020). Teaching blockchain to accounting students. *Journal of Emerging Technologies in Accounting, 17*(2), 63–74.

Stratopoulos, T. C., Wang, V. X., & Ye, H. J. (2022). Use of corporate disclosures to identify the stage of blockchain adoption. *Accounting Horizons, 36*(1), 197–220.

Tan, B. S., & Low, K. Y. (2019). Blockchain as the database engine in the accounting system. *Australian Accounting Review, 29*(2), 312–318.

Tang, Q., & Tang, L. M. (2019). Toward a distributed carbon ledger for carbon emissions trading and accounting for corporate carbon management. *Journal of Emerging Technologies in Accounting, 16*(1), 37–46.

Terando, W. D., Cataldi, B., & Mennecke, B. E. (2017). Impact of the IRC section 475 mark-to-market election on bitcoin taxation. *The ATA Journal of Legal Tax Research, 15*(1), 66–76.

Tiberius, V., & Hirth, S. (2019). Impacts of digitization on auditing: A Delphi study for Germany. *Journal of International Accounting, Auditing and Taxation, 37*, 100288.

Tyma, B., Dhillon, R., Sivabalan, P., & Wieder, B. (2022). Understanding accountability in blockchain systems. *Accounting, Auditing & Accountability Journal, 35*(7), 1625–1655.

Vincent, N. E., & Barkhi, R. (2021). Evaluating blockchain using COSO. *Current Issues in Auditing, 15*(1), A57–A71.

Vincent, N. E., & Davenport, S. A. (2021). Accounting research opportunities for cryptocurrencies. *Journal of Emerging Technologies in Accounting, 19*(1), 79–93.

Vincent, N. E., Skjellum, A., & Medury, S. (2020). Blockchain architecture: A design that helps CPA firms leverage the technology. *International Journal of Accounting Information Systems, 38*, 100466.

Vincent, N. E., & Wilkins, A. M. (2020). Challenges when auditing cryptocurrencies. *Current Issues in Auditing, 14*(1), A46–A58.

Wang, Y., & Kogan, A. (2018). Designing confidentiality-preserving Blockchain-based transaction processing systems. *International Journal of Accounting Information Systems, 30*, 1–18.

Yen, J.-C., & Wang, T. (2021). Stock price relevance of voluntary disclosures about blockchain technology and cryptocurrencies. *International Journal of Accounting Information Systems, 40*, 100499.

Yermack, D. (2017). Corporate governance and blockchains. *Review of Finance, 21*(1), 7–31.

Zhang, C. (2019). Intelligent process automation in audit. *Journal of Emerging Technologies in Accounting, 16*(2), 69–88.

Zhang, L., Pei, D., & Vasarhelyi, M. A. (2017). Toward a new business reporting model. *Journal of Emerging Technologies in Accounting, 14*(2), 1–15.

Zhang, S., Zhang, D., Zheng, J., & Aerts, W. (2021). Does policy uncertainty of the blockchain dampen ICO markets? *Accounting & Finance, 61*, 1625–1637.

Zhang, S., Zhou, X., Pan, H., & Jia, J. (2019). Cryptocurrency, confirmatory bias and news readability—Evidence from the largest Chinese cryptocurrency exchange. *Accounting & Finance, 58*(5), 1445–1468.

Ziolkowski, R., Miscione, G., & Schwabe, G. (2020). Decision problems in blockchain governance: Old wine in new bottles or walking in someone else's shoes? *Journal of Management Information Systems, 37*(2), 316–348.

CHAPTER 11

Artificial Intelligence in Accounting: Ethical Challenges and Legal Perspectives

Arif Perdana, Tawei Wang, and Saru Arifin

Introduction

The importance of automated decision-making systems (ADM) has become increasingly apparent in our society in recent decades (Helberger et al., 2020; Nalbandian, 2022). ADM systems must be developed and deployed, aligned with basic human principles and legal systems, in a manner that serves the common good. The use of artificial intelligence (AI) in ADM is now widespread in various fields, ranging from more efficient supply chain management, credit scoring, and fraud analysis to

A. Perdana (✉)
Monash University, Tangerang, Indonesia
e-mail: arif.perdana@monash.edu

T. Wang
DePaul University, Chicago, IL, USA
e-mail: david.wang@depaul.edu

S. Arifin
Universitas Negeri Semarang, Semarang, Indonesia
e-mail: saruarifin@mail.unnes.ac.id

A. Perdana and T. Wang (eds.), *Digital Transformation in Accounting and Auditing*, https://doi.org/10.1007/978-3-031-46209-2_11

more reliable recommender systems (Bakarich & O'Brien, 2021; Bandi & Kothari, 2022; Truby, 2020). However, the use of AI has raised ethical concerns. Research on technology and society highlights ADM's ethical, social, and political implications of ADM (Dignum, 2019; Siau & Wang, 2020). Some literature points out that some algorithmic systems are unaccountable because they are black boxes where the inner workings may be opaque to users. The literature also expresses concern that people may unknowingly participate in the news filter bubbles created by algorithms. In addition, critics have highlighted that ADM systems can perpetuate inequities in the system design and capture human biases in the training data (Akter et al., 2021; Belenguer, 2022).

Individuals can be harmed financially or physically by ADM systems. Technology facilitates digital transformation; however, human decisions are also critical. Technological and human decisions, and their social and ethical consequences, are critical to a company's journey toward digital transformation. People, technology, and processes work in concert to ensure that ADM is used responsibly, and that privacy, confidentiality, and avoidance of bias are maintained. This has prompted governments and policymakers worldwide to consider how the decisions and implementation of government policies can be shaped to ensure public safety, stability, and innovation in the implementation of ADM (Hsu, 2022; Wu et al., 2020).

AI poses one of the most significant privacy challenges owing to its potential to invade individual privacy. ADM often relies on large volumes of data collected from individuals, such as social media posts and location data. By analyzing this data, ADM can build profiles of individuals and make predictions about their behavior, preferences, and characteristics. While some of these data are collected with the individual's consent, concerns remain regarding whether individuals know what data is being collected about them, and how it is being used, processed, shared, and retained. Additionally, ADM systems may perpetuate or reinforce existing biases and discrimination (Akter et al., 2021). The accuracy of the systems was only as good as that of the datasets from which they were derived. ADM systems may also reflect and perpetuate data that indicate biased or discriminatory patterns. This can have severe consequences in several situations, such as when ADM is used in hiring or credit decisions and perpetuating existing inequalities and discriminatory practices.

Another potential challenge in digital transformation is data security issues (Shahim, 2021). Data breaches and hacks are becoming more common, and therefore, consumers are becoming increasingly concerned. Governments in various countries are considering or implementing laws to protect user data, partly because increasingly complex ADM systems require a tremendous amount of data, but still pose significant risks of bias and misuse (Niebel, 2021; Tamburri, 2020). Data collection methods should be scrutinized with greater care than ever before. A data breach can prompt some companies to improve their security measures, hire more cybersecurity experts, or update their internal procedures (Bana et al., 2021; Shahim, 2021). Cybersecurity breaches threaten data privacy and confidentiality through data theft. In many organizations, valuable data are managed using multiple systems. The loss of sensitive data such as personal, financial, and proprietary business information can result from unauthorized access to an organization's systems and data. Deficiencies in security measures can enable hackers to exploit insecure databases. As a result of this data theft, various crimes can be committed, such as identity theft, financial fraud, or gaining a competitive advantage (Donaldson et al., 2015). Data theft can harm both individuals and companies. Individuals may suffer financial losses and character defamation. Likewise, companies can suffer financial and reputational damage and face severe regulatory sanctions due to the improper handling of personal data (Fréminville, 2020).

In addition to technology, protecting personal and confidential data involves evaluating the behavior of individual employees and implementing robust organizational security procedures. Data security can be significantly compromised by employee behavior. For example, employees may disclose sensitive information to unauthorized parties, click on suspicious links, or use passwords carelessly, thereby putting the company's data at risk. Therefore, companies must train their employees on data security and implement policies and procedures to discourage risky behavior (Donaldson et al., 2015). Organizational security procedures also govern data security requirements. These procedures may include access controls that describe who has access to certain types of data and under what circumstances as well as response plans that specify what actions must be taken in the event of a security breach. Organizational security procedures may also include regular security audits, using security software and hardware, and applying security best practices (Kołodziej et al., 2022).

Businesses today are forced to make decisions that they do not have to make in the past. Technology facilitates a broader range of decision-making choices. However, technologies should be used ethically (Carlsson & Rönnblom, 2022). Using a set of principles, ethics determines what is appropriate and inappropriate. It focuses on how people should act, not how they should do it. When reputation and value are equally important in the marketplace, business ethics can offer a competitive advantage. Accountants and other professionals still rely heavily on ethical principles; however, their applications differ. Expectations are increasing as the profession grows. To remain relevant, accountants must evolve their profession and core competencies to align with advanced digital technology. Digital evolution can potentially threaten expertise. New ethical issues may arise from the use of digital technologies. Accountants must thoroughly understand the situation and its context before acting and making judgments. Knowledge and experience ensure professional competence and diligence. The use of digital technologies requires a clear understanding of their characteristics and the opportunities and challenges that they present. For an accountant to act ethically and gain clients' trust, they must be able to acquire new information and apply judgment to that information quickly, often in situations that they have never faced before. Professional accountants should identify information that could be valuable to outsiders and ensure that security controls are in place to protect them.

The following sections explain how accountants and auditors deal with ethical challenges and responsibly use ADM. The article begins by explaining privacy issues and potential solutions for addressing them. Next, we explain the potential bias that can occur in ADM. We then describe how ADM should be used responsibly and explain the legal issues that may potentially arise from ADM's use.

Managing Privacy Issues

Digital transformation raises several questions about the protection of personal data. Data protection generally refers to controlling who can access what data, when, where, and for what purpose (Walters & Novak, 2021). Data protection does not mean that the users remain anonymous. Instead, users can adjust their consent depending on the purpose of data use. Digitalization enables companies to collect customer data, but it may also threaten one's privacy. In many companies, access to user data is essential for facilitating data-driven decisions. For example, online shopping or search engine companies may collect and store personal data on users for advertising purposes. Therefore, these companies must ensure that their data is protected from malicious parties. Even when advanced technologies are employed to ensure the security of customer data, employees may act opportunistically by releasing sensitive customer data inadvertently.

AI can invade privacy, from data collection and processing to data analysis and interpretation (King & Forder, 2016; Perera et al., 2015). For example, AI systems often rely on the collection of large amounts of personal data to function effectively. Various data sources can be used to collect this information, raising privacy concerns. Data collection that is not properly conducted and adequately protected or used for purposes in which individuals are not adequately informed may raise privacy concerns. ADM systems may use multiple AI and machine learning (ML) techniques during data processing to analyze and gain insights. Consequently, sensitive information about an individual's habits, preferences, and behaviors may be revealed, which could invade an individual's privacy (King & Forder, 2016) primarily if this personal information is used unethically to personalize advertising based on a person's Internet activities and data. This may be useful for advertisers, but it may also invade an individual's privacy if their preferences and habits are publicized. Using these data may raise privacy concerns and may be based on assumptions or biases that may be inaccurate or unfair, even though they may be helpful in some contexts (Gouthier et al., 2022). The use of AI systems for surveillance purposes such as facial recognition and motion monitoring is another invasion of individual privacy. Privacy concerns may arise from monitoring individuals without knowledge or consent (Leslie, 2020).

With an increasingly regulated environment in multiple jurisdictions, companies that fail to protect their customers' data face ever-increasing fines and penalties. For example, the EU General Data Protection Regulation (GDPR) forces companies to strictly manage their customers' privacy and confidentiality.[1] Governments have enacted regulations to monitor and restrict data use. Privacy issues also challenge the ownership of shared information when data is collected via IoT technologies (Perera et al., 2015). Augmented reality (AR) or virtual reality (VR) devices, for example, allow a company to monitor its users' eye movements and determine what they are looking at. This allows the company to know what the

[1] https://gdpr-info.eu/

wearer is looking at and when. Companies that record images can also invade user privacy (Lecomte, 2022). Traditional data analytics/research uses a small amount of data, whereas Big Data research uses multiple data sources. Data analytics were used to identify the predictions and trends. For the data to be used, governance should be implemented to address this ethical challenge. Throughout the data lifecycle, an appropriate governance policy must be implemented (Eryurek et al., 2021; Petrella, 2021).

Before approaching privacy issues from a technological perspective, developing sound privacy practices is essential for organizations to stay ahead of change and minimize its impact (Agrawal et al., 2022). To ensure the security and privacy of personal data, sound privacy practices must include a solid set of policies, processes, and tools. Employees should be regularly notified of training or changes that could affect them (Hooi, 2019). For example, during the global health crisis, employees had to work remotely, which required new protocols for handling data. To ensure compliance, employees can benefit from processes and tools that identify and communicate these changes. In addition, ensuring sound privacy requires senior management support. A leadership approach sets the tone for interdepartmental collaboration, fosters cooperation, and forces employees to pay attention to data privacy. Multiple departments must be involved in the privacy discussions. Organizations can then assess their privacy policies regularly to identify strengths and weaknesses and highlight areas for improvement. Top management should guide a company's approach to data privacy and ensure that data privacy is used as a competitive advantage (Fréminville, 2020).

As the first step in managing privacy issues, organizations must clarify ownership, sovereignty, and access before collecting data (Walters & Novak, 2021). Organizations should carefully consider this when deciding to collect personal data. These data carry potential risks, particularly in marginalized and vulnerable communities. When organizations collect these data, they must explain how their initiative will use and protect the personal data of individuals. Informed consent was obtained before data collection (Mahanti, 2021b). Participants must understand why data are being collected, how they will be used and shared, and how they can access or modify it. Participants could also opt out of their data collected. Participants should also be aware and fully understand the risks of data sharing. The risk of sharing or accessing data should also be assessed. Organizations should be aware that risks vary widely from country to country and from population to population. Be sure to protect user privacy and ensure data security and ethical implementation by prioritizing the interests of end users. Once the data have been collected, they must be classified through proper metadata management to ensure proper privacy and confidentiality. Data classification facilitates the implementation of appropriate governance and security controls within an organization. They can also be used to improve data analysis, make informed decisions, and reduce the costs associated with data storage and maintenance. Data can be classified into public, confidential, sensitive, and personal/restricted categories. An organization can also classify data based on the extent to which their integrity and availability are essential (Mahanti, 2021a).

Cyber risk is increasing with digital transformation, with data protection being seen as the biggest challenge. At several stages of the ADM development life cycle, private and confidential data are vulnerable to theft or misappropriation. Cybersecurity practices are challenging, and some organizations may need more resources for advanced technological solutions to protect themselves (Couce-Vieira et al., 2020; Donaldson et al., 2015). Consequently, cyber threats have increased. The sensitive data of business users can lead to financial losses for an organization. As part of their data protection mechanisms, companies must also secure all their endpoints, including employees accessing software and customers using the company's platform. Organizations must ensure data security and limit access to data by following the best practices. These practices include encrypting files, using two-factor authentication, limiting access rights, storing data on secure servers or cloud storage services, and implementing corporate security policies and procedures including agreements with data-sharing partners (Donaldson et al., 2015; Fréminville, 2020). Web access administrators are responsible for controlling and monitoring endpoints because they can be used for unauthorized access. To prevent and stop malware, companies can use security software such as firewalls and antivirus programs. Companies can also educate their customers on the importance of password security and multifactor identification.

Another challenge is that fairness and privacy are often weighed against each other in ADM systems (Mehrabi et al., 2021). One trade-off arising from the specific techniques used to ensure fairness in AI systems requires access to sensitive personal data, which may pose a security risk (Kozodoi et al., 2022; Mehrabi et al., 2021). However, incorporating privacy concerns into ADM systems may make it more challenging to ensure fairness. A typical example of this trade-off is the use of demographic data to mitigate the bias in AI systems. An AI system can be made fair and unbiased by using demographic data, such as age, gender, and race. Nevertheless, the collection and use of these data raises privacy concerns because they are sensitive and can be used to discriminate against certain groups of people (Mehrabi et al., 2021). Personal data can also be used to improve the accuracy and efficiency of an AI system. Providing more context and information about an individual, personal data, such as browsing history and location data, can improve the performance of AI systems. As these data can be used to monitor and track individuals, their collection and use can raise privacy concerns. Organizations should carefully consider the potential fairness and privacy implications of their AI systems and implement appropriate safeguards to protect sensitive data from balancing these trade-offs.

Companies can balance privacy and fairness through clear consent, privacy protection techniques, data aggregation, and clear and concise policies (Eryurek et al., 2021; Gordon et al., 2022; Mahanti, 2021a). As mentioned, data governance helps companies ensure that individuals' privacy is respected before collecting and using personal data for AI purposes by issuing explicit consent. When data are collected, they can be protected by implementing differential privacy that adds noise to the data to protect individual privacy, but still allows for the extraction of useful information. Using this mechanism, ML models can be trained without requiring access to sensitive data. Organizations can also use aggregated data to train and develop AI systems. In this way, individual privacy can be protected, and fair and unbiased AI systems can be developed. Clear policies should also be established within organizations to collect, use, and retain data for AI purposes (Gordon et al., 2022; Keller & Drake, 2021; Wu et al., 2020). These policies should be reviewed and evaluated regularly.

Mitigating Bias in Automated Decision-Making

AI is often considered to be more objective than humans. In reality, AI algorithms can make biased and exclusionary decisions based on data representing social interactions. For example, because AI is trained on data, the absence of data from marginalized communities can reproduce or even exacerbate social inequalities. In this case, AI technologies may encourage stereotypical representation of the majority. This creates a negative feedback loop that leads to further loss of data from these populations, which would otherwise improve the accuracy of the AI (Akter et al., 2021). Another example can be found in the healthcare systems. As disparities already exist in our healthcare system, our predictive model dataset will contain inherited disparities (Gandhi, 2022).

AI bias is the systematic or unfair treatment of individuals or groups based on race, sex, age, or other characteristics (Belenguer, 2022). This bias can have serious consequences including discrimination and harm to individuals, groups, and society. Such a bias needs to be better governed. For example, the AI Act proposed by the European Union categorizes AI based on the risk level from unacceptable high-risk, and limited or minimal risks. While AI with unacceptable risks will not be allowed, high-risk AI levels will be required to manage potential bias through human oversight, be more transparent, and have high-quality training and testing datasets.

The AI development process can be vulnerable to bias due to data and algorithms (Holford, 2022). For instance, Suresh and Guttag (2021) showed that biases can come from the entire life cycle of machine learning. Training datasets to develop ADM systems are one of the most common sources of bias. An inaccurate representation of the population or solved task can lead to biased results. AI systems trained primarily on data from a particular sex or race are more likely to exhibit bias when applied to data from other groups. The training process may create additional biases because of the "reward" system. For example, Facebook's newsfeed needs to be upbeat, which may not only potentially bias the newsfeed selected, but also leave room for potential manipulation (Tufekci, 2016). This type of human intervention may improve the performance of the response but may simultaneously introduce the possibility of manipulation or additional biases (Wang, 2023). The algorithms and models used in AI also contribute to the bias. Some groups may be treated unfairly if these algorithms are not designed and tested carefully. For example, an algorithm that predicts the likelihood that a person will be unable to repay a loan may be biased if it is trained with data containing discriminatory patterns from the past (Jammalamadaka & Itapu, 2022). Consequently, the algorithm may indicate that individuals from racial or ethnic groups are more likely to not repay a loan, resulting in unfair treatment.

With ADM, organizations can identify causality, correlation, and other complex relationships to gain actionable insights. Putting aside the confusion of correlations and causality, ML or AI can improve the accuracy of the relationship between variables. Despite their benefits, digital transformation technologies are both biased and discriminatory. Inequalities can be exacerbated when algorithms learn about these biases. Several AI systems have demonstrated racial and ethnic biases, such as inaccurate facial recognition systems for people of color (Johnson, 2021; Wehrli et al., 2022). For instance, a digital camera may suggest that someone captured in the camera blinks simply because the camera recognizes facial characteristics (Rose, 2010). Another case study suggests that the AI system is more likely to award credit to white applicants than to applicants of other races. Gender bias has been identified in several AI systems. For example, natural language processing is used in the system to identify male pronouns in job tasks and female pronouns in household tasks.[2] In the insurance industry, AI was found to have biases such as higher premiums for women than for men and people from certain racial or ethnic groups. When making investment recommendations, AI recommends riskier investments for men than for women. In analyzing crime and fraud, AI systems exhibit biases in detecting fraud, such as a higher likelihood of detecting fraud and crime in transactions conducted by certain racial or ethnic groups.

These technological advances must be linked effectively to clear data policies. Biases can also be useful despite their harmful effects. For example, accountants and auditors can use AI detection capabilities to identify or predict potentially fraudulent behavior. In the crowdlending industry, AI determines the potential risk associated with an individual (Jammalamadaka & Itapu, 2022). Crowdlending companies use AI-based credit scoring to select projects based on their risk profile.

Companies can avoid bias by focusing on procedural and technological aspects. A company should implement proper internal control of its data. Internal controls are an integral part of accounting. It refers to an organization's processes and procedures to ensure that its financial operations are performed consistently and reliably and that its financial assets are safeguarded (Kerr & Murthy, 2013; Plant et al., 2022). In addition to accounting procedures and policies, nonfinancial controls

[2] https://www.reuters.com/article/us-amazon-com-jobs-automation-insight-idUSKCN1MK08G

may include data management, security policies, and procedures. Internal accounting controls ensure the integrity and reliability of financial data, prevent fraud, and ensure asset security. It also helps to identify and mitigate potential financial risks to an organization. Data governance, or the management and use of data, is an essential component of internal controls in accounting. Data can include financial transactions and operations such as reports and records. Organizations implement processes and procedures to ensure that data are collected, used, and stored ethically and responsibly. This includes policies on data collection, quality, security, privacy, and compliance. These policies are critical for avoiding problems in data collection, processing, and analysis (Mahanti, 2022a; Mahanti, 2022b). Data collection must be relevant and sufficient, high-quality, and comply with applicable regulations. ADM can also produce unexpected results after the data have been processed, which can pose problems. Data governance is a preventative measure that helps determine which data are relevant to the needs of the ADM system, who has access to the data, and how it is shared and stored. Data governance should be strictly enforced for ADM systems (Perdana & Lee, 2022).

Professional accountants can act as data controllers and processors for data protection (Perdana & Lee, 2022). Data controllers determine the purpose and appropriate methods for processing personal data. Accountants can assist with regulatory compliance and advise on how long data should be processed, what types of data should be analyzed, and why certain data should be further processed or analyzed. Accountants can ensure compliance by improving internal control policies for data use. Incorporating data ethics into corporate culture increases data sensitivity and transparency and mitigates risk. Accounting can ensure legal compliance, ethical data collection, and transparency in data processing. Whenever an ADM system behaves in unexpected or biased ways, accountants must explain why unintended consequences occur.

Organizations should understand how some algorithms generalize their learning from training data to identify biases in the AI algorithms. An accurate representation of the real world must be obtained by selecting the datasets for the model. Datasets based only on a population subset produce biased results. Organizations should collect data from multiple sources, use sampling techniques to ensure that the data are representative, and use data cleaning and preprocessing techniques to eliminate bias. Before aggregating the data for model training, one must know the representative data. A dataset should contain as little bias as possible regarding the population composition and data characteristics. To address these issues, organizations need to identify potential biases in datasets and document how they select and clean the data. Once an ADM system is developed, organizations should work with multiple stakeholders to ensure that AI development and deployment are transparent and accountable. This may include dialogue and collaboration with researchers, policymakers, industry, civil society organizations, and other stakeholders to ensure that AI development and use are transparent and accountable (Palladino, 2022).

From a technical perspective, AI developers must design and test algorithms and models to ensure fairness and bias. Design considerations must start from data preparation and cleansing techniques to using fairness metrics, bias detection algorithms, and debiasing methods to identify and correct biases in ADM systems (Holford, 2022). AI developers should carefully consider surrogate and other related variables. When decisions are made based on protected categories (e.g., ethnicity, race, religion, and/or gender), bias can be problematic and unfair. These variables can be excluded from the training data; however, AI developers must explore other variables that may unintentionally predict demographics. To improve the model results, these protected class labels are typically removed to comply with privacy and confidentiality laws. A mitigation algorithm can mitigate AI biases even without removing the labels. Before feeding the data into the algorithms, AI developers can encode attributes as numeric values to mitigate potential biases. Debiasing tools such as IBM AI Fairness 360 (AIF360) can be used to mitigate this bias.[3] With IBM AI Fairness 360, developers and data scientists can evaluate and improve the fairness of their artificial intelligence (AI) models. The toolkit includes a set of algorithms, codes, and other resources to identify and address potential bias. AI developers can use the toolkit throughout the AI development process from data collection to model training and evaluation. One of the critical features of this tool is the detection and quantification of bias in AI models. The tool includes algorithms and visualizations that detect bias patterns such as unequal representations.

Algorithms should be designed to mitigate bias; however, they must also be explained in terms of the effects of bias resulting from the use

[3] https://aif360.mybluemix.net/

of these algorithms (Hind, 2019). In some cases, even a sensitive algorithm can cause problems owing to unbalanced data or small changes in the data. When ADM is used with a heterogeneous population, the lack of training data may exacerbate biases. An adequate explanation of such circumstances is required to improve traceability, transparency, and interpretability. Possible explanations include the rationale behind the development of ADM, unconscious biases of developers, and appropriate communication of the development of ADM to relevant stakeholders (Bussmann et al., 2020; Rai, 2020).

Enhancing Automated Decision-Making Accountability

Accountability, transparency, and explainability are essential to ensure ADM systems are responsibly and ethically used (Bussmann et al., 2021; Hind, 2019; Rai, 2020; Zhang et al., 2022). Accountability refers to the idea that individuals or organizations are responsible for the actions and decisions of an AI system (de Laat, 2018). These responsibilities include ensuring that the system is developed and deployed fairly, ethically, and in compliance with applicable laws and regulations. To ensure accountability, the ADM systems must be able to explain and track their decision-making processes (Barredo Arrieta et al., 2020; Ribera & Lapedriza, 2019). As more ADM systems are used to make decisions, concerns about maintaining clear accountability structures have increased. Algorithmic accountability requires transparency. Transparency in algorithm development is often considered a prerequisite for trust in AI. A transparent algorithm is more than just a matter of ensuring its visibility. In general, transparency refers to the ability of system users, regulators, and those affected by algorithms to understand the various factors that influence the decisions they make, that is, the understandability and explainability of a given model (Dignum, 2019). Predictive algorithms may generate opaque decisions owing to various factors that are not always possible or desirable to eliminate. The algorithms may not be easy to understand, the cost of providing transparency may be too high, including compromising trade secrets, and privacy expectations may be violated. Several mechanisms regulate and ensure accountability in relation to organizational decisions. These mechanisms include audit, contract, and monitoring.

Explainability in AI refers to a system to explain its decision-making processes (Hind, 2019; Rai, 2020). Explainability is important because when users better understand how AI systems work and why they make certain decisions, it can help build trust between them. A bias or error in an AI system can also be detected and corrected, thereby improving the fairness and accuracy of decisions. Explainability also contributes to the responsible and ethical use of AI systems by enabling users to understand the potentially harmful consequences of the decisions made by the system. Explainability can be implemented in ADM systems in several manners. One approach to this problem is to use interpretable AI models designed to be easily understood and interpreted by humans. They typically have a more straightforward structure and use fewer parameters, making them easier to understand and interpret. An alternative approach is to use explainable AI (XAI) methods that aim to explain the decisions made by an ADM system (Linardatos et al., 2020; Meske et al., 2022). Users can use these techniques to determine which aspects of the data are most important in a particular decision, as well as a sensitivity analysis to determine how the output of an ADM system changes in response to changes in the input values.

ADM systems can be evaluated by humans and improved through feedback. When they fail, humans intervene. With human-in-the-loop (HITL), users and developers can provide feedback during development and interaction with ADM systems, which can then be monitored for efficiency evaluations and modification of the learning algorithm (Holford, 2022; How et al., 2020). For example, ADM systems can treat sex as a bias factor. The ML algorithms used must be compatible with the existing protocols and procedures to ensure that certain rights are protected. Accounting professionals can help companies mitigate the impact of bias in ADM systems as they have financial and social implications. Companies using ADM systems or regulators may also require a post hoc analysis of their automated decisions (in whole or in part). Regulators and organizations can detect discrimination patterns in ADM systems and address them before they become public by establishing a regular evaluation and tracking system. For example, mandatory audits can prevent indirect discrimination. Organizations and regulators can verify the source of training data, determine whether the design targets a particular population, and even test for predisposition by posing new customers.

AI's Legal Personhood

As explained in the previous sections, AI is currently the most advanced technology developed by computer scientists. Its existence garners considerable interest from a wide range of individuals who classify it as having advantages and disadvantages. Despite its benefits to economic development, the advent of AI has not only prompted debate in its applications, such as in the workplace, but also in the legal sector, where debates have emerged over whether AI can be defined as a legal subject, making it liable for crimes (Arifin, 2021). Concerning the presence of AI and its remarkable function in assisting human activities, the European Parliament posed a crucial question: "[r]obot autonomy raises the question of their nature in light of existing legal categories – whether they should be considered natural persons, animals, or objects, or whether a new category should be created, with its distinctive characteristics and implications for the assignment of rights and duties, including liability for damage" (Janssens, 2019).

When a system is granted legal personality, it provides circumstances that can help address problems regarding meaningful control. However, dealing with legal personhood in the context of autonomous systems is challenging and poses significant challenges (Kurki & Pietrzykowski, 2017). Who determines whether systems qualify to be considered legal entities? How, and under what circumstances, should this be performed? What happens if the system is shut off and ceases to function? (Janssens, 2019). As a result, legal experts continue to monitor the advancement of AI, and professionals in its connected sectors are still being created. Meanwhile, legal academics believe that the AI issue necessitates an ethics code to guide users (Spiegeleire et al., 2017). The ideas of various parties on an AI code of ethics are expressed in numerous models of a code of conduct, including those produced by the OECD, Canada, China, and the United Nations for military AI (Medeiros, 2020). However, legal scholars' perspectives on AI personhood differ in two major groups: those who agree that AI is an independent legal personhood, and those who disagree and prefer to address the controller as the most responsible party.

Given that the idea of personhood has seen minimal jurisprudence-based theoretical development over the past half-century, it is challenging to determine the personhood status of AI (Kurki & Pietrzykowski, 2017). The discussion on personhood status generally centers on transforming non-personal entities, such as animals, and technological breakthroughs, such as AI, into persons. Kurki and Pietrzykowski (2017) analyzed the inherent duality in conceptions of people and things. He offers nonhuman animals as an example of beings whose legal status could be altered from that of things to that of "non-personal subjects"—neither legal persons nor things. He argues that such subjects should be handled differently than traditional persons as possessors of a single subjective right—the right to be considered—that is, to have their interests evaluated and weighed in all legal decisions that may impact them. Hallevy (2013) developed a more convincing case for the personhood of animals. Hallevy believes that people and animals have coexisted for millennia. Consequently, the law treats animals as human property. Therefore, if an animal causes damage, then the owner of the animal's property rights is legally liable. The owner of the dog is legally accountable for any damage caused by the attack. In most nations, this property relationship between people and animals is governed by tort law; however, in certain nations, it is also governed by criminal law. In either event, the person, not the animal, bears legal responsibility. Kurki and Pietrzykowski (2017) explored the correct notion of legal personhood, considering New York trials to determine whether chimpanzees should be awarded a limited legal personality. Kurki and Pietrzykowski assert that trials are based on a flawed premise: legal personhood cannot be equated with the possession of legal rights, as animals possess rights despite not being legal people. In addition, Michalczak (2017) examines how practical and economic considerations could result in software agents being awarded legal personality and associated rights before nonhuman creatures.

The term "person" is only employed in a technical sense in the Universal Declaration and other international legal instruments. For instance, the 1950 Convention for the Protection of Human Rights and Fundamental Freedoms refers to the right of every person to life, and clarifies that the deprivation of life will not be considered contrary to the convention if it occurs because of the necessary use of force to defend a person against illegal violence. Here, "Person" serves as a placeholder for an individual's name. Regarding the application of biology and medicine, this technical understanding of "person" is also used in the convention to protect human rights and dignity. The term "person" does not even appear in the title, and when it does appear in the text, it is in a technical legal sense, such as when referring to the consent that must be given by a person when agreeing to medical procedures or when protecting a person who is not able to give such consent (Kurki & Pietrzykowski, 2017).

Hallevy (2013) provided a lucid opinion on the controversy surrounding AI's personality status. Hallevy concurs that AI satisfies all criminal culpability requirements, which are notably distinct from those of animals. Thus, the zoological legal concept is not applicable to AI, as—all the human interaction is emotional, but AI is more rational. In criminal law, rationality is the most important aspect, whereas emotions are rarely considered. The criminal culpability of creatures with AI may seem radical. For centuries, criminal culpability has been regarded as a component of the cosmos inhabited solely by humans. Criminal culpability necessitates strict adherence to the law and the offender: nothing more, nothing less. If an AI entity satisfies all of these criteria, there is no reason not to subject it to criminal culpability. AI entities can achieve these needs in the same manner as human and corporate criminals (but not animals).

Considering liability as the key problem in AI law, Hallevy provides specific ways of thinking through criminal responsibility for a varied array of autonomous technologies in various contexts by recognizing and selecting equivalent principles from existing criminal law. Hallevy proposed a comprehensive and legally sophisticated theory of criminal liability for AI and robotics that encompasses the manufacturer, programmer, user, and other interested parties. All sorts of criminal culpability are applicable to AI technology, and substantive arguments regarding criminal liability can be made in reference to AI entities. In addition, AI entities can be penalized in a manner comparable to that of companies (Hallevy, 2013).

Scholars have sought to examine the personhood status of artificial intelligence from several perspectives, focusing on two main directions: philosophical and moral (Bundy, 1988; Cataleta, 2020; Gordon et al., 2022; Kurki, 2017; Luccioni & Bengio, 2020; Mantelero, 2018; Pillar, 2012; Pollock, 1990; Rodgers et al., 2023; Santow, 2020; Wu, 2019). They all agree that the characteristics of AI are different from those of animals. AI works more rationally and mimics humans, whereas animals only have emotions (Hallevy, 2013; Kurki & Pietrzykowski, 2017; Michalczak, 2017; Teubner, 2006). AI is a human invention designed to assist humans in simplifying their jobs efficiently and effectively using complex data (Ashley, 2017). In this regard, however, the AI status is a human-created object, even though it can function like a human under certain circumstances. As an object, it is impossible to claim full legal responsibility for actions and consequences. This is because behind everything, the AI does is the controller. Thus, when an AI malfunctions, the controller is more likely to be held culpable.

Hallevy's (2013) theory of criminal liability analysis, which is extensive and legally sophisticated, is relevant to this argument in the context of the examination of technical legal responsibility or the responsible domain. According to this notion, the malfunctions of AI and robotics can be examined on a case-by-case basis, involving the manufacturer, programmer, user, and other interested parties. In this case, corporate legal liability is more clearly linked to AI responsibility models (Avila Negri, 2021). Based on the current work on AI personhood, Walton (2005) suggests that future studies should focus on establishing formal models for different types of debates related to communication between agents in multi-agent systems, scenarios for legal considerations, and general reasoning. Nonetheless, each country should make its own decisions about the personhood status of AI to protect its citizens from the adverse effects of AI. Given the uncertainty of an AI's personhood status, a code of ethics for AI is essential to ensure that its operations are consistent with its functions. If an error occurs, it can be investigated with the help of the public law of the country in which AI operates. Accounting bodies can also help the government formulate better regulations, standards, and codes of conduct for accountants when using ADM to better protect them from unintended consequences that may result from the use of ADM.

Conclusion

The field of AI-assisted decision-making (ADM) continues to evolve and has the potential to impact the way businesses operate and make decisions. ADM systems use advanced AI/ML algorithms and Big Data to process and analyze complex information, identify patterns and trends, and enable companies to make informed decisions. However, ADM poses some risks that need to be carefully managed to maximize the impact and minimize potential negative consequences. One important risk associated with ADM is the potential amplification of bias. The use of data- and model-driven AI can reinforce existing biases, which can negatively affect the fairness and accuracy of decisions made using analytics. For example, an ML model trained on biased data is likely to yield biased results. Similarly, if an ADM system is designed to consider only certain types of data or certain aspects, the system may produce biased or inaccurate results.

Designing and implementing ADM systems in a fair, ethical, and responsible manner can minimize these risks. Bias detection and correction can be incorporated into this process, which in turn can identify and eliminate bias in data and models. The diversity and representativeness of the data used to train the ML models can be improved through techniques such as data augmentation and data balancing. ADM Risks can also be mitigated by involving experts who know how the data are processed and how decisions are made. Accountants can address these challenges because they have expertise in managing and processing data, interpreting and evaluating nonfinancial and financial data, and creating value. Accounting professionals can help companies develop a more responsible AI environment by leveraging their understanding of the data and decision-making processes.

As a human-created object, AI cannot be held fully legally responsible for its actions and consequences, as the controller bears the ultimate responsibility. However, in the event of a malfunction, various parties such as organizations, programmers, users, and interested parties can be held accountable for AI's actions. Each nation should independently determine the status of AI to protect its citizens from its negative effects. Because there is still ambiguity about AI's status as a person, it is critical to establish a code of ethics for AI to ensure that its actions are consistent with its intended functions. If an error occurs, it can be investigated with the help of the public law of the country in which AI is used.

In addition to minimizing the risks associated with ADM, clear policies and guidelines must be established. Accounting bodies should work with the government to formulate regulations, standards, and guidelines to mitigate potential risks that may arise from the use of ADM. This will ensure that ADM systems are used transparently, accountably, and in line with the organization's goals and values. Regulating AI in decision-making and establishing appropriate laws can also ensure that the technology is used ethically and responsibly. Although ADM offers many potential benefits, it should be viewed as a tool rather than an end. Although it can process and analyze large amounts of data, it cannot replace human judgment. Therefore, ADM should be used in a way that complements rather than replaces human judgement in the decision-making process.

References

Agrawal, D. P., Nedjah, N., Gupta, B. B., & Martinez Perez, G. (Eds.). (2022). *Cyber security, privacy and networking* (Vol. 370). Springer Nature Singapore. https://doi.org/10.1007/978-981-16-8664-1

Akter, S., McCarthy, G., Sajib, S., Michael, K., Dwivedi, Y. K., D'Ambra, J., & Shen, K. N. (2021). Algorithmic bias in data-driven innovation in the age of AI. *International Journal of Information Management, 60*, 102387. https://doi.org/10.1016/j.ijinfomgt.2021.102387

Arifin, S. (2021). AI in the workplace-how should moral and legal issues be addressed? *Pro Publico Bono-Public Administration, 4*, 94–109. https://doi.org/10.32575/ppb.2021.4.6

Ashley, K. D. (2017). *Artificial intelligence and legal analytics: New tools for law practice in the digital age*. Cambridge University Press.

Avila Negri, S. M. C. (2021). Robot as legal person: Electronic personhood in robotics and artificial intelligence. *Frontiers in Robotics and AI, 8*(December), 1–10. https://doi.org/10.3389/frobt.2021.789327

Bakarich, K. M., & O'Brien, P. E. (2021). The robots are coming … but aren't here yet: The use of artificial intelligence technologies in the public accounting profession. *Journal of Emerging Technologies in Accounting, 18*(1), 27–43. https://doi.org/10.2308/JETA-19-11-20-47

Bana, S., Brynjolfsson, E., Jin, W., Steffen, S., & Wang, X. (2021). Cybersecurity hiring in response to data breaches. *SSRN Electronic Journal*. https://doi.org/10.2139/ssrn.3806060

Bandi, S., & Kothari, A. (2022). Artificial intelligence: An asset for the financial sector. In *Impact of Artificial Intelligence on Organizational Transformation* (pp. 259–287). Wiley. https://doi.org/10.1002/9781119710301.ch16

Barredo Arrieta, A., Díaz-Rodríguez, N., del Ser, J., Bennetot, A., Tabik, S., Barbado, A., Garcia, S., Gil-Lopez, S., Molina, D., Benjamins, R., Chatila, R., & Herrera, F. (2020). Explainable artificial intelligence (XAI): Concepts, taxonomies, opportunities, and challenges toward responsible AI. *Information Fusion, 58*, 82–115. https://doi.org/10.1016/j.inffus.2019.12.012

Belenguer, L. (2022). AI bias: Exploring discriminatory algorithmic decision-making models and the application of possible machine-centric solutions adapted from the pharmaceutical industry. *AI and Ethics, 2*(4), 771–787. https://doi.org/10.1007/s43681-022-00138-8

Bundy, A. (1988). Artificial intelligence: Art or science? *RSA Journal, 136*(5384), 557–569.

Bussmann, N., Giudici, P., Marinelli, D., & Papenbrock, J. (2020). Explainable AI in Fintech risk management. *Frontiers in Artificial Intelligence, 3*,. https://doi.org/10.3389/frai.2020.00026

Bussmann, N., Giudici, P., Marinelli, D., & Papenbrock, J. (2021). Explainable machine learning in credit risk management. *Computational Economics, 57*(1), 203–216. https://doi.org/10.1007/s10614-020-10042-0

Carlsson, V., & Rönnblom, M. (2022). From politics to ethics: Transformations in EU policies on digital technology. *Technology in Society, 71*, 102145. https://doi.org/10.1016/j.techsoc.2022.102145

Cataleta, M. S. (2020). *Humane artificial intelligence: The fragility of human rights facing AI* (no. 2). Humane Artificial Intelligence.

Couce-Vieira, A., Insua, D. R., & Kosgodagan, A. (2020). Assessing and forecasting cybersecurity impacts. *Decision Analysis, 17*(4), 356–374. https://doi.org/10.1287/deca.2020.0418

de Laat, P. B. (2018). Algorithmic decision-making based on machine learning from big data: Can transparency restore accountability? *Philosophy & Technology, 31*(4), 525–541. https://doi.org/10.1007/s13347-017-0293-z

Dignum, V. (2019). *Responsible artificial intelligence.* Springer International Publishing. https://doi.org/10.1007/978-3-030-30371-6

Donaldson, S. E., Siegel, S. G., Williams, C. K., & Aslam, A. (2015). *Enterprise cybersecurity*. Apress. https://doi.org/10.1007/978-1-4302-6083-7

Eryurek, E., Gilad, U., Lakshmanan, V., Kibunguchy-Grant, A., & Ashdown, J. (2021). *Data governance: The definitive guide*. O'Reilly Media, Inc.

Fréminville, M. (2020). *Cybersecurity and decision makers: Data security and digital trust*. Wiley

Gandhi, T. (2022). Introducing the responsible AI in practice series. Retrieved on March 3, 2023, from https://blog.dataiku.com/introducing-the-responsible-ai-in-practice-series-and-healthcare-use-case

Gordon, G., Rieder, B., & Sileno, G. (2022). On mapping values in AI governance. *Computer Law & Security Review, 46*, 105712. https://doi.org/10.1016/j.clsr.2022.105712

Gouthier, M. H. J., Nennstiel, C., Kern, N., & Wendel, L. (2022). The more the better? Data disclosure between the conflicting priorities of privacy concerns, information sensitivity and personalization in e-commerce. *Journal of Business Research, 148*, 174–189. https://doi.org/10.1016/j.jbusres.2022.04.034

Hallevy, G. (2013). *When Robots Kill: Artificial intelligence under criminal law.* Northeastern University Press.

Helberger, N., Araujo, T., & de Vreese, C. H. (2020). Who is the fairest of them all? Public attitudes and expectations regarding automated decision-making. *Computer Law & Security Review, 39*, 105456. https://doi.org/10.1016/j.clsr.2020.105456

Hind, M. (2019). Explaining explainable AI. *XRDS: Crossroads, the ACM Magazine for Students*, *25*(3), 16–19. https://doi.org/10.1145/3313096

Holford, W. D. (2022). Design-for-responsible' algorithmic decision-making systems: A question of ethical judgement and human meaningful control. *AI and Ethics, 2*(4), 827–836. https://doi.org/10.1007/s43681-022-00144-w

Hooi, E. (2019). *Cyber security: Beware the human factor.*

How, M.-L., Cheah, S.-M., Khor, A. C., & Chan, Y. J. (2020). Artificial intelligence-enhanced predictive insights for advancing financial inclusion: A human-centric Ai-thinking approach. *Big Data and Cognitive Computing, 4*(2), 8. https://doi.org/10.3390/bdcc4020008

Hsu, J. (2022). Europe's AI regulations could lead the way for the world. *New Scientist, 256*(3419), 9. https://doi.org/10.1016/S0262-4079(22)02307-7

Jammalamadaka, K. R., & Itapu, S. (2022). Responsible AI in automated credit scoring systems. *AI and Ethics.* https://doi.org/10.1007/s43681-022-00175-3

Janssens, L. (2019). A prospect of the future: How autonomous systems may qualify as legal persons. In E. Bayamlioglu, I. Baraliuc, L. Janssens, & M. Hildebrandt (Eds.), Being profiled: Cogitas ergo sum: Ten years of profiling the european citizen (pp. 116–121). Amsterdam University Press. https://doi.org/10.1515/9789048550180-022

Johnson, G. M. (2021). Algorithmic bias: On the implicit biases of social technology. *Synthese, 198*(10), 9941–9961. https://doi.org/10.1007/s11229-020-02696-y

Keller, P., & Drake, A. (2021). Exclusivity and paternalism in the public governance of explainable AI. *Computer Law & Security Review, 40*, 105490. https://doi.org/10.1016/j.clsr.2020.105490

Kerr, D. S., & Murthy, U. S. (2013). The importance of the CobiT framework IT processes for effective internal control over financial reporting in organizations: An international survey. *Information & Management, 50*(7), 590–597. https://doi.org/10.1016/j.im.2013.07.012

King, N. J., & Forder, J. (2016). Data analytics and consumer profiling: Finding appropriate privacy principles for discovered data. *Computer Law & Security Review, 32*(5), 696–714.

Kołodziej, J., Repetto, M., & Duzha, A. (Eds.). (2022). *Cybersecurity of digital service chains* (Vol. 13300). Springer International Publishing. https://doi.org/10.1007/978-3-031-04036-8

Kozodoi, N., Jacob, J., & Lessmann, S. (2022). Fairness in credit scoring: Assessment, implementation, and profit implications. *European Journal of Operational Research, 297*(3), 1083–1094. https://doi.org/10.1016/j.ejor.2021.06.023

Kurki, V. A. J. (2017). Why things can hold rights: Reconceptualizing the legal person. In V. A. J. Kurki & T. Pietrzykowski (Eds.), *Legal Personhood: Animals, Artificial Intelligence and the Unborn* (pp. 69–90). Springer.

Kurki, V. A. J., & Pietrzykowski, T. (2017). *Legal personhood: Animals, artificial intelligence and the unborn* (F. J. Laporta, F. Schauer, & T. Spaak, Eds.). Springer. https://doi.org/10.1007/978-3-319-53462-6

Leslie, D. (2020). *Understanding bias in facial recognition technologies*. ArXiv:2010.07023.

Lecomte, P. (2022). Companies are increasingly tracking eye movements—But is it ethical? *The Conversation*. https://theconversation.com/companies-are-increasingly-tracking-eye-movements-but-is-it-ethical-191842

Linardatos, P., Papastefanopoulos, V., & Kotsiantis, S. (2020). Explainable AI: A review of machine learning interpretability methods. *Entropy, 23*(1), 18. https://doi.org/10.3390/e23010018

Luccioni, A., & Bengio, Y. (2020). On the morality of artificial intelligence. *IEEE Technology and Society Magazine, 39*(1), 16–25. https://doi.org/10.1109/MTS.2020.2967486

Mahanti, R. (2021a). *Data governance and compliance*. Springer. https://doi.org/10.1007/978-981-33-6877-4

Mahanti, R. (2021b). *Data governance and data management*. Springer. https://doi.org/10.1007/978-981-16-3583-0

Mantelero, A. (2018). AI and big data: A blueprint for a human rights, social and ethical impact assessment. *Computer Law and Security Review, 34*(4), 754–772. https://doi.org/10.1016/j.clsr.2018.05.017

Medeiros, M. (2020). Public and private dimensions of AI technology and security. In Modern conflict and artificial intelligence (pp. 20–25). Centre for International Governance Innovation.

Mehrabi, N., Morstatter, F., Saxena, N., Lerman, K., & Galstyan, A. (2021). A survey on bias and fairness in machine learning. *ACM Computing Surveys, 54*(6), 1–35. https://doi.org/10.1145/3457607

Meske, C., Bunde, E., Schneider, J., & Gersch, M. (2022). Explainable artificial intelligence: Objectives, stakeholders, and future research opportunities. *Information Systems Management, 39*(1), 53–63. https://doi.org/10.1080/10580530.2020.1849465

Michalczak, R. (2017). Animals' race against the machines. In Legal personhood: Animals, artificial intelligence and the unborn (pp. 91–104). Springer.

Nalbandian, L. (2022). Increasing the accountability of automated decision-making systems: An assessment of the automated decision-making system introduced in Canada's temporary resident visa immigration stream. *Journal of Responsible Technology, 10*, 100023. https://doi.org/10.1016/j.jrt.2021.100023

Niebel, C. (2021). The impact of the general data protection regulation on innovation and the global political economy. *Computer Law & Security Review, 40*, 105523. https://doi.org/10.1016/j.clsr.2020.105523

Palladino, N. (2022). A 'biased' emerging governance regime for artificial Intelligence? How AI ethics get skewed moving from principles to practices. *Telecommunications Policy, 102479*. https://doi.org/10.1016/j.telpol.2022.102479

Perdana, A., & Lee, W.E. (2022, December). *AI and Digital discrimination*. Strategic Finance.

Perera, C., Ranjan, R., Wang, L., Khan, S. U., & Zomaya, A. Y. (2015). Big data privacy in the internet of things Era. *IT Professional, 17*(3), 32–39. https://doi.org/10.1109/MITP.2015.34

Petrella, A. (2021). *What is data governance?* O'Reilly Media Inc.

Pillar, P. R. (2012). Artificial intelligence reform: Social amnesia and the intelligence community. *Georgetown Journal of International Affairs, 13*(2), 177–183.

Plant, O. H., van Hillegersberg, J., & Aldea, A. (2022). Rethinking IT governance: Designing a framework for mitigating risk and fostering internal control in a DevOps environment. *International Journal of Accounting Information Systems, 45*, 100560. https://doi.org/10.1016/j.accinf.2022.100560

Pollock, J. (1990). Philosophy and artificial intelligence. *Philosophical Perspective, 4*, 461–498.

Rai, A. (2020). Explainable AI: From black box to glass box. *Journal of the Academy of Marketing Science, 48*(1), 137–141. https://doi.org/10.1007/s11747-019-00710-5

Ribera, M., & Lapedriza, A. (2019). *Can we do better explanations? A proposal of User-Centered Explainable AI*

Rodgers, W., Murray, J. M., Stefanidis, A., Degbey, W. Y., & Tarba, S. Y. (2023). An artificial intelligence algorithmic approach to ethical decision-making in human resource management processes. *Human Resource Management Review, 33*(1), 100925. https://doi.org/10.1016/j.hrmr.2022.100925

Rose, A. 2010. Are face-detection cameras racist? *Time*. Retrieved on March 5, 2023, from https://content.time.com/time/business/article/0,8599,1954643,00.html.

Santow, E. (2020). Can artificial intelligence be trusted with our human rights? *Australian Quarterly, 91*(4), 10–17.

Shahim, A. (2021). Security of the digital transformation. *Computers & Security, 108*, 102345. https://doi.org/10.1016/j.cose.2021.102345

Siau, K., & Wang, W. (2020). Artificial intelligence (AI) ethics. *Journal of Database Management, 31*(2), 74–87. https://doi.org/10.4018/JDM.2020040105

Spiegeleire, S. De, Maas, M., & Sweijs, T. (2017). *What is artificial intelligence?* Hague Center for Strategic Studies.

Suresh, H., & Guttag, J. (2021, October 5–9). A framework for understanding sources of harm throughout the machine learning life cycle. In *Equity and access in algorithms, mechanisms, and optimization* (EAAMO '21), NY, USA

Tamburri, D. A. (2020). Design principles for the General Data Protection Regulation (GDPR): A formal concept analysis and its evaluation. *Information Systems, 91*, 101469. https://doi.org/10.1016/j.is.2019.101469

Teubner, G. (2006). Rights of non-humans ? Electronic agents and animals as new actors in politics and law. *Journal of Law and Society, 33*(4), 497–521.

Truby, J. (2020). Governing Artificial Intelligence to benefit the UN Sustainable Development Goals. *Sustainable Development, 28*(4), 946–959. https://doi.org/10.1002/sd.2048

Tufekci, 2016. The real bias built in at Facebook. *The New York Times*. Retrieved on March 5, 2023, from https://www.nytimes.com/2016/05/19/opinion/the-real-bias-built-in-at-facebook.html.

Wang, B. 2023. *ChatGPT has a human team train it to be a lot better*. Retrieved on March 1, 2023, from https://www.nextbigfuture.com/2023/02/chatgpt-has-a-human-team-train-it-to-be-a-lot-better.html

Walters, R., & Novak, M. (2021). *Cyber security, artificial intelligence. Data protection & the law.* Springer. https://doi.org/10.1007/978-981-16-1665-5

Walton, D. (2005). *Argumentation methods for artificial inteligence in aw.* Springer.

Wehrli, S., Hertweck, C., Amirian, M., Glüge, S., & Stadelmann, T. (2022). Bias, awareness, and ignorance in deep-learning-based face recognition. *AI and Ethics, 2*(3), 509–522. https://doi.org/10.1007/s43681-021-00108-6

Wu, T. (2019). Will artificial intelligence eat the law? The rise of hybrid social orderings systems. *Columbia Law Review, 119*(7), 2001–2028.

Wu, W., Huang, T., & Gong, K. (2020). Ethical principles and governance technology development of AI in China. *Engineering, 6*(3), 302–309. https://doi.org/10.1016/j.eng.2019.12.015

Zhang, C., & (Abigail), Cho, S., & Vasarhelyi, M. (2022). Explainable artificial intelligence (XAI) in auditing. *International Journal of Accounting Information Systems, 46*, 100572. https://doi.org/10.1016/j.accinf.2022.100572

CHAPTER 12

Harnessing Technologies and Data to Accelerate and Operationalize Environmental, Social, and Governance (ESG) Initiatives

Arif Perdana and Seck Tan

Introduction

The concept of sustainability refers to the goal of leaving an improved standard of living for future generations,[1] where the tri-nexus of environmental, economic, and social facets is collectively addressed for the good of the society over time. Implementing sustainable corporate cultures promotes the optimization of business processes and the protection and maintenance of the environment. Businesses, investors, and consumers

[1] https://www.mcgill.ca/sustainability/files/sustainability/what-is-sustainability.pdf.

A. Perdana (✉)
Monash University, Tangerang, Indonesia
e-mail: arif.perdana@monash.edu

S. Tan
Singapore Institute of Technology, Dover Drive, Singapore
e-mail: Seck.Tan@Singaporetech.edu.sg

A. Perdana and T. Wang (eds.), *Digital Transformation in Accounting and Auditing*, https://doi.org/10.1007/978-3-031-46209-2_12

have become increasingly aware of the importance of corporate sustainability (Chouaibi et al., 2022; Li et al., 2022; Widyawati, 2020). Various factors contribute to a company's sustainability, including environmental, social, and governance (ESG) factors. A growing number of investors and other stakeholders are increasingly demanding that companies disclose their ESG-related risks, practices, and impacts to ensure that their ESG accountability is addressed (Ellili, 2022; Nicolò et al., 2022).

ESG approaches examine the relationship between corporate governance and environmental and social sustainability. The environmental dimension refers to the stewardship of nature by a company and its efficient use of natural resources, as well as the reduction of greenhouse gas (GHG) emissions generated by its operations. The social dimension assesses a company's ability to instill ethical values in its business operations and foster a culture of trust among its employees. The governance dimension examines a company's ability to act in the best interests of its shareholders, such as compliance with rules, industrial and professional standards, and governmental laws and acts (Câmara & Morais, 2022). Overall, a company that harms the environment, disregards the social and ethical consequences of its operations, does not follow sound corporate governance practices, or has difficulty implementing sustainability initiatives has shareholder accountability and survival at risk. ESG has become an increasingly prominent topic in literature (Alkaraan et al., 2022; Widyawati, 2020). ESG performance is now an essential factor in evaluating governance and social and environmental responsibilities. Investors are likely to penalize companies with low ESG scores and high ESG controversies (Broadstock et al., 2021; Ellili, 2022). ESG investing has evolved from a niche strategy and reserve for ethical investors to mainstream activities. Governments and regulators also encourage companies to become more socially and environmentally responsible (Shakil, 2021).

As an increasing number of stakeholders become interested in ESG issues, the sustainability landscape continues to expand. Data plays an essential role in ESG initiatives, regardless of the role that companies play (Dolan & Zalles, 2022). ESG initiatives face several challenges in collecting, generating, and using data. For example, Deloitte reported a disconnect between ESG data and ESG performance standards, challenges in sharing ESG data, lack of coordination in ESG reporting, and unclear incentives for managing and disclosing ESG data (Sinke et al., 2021). While practitioners have expressed concerns about these issues, academic research on how to overcome them is lacking. The quality and reliability of ESG data remain obscure (Jonsdottir et al., 2022; van Rensburg et al., 2019). For example, Van Rensburg explained that ESG data collection is a complex process. Data collection systems vary in complexity; some are automated, whereas others require manual input. Standardization, centralization, verification, and data integration are other issues in the ESG data collection.[2] Furthermore, there are multiple dimensions to each ESG dimension and demand justification of varying proxies for universal acceptance.

A key element in driving changes in ESG is identifying data problems, including collecting, measuring, analyzing, and evaluating information (Dolan & Zalles, 2022). Technologies should be used to collect data at the source, permitting companies to understand how ESG data impacts them internally and externally. In recent years, several technologies have been deployed to measure critical information, including the Internet of Things (IoT), machine learning, Big Data, robotics, edge computing, and sensors. Companies can leverage technology and data to drive ESG initiatives (Chin et al., 2022; Wu, Chen, et al., 2022a, 2022b). For example, by overcoming green technology integration challenges, management can make better data decisions, leading to robust ESG reporting aligned with a company's strategic goals. To date, companies have worked to reduce their carbon footprint by optimizing power consumption in data centers or using renewable energy sources such as solar and wind power. The weakest link to fully integrating ESG strategies is the effective use of technology to address data governance issues, ensuring that people, processes, and technology are targeted to facilitate data privacy and regulatory compliance (Jonsdottir et al., 2022; van Rensburg et al., 2019; Yin & Li, 2022). A well-designed data governance system should incorporate artificial intelligence (AI) to support responsible automated decision-making while remaining mindful of the unintended consequences of AI on ESG strategies. Ultimately, the development and deployment of AI solutions requires strong governance control to ensure social equity.

This article explores how companies can leverage technology and data to accelerate ESG initiatives. Technology has the potential to revolutionize sustainability by accelerating net-zero projects to implement more sustainable value chains. However, the effectiveness of technology

[2] https://www.accenture.com/_acnmedia/PDF-170/Accenture-ESG-Data-Challenges-Brochure-Digital.pdf.

depends on how companies develop their strategies from targeted behaviors and translate them into concrete actions.

ESG: Its History and Current Status

With the development of commercial activity centers for economic development and as a dynamic force in human society, the ESG concept has emerged over time. The rapid growth of business in the industrialized world led to the emergence of modern philanthropy in the late 1800s, which laid the foundation for early ESG initiatives (Câmara & Morais, 2022; Dolan & Zalles, 2022). The concept of corporate responsibility was developed from the realization that focusing solely on the profit motive created human costs (and climate changes) that ultimately compromised business efficiency. With the onset of the first industrial revolution, attention has been drawn to factory working conditions. To prevent worker activism, unionization, and excessive workplace regulation, companies began to implement welfare practices (e.g., employee housing, benefits, and allowances) in response to enterprise bargaining.

Corporate responsibility was previously reflected in the corporate social contract, which is still relevant today, even before the ESG concept became mainstream. These included creating jobs and maximizing corporate profits, ensuring fairness to both employees and customers, and committing to improve the living conditions of the broader community and environment in which the company operates. Several notable environmental events, such as the Bhopal gas tragedy in 1984, the Chernobyl disaster in 1986, the spill of 10.8 million gallons of crude oil from Exxon Valdez in 1989, the Ivory Coast toxic waste dump in 2006, the British Petroleum oil spill in 2010, the Fukushima nuclear disaster in 2011, and the Amazon wildfires in 2019 have made sustainable investments increasingly attractive. Additionally, rising GHG emissions and deforestation represent global environmental and societal challenges. As a result, investors and environmentalists have sparked a revolutionary movement toward greater environmental responsibility (Dolan & Zalles, 2022). Corporate social responsibility (CSR) has since become an integral part of business strategy. Integrating responsible practices into core business strategies can help develop sound decision-making capabilities. Given its extensive impact on the environment, no questions have been raised about corporate stewardship and the urgent need to reduce fossil fuel extraction and emissions control. Environmental degradation of the ecosystem is attributed to corporate excesses and practices that have largely ignored the environmental impacts. This is a strong justification for the greater corporate responsibility for the environment.

In 2004, the term ESG was coined by the Global Compact Leaders' Summit.[3] A report expressed that more than twenty of the world's largest financial institutions believe that addressing ESG issues is essential to improving corporate governance. These large corporations, with combined assets of US$ 6 trillion, collectively made this commitment. This theme was later developed through other United Nations initiatives, including the Principles for Responsible Investment, which promote ESG criteria for asset management. As they explain, companies that perform better on these issues can increase shareholder value by contributing to the sustainability initiatives of the communities in which they operate. This can be accomplished by managing risks appropriately, anticipating regulatory actions, or entering new markets to help create shareholder value. In addition, these issues can strongly influence reputation and brands, which are essential components of shareholder value.

Although the ESG movement is progressing, numerous challenges still need to be addressed. These challenges can potentially lead to social risk, including the mismatch between ESG data and ESG performance standards, challenges in sharing ESG data, lack of coordination in ESG reporting, unclear incentives for managing and disclosing ESG data, data collection, and social disruption resulting from robotics and AI.

ESG Reporting Framework, and Technology

ESG can also promote good corporate practices. It affects various decisions, such as investment decisions, advice, and risk management decisions. Sustainable organizations strive to improve governance and sustainability standards and promote environmental and social sustainability. ESG influences various decisions, including investment decisions, advice, and risk management decisions. High-quality ESG data are therefore critical to investment decisions, whether the data are self-reported, aggregated by sustainability rating agencies (SRAs), or generated using the latest technologies such as AI and machine learning. While ESG disclosure may reflect better financial performance and is an essential

[3] https://www.unglobalcompact.org/library/255.

component of investment decision-making for investors, this is not always the case (Cort & Esty, 2020). ESG information is subject to skepticism and a host of unanswered questions. For example, ESG data can contain significant noise, raising questions regarding the validity of these data. Researchers have also identified methodological weaknesses in ESG ratings and a lack of clarity in ESG data (Cort & Esty, 2020; Widyawati, 2020).

Despite these concerns, companies must adhere to the ESG Reporting Framework when reporting on their ESG performance. These guidelines help companies provide consistent, reliable, and comparable information about their ESG efforts. This framework was developed to simplify and standardize sustainability practices, goals, and performance communication. This framework will help investors, stakeholders, and the public to understand a company's ESG performance, risks, and opportunities. A number of ESG reporting frameworks exist, such as the Sustainability Accounting Standards Board (SASB), Global Reporting Initiative (GRI), Task Force on Climate-related Financial Disclosures (TCFD), Integrated Reporting Framework (ITF), and Carbon Disclosure Project (CDP). Many stakeholders, including investors, companies, analysts, and regulators, are familiar with the SASB framework. The methodology is also used by organizations that produce sustainability ratings and rankings, such as MSCI and S&P Global. The SASB framework aims to help organizations identify, manage, and communicate sustainability-related risks and opportunities relevant to their business and industry. The GRI Guidelines provide guidance to companies on how to report their economic, environmental, and social impacts. The guidelines were designed to be flexible and adaptable to different industries and geographies. TCFD is a framework designed to help companies assess the risks and opportunities associated with climate change. This framework provides recommendations for companies on how they should disclose information about their governance, strategy, risk management, and climate change-related targets and metrics. The ITF encourages companies to consider how their financial and non-financial performance are intertwined. This framework highlights ESG factors as a compelling part of a company's overall strategy and performance. The CDP is an international initiative that focuses on climate change and sustainability. Companies participating in the CDP program must disclose their GHG emissions, energy use, and strategies to address climate change.

The reporting frameworks require companies to manage their data better and present information generated in a standardized manner. Given the complexity of ESG data, companies can leverage digital technologies from data collection to information disclosure and reporting. A variety of technologies can be used to capture and manage the large amounts of data needed for ESG reporting, including cloud-based software; ERP systems; and environmental, health, and safety management systems. Data collection using these technologies can be automated to ensure their accuracy and consistency. The ESG data can also be presented clearly and transparently using this technology. Companies can create ESG-compliant reports using dashboards, visualization tools, and report templates. Through digital platforms, companies can engage with stakeholders such as investors, employees, and customers to gather ESG feedback. Companies can utilize this information to improvetheir ESG reporting. They can use technology to track sustainable progress over time and monitor their ESG performance. Companies can also use sensors and monitoring systems to collect real-time data on energy use, emissions, and resource consumption.

Organizations and investors are increasingly seeking alternative data. These alternative data can be obtained from the Internet of Things (IoT) such as CCTV, digital sensors, satellites, and smartphones. Data from this source are available in real time and can be used to improve organizations' ESG initiatives, better manage risk, and maximize long-term returns on investments. For example, companies can use digital tools to track and report their GHG emissions and energy consumption. This can include using sensors and monitoring systems to collect real-time data as well as software to manage and analyze the data for reporting. digital technologies, such as smart-building management systems and energy efficiency software, to monitor and improve energy use and reduce emissions. This information can be used to demonstrate progress toward sustainability goals and inform the ESG reporting process. However, ESG data can be voluminous and originate from various sources. While the IoT can enable organizations to collect data effectively, data quality issues can still arise. Organizations need to understand the structure and use of corporate data and information as well as their decision-making processes. The concept of data governance, which focuses on implementing decision-making around the data infrastructure, is critical for implementing ESG. Data governance includes appropriate data architecture, sound data modeling and design, properly arranged data storage and operations, ensuring data quality and security, data integration and interoperability, and metadata management (Sinke et al., 2021; Yin & Li, 2022).

The lack of standards for ESG reporting is another critical issue in the ESG initiative that requires a technological solution. Various guidelines and standards have negatively affected data collection, sharing, processing, and disclosure. Ultimately, it is complicated to define, uphold, and measure progress, and many organizations get it wrong by accident, or because there is no consensus on what getting it right actually means. Blockchain can potentially solve this problem (Chin et al., 2022; Parmentola et al., 2022). This technology enables the immutable storage and reporting of a company's ESG data points. By encrypting complex transactions across organizational boundaries, blockchain facilitates enterprise-wide transparency and openness, which are necessary for collaborative innovation. When multiple data points come from different sources and are managed on a blockchain, the process can be dramatically reduced in terms of time and cost, facilitating data sharing and communication between stakeholders and reducing the friction associated with coordination. In addition, blockchain technology can help ensure that the data entered are accurate, verifiable, and traceable, eliminating inaccuracies and providing an alternative source of truth for all participants in the network. With blockchain and big data analytics, organizations can track and assess the environmental impact of their supply chains. This can help organizations identify areas for improvement and reduce their carbon footprint.

Internet of Things (IoT) and ESG

The Internet of Things (IoT) is gaining paramount significance with the growing integration of physical objects and smart devices into the digital ecosystems. Essentially, IoT serves as an interface between the community of information and the world at large. It is a network of physical objects that can communicate with one another and have digital identifiers. The IoT now encompasses virtually every aspect of modern life, enabling individuals to live more comfortably and work more efficiently owing to the development of next-generation wireless technologies. Technically, the IoT represents a standardized and integrated digital identification system that uses Internet protocol (IP) addresses and other protocols such as Message Queue Telemetry Transport (MQTT), HyperText Transfer Protocol (HTTP), Constrained Application Protocol (CoAP), Data Distribution Service (DDS), WebSocket, Advanced Message Queue Protocol (AMQP), Extensible Messaging and Presence Protocol (XMPP), and OPC Unified Architecture (OPC UA) to connect IoT devices. Several wireless network devices and protocols, such as RFID (EPCglobal protocol), Bluetooth, Wi-Fi, Zigbee, Cellular, 6LoWPAN, and PROFINET, are also used to connect IoT devices. As technology advances, new possibilities and opportunities are emerging for the development of smarter devices to support intelligent applications, such as smart manufacturing, smart facilities, smart agriculture, smart metering, healthcare monitoring devices, physical asset management, and environmental surveillance.

An analysis by the World Economic Forum (WEF) shows that 84% of IoT implementations are aligned with, or have the potential to achieve, the United Nations Sustainable Development Goals (SDGs), supporting companies' efforts to improve their ESG performance.[4] Through IoT, sustainable business and ESG assessment can be done more effectively across various industries, enabling them to monitor, measure, and improve their ESG initiatives. Companies can use IoT to monitor utilities and energy systems, design and manage property and facilities, and manage supply chains and transportation. Using IoT to collect data can help reduce vehicle emissions by manually collecting meter data. This automation allows for the early detection of sources of error, minimization of outages, and reduction of waste. Consequently, this improves the operational efficiency, resiliency, and service delivery. Remote meter readings and the early detection of errors can make business operations more efficient and reduce costs. Remote monitoring of corporate buildings, such as air quality, water leaks, pest control, and water leaks, can also be done using IoT technology, resulting in better management, lower costs, and increased safety for employees, which in turn leads to a better workplace. If water leaks are detected early, they can be prevented from causing damage to buildings and minimized. Smart heating, ventilation, and air conditioning (HVAC) systems and smart lighting allow occupants and businesses to have a more dynamic work environment by cooling

[4] https://www3.weforum.org/docs/IoTGuidelinesforSustainability.pdf.

and heating spaces, as needed, creating flexible living and working conditions.[5] Using sensors, smart-building IoT systems can create detailed maps of energy and space usage within a property, and analytics tools can generate information based on these maps. This allows buildings to optimize their energy consumption and improve their indoor air quality.[6] These environments provide real-time data and can be expanded to provide smarter, more dynamic, and more responsive environments and workspaces. This also has a positive impact on ESG ratings.

By using IoT solutions in the supply chain, companies can monitor carbon footprints in real time and provide visibility during transportation. Exporters, importers, retailers, and manufacturers can use this data to better understand the impact of their supply chain activities. With IoT tools, companies can measure the carbon footprint of their logistics supply chains at a granular level that was previously impossible (Wu, et al., 2022a, 2022b). This helps measure the impact of their operations on the environment, society, and governance at a new level. In addition, AI-based IoT solutions have assisted retailers in implementing next-generation sustainability programs that have the potential to transform the entire supply chain. IoT tools can improve supply chain management in several ways. These include reducing energy consumption and carbon footprints, supply chain optimization, responsible sourcing, and waste reduction.[7]

The IoT has also proven to be helpful in the field of environmental protection. It can monitor and control various environmental objects to conserve natural resources and protect the environment for future generation. This technology can address the challenge of promoting a sustainable environment. Recent advances in smart agriculture, for example, have shown that technology is instrumental in making the environment livable for people. For example, using sensors to collect and record information on agricultural systems allows organizations to improve productivity and the quality of production by modifying equipment operations based on real-life situations (Doshi & Varghese, 2022). Table 12.1 presents the relevant ESG key performance indicators (KPI) and IoT that can be used to achieve these KPIs. The table also shows the

[5] https://www.forbes.com/sites/forbestechcouncil/2022/11/18/how-iot-can-improve-esg-for-companies-and-communities/?sh=4bd9274e1fa2.

[6] https://www.techtarget.com/iotagenda/post/How-IoT-helps-environmental-social-and-governance-goals.

[7] https://www.microshare.io/2019/11/22/esg-as-easy-as-iot/

Table 12.1 ESG and Relevant IoT

ESG Related Areas	*Relevant IoT*	*Data types*
Utilities and energy efficiency	Smart thermostat, smart metering, water level sensor	Numeric
Carbon footprint	Route optimization, location intelligence, Zero-emission autonomous robots	Numeric, Spatial, Vector
Environmental management systems	Environmental sensor, fill level sensor, water level sensor, airflow sensor, CCTV	Numeric, Vector, Raster/Grid, Images/Pictures
Supply chain management systems	RFID, sensors, satellite communication technologies, CCTV, location intelligence, route optimization	Numeric, Vector, Raster/Grid, Images/Pictures
Occupational health and safety	Smart window control, smart zoning, smart lighting	Numeric

Source Author

types of data collected from the IoT, which are universally understood and easily used by end-users.

While IoT can help companies automate data collection, problems can arise from cybersecurity threats and vulnerabilities. Networked IoT devices allow hackers to penetrate enterprise networks and compromise the data integrity. Therefore, organizations must consider implementing cybersecurity policies and technologies to secure and protect traffic in systems and networks. This includes establishing a sound corporate policy for managing IoT and equipping the corporate network with sufficient hardware and software specifications, such as intrusion detection systems and authentication, to prevent cybersecurity incidents.

Artificial Intelligence (AI), Data Governance, and ESG

In the previous section, we discussed the role of the IoT in ESG data collection. Most large companies are already making extensive use of IoT. Smaller industries also follow this trend and shift their focus to the IoT. Companies collect more data from IoT devices than ever before, allowing them to stream data. Factories and utilities that deploy these devices in their factories have a unique opportunity to leverage the data collected. However, companies may also fail to take advantage of this opportunity because they may be inundated with noisy and irrelevant data. The use of AI can help solve this problem by filtering out irrelevant alerts, so that operators receive only the information they need. The advancement of AI, which includes many new technologies, has revolutionized the way businesses work with data, making it easier for computers to perform complex tasks at incredible speeds and volumes.

AI applications are increasing globally owing to technological advancements, and their applicability, including its applications in ESG, will significantly increase. A combination of AI and IoT can be an effective tool for gaining actionable insights from the data (Fang et al., 2023; Ketter et al., 2020). Just as humans collect data and responses via their five senses from their interactions with the environment and process these data and responses with their brain, IoT devices collect data and responses from the environment, whereas AI acts as a brain to process these data and responses to guide actions and behaviors by processing them further. For example, AI can facilitate the identification of trends and patterns related to ESG performance such as energy consumption, resource use, emissions, and stakeholder engagement. Data visualization and reporting tools generated from AI can also be used to communicate project progress and impact stakeholders. AI is particularly useful in keeping organizations informed in real time about their ESG initiatives, such as water leaks, that drive up the facility's resource consumption. The data collected from smart metering can then be used to predict future utility consumption, leading to a more efficient resource allocation. Using AI to monitor facilities can help managers to maintain their facilities and anticipate potential failures. AI can be used to predict and mitigate ESG risks such as supply chain disruptions and environmental disasters. By using chatbots and other digital platforms, companies can improve their communication with stakeholders and solicit feedback.

The above examples illustrate how organizations can use AI to leverage their data collected from the IoT. Investors are exploring a variety of alternative data sources to supplement financial metrics with non-financial data. Many unstructured ESG data, such as news articles, annual integrated sustainability reports, sustainability investment announcements, bond prospectuses, and ESG disclosures, are underutilized in evaluating corporate ESG performance. Using natural language processing (NLP) techniques, AI has paved the way for innovative approaches to analyzing unstructured text data, such as determining the tone of a conversation (Luccioni et al., 2020). Analyzing the tone of a particular type of conversation can be achieved by training algorithms to read and analyze the conversation by comparing the words used with a reference set of existing knowledge (i.e., a corpus). For example, an AI-based application can be developed to read transcripts of corporate quarterly reports. Based on the terms used, algorithms can determine whether a company is serious in mitigating ESG risks. Investors can then determine which companies are at high ESG risk and are well-positioned to transition to green business activities. This information can also help investors manage resources and technical capacity, set priorities, identify mitigation actions, and define the scope of their engagement activities.

While AI can help companies analyze their data and lead to more accurate predictive analytics and optimizations that result in improved KPIs in the environmental dimension of ESG, AI can also cause problems in the social and governance pillars of ESG. These problems can arise when companies use AI to manage their customer data and use it for product development, risk management, and marketing. Privacy and confidentiality are common concerns in AI model training. Companies must be prepared to share how their use of data and AI will affect people and society (Ryan & Stahl, 2021). When using AI, companies must consider the following questions: What is a company's policy on using personal data? What steps should be taken to ensure that customer privacy is protected? Are existing or potential customers treated fairly or are existing inequities repeated or even reinforced? Do AI-based applications place people at the center of their development? How will AI impact stakeholders including customers, employees, and society? AI should be designed to avoid unintended consequences, such as discrimination, invasion of privacy, loss of autonomy, social exclusion, and profound distortions.[8,9,10] These consequences can violate human rights and have severe financial and reputational implications for companies, which are inextricably linked to the social and governance dimensions of ESG. Therefore, AI's ethical and responsible use of AI is an integral part of ESG initiatives and reporting processes. To achieve responsible AI practices, data governance is a critical area that organizations must address. A data governance framework must be in place from the point of collection and generation of data through its archiving and destruction.

[8] https://ec.europa.eu/futurium/en/ai-alliance-consultation.1.html.

[9] https://unesdoc.unesco.org/ark:/48223/pf0000381137.

[10] https://ai.google/principles/

The Role of Data Governance in ESG

Data governance has no single definition or is broad concepts. Generally, data governance is an umbrella term that encompasses a variety of components, including data treatment, employee roles, processes, communications, metrics, and tools that help organizations manage and better control data assets. Traditionally, data governance programs have focused on preventing data misuse and loss, which were accomplished by locking and securing data and complying with regulatory requirements.[11] For example, in the 2000s, many organizations focused on managing risk, protecting data from misuse, and simplifying audits and reporting. Numerous regulations require companies to implement data governance, including the Payment Card Industry Data Security Standard (PCI-DSS), Sarbanes–Oxley, and Health Insurance Portability and Accountability Act (HIPAA). Between 2010 and 2020, government regulations, including the General Data Protection Regulation (GDPR), California Consumer Privacy Act (CCPA), and Personal Data Protection Act (PDPA) in Singapore, were implemented. These regulations enforce companies to comply with privacy and confidentiality regulations and to avoid violating consumer trust. Efforts must be made to ensure that data are used ethically and responsibly from 2020 onward. If companies misuse data or use it to train AI models that can negatively affect society, they will face severe consequences. The European Union has proposed the AI Act.[12] This regulation applies to all sectors (except the military) and establishes a common legal and regulatory framework to ensure that AI is safe and compliant with regulations.

Every successful company must have a data governance program. A data governance program is not only about ensuring the security of data but also about creating a process for accessing and using data that serves the strategic goals of the organization (Bollweg, 2022). Ideally, data governance should be implemented in a manner that breaks down silos and enables insights from multiple data sources as part of the data governance process. A company should take special care to ensure the accuracy and quality of its data when some of its reporting requirements, such as ESG, rely on external data sources. In such cases, a company may need

[11] https://www.informatica.com/blogs/accelerating-data-governance-for-esg-A-fireside-chat-with-federated-hermes.html.

[12] https://artificialintelligenceact.eu/.

to help control data quality and accuracy. Its integrity must be ensured for downstream applications and processes to rely on such data. In addition, effective data governance includes the ability to track and manage the movement of data within an organization and to access and analyze the data quickly and easily (Mahanti, 2021a). Organizations can improve their data reliability, accuracy, and usability by implementing robust data governance policies and procedures.

In addition to protecting the data, data governance is vital for AI development. Managing data is critical to AI because the most important component of AI development is not only the computational power and sophistication of the algorithms but also the quality of the data. The data are the be-all and end-all of an AI-based application. Garbage in, garbage out (GIGO) where the poorer the quality of the data that companies use to train their AI models, the poorer the outcome of the AI. Conversely, the higher the quality of the data, the better the results. Even if the data used to train the AI models are of high quality, if the data contain biases due to existing social practices (e.g., gender bias and discrimination against minorities), the results will amplify the existing biases. Thus, one strategy for mitigating these biases is to implement data governance.

Data governance starts with clearly defined data policies and procedures, standards for integrating and sequencing data, and processes to ensure quality and outcomes (Bollweg, 2022; Mahanti, 2021b). An enterprise governance body must provide data quality assurance, and policies must be strictly enforced for all data collection, acquisition, preparation, and cleansing mechanisms. First, the data policies must ensure that the data profiles are up-to-date, clear, and unambiguous by setting up an enterprise data dictionary (Eryurek et al., 2021). This dictionary contains information about different types of data (infotypes) with a clear, unambiguous meaning for all organizational members. For example, related to ESG data, this infotype can be "water usages" or "electricity usage." This allows everyone to use the same definitions and understanding of the data, thereby ensuring the accuracy and integrity of the insights derived from the data. Organizations can then classify their data into multiple categories such as person identifiable information, financial, business intellectual property, resource use, employee experience, and ethical conduct.

Organizations must also manage the metadata. The purpose of metadata is to provide context and understand other data. This document contains structural and descriptive information about the data elements, relationships, and other attributes. Metadata also allows data to be associated with personal information. To be valid, metadata should be securely linked to the described data and subject to verification. This data classification and metadata management can also be aligned with the ESG data taxonomy. This, in turn, improves comparability and the level of granularity of the data for ESG disclosures. Organizations must ensure that their data are of high quality in terms of accuracy, timeliness, completeness, and trustworthiness (Petrella, 2021). In addition to careful data collection and knowing where the data physically came from, metadata can help improve data quality by providing detailed information that enables better understanding and use. This is particularly important for ESG data from various external parties to multiple IoTs. Metadata describes the data and answers important questions about the data, such as who collected it, when it was created, and why it was collected. Defining the entire lifecycle of data, from production to decommissioning, is also important to ensure that the data are used effectively in downstream applications such as AI development. When issues arise related to data, the data governance mechanism should address them appropriately. For example, inconsistencies between systems must be resolved, and protocols should be established to communicate changes between data owners. Finally, data-monitoring processes should be used to assess the overall quality of the data against predefined data guidelines.

As part of the data governance mechanism in training AI, organizations can also use a datasheet for detailing information about a particular dataset (Gebru et al., 2021). This document typically includes information about the source, format, scope, and content of the data as well as relevant guidelines or restrictions on its use. A datasheet is essential because it provides AI developers with the information they need to effectively use a dataset. By understanding the source, format, and content of a dataset, users can determine whether it is appropriate for their needs and plan how to use it in their research or analysis. In addition, the datasheet can help users avoid pitfalls or errors resulting from incorrect use of a dataset. Some common elements of a datasheet are (1) the name and description of the dataset; (2) the source of the data (e.g., a specific study or survey); (3) the format of the data (e.g., CSV, JSON); (4) the scope of the data (e.g., number of records and attributes); (5) the types of data included in the dataset (e.g., numeric, categorical, ratio, and interval); and (6) any relevant rules or restrictions on the use of the data (e.g., copyright and licensing).

When properly implemented, data governance can save organizations' time and effort in developing AI applications, from data collection to application deployment to interpreting results to business decisions. By implementing data governance, companies can convert their data into valuable assets that can otherwise become liabilities to their business if not handled properly.

Blockchain and ESG

Blockchains are a type of distributed ledger technology (DLT) that stores transaction records in chronological order using a chain of hash data. DLT networks are characterized by equal privileges and connections between all participants; therefore, no central authority is required to manage the network. By distributing the control across many nodes, a single point of failure can be avoided. Because DLTs enable the full disclosure of transactions and provide a single source of truth, they ameliorate transaction uncertainty, insecurity, and ambiguity (Hancock & Vaizey, 2016). Blockchain is a continuously growing chain of hashed data through which a series of records or transactions can be chronologically added by combining them into blocks. A single transaction block contains important information such as the timestamp and hash value for a group of completed transactions. A timestamp determines the chronological order of transactions, whereas a hash value links a block to a blockchain. The addition of blocks to a chain depends on cryptographic mechanisms. This ensures immutability and security as the new block is always linked to the previous block, allowing ownership to be established (Raval, 2016).

Blockchains can be divided into public and private. Anyone can participate in a public blockchain as a node in a decentralized network. Any person can read, write, or validate transactions in a public blockchain. Cryptocurrencies, such as Bitcoin, use this type of blockchain and allow anyone to participate in the network and trade the currency. The validity of a transaction is determined by the consensus of network participants. Several methods exist to establish consensus mechanisms in public blockchains, including Proof of Work (PoW), Proof of Stake (PoS), Delegate PoS (DPoS), Proof of Luck (PoL), Proof of Elapsed Time (PoET), Proof of Activity (PoAc), Proof of Capacity (PoC), Byzantine Fault Tolerance (BFT), Practical Byzantine Fault Tolerance (PBFT), Federated Byzantine Agreement (FBA), Delegated Byzantine Fault Tolerance (DBFT), Proof of Authority (PoA), Proof Importance (PoI), Proof

Burn (PoB), Proof Believability (PoBLV), Proof Devotion (PoD), Proof Reputation (PoR), and Proof of Weight (PoWe) (Bada et al., 2021).

Unlike public blockchains, private blockchains are controlled and approved by a central authority. Nodes in a private blockchain can only be configured by specific users or organizations. Companies and organizations that want to maintain control of their networks and restrict access to ledgers often use this type of blockchain. A private blockchain is more efficient and scalable than a public blockchain. Although private blockchains may use consensus mechanisms, they are controlled by a central authority, which may not use consensus mechanisms to verify transactions. The central authority determines the transactions that are accepted and added to the ledger. Consequently, transactions do not need to be individually verified by each node in the network, making the network more efficient and scalable. However, private blockchains forgo some of the decentralization and security benefits associated with public blockchains that use consensus mechanisms to maintain the integrity of their ledgers. Private blockchains may use a consensus mechanism in some cases; however, they are usually tailored to the needs of a particular network. For example, a consortium of companies may use a consensus mechanism tailored to specific needs before implementing a private blockchain. The consensus mechanism would be tailored to the needs of the consortium, rather than the decentralized, open mechanism used in public blockchains.

Blockchain is not just a disruptive technology but must be viewed as an innovative, integrative solution that can improve a variety of business processes. Blockchain technology enables companies to develop new business models and digitize assets, leading to higher profits. As a foundational technology, blockchain is a building block for a wide range of business processes and enables industries and companies to structure their interactions and processes in fundamentally different ways. The blockchain technology can create a trusted ecosystem by establishing a single version of the truth. Blockchains provide a logical system through which companies can collaborate with each other, rather than requiring separate systems for each company to manage processes and store data. This created a trusted environment between participants, where a high level of manual verification and reconciliation would have been required (Liu et al., 2021).

Blockchain technology has the potential to be used in various ESG initiatives. For example, blockchain can be used as a gateway infrastructure for data collection. Digital identity tools and IoT sensors can be used to transparently and confidently transmit data to blockchain networks. This gateway provides organizations with a comprehensive middleware solution for capturing, processing, and analyzing enterprise sustainability data. The Blockchain Gateway served as an input node for the blockchain network. Sensitive information can also be protected by one-way data encryption. In doing so, blockchain can be used to create immutable records of environmental data, such as carbon emissions or water consumption, so that companies can track and reduce their environmental impacts over time.

Smart contracts can be developed from blockchain technology for supply chain traceability and regular audits. Blockchain-based smart contracts enable a disparate group of network actors to share data relatively easily and from anywhere in the world in near real time, increasing efficiency and improving the environmental sustainability of the supply chain. A smart contract allows automated verification of contract requirements in the supply chain. This results in transparent and verifiable supply chain systems that track the origins and sustainability of products. Consequently, this helps businesses and consumers make more informed decisions about the products they buy and ensures that they support sustainability initiatives and ethical practices. Smart contracts can also be used to automate and secure inventory management, resource replenishment, invoicing, and data exchange processes, such as tokenization for supply chain resilience. Using blockchain technology, every item can be traced back to its source. This approach can identify bottlenecks and discrepancies in ESG across the supply chain in real time. Blockchain can also be used to facilitate voting and decision-making in organizations, ensuring that all stakeholders have a say and that decisions are made in a transparent and fair manner. Overall, the use of blockchain in ESG initiatives can help organizations operate in a more transparent, accountable, and sustainable manner (Parmentola et al., 2022).

Blockchain Consensus Mechanisms and Energy Used

One of the main drawbacks of blockchain is its high energy consumption owing to its proof of work (PoW) consensus mechanism (Auhl et al., 2022). As explained in the previous section, a public blockchain relies on a consensus mechanism to establish trust between the nodes. Although other consensus mechanisms have been introduced that either mitigate the disadvantages of PoW or are more suitable for certain uses of blockchain, the efficiency and sustainability of blockchain will inevitably be affected by these consensus mechanisms, which have both advantages and disadvantages.

The PoW algorithm is one of the most widely used consensus algorithms for this purpose. As a result, it is highly energy intensive and requires miners to perform complex computational tasks to validate transactions and create new blocks. To validate transactions and earn rewards, miners must run powerful computers around the clock, which consumes a significant amount of energy. Because the PoW algorithm consumes a significant amount of energy, it has a negative effect on the environment. PoW mining requires fossil fuels to run computers, which contributes to GHG emissions and climate change. In addition, PoW systems consume varying amounts of energy over time depending on the difficulty of the computational tasks, leading to fluctuations in energy consumption (Platt et al., 2021).

Alternative consensus algorithms have been developed to address the energy efficiency issues of PoWs. For example, a PoS algorithm relies on users to validate transactions and create new blocks, instead of performing computations. Compared to PoW, this approach is more energy efficient. However, the PoS algorithm can also introduce tradeoffs and challenges. One potential problem with PoS is that it can lead to centralization. This is because users who hold the most tokens can exert the greatest influence over the network. Consequently, power and wealth can become concentrated, leading to injustice and inequality (Bada et al., 2021; Platt et al., 2021; Wadhwa et al., 2022).

In addition, several consensus mechanisms in the blockchain industry are more energy efficient than those in PoW. DPoS, POA, and PoC are examples of these mechanisms. The Delegated Proof of Stake system allows users to delegate their voting rights to "delegates" who verify transactions and create new blocks on behalf of users. Because not all users must participate in the validation process, this can be an energy-efficient approach. For PoA systems to work, a select group of "authorities" must validate transactions and create new blocks. Authorities are often selected based on their reputation and trustworthiness, and the validation process is typically less energy intensive than PoW or PoS. PoC systems use free storage space on user devices to store data and verify transactions. The advantage of this approach is that it requires less computing power than PoW and can therefore be an energy-efficient method (Bada et al., 2021).

The use of blockchain technology as an IT solution should be environment friendly. Its use does not contribute to global warming or environmental degradation. When implementing a blockchain solution, companies should prioritize ESG factors, especially considering the existing campaign to reduce the carbon footprint and use environmental resources efficiently. To deploy a green blockchain, companies must consider the following factors: (1) Is a blockchain necessary for the organization? If so, what is the most environmentally sustainable blockchain solution that can be applied? (Bada et al., 2021) Blockchain knowledge enables organizations to select the most appropriate and sustainable solutions for their use cases and avoid wasting computing resources on failed blockchain initiatives.

Table 12.2 and Fig. 12.1 illustrate the relationship between the energy consumption of different blockchains and their consensus mechanisms. When deciding whether to use blockchain for a particular project, a few factors must be considered. These factors include the energy consumption of the blockchains, which differs significantly from one to another. In addition, the trust requirements should be considered. A blockchain can only be considered a suitable solution for a use case if there are multiple instances that generate transactions and there is a certain level of distrust between these instances. Blockchain technology was developed to solve the problem of databases with multiple, untrusted authors. In cases where there is only one instance generating transactions, or when there is a high level of trust between instances, a centralized database may be the best solution.

Blockchain and Carbon Credit

The use of carbon credit markets reduces GHG emissions by mobilizing resources and reducing the cost of production. Carbon credits are purchased from the carbon market and are the prices to pay for GHG emissions. The goal of the carbon market is to ensure that producers are responsible for their polluting acts and to encourage environmentally friendly production methods. Thus, the development of these markets can help reduce carbon consumption and achieve neutrality. However, the carbon credit market is currently largely closed to the public and is accessible only to large corporations and government agencies. In addition, the lack of quality controls in which carbon credits are invested and poor transparency in the voluntary carbon market have also led to criticism. Blockchain technology can be used to buy and sell carbon credits, which is a market-based approach to reducing carbon emissions. Blockchain technology has the potential to increase transparency in the voluntary carbon

Table 12.2 Consensus mechanisms in blockchain and its energy consumption (Bada et al., 2021)

Consensus mechanisms	*Blockchain platform*	*Light energy consumption*	*Energy efficient*	*Energy intensive*
Proof of Authority (PoA)	Hyperledger Fabric, Quorum, VeChain, POA network	•		
Delegated Byzantine Fault Tolerance (DBFT)	NEO	•		
Practical Byzantine Fault Tolerance (PBFT)	Hyperledger Sawtooth	•		
Byzantine Fault Tolerance (BFT)	Ripple	•		
Proof of Elapsed Time (PoET)	Hyperledger Sawtooth	•		
Federated Byzantine Agreement (FBA)	Stellar	•		
Proof of Capacity (PoC)	Burst, Storj, Chia, Spacemint	•		
Proof of Reputation (PoR)	gochain	•		
Proof of Believability (PoBLV)	IOST	•		
Proof of Devotion (PoD)	Nebulas	•		
Proof of Luck (PoL)		•		
Proof of Weight (PoWe)	Algorand	•		
Delegate PoS (DPoS)	TRON, Steem		•	
Proof of Stake (PoS)	Tezoz, Cardano, Hydra, Ethereum 2.0		•	
Proof of Importance (PoI)	NEM		•	
Proof of Activity (PoAc)	Decred			•

(continued)

Table 12.2 (continued)

Consensus mechanisms	*Blockchain platform*	*Light energy consumption*	*Energy efficient*	*Energy intensive*
Proof of Burn (PoB)	Counterparty			•
Proof of Work (PoW)	Bitcoin, Monero, Litecoin			•

Source Author

credit market and to facilitate access to the mandatory market for all participants (Muzumdar et al., 2022; Woo et al., 2021).

Blockchain technology can facilitate the buying and selling of carbon credit. First, blockchain can be used to track and verify the origin, ownership, and transfer of carbon credit. This ensures that the traded carbon credits are authentic and that the emission reductions they represent are real and verifiable. Second, smart contracts on the blockchain can be used to automate carbon credit transactions. Thus, carbon credit transactions can be simplified for buyers and sellers by reducing costs and complexity. Third, blockchain facilitates peer-to-peer carbon credit markets. By creating peer-to-peer markets for carbon credits, individuals and organizations can buy and sell carbon credits directly, without relying on a centralized intermediary. Finally, blockchain technology can be used to create a more transparent and verifiable market for carbon credit. This leads to more accurate pricing and reduces the possibility of fraud or manipulation. Overall, blockchain technology can contribute to global efforts to reduce CO_2 emissions by improving the efficiency and effectiveness of the carbon credit markets (Sipthorpe et al., 2022).

There are two different approaches to using blockchain technology to facilitate the buying and selling of carbon credits: mining- and NFT-based. Mining-based carbon credits were generated by mining cryptocurrencies. This involves the use of computers to solve complex mathematical problems and validate transactions in the blockchain. Miners receive a certain number of carbon credits for mining, which can then be traded on a carbon credit market, similar to other cryptocurrencies. On the other hand, NFT-based carbon credits are unique digital assets that represent a specific number of carbon credits. They are based on blockchain technology and use non-fungible tokens (NFTs) to represent carbon credits. NFTs are unique digital assets that cannot be replaced or exchanged with

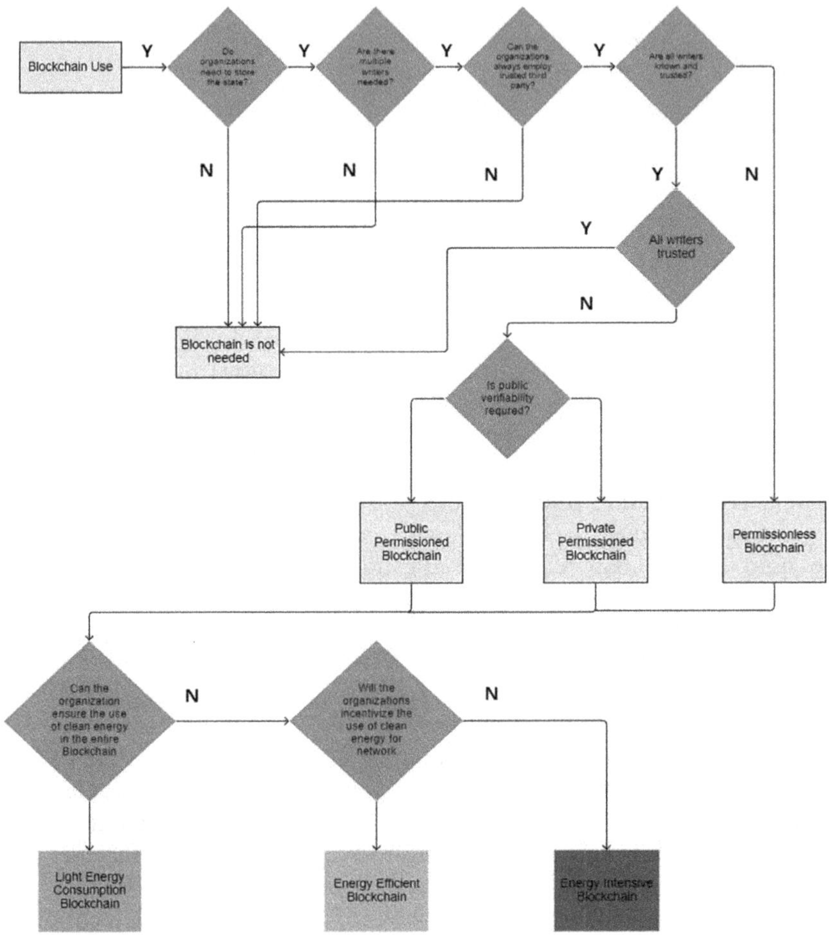

Fig. 12.1 Flowchart of blockchain platform selections (Adapted from Bada et al., 2021)

other assets. Similar to how other NFTs are traded, carbon credits represented as NFTs can be bought and sold in a carbon credit market. Both mining-based and NFT-based carbon credits have the potential to facilitate the purchase and sale of carbon credits in a transparent and verifiable manner through the use of blockchain technology. However, they differ in the specific approach used to represent and trade carbon credit.

Despite the potential advantages of using blockchain to issue carbon credits, there are also some potential disadvantages. The first disadvantage is that the implementation and use of a blockchain system can be complex and require specialized technical expertise. A lack of resources can be a barrier to adoption, especially for smaller organizations and individuals. Second, implementing and maintaining a blockchain system can be costly, requiring specialized hardware and software, and ongoing maintenance and support. Third, some blockchain systems may not meet the requirements of large global carbon credit markets. This could limit their effectiveness in reducing carbon emissions globally. Fourth, although blockchain technology is generally considered secure, it is not immune to cyberattacks such as hacking. Consequently, carbon credits can be lost or stolen, thereby undermining the integrity of the system. Fifth, blockchain technology for carbon credits is a relatively new and rapidly developing field, and regulatory hurdles or uncertainties must be resolved to ensure the integrity and fairness of the system. One final point: for a blockchain-based carbon credit system to be effective, it must be adopted by individuals, organizations, and governments worldwide. This can require a significant amount of time and effort.

Conclusion

Technology plays an important role in supporting ESG initiatives. Using the Internet of Things, data on environmental impacts, social responsibility, and governance practices can be collected and analyzed. Companies can use this information to identify areas of improvement and track progress over time. With technology, information about ESG initiatives can be communicated and shared openly with stakeholders including investors, customers, and the public. In this way, companies can build trust and credibility, and identify potential risks and opportunities. Processes and systems can be automated using technology, which helps reduce waste, increase efficiency, and minimize negative environmental impacts. Organizations and other stakeholders can benefit from technology-enabled collaboration and partnerships, leading to greater progress and positive outcomes toward ESG responsibilities.

As part of their ESG initiatives, organizations should implement data governance policies that cover all aspects of data collection, classification, processing, storage, and deletion. A data management program can help organizations ensure that data are collected and reported in a consistent and accurate manner and in accordance with industry standards and best practices. Data management tools and systems can be implemented to track and measure performance in key areas such as GHG emissions, water use, and employee diversity, so that data can be used for ESG initiatives. Data governance builds trust and credibility with stakeholders such as investors, customers, and the public. Finally, effective data governance is essential for making data-driven decisions and continuously improving competency toward ESG accountability.

References

Alkaraan, F., Albitar, K., Hussainey, K., & Venkatesh, V. (2022). Corporate transformation toward Industry 4.0 and financial performance: The influence of environmental, social, and governance (ESG). *Technological Forecasting and Social Change*, *175*, 121423. https://doi.org/10.1016/j.techfore.2021.121423

Auhl, Z., Chilamkurti, N., Alhadad, R., & Heyne, W. (2022). A Comparative study of consensus mechanisms in blockchain for IoT networks. *Electronics, 11*(17), 2694. https://doi.org/10.3390/electronics11172694

Bada, A. O., Damianou, A., Angelopoulos, C. M., & Katos, V. (2021). Towards a green blockchain: A review of consensus mechanisms and their energy consumption. *2021 17th international conference on distributed computing in sensor systems (DCOSS)*, 503–511. https://doi.org/10.1109/DCOSS52077.2021.00083

Bollweg, L. M. (2022). *Data governance for managers*. Springer. https://doi.org/10.1007/978-3-662-65171-1

Broadstock, D. C., Chan, K., Cheng, L. T. W., & Wang, X. (2021). The role of ESG performance during times of financial crisis: Evidence from COVID-19 in China. *Finance Research Letters, 38*, 101716. https://doi.org/10.1016/j.frl.2020.101716

Câmara, P., & Morais, F. (Eds.). (2022). *The Palgrave handbook of esg and corporate governance*. Springer International Publishing. https://doi.org/10.1007/978-3-030-99468-6

Chin, T., Shi, Y., Singh, S. K., Agbanyo, G. K., & Ferraris, A. (2022). Leveraging blockchain technology for green innovation in ecosystem-based business models: A dynamic capability of values appropriation. *Technological Forecasting and Social Change, 183*, 121908. https://doi.org/10.1016/j.techfore.2022.121908

Chouaibi, S., Chouaibi, J., & Rossi, M. (2022). ESG and corporate financial performance: The mediating role of green innovation: UK common law versus Germany civil law. *EuroMed Journal of Business, 17*(1), 46–71. https://doi.org/10.1108/EMJB-09-2020-0101

Cort, T., & Esty, D. (2020). ESG standards: Looming challenges and pathways forward. *Organization & Environment, 33*(4), 491–510. https://doi.org/10.1177/1086026620945342

Dolan, C, & Zalles, D. B. (2022). *Transparency in ESG and the circular economy*. Business Expert Press, LLC.

Doshi, M., & Varghese, A. (2022). Smart agriculture using renewable energy and AI-powered IoT. In *AI, edge and IoT-based smart agriculture* (pp. 205–225). Elsevier. https://doi.org/10.1016/B978-0-12-823694-9.00028-1

Ellili, N. O. D. (2022). Impact of ESG disclosure and financial reporting quality on investment efficiency. *Corporate Governance: The International Journal of Business in Society*. https://doi.org/10.1108/CG-06-2021-0209

Eryurek, E., Gilad, U., Lakshmanan, V., Kibunguchy-Grant, A., & Ashdown, J. (2021). *Data governance: The definitive guide.* O'Reilly Media, Inc.

Fang, M., Nie, H., & Shen, X. (2023). Can enterprise digitization improve ESG performance? *Economic Modelling, 118*, 106101. https://doi.org/10.1016/j.econmod.2022.106101

Gebru, T., Morgenstern, J., Vecchione, B., Vaughan, J. W., Wallach, H., III., & H. D., & Crawford, K. (2021). Datasheets for datasets. *Communications of the ACM, 64*(12), 86–92. https://doi.org/10.1145/3458723

Hancock, M., & Vaizey, E. (2016). *Distributed ledger technology: Beyond blockchain*. UK Government Office for Science. https://www.gov.uk/government/uploads/system/uploads/attachment_data/file/492972/gs-16-1-distributed-ledger-technology.pdf

Jonsdottir, B., Sigurjonsson, T. O., Johannsdottir, L., & Wendt, S. (2022). Barriers to using ESG data for investment decisions. *Sustainability, 14*(9), 5157. https://doi.org/10.3390/su14095157

Ketter, W., Padmanabhan, B., Pant, G., & Raghu, T. S. (2020). Special issue editorial: Addressing societal challenges through analytics: An ESG ICE framework and research agenda. *Journal of the Association for Information Systems, 21*(5), 1115–1127. https://doi.org/10.17705/1jais.00631

Li, C., Wu, M., Chen, X., & Huang, W. (2022). Environmental, social and governance performance, corporate transparency, and credit rating: Some evidence from Chinese A-share listed companies. *Pacific-Basin Finance Journal, 74*, 101806. https://doi.org/10.1016/j.pacfin.2022.101806

Liu, X., Wu, H., Wu, W., Fu, Y., & Huang, G. Q. (2021). *Blockchain-enabled ESG reporting framework for sustainable supply chain* (pp. 403–413). https://doi.org/10.1007/978-981-15-8131-1_36

Luccioni, A., Baylor, E., & Duchene, N. (2020). *Analyzing sustainability reports using natural language processing*. https://doi.org/10.48550/arXiv.2011.08073

Mahanti, R. (2021a). *Data governance and compliance*. Springer. https://doi.org/10.1007/978-981-33-6877-4

Mahanti, R. (2021b). *Data governance and data management*. Springer. https://doi.org/10.1007/978-981-16-3583-0

Muzumdar, A., Modi, C., & Vyjayanthi, C. (2022). A permissioned blockchain enabled trustworthy and incentivized emission trading system. *Journal of Cleaner Production, 349*, 131274. https://doi.org/10.1016/j.jclepro.2022.131274

Nicolò, G., Zampone, G., Sannino, G., & de Iorio, S. (2022). Sustainable corporate governance and non-financial disclosure in Europe: Does the gender diversity matter? *Journal of Applied Accounting Research, 23*(1), 227–249. https://doi.org/10.1108/JAAR-04-2021-0100

Parmentola, A., Petrillo, A., Tutore, I., & de Felice, F. (2022). Is blockchain able to enhance environmental sustainability? A systematic review and research agenda from the perspective of Sustainable Development Goals (SDGs). *Business Strategy and the Environment, 31*(1), 194–217. https://doi.org/10.1002/bse.2882

Petrella, A. (2021). *What Is data governance?* O'Reilly Media Inc.

Platt, M., Sedlmeir, J., Platt, D., Xu, J., Tasca, P., Vadgama, N., & Ibanez, J. I. (2021). The energy footprint of blockchain consensus mechanisms beyond proof-of-work. *2021 IEEE 21st International Conference on Software Quality, Reliability and Security Companion (QRS-C)*, 1135–1144. https://doi.org/10.1109/QRS-C55045.2021.00168

Raval, S. (2016). *Decentralized applications: Harnessing bitcoin's blockchain technology*. O'Reilly Media.

Ryan, M., & Stahl, B. C. (2021). Artificial intelligence ethics guidelines for developers and users: Clarifying their content and normative implications. *Journal of Information, Communication and Ethics in Society, 19*(1), 61–86. https://doi.org/10.1108/JICES-12-2019-0138

Shakil, M. H. (2021). Environmental, social and governance performance and financial risk: Moderating role of ESG controversies and board gender diversity. *Resources Policy, 72*, 102144. https://doi.org/10.1016/j.resourpol.2021.102144

Sinke, G., Duijze, G., Wouda, H., Eppink, J., Pott, M., & Cammeraat, M. (2021). *The importance of ESG data management challenges and opportunities for the real estate ecosystem*. Deloitte.

Sipthorpe, A., Brink, S., van Leeuwen, T., & Staffell, I. (2022). Blockchain solutions for carbon markets are nearing maturity. *One Earth, 5*(7), 779–791. https://doi.org/10.1016/j.oneear.2022.06.004

van Rensburg, H. M. M. J., Gous, A. G. S., Vosloo, J. C., & van Heerden, M. (2019). Improving data management for environmental reporting in the gold mining industry. *South African Journal of Industrial Engineering*, *30*(3). https://doi.org/10.7166/30-3-2236

Wadhwa, S., Rani, S., Kavita, V., & S., Shafi, J., & Wozniak, M. (2022). Energy efficient consensus approach of blockchain for IoT networks with edge computing. *Sensors, 22*(10), 3733. https://doi.org/10.3390/s22103733

Widyawati, L. (2020). A systematic literature review of socially responsible investment and environmental social governance metrics. *Business Strategy and the Environment, 29*(2), 619–637. https://doi.org/10.1002/bse.2393

Woo, J., Fatima, R., Kibert, C. J., Newman, R. E., Tian, Y., & Srinivasan, R. S. (2021). Applying blockchain technology for building energy performance measurement, reporting, and verification (MRV) and the carbon credit market: A review of the literature. *Building and Environment, 205*, 108199. https://doi.org/10.1016/j.buildenv.2021.108199

Wu, W., Chen, W., Fu, Y., Jiang, Y., & Huang, G. Q. (2022a). Unsupervised neural network-enabled spatial-temporal analytics for data authenticity under environmental smart reporting system. *Computers in Industry, 141*, 103700. https://doi.org/10.1016/j.compind.2022.103700

Wu, W., Fu, Y., Wang, Z., Liu, X., Niu, Y., Li, B., & Huang, G. Q. (2022b). Consortium blockchain-enabled smart ESG reporting platform with token-based incentives for corporate crowdsensing. *Computers & Industrial Engineering, 172*, 108456. https://doi.org/10.1016/j.cie.2022.108456

Yin, J., & Li, C. (2022). Data governance and green technological innovation performance: A curvilinear relationship. *Journal of Cleaner Production, 379*, 134441. https://doi.org/10.1016/j.jclepro.2022.134441

CHAPTER 13

Digital Transformation in Audit-Japan's Current Situation in Advantages and Challenges of Adopting Digital Technology

Keiji Yumiba

Introduction

Early in my auditing career in the early 1990s, the accounting profession needed help to fully integrate technology into its routine activities. At that time, laptops began to make their presence feel in the market. However, because of their heavy weight and inferior performance, they are considered unsuitable for mobile device use, especially with regard to audits. Therefore, computers played a minor role in the audit during this period.

At the beginning of my tenure at the accounting firm, I noticed a lack of access to technological resources. Computer resources on each office floor were scarce, and only a handful of competent employees had the

K. Yumiba (✉)
Sankei Biz Consulting, Corp., Tokyo, Japan
e-mail: keiji.yumiba@sankei-bc.co.jp

A. Perdana and T. Wang (eds.), *Digital Transformation in Accounting and Auditing*, https://doi.org/10.1007/978-3-031-46209-2_13

skill to operate them optimally. Despite this limitation, I was honored to work with a team that was enthusiastic about harnessing the potential of computer technology. The vanguard of this challenging group was led by a certified public accountant who was working to integrate computerized systems into our audit procedures. Our supervisor was invaluable in supporting his innovative initiatives through collaboration with us. Motivated by a shared passion for technology, I began a professional journey that culminated in earning my CPA license and integrating computerized auditing methods into my work.

My first encounter with a personal computer (PC) occurred during a standard audit process, also known as checking totals of account receivables. Previously, I had painstakingly checked the totals of voluminous paper account books manually using a calculator. This process involves considerable effort and is time consuming. The integration of PC into this process has resulted in consistent changes. I was impressed by the system's efficient delivery of results as I entered the data. This consistent interaction underscored the ability of the technology to optimize the effectiveness of our processes.

The second half of the 1990s saw a significant change in the auditing industry as firms began equipping their staff with portable computers. This change has given the accountants the ability to transport their essential work tools, representing a remarkable advance in the adoption of technology in the industry. The development of a technology-driven approach gained momentum in the early 2000s when the Audit Standards Board of the American Institute of Certified Public Accountants issued Statement on Auditing Standards No. 99. This established standard emphasizes the compelling need for personal computers (PCs) to perform audit procedures. Consequently, the Japanese auditing sector has proactively adopted digital technology to conduct audits in response to global advances.

The audit sector is currently undergoing a change that presents challenges that need to be addressed. Nonetheless, effectively identifying and addressing these obstacles will play a critical role in determining the future of the profession. By continuing to integrate technologies into our work, we are driving progress toward a future characterized by innovative advances and improved efficiency. This paper analyzes the complicated challenges of merging digital technologies, including PCs, with audit procedures in Japan, considering both past and current viewpoints. It also initiates meaningful dialogue on the potential impacts and obstacles that may arise. A thorough analysis of past experiences provides the fundamental basis for addressing future issues. The more we search into the complexities of integrating technology into the audit process, the clearer it becomes that this integration is not just a matter of discretion, but a necessity for the continued expansion and progress of the audit industry.

The Current State of the Japanese Auditing Industry

Number and Scale of Auditing Firms

In July 2022, the Certified Public Accountants and Auditing Oversight Board (CPAAOB) released "the 2022 Monitoring Report," which provides an in-depth analysis of audits conducted in Japan and a comprehensive assessment of the country's auditing industry.[1] According to the report, 2376 accounting firms in Japan provided audit and assurance services at the end of March 2021. The scope of audit and assurance services is comprehensive, covering a wide range of activities that may include mandatory audits and voluntary audits but are not limited to. Mandatory audits, as required by law, cover various assessments, including audits related to the Financial Instruments and Exchange Act, the Enterprise Act, financial audits of educational institutions under the Private School Subsidies Act, and other relevant legislation. Conversely, discretionary audits comprise a category of services that organizations may use without statutory requirements.

Organizations that provide audit services have various structural frameworks. One example is audit firms, which are formally organized legal entities that provide structured audit services. In addition, partnerships are usually formed by professionals who pool their expertise to offer a comprehensive range of solutions. Finally, it should be noted that a significant part of this field comprises independent professionals. These are experienced auditors who offer customized audit and attestation services. Depending on their scope, accounting firms are further classified by CPAAOB. This classification considers various elements, including the firm's size, number of licensed experts, and range of services offered.

[1] https://www.fsa.go.jp/cpaaob/english/oversight/20221223/2022_monitoring_report_en.pdf.

Overarching classifications include large audit firms,[2] mid-size public accounting firms,[3] and small-to mid-sized public accounting firms.[4] Each category of accounting services has a unique function within the ecosystem, and is tailored to a diverse clientele with varying needs and subtleties.

The comprehensive analysis of the auditing environment in Japan, prepared by the CPAAOB, highlights the dynamic and multilayered dimensions of the sector. Both providers and demanders of audit services must understand the scope and diversity of these services. The consequences of this categorization can significantly impact various aspects ranging from ensuring compliance with regulatory standards to designing the most effective methodologies for the audit sector. It also highlights the prospects of expanding and developing this critical industry in the Japanese economic apparatus. The tabular representation provides an overview of the distribution of audit firms and the scope of their assurance services. It provides a comprehensive overview of Japan's audit industry and essential insights into its operational dynamics.

The market includes four large accounting firms and five medium-sized firms of significant size. These firms perform various statutory and voluntary audit services, including Financial Instruments and Exchange Act (FIEA) audits, Companies Act audits, and various additional audits. Firms in these categories provide comprehensive auditing services and hold a significant market share in Japan's auditing industry. In contrast, a significant number of accounting firms that fall under the small- and medium-sized categories (2367) are engaged in performing similar audits. Nevertheless, it is essential to distinguish between two subgroups in this category: partnerships, which comprise 253 firms, and solo practitioners, which account for a significant number of 2060 firms. Individual practitioners may encounter constraints that require them to work with other auditors to provide audit and attestation services to publicly traded companies. According to Table 13.1, there are 262 audit firms, a total of

[2] Large-sized audit firm: An audit firm that has more than approximately 100 domestic listed audited companies and whose full-time staff performing actual audit duties total at least 1000.

[3] Mid-tier audit firm: An audit firm whose business scale is second only to large-sized audit firms.

[4] Small and medium-sized audit firm: An audit firm other than large-sized and mid-tier audit firms.

Table 13.1 Classifications of audit firms (as of March 31, 2021)

Classification		*Statutory Audits*			*Non-statutory audits*
	Number of firms	*FIEA audits[4]*	*Companies act audits*	*Other audits*	
Large-sized audit firms	4	o	O	o	O
Mid-tier audit firms	5	o	O	o	O
Small and medium-sized audit firms	2,367	o [4]	O	o	O
• Small and medium-sized audit firms	(253)				
• Partnerships[1]	(54)				
• Solo practitioners[1]	(2,060)				

(Based on "The 2022 Monitoring Report"—CPAAOB)

[1] The number of audit offices in fiscal year 2020 (book closing date from April 1, 2020 to March 31, 2021) listed in copies of audit summaries or audit implementation reports submitted to the JIPCA

[2] The symbol "Yes" in the table means that the audit firm classification can conduct the respective audits

[3] Audit firms must register with JIPCA to audit domestically listed companies. For more information, see the column "JIPCA's Registration System for Listed Company Audit Firms" (page 23)

[4] To provide audit and attestation services to listed companies, Solo practitioners are mandated by law and each exchange's securities listing regulations to offer them in conjunction with other CPAs

Large-sized, Mid-tier, and Small- and medium-sized firms, as of March 31, 2021, and the breakdown by the number of CPAs belonging to audit firms is shown in the diagram. The chart shows that more than 90% of audit firms have fewer than 25 CPAs, and the majority consist of solo practitioners, as shown in Fig. 13.1.

Status of Audit Attestation Services by Entity

The figures describe the different obligations of various audit firms operating in the Japanese industry and provide valuable perspectives on allocating audit engagements for fiscal year 2020. According to the data, audit firms of significant size, representing a critical segment of the audit industry, performed nearly 70% of the audits required by the FIEA and

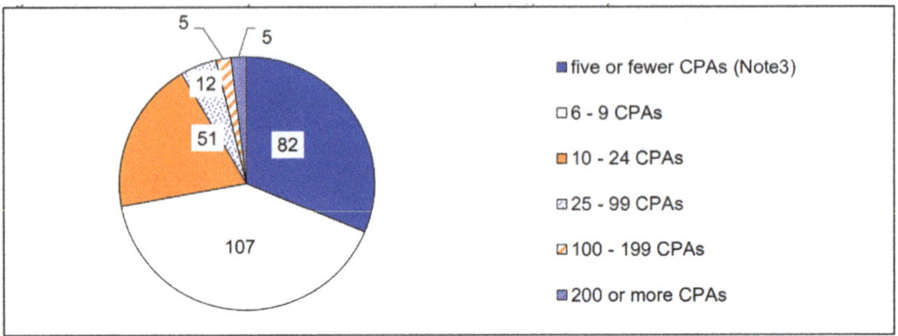

(Note 1) The number of full-time CPAs is the total of partners who are CPAs and full-time staff who are CPAs.
(Note 2) Data on 262 audit firms was collected from operational reports submitted by these firms in FY2020(Note 3) An audit firm where the number of partners who are CPAs drops to four or fewer should be dissolved, but six months is granted as suspended term as stipulated in the CPA Act.

Fig. 13.1 Number of audit firms by scale in terms of full-time CPAs (Based on "The 2022 Monitoring Report"—CPAAOB)

Companies Act. This underscores the preeminent position of these firms in the critical areas of audit work that they oversee.

The prevalence of larger firms in these industries can be attributed to the complexity and large scale of their auditing operations. Organizations covered by the FIEA and Companies Act tend to be significant and have complex business environments that require more comprehensive and methodical audit procedures. Smaller companies or independent practitioners may not have the resources to effectively manage transactions with a global reach that exceeds their size. In contrast, an examination of audits conducted under the Private School Subsidy Act reveals a clear trend. In fiscal year 2020, the vast majority of audits of educational institutions, or about 70%, were conducted by individual practitioners. Generally, these audits focus on compact educational enterprises such as preschools. Although these entities are significant, their procedures and transactions are less complex than those of the large entities. Figure 13.2 presents this information.

Smaller educational institutions have similar business profiles, making them suitable for individual accountants who can provide services tailored to their needs. This shows that independent auditors, even if they cannot perform complicated corporate audits, make a remarkable contribution to auditing by responding to the specific needs of the educational sector. This dichotomy in the Japanese auditing industry highlights the importance of promoting a diverse pool of firms. Each category, including

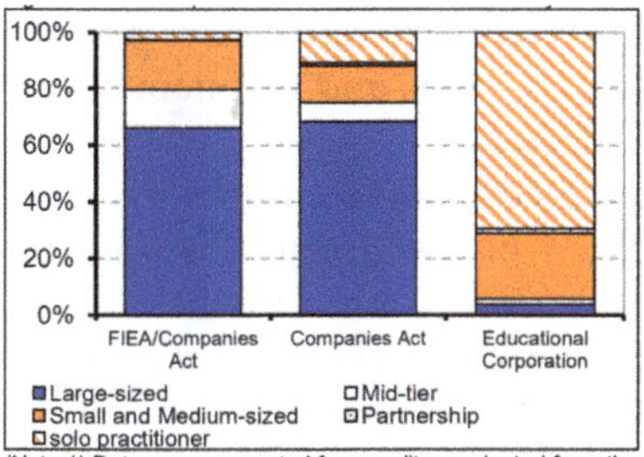

Type		FIEA/Companies Act	Companies Act	Educational Corporation
Audit firms		4,035	5,395	1,486
(Breakdown)	Large-sized	(2,748)	(4,172)	(199)
	Mid-tier	(555)	(415)	(92)
	Small and medium-sized	(732)	(808)	(1,195)
Partnership		9	51	85
Solo practitioner		107	659	3,556

(Note 1) Data was aggregated from audits conducted from the term ended April 2020 to the term ended March 2021. The figures do not match with the figures in Figure I-3-1 because the collection period is different.

(Note 2) The figures in the column "FIEA/Companies Act" include services requiring audit and attestation only under the FIEA, in addition to services requiring audit and attestation under the FIEA and the Companies Act.

(Source) Prepared by the CPAAOB based on data from the JICPA

Fig. 13.2 Principal audit and attestation services by audit firms (Based on "The 2022 Monitoring Report"—CPAAOB)

prominent firms and independent providers, is essential to ensure a complete, competent, and fair audit of various industries and company sizes and contributes to the credibility and reliability of economic documentation.

Share of Audit Firms in Charge of Companies Listed in Japan by Size

The audit environment for listed companies in Japan during fiscal year 2021 provides an exceptional opportunity to observe changing industry patterns and habits. According to available data, the country hosts 3866 listed companies. Interestingly, over the past five years, it has been observed that the percentage of companies audited by audit firms of significant size has decreased by approximately 8%. This remarkable progress is significant in that it draws attention to the traditional market structure of the audit sector, where large companies such as those listed on the stock exchange tend to occupy a dominant position.

This decline could be due to a combination of factors, and it is essential to understand the possible relationships among these factors. I propose a plausible rationale that involves rethinking and improving risk-mitigation methods by prominent accounting firms of significant size. Given the complicated nature and potential risks associated with auditing publicly traded companies, it is likely that firms will see a need to increase their audit fees. Simultaneously, they may exercise caution in their client selection and choose not to renew contracts with companies considered particularly risky. The proposed strategic approach demonstrates a deliberate intent to control risk, achieve financial stability, and maintain a solid commitment to providing exceptional services.

Conversely, the number of publicly traded companies audited by small- to medium-sized accounting firms increased proportionally by approximately 5% over the five years noted above. This indicates these firms' increased capabilities and notoriety, thus solidifying their central role in the provision of audit services. Small and medium-sized firms demonstrate strategic foresight by taking advantage of the market space freed up by larger organizations and demonstrating their adaptability and responsiveness to evolving market trends. The increasing participation of small- and mid-sized accounting firms in this space is a sign of a positive move toward inclusiveness and a bright outlook for the long term. This would lead to the availability of a broader range of accounting services to meet the diverse market needs. Adaptation and diversification tactics in the industry are essential to provide all companies with comprehensive, accurate, and timely audits, regardless of their size and market segment. The table shows the distribution of audit firms responsible for managing publicly traded companies, based on their size. Figure 13.3 shows the number of listed domestic companies classified according to auditor scale.

Given the highly complex structure and extensive operations of publicly traded companies and their frequent involvement in global transactions, auditing these companies requires advanced expertise and robust

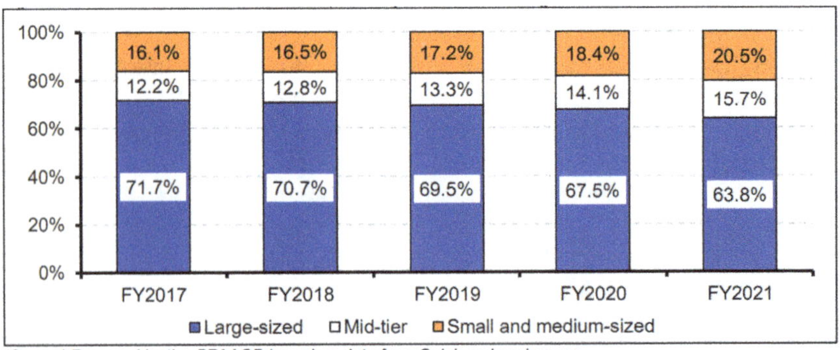

(Source) Prepared by the CPAAOB based on data from Quick and exchanges

Fig. 13.3 Number of listed domestic companies by scale of accounting auditor (Based on "The 2022 Monitoring Report"—CPAAOB)

quality assurance systems. Auditors entrusted with these accounts are expected to demonstrate a high level of skill and effective management of an all-encompassing audit organization that illustrates the due diligence required in auditing these large companies.

The Japanese Institute of Certified Public Accountants (JICPA) has recognized the significant demands and challenges associated with auditing listed companies and has taken proactive steps to strengthen the capabilities of small and medium-sized accounting firms.[5] Tailor-made measures have been introduced to increase the efficiency of such firms in conducting audits of listed companies. The JICPA established a special committee focused on improving the quality control mechanisms in these firms. Our committee is dedicated to developing human resources, thus strengthening the competence of firms with highly qualified personnel who can meet the demanding requirements of auditing listed companies.

In addition, the JICPA adopts a proactive approach by encouraging the adoption of modern auditing methods. We are committed to promoting the adoption of electronic audit documentation to enable the streamlined and efficient processing of audit information. It also supports the introduction of data auditing, an essential digitalization technique that uses cutting-edge technologies to audit complex financial information. By implementing these initiatives, the JICPA strives to provide small and medium-sized accounting firms with tools and resources to deliver world-class auditing services to publicly traded companies. Thus, we aim to uphold the credibility and ethical standards of the Japanese auditing industry.

Relationship and Transition Between Audit Objectives and Audit Techniques

The role of PCs in various business settings, particularly in the context of Japanese auditing, can be categorized into three primary functions, each of which caters to specific requirements. Initially, PCs served as an essential component in the performance of mathematical computations. This feature involves the agile and accurate execution of complex calculations, frequently achieved by amalgamating the four primary arithmetic

[5] https://www.fsa.go.jp/cpaaob/english/oversight/20230330/2022_jireisyu_en.pdf.

operations (addition, subtraction, multiplication, and division). The aforementioned computations encompass diverse business operations including payroll processing, interest rate evaluation, and cost accounting analyses. The efficient execution of computations by the PC plays a crucial role in driving various business operations, thereby augmenting the overall productivity. PCs also play a crucial role in data-processing tasks. This involves the manipulation of data to align it with the unique requirements of a given project or aim. Data processing may involve merging multiple datasets into a consolidated format or selectively extracting data elements that satisfy predetermined conditions from a more extensive dataset. PCs allow businesses to transform unprocessed information into valuable insights, effectively supporting well-informed decision-making.

Finally, PCs enable seamless exchange of information, which is a critical requirement in any organizational context. This task aims to facilitate the dissemination of data created or owned by an individual throughout the organization to enhance operational productivity and effectiveness. Technological advancements have improved this functionality by incorporating local area networks (LANs) and wide area networks (WANs) to facilitate effortless information-sharing within establishments. Moreover, with the emergence of the Internet, this ability has expanded, allowing the sharing of data internally and across organizational borders. Fundamentally, the trio of numerical calculation, data processing, and information-sharing activities performed by PCs exemplifies the crucial role of technology in current business practices by enhancing efficacy, facilitating collaboration, and enabling informed decision-making.

Here, I propose a conceptual framework that describes the interdependence between the three aforementioned functions, PC, and their impact on the audit process. To create a more coherent structure, I integrated these functions into two overarching classifications: numerical computation/data manipulation and information dissemination. First, the relationship between "numerical computations/data manipulation" and auditing practices was explored. To make this connection, I thoroughly analyzed the intersection between PC capabilities and auditing from two perspectives. This study was conducted from the perspective of the audit objectives and techniques. The purpose of the analysis from two perspectives is to provide a thorough understanding of the role that the "numerical computation/data processing" capabilities of PCs play in facilitating the audit process. A nuanced understanding of its role in the audit process can be achieved through a comprehensive assessment of how this PC functionality aligns with and supports audit objectives, and its potential for seamless integration with established audit methodologies.

Audit Objectives

Prior to the 1990s, the primary purpose of an audit was to provide expert opinion on whether a company's financial statements accurately reflected its financial position and performance results. The main objective of the audit was to ensure the accuracy and reliability of a company's financial statements, following auditing standards. Thus, investors should be protected from losses caused by the misrepresentation of the company's financial position and operating performance. Nevertheless, the report did not wholly guarantee no fraudulent acts or inaccuracies in financial statements. This approach resulted from the "dual responsibility principle," which states that management is responsible for preparing financial statements, while the auditor is responsible for issuing the audit opinion. Since auditors do not have the authority to conduct mandatory inquiries, this could result in the intentional concealment of fraudulent acts by management going unnoticed by the auditor. The prevailing view of auditors has conventionally embraced this view. Nonetheless, significant accounting scandals that have had a societal impact have led to rigorous public scrutiny of the audit process, and thus to questions such as "What specific aspects are auditors evaluating?".

As a result of increased scrutiny and recognition of the need for more stringent measures to prevent fraudulent acts, a significant change occurred in 2013 with the publication of the "Standards for Mitigating the Risk of Fraud During Audits".[6] This introduced a new objective for the audit process, which emphasizes the importance of identifying incidents of fraudulent practices. This emphasizes the importance for auditors to carefully investigate fraudulent activities that may result in material misstatements and affect the fairness of financial statements. Consequently, this has introduced an additional layer of attention and scrutiny into the audit process, ultimately leading to increased accountability and assurance in financial reporting.

[6] https://jicpa.or.jp/english/accounting/system/pdf/0-99-0-2-20130919.pdf.

Audit Techniques

There are four categories of audit methods: conventional, technology-assisted, continuous audits (CA), and artificial intelligence (AI) audits. As defined above, conventional auditing involves the use of statistical sampling to examine historical transactions over several months. Statistical sampling is a viable method for auditing financial statements for accuracy because it allows auditors to assess the entirety of a dataset against a representative subset. However, traditional auditing methods have two significant limitations. First, the use of random sampling poses a limitation in comprehensively extracting all transactions, particularly those involving fraudulent activity, making fraud detection a significant challenge. In addition, reviewing past transactions spanning several months can hinder the timely detection and prevention of fraudulent activities.

Contemporary audit methods or technology-assisted audits include CAATs, which leverage the power of computers and data to improve the efficiency and effectiveness of auditing procedures. These methods facilitate the evaluation of all transactions and identify those that show signs of possible fraudulent behavior. However, the challenge with computerized audits is ensuring timely audits while examining transactions that date back several months, similar to standard audits. They also face obstacles in formulating appropriate analytical scenarios to identify fraudulent activities based on organization-specific assumptions.

In addition, CAs represent a more sophisticated iteration of CAATs that systematically execute automated software programs generated by data analytics tools. Timely identification and disclosure of potential fraud indicators by the CA leads to significant changes in the audit approach and methodology. Auditors are promptly notified when transaction irregularities are identified, allowing timely auditing, immediate detection, and mitigation of fraudulent activity. Despite the implementation of CA, the task of developing analysis scenarios that accurately reflect an organization's unique circumstances is a persistent obstacle.

Finally, AI audits rely on artificial intelligence (AI) and offer numerous benefits, such as incorporating machine learning and natural language processing. Currently, in Japan, there is no generally accepted and standardized process for conducting AI audits, yet the public expects the use of AI in auditing. Various technological advances such as machine learning and natural language processing can effectively support AI in auditing. By applying machine-learning techniques, computer systems are expected to gain the ability to understand historical data, independently identify signs of fraudulent activity, and systematically extract transactions that match these identified criteria. Additionally, by applying natural language processing, computers can understand the semantic content of a sentence. Consequently, computers are expected to search for internal records, such as the minutes of previous board meetings and approval documents, and extract relevant documents.

As auditing techniques continue to advance, CPAs must adapt their knowledge and skills to meet the changing professional demands. This includes combining accounting and auditing expertise with computerized data analysis skills. Auditors must keep pace with ever-evolving audit techniques, with a growing trend toward CAATs, CA, and the potential integration of AI. In particular, they need to focus on developing more efficient and tailored analysis scenarios to increase the added value and precision of their audit services.

Auditing and Information Sharing

In the second half of the 1990s, accounting firms began to use PCs to communicate via e-mail, electronic bulletin boards, and distributed laptops to their staff. During a similar period, accounting firms began experimenting with digitizing and archiving audit documents in electronic media to replace traditional paper-based methods. This innovation eventually led to the introduction of electronic auditing documents. After introducing e-mail and electronic bulletin boards in the audit firm where I was employed, several CPAs, especially older ones, preferred direct communication because they found it more convenient and efficient in transmitting instructions. This delay was due to the fact that the individuals in question were unfamiliar with the operation of computers, including the use of keyboards. Over time, the proliferation of electronic communication channels, such as e-mail and electronic bulletin boards, has made these voices less common.

Initially, there was some concern about the feasibility of implementing electronic audit documentation, because physical documents still predominated. Most of the company's documentation is paper, making large-scale scanning and digitization initiatives impractical. With the introduction of electronic audit documentation, auditors have overcome time and space constraints imposed by paper documents. This development has led to

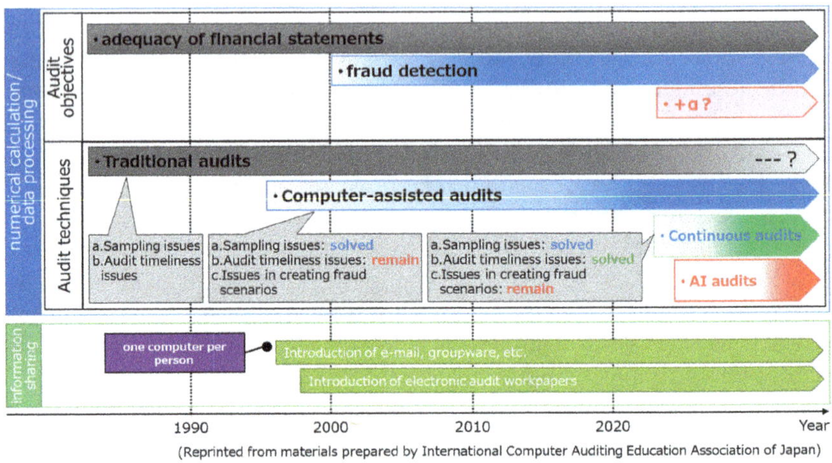

Fig. 13.4 Auditing and information sharing (Based on ICAEA material—https://www.iacae.org/English/index/index.php)

streamlining audit processes, which has contributed significantly to the growing popularity of electronic audit documents.

Considering the current scenario, it can be said that electronic audit work papers have taken a permanent place in auditing firms of considerable size. Moreover, electronic workpapers are currently being adopted by small- and mid-sized audit firms. Electronic audit workpapers are tools for developing audit procedures that align with a risk-based approach. This increases the efficiency and has the added benefit of improving the overall quality of the audit process. The chart shows the above content arranged in chronological order (Fig. 13.4).

Computer-assisted Audit Techniques (CAATs) Flow

CAATs involve a more extensive range of procedures than do traditional perceptions. Often, they are limited to encompassing only the tools that enable data analysis. However, this perception weakens the all-encompassing nature of CAATs. CAATs represent a complete process flow, referred to as "CAATs Flow," with data analysis tools only being part of that process.

CAATs flow involves a systematic approach, in which each phase adds value to the overall effectiveness of the audit. The process begins with setting audit objectives and identifying foreseeable risks. In the subsequent phase, we determined the appropriate actions, timing, and scope to mitigate the identified risks. The data were then extracted and processed to facilitate the subsequent analytical procedures. The phase of using data analysis tools is commonly called "data analysis." However, it is essential to note that this phase should not be confused with the CAATs. By performing this step, auditors can thoroughly examine transactions and detect irregularities, streamlining the fraud detection process. Following data analysis, the results were thoroughly evaluated and communicated (Figure 13.5).

The first step in implementing CAATs is "event perception." This process involves identifying potential risks or issues that could impact a business, such as changes in applicable laws, regulations, and incidents related to fraudulent activity. We then proceed to the process of identifying and evaluating potential areas of focus for the audit, commonly referred to as "selecting audit themes (risks/issues)." This process includes an evaluation to determine whether it is possible to

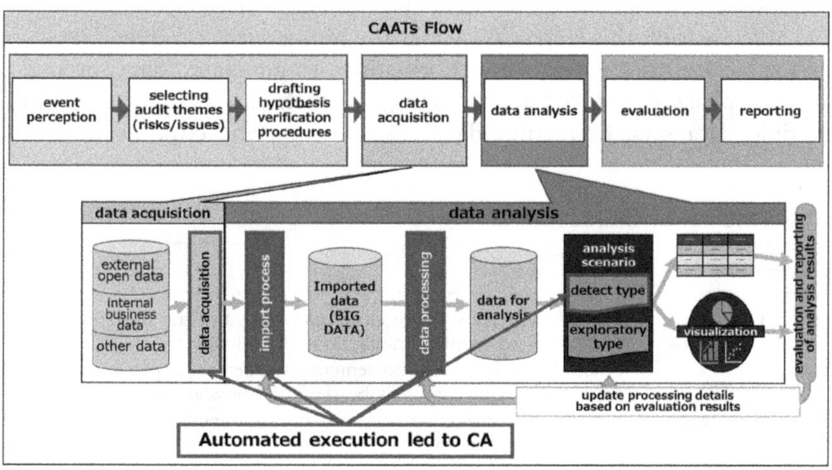

Fig. 13.5 CAATs flow (Based on ICAEA material—https://www.iacae.org/English/index/index.php)

prevent the identified event through internal controls or other measures. If it is determined that prevention of an event is not possible, it is deemed appropriate to select the event as an audit topic. Once the audit topic is determined, the next step begins with the development of hypothesis testing procedures. During the audit process, auditors develop hypotheses about the data to be audited, and prepare a statement explaining the circumstances and events necessary to verify that these events are consistent with the hypotheses. This statement can be called an analytical scenario, and can be classified into the following two categories (Table 13.2):

The audit process uses CAATs and proceeds through several clearly defined phases. The journey begins by creating an analysis scenario, the blueprint for subsequent auditing procedures. Once this scenario is developed, auditors move into the "data-sourcing" phase. They obtained the source data required for the planned analysis. Much of this data are typically internal business data from various enterprise systems, such as accounting or sales management. Auditors, however, also have the flexibility to include external open data such as stock prices and exchange rates, or other data such as e-mails as source data.

Once the required data are available, auditors begin the "data analysis" phase. This phase is initiated by importing the source data into a data analysis tool; this step is known as the import process. The data were then subjected to a series of transformations to generate "data for analysis" in a phase called "data processing, " which can include combining multiple data sets, extracting data based on specific conditions, filling

Table 13.2 Analytical scenario

Classification	*Definition*
Detect-type	Analytic scenarios where clear rules exist and the purpose of the scenario is to identify transactions that violate the rules Examples: double reimbursement of expenses, expense applications and approvals by the same person, etc
Exploratory-type	Analytical scenarios created to extract transactions that show signs of fraud or error based on deviations from the same category or analysis of time series trends Examples: large/frequent expense reimbursements, clients with continuously increasing accounts receivable turnover, etc

Source Author

Table 13.3 Process and software requirements

Process	*Examples of software*
Data extraction Import processing Processing Data analysis based on detect-type analysis scenarios	RPA (Robotic Process Automation) CAATs-dedicated tool (ACL™ Analytics, IDEA®, etc.)

Source Author

in missing data, and formatting the data to simplify analysis. After this preparatory work, the fundamental data analysis began. The previously created scenarios guide the analysis and increasingly use data visualization techniques, such as charts, to gain insights and test hypotheses.

The results of this analysis were evaluated and led to revisions of the analysis scenario as needed. The process is not unidirectional, but often includes cyclical iterations that refine the hypothesis and corresponding data identification and analysis scenarios. The final analysis results were then reported. A subset of these processes—data extractions, import processing, data processing, and the application of detect-type analysis scenarios can be programmed in advance to be executed automatically by a computer scheduler, thereby realizing a CA. The integration of each process with specific software for automatic execution is summarized in Table 13.3. These software tools have been proven to position CA as a viable and technologically supported auditing technique. Table 13.3 summarizes the combinations of each process and software to be executed automatically. Because the example software has a proven history, CA can be considered a viable audit technique using existing technology.

Japan's Current Situation in Advantages and Challenges of Adopting Digital Technology

In 2018, the Japanese Ministry of Economy, Trade and Industry published a seminal document called the "Guidelines for Promoting Digital Transformation" (Broeckaert, 2022). This strategic plan describes how digital transformation (DX) refers to companies using digital technologies and data to manage significant changes in their business environments. It encourages companies to redefine and innovate their offerings, organizational frameworks, and strategies to meet the dynamic demands and expectations of customers and society. DX goes beyond external appearance and emphasizes fundamental changes inside companies, including their operations, organizational structures, processes, and corporate culture. All of these changes aim to secure a sustainable competitive advantage.

Examining this DX context provides a broader perspective for understanding the importance and impact of CA and CAATs. Incorporating CAATs into the audit framework significantly transforms the process by aligning it with the modern DX principles. The use of technology and data in audit processes by chartered accountants (CAs) and CAATs signifies a shift toward digital transformation that optimizes audit quality and efficiency.

Another critical component of the digital transformation of auditing is the introduction of electronic auditing documentation. By removing time and location constraints, this innovative digital solution enables auditors to create and retain audit documentation with greater accuracy and precision, thereby improving audit quality. Considering these recent developments, DX has become a topic of great importance and applicability in Japanese accounting firms.

Leading accounting firms have gradually integrated CAATs into their practices. However, not all auditors are familiar with data analytics tools and their applications. To address this disparity, leading firms methodically integrate information technology experts into their staff or create specialized teams dedicated solely to data analytics. Audit departments are taking the expertise of professionals and working to create combined audit teams comprising IT specialists and Certified Public Accountants (CPAs). Such teams adhere to the prescribed process for CAATs with data collection and analysis typically performed by IT specialists or data analysis teams. Owing to the iterative nature of any process involved in the CAATs flow, clear and effective communication is critical, although this may present certain difficulties. There is also a growing trend among small- and medium-sized accounting firms to embrace the use of CAATs with great enthusiasm. However, because these firms typically have limited resources compared with their larger counterparts, they tend to invest in extensive CAATs flow training for their CPAs rather than hiring outside IT experts. Currently, the use of CA is limited, especially for leading accounting firms. Two main factors contribute to this situation. First, the essential requirements for CAATs may not yet be deeply ingrained in the industry. In addition, the infrastructure required to automatically retrieve data from companies undergoing audits is yet to be fully developed.

The adoption of electronic audit documentation reached a high level of maturity among large audit firms after a prolonged period of use. However, smaller- and mid-sized audit firms have experienced varying levels of adoption. Although traditional paper-based audit documentation systems still exist, an increasing proportion of professionals use digital audit documentation. One impetus for this trend can be attributed to the prominent role of the Japanese Institute of Certified Public Accountants, which has been actively promoting the adoption of digital audit working papers through services provided by firms supported by smaller and mid-sized audit firms. While adopting these smaller firms is still cautious, it is expected to increase in the future.

Future Tasks

Three critical aspects are related to the digitization of audits: the effective implementation of CAATs, the use of CA, and the use of electronic audit workpapers. Electronic audit papers have become commonplace among large accounting firms, and small and medium-sized firms are expected to adopt this trend soon. However, two main obstacles require attention in order to fully adopt CAATs and CA.

The first obstacle is the implementation of appropriate data analysis tools. Audit firms in Japan typically use a combination of general-purpose software, such as Excel® and Access®, and CAATs-specific tools, such as ACL™ Analytics and IDEA®, to perform audit procedures that require CAATs. Multi-functional software solutions offer the advantages of cost-effectiveness and wide availability, as they are installed everywhere on auditors' computer systems. Nevertheless, it should be noted that the suitability of this software for CAATs and CA is questionable because of inherent limitations such as the susceptibility of the data to change, limitation of data elements, slow processing speed, and need for advanced programming language skills.

On the other hand, dedicated software for CAATs solves all the above limitations of generic software, making it the preferred alternative for performing tests with CAATs and CA. A major limitation of using this software is its comparatively high cost of ownership, which hinders its use at all examiners' workstations. Consequently, only a limited group of auditors can use this tool, which hinders the accumulation, dissemination, and sharing of knowledge factors fundamental to successfully adopting CAATs and computer auditing (CA). Therefore, it is critical to develop CAATs-specific software that is economically viable and that ensures broader accessibility and use within the auditing community.

Additionally, barriers to education pose a major challenge. There is a lack of professional training opportunities for auditors in Japan regarding the effective use of CAATs. Although auditing firms have introduced some training programs, they are often limited in scope and do not provide comprehensive instructions on the software used for CAATs. In addition, the lack of competent CAATs professionals within the audit firm inevitably leads to inadequate knowledge dissemination and training.

To address this challenge effectively, it is essential to establish a system that promotes the dissemination of CAATs knowledge in society. One possible solution is to raise the level of training in accounting firms while ensuring that CAATs courses are included in the college and graduate school curricula. This approach makes it possible to disseminate and distribute knowledge about CAATs promptly and widely.

References

Broeckaert, L. (2022). *Digital Transformation in Japan: Assessing Business Opportunities for EU SMEs*. EU-Japan Center for Industrial Cooperation, Tokyo.

Certified Public Accountants and Auditing Oversight Board. (2022). *2022 Monitoring Report*. https://www.iacae.org/English/index/index.php

Index

A. Perdana and T. Wang (eds.), *Digital Transformation in Accounting and Auditing*, https://doi.org/10.1007/978-3-031-46209-2